FETCH THE DEVIL

Clint Richmond

Fetch
the
Devil

The Sierra Diablo

Murders and

Nazi Espionage

in America

ForeEdge

ForeEdge
An imprint of University Press of New England

www.upne.com
© 2014 Clint Richmond
All rights reserved
Manufactured in the United States of America
Designed by Mindy Basinger Hill
Typeset in Garamond Premier Pro
University Press of New England is a member of the
Green Press Initiative. The paper used in this book meets
their minimum requirement for recycled paper.
For permission to reproduce any of the material in this book,
contact Permissions, University Press of New England,
One Court Street, Suite 250, Lebanon NH 03766;
or visit www.upne.com

Hardcover ISBN: 978-1-61168-534-3
Ebook ISBN: 978-1-61168-561-9
Library of Congress Control Number: 2013954951

5   4   3   2   1

Texture on title and part title pages by
HA! Designs - Artbyheather

For Judith Morison

AND IN LOVING MEMORY OF

Johanna, Jonas, and Joy

THE CHIEF WANTS YOU TO

BECOME A BAND OF ROBBERS—

READY, IF NEED BE,

TO FETCH THE DEVIL FROM HELL.

Provocative challenge by an Abwehr commander under Nazi spymaster
Admiral Wilhelm Canaris, when dispatching German agents
on missions to foreign countries (Ladislas Farago, *The Game of the Foxes*).

CONTENTS

PREFACE

*Hindsight is not only clearer than perception-in-the-moment, but
also unfair to those who actually lived through the moment.*
Edwin S. Shneidman, *Autopsy of a Suicidal Mind*

I first heard of the murders near the Sierra Diablo Mountains in Far West
Texas while working as a criminal-courts reporter in Dallas, in the 1960s.
I was lucky to be part of a small audience of newsmen, deputies, and other
courthouse denizens for some of legendary sheriff Bill Decker's rare story-
telling sessions about the Depression-era bad guys he had personally faced
down. He held a grudging belief that the desperados of the day lived by a
code. Though they might readily use lethal force if they were cornered, or
to expedite a getaway, they did not kill for thrills.

The atypical torture-murders of California socialites Hazel and Nancy
Frome in 1938 were, at the time, and still remain, the biggest unsolved
crime in the history of the Southwest. Sheriff Decker, like almost every
Texas lawman of the period, played a part in that sweeping investigation.

Generations of Texas newsmen have revisited the mystery, including
one of my editors when I was a reporter at the *Dallas Times Herald*. Felix
McKnight, then the paper's executive editor, had looked into the case in the
1940s, as a young reporter himself, and concluded it might never be solved.

Little did I know that, when Sheriff Decker was regaling us with tales
of his encounters with Bonnie and Clyde and his capture of the notorious
cop killer Raymond Hamilton, the Frome murders would become such
a time-consuming quest of my own writing career at the turn of this new
century.

In late March 1938, the California matron and her beautiful daughter
set out alone on a cross-country drive from their Bay Area home to the
East Coast, with scant regard for the dangers lurking on the highways they
would traverse. They soon became the most famous victims of that era.

The brutal torture and murders of Hazel Frome and her sorority-president daughter Nancy in the desert east of El Paso baffled local sheriffs, Texas Rangers, and federal agents for decades.

New evidence, gleaned from several sources unavailable until long after the women's near-nude bodies were found, is compiled and compared in this book for the first time, to provide a plausible answer to this more than seven-decades-old mystery.

Law enforcement officers working on the Frome murder case were largely unaware of information gradually building in the files of federal agencies about the Nazi spy network operating under deep cover in the western United States. The investigators certainly had no knowledge that these clandestine activities could have been linked to the crime.

In building this story I had the advantage of hindsight gained through the declassification, in the late 1990s, of secret government files. Access restrictions were lifted after my own Freedom of Information Act (FOIA) requests regarding specific individuals and events pertaining to pre–World War II Axis spying. My requests covered old files of the FBI, the Justice Department, the immigration service, and military intelligence agencies. I also found considerable relevant information about persons believed to be involved in the Frome murders in the archives of the criminal division of the American Medical Association (AMA).

Also of significance to this case were the voluminous Nazi spy files seized after the war and shipped in crates from Germany to the National Archives in Washington, D.C. This rich source of information was not made public until 1967, when military historian and journalist Ladislas Farago stumbled across the cache of Abwehr documents after a decade of research.

My chance discovery, in 1995, of a massive, forgotten cold-case file personally penned by the original Frome case coordinator, the late sheriff Chris P. Fox, and carefully stored at the El Paso Sheriff's Office, offered the final pieces needed to provide the link between the murders and Nazi espionage activities.

In fairness to those Old West lawmen who so diligently worked to solve the Frome case, connecting the murders to unknown German espionage operations from California to the Texas-Mexico border would have been impossible in the late 1930s and early 1940s, indeed, until long after the end of World War II.

Only in recent years, after files in the possession of the U.S. government were declassified, was I able to connect the germane incidents described in this book that were occurring contemporaneously in El Paso, Mexico, Los Angeles, and the San Francisco Bay Area at the time of the murders. The newly revealed associations, mostly unintended, between the Frome family's fate and subversive Nazi elements, became too numerous to be simply coincidental.

Clint Richmond

FETCH THE DEVIL

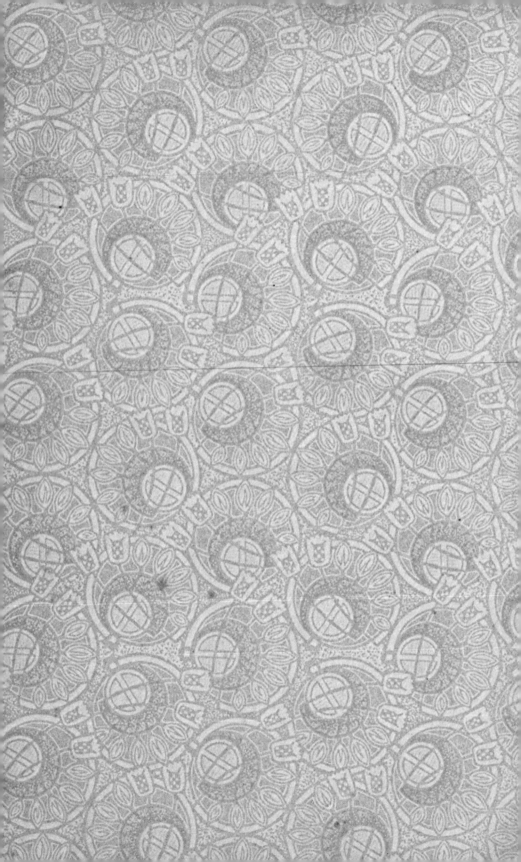

AN UNFORGIVING PLACE

Her pampered skin was more accustomed to the caress of perfume than the rivulets of hot, wind-driven desert sand abrading her naked back. Only two weeks earlier the beautiful young woman had been dancing in the arms of admiring suitors at the spring ball of her Bay Area sorority.

A large-eared pack rat darted back and forth from the safety of its midden-lined nest in a nearby crag, to tug at the glinting diamond wristwatch that the older woman wore on her left arm. The rodent was answering some inexplicable instinct to collect such bright trinkets to decorate its burrow, more driven by primordial addiction than fear of approaching the human corpses intruding on its natural habitat.

The journey of Nancy and Hazel Frome, missing four days on their coast-to-coast schedule, had ended in this shallow caliche pit in the Chihuahuan Desert, six miles east of the hamlet of Van Horn, Texas.

The great desert covering much of northern Mexico and Far West Texas is an unforgiving place for those who enter unprepared. In all seasons, a relentless sun makes for searing days that rapidly turn to freezing nights, soon after it sets. The extremes of temperature swung that day, on April 3, 1938, in a violent pendulum of more than fifty degrees, enough to cause tiny, eroding fissures in rock surfaces.

The women were not prepared, nor did they intend, to come to this spot. Cruel men, some would later say maniacs, had delivered them here, to execute them and leave their fragile remains to be consumed by the creatures and elements of the harsh desert. They lay side by side in death, as they had always been in life, mother and daughter, waiting for someone to find them. They were oblivious, in morbid stillness, to a hundred kinder men ranging for miles over the sere plain in search of them.

PART I

MURDER IN
THE DESERT

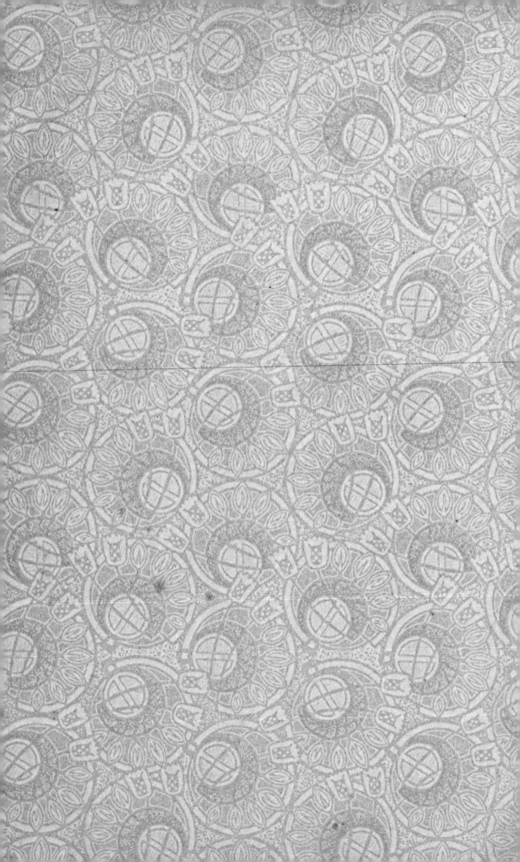

There were two ways guaranteed to ruin a perfectly swell day in the spring of 1938. One was to make eye contact with the ragged little urchins riding in the back of an Okie family's dilapidated pickup truck. The other was to read a front-page story about what was going on with the Jews in Germany.

The Tri Delta sisters at the University of California, Berkeley, avoided both, as they planned for the annual spring sorority gala to be held on March 22. There had been enough gloom in the almost decadelong Great Depression to last a lifetime. Hitler had only been in control for a few years, not really enough time to be blamed for every bleak headline coming out of Europe.

The goal was to make the spring dance such a festive occasion that everyone could forget the negative news and have some fun for a while. Delta sisters, alums, and their beaus eagerly anticipated the event — none more than the vivacious former sorority president Nancy Frome, who had remained active as an adviser long after her own graduation.[1]

Making ends meet was the national obsession of most Americans during the second phase of the economic crisis, with almost 20 percent of the workforce still unemployed. Keeping up appearances, not simple survival, was the primary concern of Nancy's family, residing in the comfortable home at 2560 Cedar Street in Berkeley. The white stucco house with its red-tiled roof was of a Spanish style more popular in Southern California nearer the Mexican border than in the San Francisco Bay Area. Likewise, the family that owned the house seemed more in tune with the Hollywood lifestyle.

The property was landscaped to avoid the need for much maintenance, with a thirty-foot palm tree in the front yard, surrounded by overgrown succulents and cacti. The rest of the place was encircled by a five-foot brick-and-mortar wall, ensuring that whatever went on inside the property was hidden from view of the casual passerby.

The home, where twenty-three-year-old Nancy lived with her father, mother, and younger sister Mada, was in a hilly section of town, overlooking Berkeley central, with vistas across the bay to San Francisco. It was a genteel college neighborhood within easy walking distance of the University of California campus.

The views of the bay were spectacular, including one panorama of Alcatraz Island. The austere, gray-walled federal prison had housed its most famous inmate, Alphonse Gabriel "Al" Capone, for the past three and a half years. The concrete penitentiary, which also held many of Capone's fellow gangsters from the recently ended Prohibition era, loomed through the morning fogs like a castle perched on an islet in a misty sea. The misery held captive on that island could scarce be imagined from those lofty Berkeley heights.

The university neighborhood, though filled with upscale homes, was only marginally upper class, befitting the professors, business executives, and other professionals in residence there. While comfortable, it was not considered the most exclusive neighborhood in the bustling Northern California metropolis. Southern California laid claim to flashy glitz and glamour, but the Bay Area was home to most of California's old money. Stately mansions graced the city of San Francisco, and many of the cross-bay suburbs were resplendent with near-palatial homes of the heirs to timber, mining, shipping, and railroad empires.

If the Fromes had not quite attained the status of Bay Area aristocracy, they were doubly blessed in avoiding the worst of the Great Depression. The immediate family not only shared in the community weal from the university but also enjoyed the exceptionally good earnings of its breadwinner, Weston G. "Pop" Frome. A self-made success, the father was a top executive at Atlas Powder Company, a leader in the international explosives industry. That industry was booming, despite the Depression. Construction contracts for the military and the Works Project Administration (WPA) required enormous supplies of the blasting materials his company manufactured and distributed.

Frome most often referred to his position as "regional sales manager." But working in the secretive high-explosives industry, it came naturally to him to downplay his role in the company's operations. At age 50, he wore several hats in Atlas Powder's top management.

The headquarters of Atlas Powder was at Wilmington, Delaware, in an industrial complex adjacent to E. I. DuPont de Nemours and Company, its former parent. Atlas had been formed in the early 1900s, as a spinoff from DuPont after a court-ordered divestment under the Sherman Antitrust Act. Business and personal connections between executives of the two companies remained cozy, despite the split. And while Atlas did not have a monopoly in the explosives industry, the company was an international leader in its field. The division Frome managed had cornered much of a vast market in the western United States, the Pacific region, and Latin America.

Frome's base salary in 1938 was a whopping two thousand dollars a month. At the time, a set of four of the best automobile tires could be bought for less than forty dollars, with the spare thrown in free; a pound of coffee went for twenty-seven cents. A U.S. senator's salary was ten thousand dollars a year.

Weston Frome was born in rural eastern Pennsylvania on May 1, 1888, to first-generation German American parents. His father and mother owned and operated a small German inn, with accommodations for eleven guests, in the hamlet of Pen Argyle. His grandparents had emigrated in the mass wave of Germans known as the "Forty-eighters," a huge talent exodus of educated professionals and tradesmen fleeing European wars in the 1840s.[2]

As the first college-educated member of his family, Weston Frome was now long removed from the time when he washed dishes in the family business during his public-school years. His German lineage mattered little as far as his Bay-area peers were concerned. Of primary importance was the fact that his company brought a substantial payroll to town. His plant employed three thousand workers, no small contribution to the local economy during the Depression.

A dour, heavy-set man of medium height, Pop did not participate much in local civic activities. Although he kept his main office at One Montgomery Street in downtown San Francisco, his focus was global.

To all appearances, his work was his life. His only social connection in the community was membership in the Benevolent and Protective Order of Elks at nearby Richmond, where he occasionally dropped by the lodge for drinks and gaming with a close-knit group of cronies.

Frome had joined DuPont at one of its plants in Missouri as a twenty-two-year-old chemist shortly after college. He graduated from Lehigh University in 1908 and was hired by DuPont two years later. When the blasting powder business was split off from DuPont, he went with the emerging Atlas Powder Company; in 1913, he was one of the original managers to help create the spin-off.

While working in Missouri, he met an attractive, auburn-haired school-teacher named Hazel Eva Johnson. After graduating from Milwaukee State Teachers College, Hazel had found a job at a public school near Frome's plant in Webb City, Missouri.[3] She taught in public schools at Fort Atkinson and Washburn before marrying Weston in October 1913. They were both twenty-five years old when they wed.

Hazel, born July 29, 1888, in Stoughton, Wisconsin, was the daughter of first-generation immigrants from Norway. Her father was a carpenter by trade.[4]

Weston and Hazel settled at Webb City, Missouri, close to his job with Atlas Powder, where he rapidly climbed through the ranks. Two daughters were born at nearby Carthage — Nancy Eudora, named after Hazel's mother, in July 1914, and Mada Margaret in September 1915.

The Frome family moved from Missouri when Pop was promoted to the regional management position and transferred to the Bay Area in 1932. When he wasn't traveling his territory, Frome divided his time between the office in downtown San Francisco and an office at the sprawling manufacturing plant in nearby Giant, California. Giant was a township formed by the company and named for its dynamite brand, Giant Powder.[5] It was situated in a waterfront industrial enclave of the City of Richmond. Despite the proximity of these Atlas facilities to their residence in Berkeley, Pop's travel schedule and work demands meant he was rarely at home.

With the family patriarch personally aloof and physically away so much of the time, the Fromes were perhaps best known in the community for their beautiful women. They were frequent "items" in the society pages of the local newspapers for their travel adventures and their prominent roles in the more fashionable events of the East Bay.[6]

Although Hazel often boasted about her husband's executive position, she was not a heavy spender; she was, in fact, considered frugal when it came to purchases for herself. Her chief vice, if anyone considered it that, was enjoying the highballs she imbibed during her regular bridge outings at a women's club in Richmond. She was known to get a bit intoxicated from time to time.

Family life, such as it was, centered on the university, where the daughters were among the most popular coeds on campus. Each girl was elected president of the Delta Delta Delta sorority in her junior year. Throughout college, the sisters, just one year apart, were inseparable and shared many of the same Tri Delta friends.

They were pretty in different ways. Nancy, who stood five foot four, wore her dark blonde hair in a short, curly bob. Mada, a bit taller, had brunette hair, almost to her shoulders. Whereas Nancy's personality was bubbly and extroverted, Mada was contemplative and serious. In general, she was more cautious and practical than Nancy, who was considered a bit of a risk taker.

They both loved dancing and parties, and were as popular with the boys as they were with their loyal girlfriends. Droves of swains came courting from the time Nancy and Mada returned home from finishing school back east to complete their education at Berkeley.

Nancy spent her money freely. She knew if she ran short she could ask her more frugal sister for a loan. The girls had never held jobs — they could always hit up Pop for whatever cash they needed.

Mother Hazel assumed responsibility for maintaining the family's proper social appearances. Pop was glad to leave that chore to his wife and, for all practical purposes, was just the family meal ticket.

As the girls matriculated through prep school and college, Hazel dedicated herself to one goal that seemed to override many other decisions made by the family — preparing her daughters for proper marriages. Other than her occasional bridge game, the mother spent most of her time shepherding her daughters toward that end. As part of that grooming the girls were given everything the former schoolmarm could never afford during her own working-class, Midwestern upbringing.

Both sisters finished boarding school as high achievers at Bradford Academy near Lowell, Massachusetts, prior to attending college. They were expert equestrians and musically talented. At Bradford, Nancy won high honors for her virtuosity on the piano.

The Frome daughters were German in name only. In every other way they were all-American coeds.

However, it was not as if German lineage bore any particular stigma, since nearly 60 percent of the American population traced at least part of its heritage back to the fatherland. German ancestry was second only to Anglo-Saxon-Irish in the population as a whole, with about 60 million of the 132 million Americans claiming some German kinship.[7] Another

1.9 million Germans immigrated to the United States between the end of World War I in 1919 and 1938.

The 1935 Cal Berkeley yearbook, at the time Nancy was sorority president, tellingly featured a full-color rendering of a Nazi swastika and artist's concept of an iron-fisted storm trooper, surrounded by citizens raising their arms in the "Heil Hitler" salute.

The theme of the class book that year was "The International House, symbol of worldwide amity and unity." In their illustrations, the student artists had romanticized the emerging dictatorships in Germany and Russia with the same credibility afforded the other industrialized nations of the world.

A full page of symbolic Nazi Germany artwork introduced the section on varsity athletics. The caption read, "The blazing defiant Swastika stands out in bold relief. Germany's progressive commercial spirit is shown by its air carrier, its ocean liner, rebirth since the war, and its glory in the (upcoming) 1936 Olympic games."

Naively ecumenical, the yearbook section on campus organizations, which included the school's fraternities and sororities, was illustrated with a Soviet peasant soldier, complete with Communist hammer and sickle.[8] The caption read, "Russia signifies life and experiment, hence the main movement of the workers and soldiers is shown on a diagonal moving plane. The borders indicate the gay decorations typical of things Russian."

These political impressions about Europe's most repressive governments, held by many of the collegians preparing to assume positions in the changing new world, were likely outgrowths of their parents' bitter memories of the recent Great War. Most Americans and a good percentage of their leaders were adamant isolationists.

Nancy, who majored in philosophy, graduated with honors in 1936; Mada graduated a year later. Their college years had been a time of sheltered innocence, spent among privileged peers.

The Frome girls were typical students of the day, deafened — by the sounds of jazz and big ballroom dance bands — to the martial music of foreign armies marching abroad. It was a time of cynical denial and isolation, rather than the world of amity and unity the college yearbook portrayed. In the real world, clouds of another war were already forming just over the horizons of the oceans that were supposed to make America a fortress against such foreign intrigues.

2

Hazel, Nancy, and Mada Frome were college educated, avid newspaper readers, and unusually well traveled for the day. Undoubtedly, they were more aware of foreign and domestic troubles than the average citizen. Yet, like most Americans, they seemed somehow inured to the gathering storms abroad and the potential perils caused by the grinding poverty of unemployment at home.

They had sailed around the world twice and had actually visited Nazi Germany on their last trip to Europe.[9] They took world cruises in 1934 and 1936 aboard the Dollar Steamship Company's luxury ocean liners, which were named for American presidents. Friends staged a bon voyage dinner for the three women at the Athens Athletic Club in Richmond on the eve of the earlier sailing. Hazel and her daughters had also driven on vacations all over the United States, Canada, and Mexico. Even more unusual for the times, they had made these trips on their own, unescorted by Pop or any other male relative or friend.

The women's ocean voyages conveniently originated close to home, at the Port of San Francisco. While most local residents could only dream of boarding one of the majestic ocean liners sailing under the newly built Golden Gate Bridge, the Fromes' travel adventures, on both land and sea, were regular items in local society columns. San Francisco was one port of call for the steamship line's round-the-world cruises. Other stopovers included Honolulu, Yokohama, Kobe, Hong Kong, Manila, Singapore, Penang, Colombo, Bombay, Suez, Port Said, Alexandria, Naples, Genoa, Marseilles, New York, Havana, Cristobal, and Balboa.[10]

The 1934 world cruise was advertised as "14-countries, 104-days and costs $1,033 — complete." In this case, "complete" included all meals, entertainment, and amenities aboard ship, with a spacious first-class cabin.

The Frome women took a more leisurely, four-month cruise in 1936, with layovers for side trips in Asia, North Africa, and Europe. These longer stops required debarking one ship and catching the next Dollar Steamship arriving in port after their sojourn on land. This time they debarked in Italy for an extended tour of the Continent.[11] Hazel, Nancy, and Mada spent several weeks traveling through Europe by rail and motor coach, and attended events at the Berlin Summer Olympics, Hitler's grandly staged extravaganza to introduce the world to the New Germany.[12]

All three were considered unusually liberated for females of the day, even by many of the sisters' contemporaries. They drank socially, smoked cigarettes, and thought nothing of joining in casual conversation with male strangers they met along the way.

In one respect, at least, Nancy and Mada appeared to be following a more traditional path when they both became engaged to well-to-do young bachelors while they were still in college. That pattern of stability was to be relatively short lived when both girls broke their engagements within months of one another.

Mada's seemingly impulsive decision to end her engagement to the scion of a wealthy Southern California family in May 1937 threw the Frome household, especially the matron, into an uproar. Hazel had invested a great deal in her hopes of a good marriage for each of her beautiful, talented daughters.

Now Mada, generally considered the more levelheaded of the two, had dissolved an enviable courtship, seemingly out of the blue. Her engagement to Cal football star John R. (Jack) Brittingham had lasted through her junior and senior years in college, and everyone assumed they would marry when she graduated.

Jack's family was fabulously wealthy, with California ranching and oil interests, and vast land holdings in northern Mexico. His brother Robert had also been a gridiron star on the Cal Golden Bears football team when Nancy and Mada were at university.[13]

There was never any doubt that the boys and their parents would remain friends with the Fromes. Despite the breakup, Hazel and the girls went through with plans to visit the Brittinghams at their ranch and hacienda near Torreon that July, as part of a three-month driving tour of Mexico. The family patriarch, Edward Brittingham, also wined and dined the women when they later passed through Mexico City, after they had spent some time at a Santa Engracia ranch in Tamaulipas and several weeks in Acapulco.[14]

During these visits, Hazel had hatched the notion that a union with one of the Brittingham boys could still be in the cards. The girls had spent many hours with Jack and Robert horseback riding. The young men took them on sightseeing tours and outings, and escorted them to local fiestas. Hazel thought both Jack and Robert were especially attentive toward Nancy.[15]

As luck would have it, Nancy had also inexplicably, but amicably, nullified her own engagement to a university classmate. Nancy's former beau had graduated to become a Bay Area eye doctor.

While Mada surprised the family by breaking what everyone considered to be the ideal engagement, they were even more stunned when, early that autumn, she announced she would wed a young marine second lieutenant she had only recently met.

Her December 1937 wedding to Lt. Benjamin L. McMakin, though conducted with all the formal trappings of a sanctioned ritual, remained a bone of contention between mother and daughters. Nancy was almost giddy with excitement over her sister's marriage and her new brother-in-law, while Hazel remained passively disappointed with Mada's choice. Dashing though he might be, the young man's pursuit of a military career offered little prospect for future wealth.

The newlyweds were living in married officers' billets on the Parris Island Marine Corps base in South Carolina. No sooner had they settled in than Nancy began talking about an extended trip back East to visit her sister. Her idea was to go by train, alone.

When Hazel insisted on chaperoning, a running argument over travel plans ensued.

Hazel had several reasons for wanting to take charge, not the least of which was keeping an eye on her only remaining marriageable daughter. She was not about to let Nancy take off alone to Parris Island for unsupervised attendance at social events featuring handsome navy and marine bachelors in their splendid uniforms.[16] One military man in the family was quite enough.

Since Pullman train fare for two would be expensive, Hazel suggested it would be more economical to drive. This would serve another purpose as well. By the mother's calculation, a swing through northern Mexico on the return trip, with a stopover at the Brittingham hacienda, might provide the opportunity to bring Nancy and the eligible bachelors in contact again.

Nancy's desire to go solo for a reunion with her sister remained a topic of contention in the household for several weeks in February and into early March. She was twenty-three, after all, and trying to be her own, grown-up person. But Hazel adamantly insisted on accompanying her. And Nancy was unable to ally her father on her side of the argument that she was old enough to go by herself.

Pop seemed to settle the question of transportation with a rare intervention, unusual for him in such matters. He confided that the family was experiencing an unspecified, temporary financial setback. He could not afford the high cost of first-class Pullman fares for two. For the same reason, commercial air carrier was also out of the question.

For a while, they were at an impasse and even talked about calling it off altogether. But Nancy's eagerness to go on the trip at that time played well into Hazel's ambitions, and they finally agreed on a plan.

It was an earlier stroke of good fortune that ultimately made the trip feasible. Pop Frome had recently won a spanking new luxury car in a charity raffle, after buying two twenty-five-cent tickets while on a business trip back to corporate headquarters in Wilmington. The prize was a 1937 Packard sedan.

The Fromes were already a two-car family, uncommon for the time. When he won it, Pop gave the car to Nancy. It was sitting in the garage with just 4,500 miles on the odometer, two-thirds of which had been driven by one of Pop's DuPont friends, when he delivered it from Delaware to the West Coast. Nancy had so far put it to little use, making short trips around the Bay Area.

The car would save money over train fares, as well as make the mother an indispensable travel companion. There would also be plenty of room to carry the considerable amount of luggage required for such an extended vacation.

A date was set. Hazel and Nancy would leave a day after the Delta Delta Delta spring gala, scheduled for March 22, which Nancy would chaperone. They planned to return by way of Mexico in early June.

But for Pop's good fortune in winning the car, the fateful trip might never have happened. Winning any car, let alone a luxurious model like the Packard, was a dream come true. The country's love affair with the automobile was in full bloom well before the onset of the Great Depression. Americans owned almost 80 percent of the world's automobiles.[17]

The Packard was the undisputed leading luxury car made in America throughout the post–Great War period. This one was a Packard Eight Series, seven-passenger sedan, which retailed for a manufacturer's suggested price of $1,900.[18] With an eight-cylinder engine and a wheelbase of eleven and a half feet, it weighed slightly less than two tons, at 3,835 pounds. While not as prestigious as Packard's larger, twelve-cylinder Super Twelve, it was quite luxurious, considering the average cost of a new car in 1938 was $763.

It was the ideal touring car, providing, of course, there were two drivers to spell one another and break the monotony of the three-thousand-mile trip. While the Packard got only about ten miles to the gallon, its twenty-five-gallon fuel tank allowed for long stretches between refills. Gasoline had dropped to about ten cents a gallon from seventeen at the beginning of the Depression.[19] Occasionally, price wars drove that cost to as low as a nickel, especially when hot crude from the vast new East Texas oil field glutted the market.

Packard Motor Car Company touted the car as one of the most comfortable ever built, with its "Completely-Balanced Design." For the traveler's enjoyment on long trips, Packard wired in an antenna that promised the clearest and most powerful reception for a separately installed radio. A radio made by Galvin Corporation was specially designed for use in automobiles. The new radio was named Motorola, adding the word motor to the suffix "ola" that designated most popular audio equipment during the early twentieth century.

There was plenty to listen to on the radio, from music, variety broadcasts, and serialized dramas and adventures, to the troubled news of the nation and the world. Preachers fulminated on the air, with demagogues like Father Charles Coughlin, the pro-Nazi radio priest, haranguing millions of listeners, coast to coast. The first leg of the trip would also be in constant range of the "border blasters." These English-language stations in Mexico trumpeted unregulated messages over the border, on 100,000-watt transmitters, twenty-four hours a day.

The first day of spring 1938 found Nancy and her mother busily packing for their new adventure. Such a motor trip without male escort would have been fraught with concern for most women of the day. For the intrepid, globe-traversing Frome women, it was a lark. Hazel could also be smugly satisfied that the vacation promised the potential for more than just another enjoyable outing.

3

Flooding and mudslides in Southern California postponed the departure hour for the women's cross-country motor trip to visit Mada. The on-again, off-again trip was finally underway shortly before noon on Wednesday, March 23. Perhaps the delay was just as well, since Nancy had been out late the night before, attending the Tri Delta spring dance.

Monsoon rains all along the California coast during the first week of March 1938 were blamed for more than two hundred deaths and millions of dollars in damage to homes and businesses, highways, and bridges. The storms were so severe that the Academy Awards ceremonies in Los Angeles, originally scheduled for March 3, had been postponed a week.

The Frome women were not about to let a little weather interfere with their plans. They had a nearly new car and could choose from several recently built, coast-to-coast highways, which had been constructed to make work for thousands of unemployed men and boys.

The most direct route, US Highway 50 from San Francisco to Ocean City, Maryland, crossed the Midwest with a network of excellent, multilane roads that would deliver them almost door-to-door from their home in Berkeley to Parris Island, South Carolina. It was one of the most scenic routes in the new network of highways, taking the traveler on modern roads through the Sierra, Wasatch, and Rocky Mountains of California, Utah, and Colorado, and across the prairie lands of Kansas and Missouri, before veering south to the eastern seaboard. Hazel's mother and five sisters lived in Missouri, so such a route could have also offered an opportunity for a reunion with Nancy's grandmother and aunts.

An alternative was a less coordinated southern route, roughly following the newly designated and uncompleted US 80, originating in San Diego and terminating at Tybee Island, Georgia. Only the eastern portion of that system, named the Dixie Overland Highway, had been finished, from the east coast to Dallas. To connect to that route from San Francisco, the women would have to drive nearly four hundred miles south in California and then cross Arizona, New Mexico, and hundreds of miles into Texas, before picking up the new highway. With the March rains having caused considerable damage to roads and bridges in Southern California, that alternative seemed problematic.

But for some unexplained reason, they chose the longer, southern route that would take them along the Mexico border and through El Paso, Texas, to connect with US 80.

Whether it was because of the many high mountain passes on US 50, some of which were still heavily snow packed that time of year, or another unknown reason, Hazel most likely made the final choice of the southern alternative. Pop was not consulted in the matter. The Frome women seldom bothered him about their extensive travel schedules, conferring only about the financing of their trips.

They were undeterred by the reports of recent flooding in the state, having traveled through other deluges, in far worse terrain than modern California. While motoring from Monterrey to Santa Engracia on their Mexico trip the previous summer, Hazel, Nancy, and Mada found themselves stranded on a muddy road, miles from nowhere. A friend who was also vacationing in the area would later attest to their resourcefulness.

"It was raining and the Frome car was stuck in a ditch approaching the ranch," recalled Mrs. T. B. Chattam, about finding them on a desolate stretch of Mexican countryside in the summer of 1937. She described how the women had managed the situation quite well. Hazel had hired a donkey cart for her own transportation and horses for Nancy and Mada to ride bareback to continue their journey. When Mrs. Chattam last saw them they were riding off toward the guest ranch — the girls on horseback and Hazel huddled under a serape in the cart.[20]

Pop also boasted that, on their motor trip through Europe, the women had never run into a problem they couldn't handle, be it in the bistros or the backwaters of the Continent.

So, despite the road conditions, Nancy and Hazel chose to head out into the storms on the cross-country drive to visit Mada and her new husband.

Since they intended to be gone several months, selecting the appropriate clothing and accessories took considerable planning. Hazel's intuition that she should accompany Nancy on the extended visit seemed borne out by the choices her fun-loving daughter had made. Nancy clearly planned to go partying. At the top of her clothing list were three evening gowns: a backless, maroon taffeta formal with rhinestone straps; a V-neck dress with a slit down the back in deep coral crepe; and a turquoise chiffon formal.[21] The rest of Nancy's trip attire included assorted dresses, coats, skirts and blouses, shoes, hats, lingerie, and bathing suits, in addition to toiletries. Altogether, she packed forty-five items of clothing and accessories; her mother, only half as much. Both women took flowered silk, Japanese kimono-style negligees, acquired on their most recent world cruise.

Their best jewelry was in a safety deposit box at the local bank, but they did wear some expensive, smaller pieces.

It took six pieces of luggage to hold everything, including two well-worn wardrobe trunks. Hazel's trunk was festooned with stickers from European hotels and painted with her initials, "H. F." Nancy's bore her initials, "N. F.," but no travel stickers. They also took large leather suitcases, a cosmetics case, and a sizable, hard-sided hatbox.

On the morning of their departure, Pop Frome loaded the trunks in the Packard's spacious rear luggage compartment, above the spare tire and tire tools. The car's storage area provided nearly eight cubic feet in a carpeted space above the spare. Pop left for work while Hazel and Nancy were putting the finishing touches on their packing. He didn't know exactly what time they took off, only that it was later than originally planned.[22]

Along with their luggage, the women took a heavy brown army blanket, a light yellow blanket, and a red cotton Navajo blanket. The bedding was arranged in the wide, velvet-covered backseat of the car, to provide a sleeping area for one of them to rest when they took turns driving. They did not intend to stop, except at night, and hoped to make the trip across country in six days of hard driving. They planned to arrive at Mada's home at Parris Island on Tuesday, March 29.[23]

On their way, they had to drop off the family dog at a veterinarian kennel where it would be boarded during their absence. They were apparently feeling harried, because they forgot to go by the bank for traveler's checks. Nancy was carrying $50 in cash, and Hazel had about $150, which, in a habit developed through years of travel, she had pinned inside her bra. Pop had reminded them that they could replenish their cash by writing checks at key cities where Atlas agents would vouch for them.[24]

The women were not far into their journey before signs of the devastating floods became obvious. They drove the car along normally excellent highways with lanes and sections of bridges now washed out. The forced detours soon obliterated their previous itinerary.

They originally planned to intersect a highway connecting to US 80 on the California-Arizona border, in the vicinity of the desert hamlet of Needles, on the first day. This is what they told Pop. But their late departure and the unexpected detours disrupted their schedule. At some point they decided to drive far off their intended route and stop for the evening in Los Angeles, only 380 miles into the initial leg of the trip.[25]

Atlas Powder Company kept a corporate suite at the magnificent Los Angeles Biltmore Hotel, which the Frome women, as well as Pop and his business associates, frequently used free of charge. An unplanned layover at the Biltmore would offer a splendid start to their trip, since it was internationally known as the finest hotel in the western United States. There they could enjoy a luxurious room and excellent service without depleting their travel budget.

Pop had spent forty nights at the Biltmore the previous year. It was his home away from home. The women were also no strangers to the hotel. They had stayed two nights as recently as late January. This followed closely on a ten-day stay when the whole family went to Los Angeles to attend the 1938 Rose Bowl, where Nancy's team, the Golden Bears, handed the Alabama Tide a stunning 13–0 defeat. They had checked into the Biltmore for the Pasadena football festival on December 27. Pop left the following day; Hazel and Nancy stayed on until January 8.

On the current visit, the women did not take time to enjoy the many amenities of the fabulous hotel they had used so often in the past. However, the grand trappings of the Italian Renaissance–style lobby and galleria set a fine stage for their first night on the road. As attendants took care of parking their loaded car, they were whisked by a liveried bellman to one of the 1,400-plus luxury rooms in the eleven-story hotel.

Just staying at the Biltmore was an exciting experience, because the facility was frequented by movie moguls and stars, corporate executives, and the international glitterati of the traveling world.

Less than two weeks earlier, the Tenth Annual Awards of the Academy of Motion Picture Arts and Sciences had been staged for the fifth time in the hotel's grand, subterranean Biltmore Bowl. Spencer Tracy and Bette

Davis had accepted Oscars for best actor and best actress, for their roles in *Boy's Town* and *Jezebel*, respectively.

It had been a controversial year for the Oscars.[26] The epic movie *The Adventures of Robin Hood*, starring Errol Flynn, and the actor himself, were all but boycotted in Oscar nominations due, many believed, to the star's brazen association with openly pro-Nazi characters then frequenting the Hollywood nightclub scene.[27]

HAZEL AND NANCY had their Packard brought around early on the morning of the twenty-fourth, hoping to make up for time lost on the first day out. They had another choice of excellent roads. From Los Angeles they could have proceeded directly east on US Route 66, the famed "Main Street of America," which offered wide-lane highways all the way to Amarillo. Instead, they again chose a more southerly route that would take them closer to the Mexican border, via Phoenix and El Paso. This route was a little longer but promised drier weather, being largely desert all the way to Texas.

Unfortunately, the women soon found road conditions further south were no better than those they had encountered the previous day. Almost immediately they were forced to detour, due to flooding and damage along the mountainous and desert roadways. They were all the way to Arizona before they drove out of the devastation caused by the storms.

The sun burst through the clouds as they entered the scenic, but sometimes frighteningly lonely, Sonoran Desert. The isolation of the desert expanse and sparse traffic would most certainly heighten the sense of danger for lone female travelers. The rigors of driving around road hazards soon took a toll, and the trip was no longer the lark it was planned to be.

Although Packard advertised the Touring Sedan as the most comfortable ride of any automobile in America, Nancy began suffering severe cramps in her right leg from long stints pushing the gas pedal, manipulating the clutch, and braking. The chrome-plated, treadle-type accelerator did not really "rest the foot," as the brochure promised. Then Nancy came down with a cold, which seemed to grow worse with each grueling hour. Finally, she was forced to give up her turns at the wheel to her seemingly indomitable mother, who no doubt took over that responsibility with a few well-placed reminders about how indispensable she was on such a long journey.

By the time they reached Phoenix, just over four hundred miles from Los Angeles, late on Thursday afternoon, they were ready to call it a day. Exhausted from hours of unbroken desert motoring and already getting on each other's nerves, they stopped for the night at a motor court just outside the city. The place was called the Sea Breeze, oddly misnamed for a motel in the middle of a desert.

The next morning they tried again to get an early start. Nancy's cold was worse, and the leg cramps still troubled her, even after a night's rest. Adding to their road jitters, a scruffy looking motorcyclist tried to engage Nancy in conversation while the women ate breakfast at the motel's greasy spoon café. The man lingered outside longer than seemed necessary and did not ride off until they had checked out and entered the highway themselves at about 8:00 a.m. They had the car serviced, gas tank filled, and tires checked at a Conoco station near the motel.

Leaving Phoenix, the travelers soon drove out of the Sonoran Desert, only to enter an even harsher terrain. The Chihuahuan Desert was far less scenic and more foreboding, with great stretches of highway devoid of roadside services.

At 2:00 p.m., the women stopped to refuel at Cal Taylor's Texaco Super Station in Safford, Arizona. Hazel told Taylor they were having minor car trouble, which had developed soon after leaving Phoenix. After refilling the tank he checked on the problem. The car was making a rapid backfire noise. He suggested it might be a valve sticking or a camshaft belt slipping, but he had no mechanic available. He told Hazel he did not think it would cause a breakdown before they could drive the two hundred miles to El Paso, which she mentioned would be their next layover.[28]

4

The first glimpse of Paso del Norte could be as welcome as the discovery of one of Coronado's fabled Seven Cities of Gold, when travelers caught sight of the skyline shimmering above the Rio Grande River. The glow of the setting sun painted the city's tall buildings, as the Frome women drove their sputtering sedan off the desolate desert into the city limits of El Paso, just before dark on Friday evening.

The municipal oasis on the border had been known for centuries by conquistadors and cowboys as the passage to the North. It wasn't really much of a city, with a population that had declined during the Depression to about ninety thousand. Compared to the glitter of the West Coast metropolises, it looked rather seedy and alien. But it provided temporary sanctuary to the weary travelers. They had been on the road three days, and already the trip was beset by floods, detours, car trouble, and illness.

Shortly after 6:00 p.m., they pulled up to the curbside entrance of the Hotel Cortez in the center of town. After they registered, an eager bellhop insisted on carrying their two overnight bags to suite 814, even though the women indicated they didn't need help with this small amount of luggage. The bellhop, a Mexican lad from Juarez, said he would be available to assist them at any time, with anything they might need during their stay.

Their accommodations included a sitting room with a separate bedroom and large bath. Hazel complained to the concierge about the car trouble, and he had the car taken from in front of the hotel to a nearby parking garage called Hitching Post #2.[29] It was too late in the evening to have the problem diagnosed, because the local Packard dealership was closed until morning.

With the car and most of their luxury items safely stowed for the night, Hazel turned her attention to her ailing daughter. The forced stopover for car repairs would give Nancy a chance to have her health problems — the severe cold and leg cramps — tended to as well.[30] Hazel inquired at the front desk about the house physician and was told the hotel's regular doctor was not on call during evenings and weekends. The prestigious position of hotel doctor to a grand establishment like the Cortez became somewhat less glamorous after hours, when the treatment of celebrity guests was more likely to involve illness or injury caused by overimbibing.

The same bellhop who had carried their luggage to the room overheard the mother's inquiry and approached her, out of earshot of other employees. He knew of a doctor with offices and residence nearby, who made evening and weekend calls for the guests at the Cortez and other downtown hotels. An enterprising bellboy could expect a generous tip from both the ailing hotel guest and the substitute doctor he referred. Hotel management was not aware of the arrangement.

The unauthorized doctor arrived in short order to attend to Nancy in the sitting room of their quarters. He was wearing a cleaned and pressed, though inexpensive, business suit and tie. He was an odd-looking man, with unusually large eyes. When he removed his felt dress hat he revealed scars on his forehead, made more prominent by his closely cropped, military-style haircut.

After a brief examination, the doctor assured the women that Nancy's ailments were not serious. In answer to Hazel's fretting about their plight, he pointed out that, while the delay caused by car trouble was regrettable, the girl would certainly benefit from a day or two of rest from the road. He pulled from his satchel a cold tonic and a bottle of muscle relaxant pills, which he promised would cure the leg cramps. Both medications were labeled as manufactured in Mexico and not likely prescribed north of the border.

The man was perfunctory but amiable. Hazel noted that the doctor was probably an immigrant, as his English was tinged with a German accent. Ever the chatty one, she told him about their visit to Berlin to attend the Olympics. He also seemed mildly interested when she mentioned her husband was a second-generation German American, with an important position as a West Coast executive in the explosives industry.

The doctor took his fee in cash and left as quickly as he had arrived.

Getting off the road and into a luxurious hotel had already rejuvenated Nancy. She and Hazel dined that evening at the hotel's main restaurant, which offered a menu of fine cuisine to its guests and was also a favorite eatery among El Paso's elites. There was no need to leave the hotel to enjoy excellent food in a pleasing milieu, as the restaurant was an extension of the grandly decorated, Spanish Colonial–style lobby. The Frome women were used to the luxury afforded by fine hotels, and in the Cortez they had picked one of the best in the Southwest.

Greatly refreshed after being anywhere but behind the wheel of the car, the women decided to relax by taking in a movie. The bellhop provided directions to a nearby theater, assuring them it was safe to walk to and from the hotel.

The unexpected breakdown of their car and the detours due to inclement weather were a big disappointment for the women. After driving hard for days, they had covered fewer than twelve hundred miles of their three-thousand-mile trip. Now, stuck on the far western tip of the broad state of Texas, their carefully made plan was out the window. They should have been somewhat consoled, looking at the road map, that they had broken down in what seemed to be the only civilized place for hundreds of miles. El Paso, it turned out, was not a bad place to be stranded. It was an oasis in a vast desert.

Before turning in for the night, Nancy penned a short letter on hotel stationery to her best friend and sorority sister, Alison Dodge:

Al dear,

Just a note before I go to bed. Excuse the terribly large paper but beggars can't be choosers.

We arrived here tonight with car trouble and still aren't sure what time we'll get away tomorrow. We want to leave early, as Dallas is 650 miles and we want to get as close as possible. So far we have had quite a few detours. The flood in Calif. took out so many bridges and made lots of the road impassable. After we left L.A. it began to get warmer until now I'm really practically roasting. Of course, it isn't like the summers here — but just to help things along Mom won't let me wear a wash dress because of my cold so I've been wearing that cute grey number plus my brown coat. . . .

South Carolina still seems miles away and I'm getting more impatient every minute. As we have figured now we will get in sometime Tues — we hope early in the afternoon.

My "scotch blood" is coming out now that we're in Texas where cigarettes are 18¢ a pkg. and of course we arrived without any. We're practically ready to give up smoking.

Do write and have fun.

Lots of love,

Nancy

She told her friend they had "splurged" on a movie that night, which was followed by a short Movie-tone News report about Hitler's annexation of Austria.

"It [the feature film] was cute, but it was so hot and stuffy in the show — and the place was full of 'smelly' Mexicans," she wrote.

The movie Hazel and Nancy had chosen that evening was *Bluebeard's Eighth Wife*, starring Gary Cooper and Claudette Colbert.

5

The stranded women woke on Saturday to a serious international incident roiling not far from their hotel. Throngs of Mexican protesters carrying anti-gringo signs could be seen in Juarez just across the river from their eighth-floor window. The day they arrived in El Paso, Mexican president Lazaro Cardenas had expropriated most of the large, foreign-owned, mineral-extraction businesses in Mexico. His decree covered mining operations but was primarily aimed at oil company holdings. The Mexican army was dispatched throughout the country to occupy drilling sites and seize physical assets, including crude oil stores, drilling rigs, oil pipelines, tank trucks, and rail tank cars.

Most of the seized property belonged to American petroleum companies. These monopolies were so powerful that they would not allow crude oil taken from the ground in Mexico to be refined into gasoline there. The oil was shipped to the United States for refining and returned to Mexico, to be sold at escalated prices to the Mexican people.

In Juarez, just minutes from the Hotel Cortez, the Mexican army was in the process of seizing hundreds of oil-tanker cars belonging to Standard Oil of Texas and Sinclair Oil. President Franklin Roosevelt reacted immediately by demanding that Mexico compensate the Americans for their losses.[31]

The action sent hundreds of Mexican workers into the streets of Juarez to protest their lost jobs with the "gringo" employers. But far larger crowds reacted joyously to taking back the country's mineral wealth. Wherever the two groups crossed paths, fights erupted. A number of ugly incidents of unruly mobs menacing American tourists were reported, and visits south of the Rio Grande border river were discouraged.

Hazel Frome had more personal problems on her mind when she called Harold White, the resident manager of Atlas Powder Company for the El Paso district, shortly after 7:00 a.m., Saturday. White was the powder company's top mining and explosives engineer for West Texas, New Mexico, and northern Mexico. He was only too glad to assist the boss's wife and daughter with their problem.

White picked up the Frome car at the parking lot and drove it to the local Packard dealership, Stone Motor Company, six blocks from the Cortez. He waited while the shop foreman and a factory-trained mechanic named Bill Hollum diagnosed the problem. The "scraping sound" and other motor noises were not too serious, but minor parts needed for the repair were unavailable in El Paso. This type of mechanical failure was rare. In technical terms, Hollum told White, "the mushroom had broken off the push rod and the eccentric on the camshaft was badly scored."[32] While the defect made a worrisome noise, the mechanic assured White it would be safe for a male operator to drive the car on to Dallas. He did not think it advisable for two lone women to take such a risk, no matter how slight.

Packard offered a four-thousand-mile, ninety-day warranty on new cars, but both had already expired. The foreman told White that the charge, including shipping, would be under fifty dollars. Repairs would take an extra day while they waited for the part to be flown in from the factory in Detroit.

White called Hazel to explain. He said they would be taking a serious risk to set out on the drive from El Paso to Dallas, which was mostly through desert and sparsely populated plains.

Hazel prudently agreed not to take off in the damaged Packard. She authorized the extra charge for airfreight and asked White to bring the rest of their luggage to the hotel. By the time he accomplished that errand around midmorning, the women had already left their room.

The Atlas rep dropped off their luggage with a solicitous bellhop who assured him he was personally in charge of the ladies' welfare while they stayed at the Cortez.

Considering the riots across the border, White was surprised to learn from the bellhop that the women had left the hotel for a shopping jaunt to Juarez. While Hazel and Nancy seemed oblivious to the turmoil, White, along with the other local residents, was keenly aware of the increased potential for danger.

Even under normal circumstances, the border area, particularly on the Mexican side, could be hazardous for the casual traveler. The El Paso–Juarez community had always harbored the usual collection of border-town desperados, but in recent years an even more sinister human denizen had arrived on the scene.

By 1938, El Paso–Juarez had become a hub of international intrigue. A thriving hotbed of agents provocateurs had massed at the border, to incite discord between the United States and Mexico. This group included propagandists and labor troublemakers, as well as spies and saboteurs. Most of the agents were German, but some were from Japan, Italy, and the Soviet Union.

The sudden availability of vast stocks of the newly confiscated American and British crude oil was an unexpected bonus. Mexican authorities announced within days of the seizure that Germany, Japan, and Italy would be the main customers for that oil in the future.

The intrepid Frome women, theoretically, had no reason to attract the attention of these unsavory characters. The women were apolitical. They had traveled freely all over the world, with little thought or care about the subtle dangers festering along their routes from political unrest and poverty.

THE "SUBSTITUTE" DOCTOR'S MEDICINE and advice seemed to work wonders on Nancy's ailments, and after a good night's rest, the women were raring to go exploring. They were apparently unconcerned about the turmoil on the border when, Saturday morning, they boarded the Juarez-bound trolley for the short ride that would take them from the greatest industrial nation into one of the most undeveloped, agrarian countries in the world.

As short as the ride was, Hazel managed to strike up a conversation with a stranger on the trolley — a salesman — who recommended some places to buy perfume.

Later that afternoon, the women were observed walking through the lobby of the Hotel Cortez with a number of shopping bags. Nancy stopped to play with a small terrier another guest was taking for a walk across the street, in San Jacinto Plaza. The square-block park was a duplicate of the promenades found all over Mexico, with its circular, tree-covered, stone walkway, heroic statuary, and sculpted benches.

By this time the presence of the Frome women at the luxurious hotel was well known. Bellboys and male guests alike were hoping for a glimpse or brief conversation with the attractive, obviously worldly daughter.

It wasn't as if they were damsels in distress, cast ashore on some deserted island. Except for the inconvenient delay, the women endured their plight in relative opulence. They were stuck, at least for the weekend, on an isle of plenty, in a sea of despair. Still, both Hazel and Nancy complained of the inconvenience to everyone they encountered. Their complaints evoked little more than polite sympathy, since most of their listeners were struggling hard just to make a living in the sluggish recovery of the late thirties.

The hotel where they were marooned was only a dozen years old, having been built in 1926 at the corner of Mesa and Mills Avenues, in the heart of downtown El Paso. The eleven-story edifice was decorated in Spanish Colonial Revival style. Its stately entrance was flanked by five-story-high casement windows, extending the entire block of the building. Above the arched windows were grilled balconies, which added to the building's grandeur.

The reception area was framed by the coats of arms of Spanish conquistadors.[33] From the time of its opening, the hotel was known as the "Castle of Old Spain on the Plaza." The restaurants, clubs, and breakfast rooms, as well as the entrance to the elevators, all echoed the Spanish Colonial theme. Because these public facilities abutted the lobby, foot traffic was usually heavy, and hotel guests were barely distinguishable from the general public.

The guest rooms were all built around a utility core in the center of the building, providing the upper floors with panoramic views of the territory surrounding El Paso. Rooms on the north side looked out over the nearby, starkly bare Franklin Mountains, with the white sands of the Chihuahuan Desert farther out from the city.

The south side of the building, where the Fromes' eighth-floor suite was located, offered views of the valley of the Rio Grande River. Across the muddy stream, the sprawling hills of Mexican Juarez were covered in densely packed slums. From this height, even the tin-roofed shacks seemed colorful and picturesque.

6

All eyes were on the fashionably dressed California mother and daughter from the moment they crossed the luxurious lobby of the Hotel Cortez. Soon most of the staff and many of the guests were aware of the two women traveling alone across the country and now stranded in their midst by car trouble.

The women's urbane sophistication was obvious to the hotel staff from their dress and demeanor. Some employees noted that both mother and daughter were almost never seen without cigarettes, cork tipped, daintily held in sometimes-gloved hands. Hazel talked enough to other guests and within earshot of the wait staff that everyone knew of their plight. Eavesdroppers also knew, from snatches of her conversations, that these were the relatives of an important West Coast executive. Nancy seemed uncomfortable with her mother's boasting to complete strangers, but before long Hazel had everyone believing that her husband was a major decision maker in America's explosives and munitions industry.

. When the Fromes returned to the hotel from their Saturday shopping spree in Mexico, a telephone message from Harold White was waiting at the hotel desk. White briefed the women on the status of the car and the fact that it would not be ready until midweek. He also invited them to join his family for an outing the following day.

On Sunday, the Whites picked up Hazel and Nancy in the hotel lobby and took them on a sightseeing tour of El Paso's parks and landmarks. After lunch they all went to the midget car races. That evening they ventured across the border bridge and enjoyed a sumptuous dinner in one of the best restaurants. Where quail was a rarity in the States, in Juarez it was served almost as a side dish.

While making the rounds of El Paso, Mrs. White asked if the women were not afraid to travel so far alone. Mrs. Frome laughed at the hazards of the road and said, in all their travels around the world, she and her daughters never had to so much as change a tire. "There is always some gallant gentleman nearby to take care of any problem that might arise," she said.[34]

On Monday, Hazel checked on the car herself and was told the same thing that White had reported. For all her social status, the parts simply could not get to El Paso any sooner. The car would be ready either late Tuesday or early Wednesday.

Before leaving the hotel Nancy penned another letter to friend Alison Dodge and gave it to a bellhop to be mailed. It was dated Monday, March 28, 1938, and written in neat, tight longhand on Hotel Cortez stationery:

Dear Al,

Well, we're still sitting in El Paso when we should be arriving at Parris Island tomorrow. Our car trouble was much more serious than we thought. The camshaft was broken — something that happens only with a defective part, so therefore no one carries such parts. They had to wire Detroit and have it sent from there, so we can't be sure when we will get away from here. If they send it airmail we will possibly get away from here tomorrow afternoon or Wed. It will take us at least three and a half more days of hard driving. I'm terribly disgusted at this point, but I'm glad we're in a decent place instead of some little funny town.

Sat. Mom and I took the street car over to Juarez, Mexico — only about a 15 mins. ride. It isn't much of a place but we did buy some perfume.

Yesterday, the salesman for the Powder Co. and his wife took us around the city and then to the midget auto races. Then to a night club in Juarez for dinner. It was fun but we're terribly tired.

I'll write again when I get there. Don't forget to write us.

My love,

Nancy.[35]

Monday evening the women again went across the bridge into Mexico. This time they decided to venture a little deeper into the border town's nightlife. Keno Smith, floor manager of the Café Juarez Lobby #2, seated the ladies for dinner.

Halfway through the meal, two smartly dressed, Anglo men in business suits approached Nancy and Hazel's table and asked them to dance. The women weren't offended by the approach and, in fact, chatted quite pleasantly. Hazel suggested she might have seen or even met one of them before, in California. She said she thought he was "a salesman on the West Coast."

After the women declined the invitation to dance, the two men left the nightclub.

At around eleven o'clock Monday night, the hotel desk clerk, James O'Reilly, was dozing off, when the rapid pinging of the counter bell startled him awake. Mrs. Frome brusquely asked for her room key and inquired if she had any phone messages.

O'Reilly checked their box for messages and found none.

ON TUESDAY, Hazel and Nancy passed much of the day waiting for the car, reading, and listening to the radio. Nancy was embroidering pillow linens that she kept in a large cardboard box in the sitting room of their suite. As the maid was finishing her chores, Hazel left for a hair appointment at a nearby beauty salon run by E. L. Bradford. She ordered a shampoo, rinse, trim, and set.

While she was in the salon, a major crime drama was unfolding less than a block from the Cortez. At 11:25 a.m., two well-dressed gunmen walked into the lobby of the State Loan Company at 206 North Mesa, bound and gagged manager B. H. Johnson, and fled with $350 in cash. The strong-armed robbery created quite a stir among the locals, but neither Hazel nor Nancy seemed troubled by the brazen crime committed so close to their hotel.

On Tuesday afternoon, Mrs. White talked to Hazel and Nancy, who were in high spirits. The parts for their car had arrived, and it appeared they would be able to continue on their trip the next day.[36]

Earlier, Nancy had asked doorman Tex Riccard about a barn dance planned by the hotel that evening at the Old El Paso Club. When he said the dance wouldn't begin until 9:00 p.m., she and Hazel decided to go back to Juarez for dinner and entertainment.

Despite the violent crime so close at hand, the intrepid mother and daughter again took the trolley across the border to Mexico. That night they ate at the Spanish Town Café and went to at least one nearby club after their meal.

When they returned to the hotel later in the evening, Hazel again stopped for the key, and night clerk O'Reilly checked their box for messages. This time he found a large, plain envelope with no stamps or address. The only marking at all was the word "Frome," scrawled in longhand. Hazel stared at the envelope for a few seconds and asked the clerk who left it. He said he did not know.

Apparently unconcerned about the odd delivery, or perhaps wanting to read it in private, Hazel stuffed the envelope into her purse without opening it. She was a little unsteady on her feet as the women made their way to the ornate elevators to return to their lofty suite.

At 9:30 the following morning, the Packard was repaired and ready to go. A mechanic delivered the car to the front entrance of the Cortez. More than two hours passed before Hazel called down to the bell captain to have their luggage picked up. Doorman Riccard was visibly annoyed that the car was left blocking the hotel entrance for such a long period during the busy checkout time. Important patrons often treated the loading area like their own private driveway, oblivious to the inconvenience they might be causing other arriving or departing guests.

While the bellboy was loading the luggage, Tex Riccard engaged Nancy in casual conversation. She was wearing a knee-length dress and black straw, sailor-type hat, with thick anklet socks and sports shoes. Asked if she would be driving, she told the doorman that her mother always started out driving on their trips and then they switched off every hour or so. Nancy's normally cheery demeanor was absent in that brief exchange, but it was understandable; there was tension throughout the hotel that morning.[37]

About the time the Fromes were having their car loaded to resume the trip, another ominous event was occurring just a few miles away in Juarez. The entire lobby of the hotel was abuzz with the latest news that an assassin's bomb had gone off at a Juarez government building, killing Mayor Jose Borunda and his bodyguard, Domingo Barraza. The already tense situation in Mexico was growing more dangerous. A long stretch of Hazel and Nancy's trip to Dallas would be driven on a desolate stretch of highway abutting the river that formed the troubled border.

They left the hotel on North Mesa shortly before noon, mountain standard time, on Wednesday, March 30. On the way out of town, they stopped at the Texaco Service Station at Myrtle Street and Alameda Avenue to fill the Packard's oversized tank. Mrs. Frome declined attendant C. C. Lampkin's offer to check the oil and tires, explaining that the car should be in perfect shape since it had just come from the garage. She complained the repairs had cost her forty-six dollars.[38]

She wanted to know how the roads were to the east. When Lampkin asked what route they were taking, she said they were going by way of Fort Worth and Dallas. They had originally hoped to complete the long drive to Dallas in one day. To further complicate the late departure, they would lose another hour when they crossed into the central time zone soon after leaving El Paso.

Hazel asked Lampkin if there was any other road circling the city that might make a connection with Route 80, some miles away from the city limits. She was disappointed when he told her this was the only street out of town that linked directly to the highway.

After paying the attendant for the gasoline, Hazel and Nancy Frome drove off into the great Chihuahuan Desert.

Ahead of them was US Highway 80, an almost perfectly straight tarmac ribbon traversing some of the most hostile terrain in North America. Any motorist straying off this lonely route would most likely become lost in a high desert, where the flat, parched earth was broken only by occasional arroyos and low, treeless mountains. The terrain for miles on either side of the road was unpopulated, except in tiny hamlets strung at far intervals. Dirt roads led off to the few lonely ranches out of sight of the main highway. But even most of those old homesteads were now derelict shacks that had long ago been abandoned.

This leg of the trip was actually a continuation of their earlier drive through this great desert. They had successfully crossed the western half in Arizona and New Mexico before arriving at El Paso five days earlier. Now they planned to speed nonstop through the remaining two hundred miles of the treeless expanse east of El Paso. The car was filled with enough gasoline to drive without stopping until the desert was behind them. Their next planned break was just across the Pecos River, at the hamlet of Monahans, Texas. The town was the gateway to the White Sand Hills, a region of drifting dunes popular with passing motorists. But the Fromes were not out for sightseeing.

As the station attendant had told them, the only road through this bleak plain east of El Paso was Route 80. Hazel and Nancy had no choice except to take that highway all the way to Dallas, almost 650 miles away.

Their nearly new Packard was more than a match for the desert. Its eight-cylinder engine was capable of sustained, high speeds. And Route 80, called Broadway of America, was a good, wide-open section of the national highway system. The weather was clear and crisply cool.

They had set out later than planned, which meant if they drove straight through to Dallas, they would arrive well into the wee hours of the following morning.

7

On Thursday afternoon, March 31, two army engineers surveying land near the intersection of US 80 and US Highway 290, almost two hundred miles east of El Paso, came upon an abandoned, silver-gray Packard. The place was called Phantom Lake, eleven miles west of Balmorhea. The soldiers had seen the car there late in the afternoon the day before but guessed the owner might be trekking around the desert nearby and thought nothing unusual of it. Cactus collectors often parked on the roadside and roamed, with shovel in hand, short distances into the brush, searching for rare succulents to add to their gardens or sell at a farmer's market.

When the soldiers saw the car in the same spot on the second day, they grew concerned. Back at camp they told their sergeant, who placed a call to the Reeves County Sheriff's Office. Deputy Sheriff Sam Davis and another deputy were dispatched from Balmorhea to check out the abandoned Packard.

What the deputies found was a car almost begging for someone to drive it away. The doors were unlocked, and the key was in the ignition, with other keys dangling from a chain. Otherwise, the interior of the car was completely bare.[39]

Taking note of the California license plate number, Davis began a careful examination of the car's exterior. It appeared to have been driven roughly through the brush country. Dirt, cacti, and creosote brush were caught in the bumper and undercarriage, and thorns were embedded in the sides of the tires.

The car cranked right up, and the engine seemed in perfect running order, with plenty of gasoline in the tank. But the spare tire in the trunk showed damage, and there were long cactus spikes sticking through the walls. The inner tube required to inflate the tire was missing from the trunk. The tire had been changed recently and a spare placed on the car. Oddly, the tire change kit was still in its original packing, indicating that another bumper jack and tool had been used to remove and replace the damaged tire.

After recording the vehicle's mileage from the odometer in his report, the deputy drove the car into the small town of Balmorhea. He called his boss, Sheriff Louis Robertson, top lawman for Reeves County, at the courthouse in Pecos to report recovery of the car.

On Friday morning, Deputy Davis ordered the car washed and thoroughly cleaned, inside and out. The vehicle seemed in perfect condition except for a green, paint-streaked dent in the right front fender. The damage was so minimal he did not include it in his written description.

From the license plate, a clerk in Pecos was able to determine that the car was registered in Berkeley, California. An assistant in the sheriff's office called the California highway patrol. The state authorities dispatched an officer to the Frome residence, but no one was home. Since the Texas sheriff's call did not sound especially urgent, no further effort was made to track down the car's owners that afternoon.

Weston Frome was traveling on business in Southern California. Finally, at 11:30 Friday night, a Berkeley city patrolman encountered him returning to his house. He informed him that the family car had been found abandoned in the desert in Texas.

Frome immediately raised an outcry that something serious was amiss. Only then did the first alarm bells go off. Visibly shaken, he explained that his wife and daughter were traveling without male escort on a cross-country motor trip. They had planned to leave El Paso on Wednesday, to drive as far as Dallas. He said he had not heard from them since Tuesday.[40] The officer noted in his report that Frome was more than upset. He was also obviously drunk.

Frome's first reaction struck the patrolman as a little odd. The distraught man immediately expressed certainty that his wife and daughter had been "kidnapped and murdered."[41] The officer had told him the car was completely bare of luggage when it was discovered and searched by deputies in Texas. Frome said the car should have been loaded down with baggage when it left El Paso.

Since nothing at the scene indicated foul play — there were no bloodstains, signs of struggle, or broken windows in the automobile — Texas and California authorities were still treating the mystery as a simple "missing persons" case, as of late Friday night. It was two and a half days since the women had left the Hotel Cortez.

On Saturday morning, Sheriff Robertson set out to backtrack the car's known path, to determine if anyone along the route to El Paso might know something about the missing occupants. Driving the car himself with two other Pecos residents for company, the sheriff headed from Balmorhea to US 80 and then westward, checking in at filling stations, cafés, and auto courts. He asked employees at every service business along the route if they had seen the big silver car he was now driving. No one recalled the car stopping at their location or knew anything about the owners' whereabouts.[42] He and his passengers smoked during the ride, filling the front and back ashtrays with cigarette and cigar ashes and butts.

The sheriff did run across an army officer having his car serviced who had heard about the women secondhand. Some of his men had seen two women on Wednesday afternoon, parked in the vicinity where the car was reportedly found. He said his soldiers, on maneuvers in the area, were making cracks about two attractive gals parked on the side of the road, "who gaily waved handkerchiefs and sent big smiles," as their truck rolled past. The soldiers had responded with wolf whistles and shouts for the women's phone numbers. The officer said he only recalled the incident because he had chewed out the platoon sergeant for allowing the soldiers to behave so boorishly.

Having traveled the entire route to El Paso without learning anything about the whereabouts of the car's occupants, Sheriff Robertson called on the local office of the Federal Bureau of Investigation. By Saturday afternoon, FBI agent Burt Dameron of the El Paso office had entered the case, taking jurisdiction of the hunt for the women as a possible violation of the federal kidnapping law.

A bulletin was issued, and by late Saturday a twenty-five-member posse was assembled to begin scouring the desert outward from the point where the car had been found. On Sunday morning, a coast guard airplane was used to broaden the search, flying low and further out from the highway, into the desert and nearby mountains. If the women had abandoned their car and hiked off the road into the desert, there was little hope they could have survived this long. It was three days since they were last seen by anyone of record.

Early Saturday evening, reporters at local papers, including those in El Paso, had received telephone briefings from the FBI and Sheriff Robertson.

Only the *El Paso Times* was able to replate its front page for the Sunday edition deadline. The story was featured under a banner headline. Of less value to the search effort, since it was hundreds of miles from the scene, the *Dallas Morning News* ran an Associated Press wire story on page 1, under the headline

MOTHER, DAUGHTER, ON WAY TO DALLAS,
VANISH IN HILLS/FOUL PLAY FEARED

Meanwhile, Frome contacted his El Paso manager, Harold White. White, who had already been in touch with the local FBI office, updated Frome on everything the authorities relayed to him. He also repeated what little he knew about the movements of Hazel and Nancy before their departure from El Paso.

"Things look pretty bad down here. You'd better come," he said.

After Frome conferred with some of his fellow Atlas Powder executives, the manager of his San Francisco office, R. K. Gottshall, made arrangements for the two of them to leave for Texas. American Airlines had a direct flight from San Francisco to El Paso, which they could just catch if they left immediately for the airport.

The flight arrived in El Paso at 4:30 a.m., Sunday. They were met at the airport by El Paso district attorney Roy Jackson and the local Atlas Powder Company manager. Witnesses to the arrival said both men from California appeared inebriated when they deplaned, but they didn't make much of it, considering the terrible circumstances surrounding the trip.

The three Atlas executives and the local DA piled into White's car and headed out on the long drive to Pecos, where the search effort was headquartered. By this time, Sheriff Robertson had left the Frome Packard in El Paso for the G-men to examine further and hitched a ride with a highway patrolman back to Pecos. The federal authorities were convinced they had a kidnapping on their hands.

Arriving in Pecos, the California executives insisted on joining one of the search parties in the wild desert lands near where the car had been discovered. Sheriff Robertson urged them to stay in town and get some rest, but Weston Frome and his associates were adamant about participating in the hunt.

"We started to walk around the area," Frome said, describing it later to a Ranger. "We walked up to the edge of a cliff and looked out. I told Harold I believed they had been murdered. He said I should not look at it that way. I said that's just the way I feel about it."[43]

After several hours of painfully hiking around the bleak landscape, the exhausted executives decided to return to Pecos and check into a motel. Robertson assured Frome he would call him the minute there was any news about his family.

Nobody in law enforcement had suggested that his wife and daughter might be dead, but Pop Frome pointedly demanded that, "if the murderers" were ever caught, he wanted to talk to them first. It was an unusual statement to make at the time, since there was no evidence the women were not still alive.

Sheriff Robertson let the strange request pass, with only a weak attempt to console the agitated man.

In those parts, and in much of the rest of rural America, it was considered odd, if not downright stupid, for women to travel without male escort on the highways and roads. Thus, the headline in the *El Paso Times* on Sunday, April 3, 1938, drew extra special attention from readers and officials.

EL PASO WOMEN VISITORS DISAPPEAR:

MOTHER, DAUGHTER FROM CALIFORNIA OBJECTS OF SEARCH

Lawmen from several local, state, and federal agencies in a half-dozen southwestern and western states had been on the lookout for the women at least twenty-four hours before the general public learned of their disappearance. The ever-widening search along US 80 was well underway. Citizen volunteers, workers from the Civilian Conservation Corps (CCC), local ranch hands, and soldiers bivouacked in the area added manpower to the hunt.

Mayhem on the nation's highways was not unusual in this lawless, late-Depression period, but the disappearance of socially prominent female travelers — especially because one of them was a winsome, young sorority girl — struck a sensitive national nerve. Across the country, the wire-service accounts of the strange disappearance were being set in type for the Monday-morning editions of hundreds of newspapers, ranging from metropolitan publications on both coasts to the small-town dailies serving every corner of the nation's heartland.

Closer to home, the disappearance of Hazel and Nancy Frome created near hysteria. The San Francisco and Los Angeles metro papers and the myriad of California dailies prepared sensational headlines for their Monday editions, as wire reports from Texas were frequently updated to reflect breaking events from the weekend.

As it turned out, one man held the key to the emerging story, and that source was a most reluctant and unreliable eyewitness.

8

He was a hulking man with a pie-plate-flat face, broad nose, and close-set eyes in a large head supported by no discernible neck. A wart on the side of his nose and gaps between tobacco-stained front teeth further marked his hard lot in life. His usual attire did little to improve the first impression of many who met him that Jim Milam was a galoot.

A grayish fedora, grime stained around the band from years of soaking up sweat and the petroleum products he handled on the job, mixed with dust from countless sandstorms common to the region, topped the head that protruded between the shoulder straps of faded bibbed overalls. His wife, with skillfully applied patches, kept the oversized denim overalls in service long after they should have been retired. Getting the most use out of clothing was a necessity in a household supporting ten children in the waning years of the Great Depression. Idle youths — and there were many in the desert towns on his delivery route — regularly taunted him about gypsy bands camping in the seat of his pants. He chalked up their insults to jealousy over his having a steady job when most of their dads were on the dole.

It was not necessarily due to poor hygiene that he appeared always in need of a bath. He was a loyal employee of the Pelton Oil Company of Wickett, Texas. Handling the gasoline, oil, and lubricants he delivered by tanker all over his sales territory kept him looking perpetually soiled. Unfortunately, the negative impression conveyed by his physical appearance was not improved by his personal demeanor. When it was convenient, he claimed he could neither read nor write. Now he wished he had also played dumb about what he saw four days earlier, along a desolate stretch of US Highway 80, between Van Horn and El Paso. If he had just kept his mouth shut, he would not be out here on his one day off, tromping around in the heart of the Chihuahuan Desert trying to avoid the fangs, stingers, and stickers of every plant, insect, reptile, and animal native to the area.

For all his clumsiness, it was not his fault when he stumbled over the edge of the shallow gravel pit and landed painfully on his knees in a viciously thorny bush. The slight fall ripped a large hole in the already patched knee of his overalls.

His search companions were too far away to witness his embarrassment. Not that he needed an excuse for losing his footing. The last rays of the sunset would have blinded anyone to the approaching crevice. The setting fireball was directly in his eyes as he trudged west, and when it dipped behind the Sierra Diablo Mountains, it was impossible to see the old diggings in the gloom cast across the desert floor. Luckily, he tumbled only a couple of feet into the quarry, which had not been visible from the highway a half mile away when they started searching. The abandoned pit was actually little more than a scraping on the surface of the desert, from which an enterprising soul had tried to extract enough gravelly rock to earn a few dollars on some long-ago construction project for a house or road.

Milam was picking himself up, with only a few thorn pricks from the tasajillo bush to show for his clumsiness, when he noticed the two bundles that looked like rag piles, several yards further down the depression.

The truck driver, along with Culberson County sheriff Albert Anderson and a local volunteer named Joe Schneider, a service-station operator and ambulance driver, had been searching the desert six miles east of Van Horn for a couple of hours before he stumbled into the pit and made the gruesome discovery.[44] Like all the others, they were hoping to find some trace of the two California socialites, or a sign that the wealthy matron and her sorority daughter had been in the area.

In a twist of fate, this was not Milam's first encounter with the women.[45] Now he had come upon them for the second time. Their bodies were lying in the middle of the gravel quarry. Four days earlier, he had seen them in a fancy new car capering along the desert highway, apparently playing high-speed chase with one, then two, smaller and older-model cars.

As soon as the trucker's eyes adjusted to the shadows in the pit, there was no question about what he had discovered. His throat was so parched that his first outcry was only a croak, but he quickly found voice to summon his fellow searchers. His usually flat, staring eyes bulged at the sight of two nearly nude female bodies lying face down, motionless, side by side. When he glimpsed the blood-covered heads, fear seized his lungs, causing panic as he called louder and more urgently for his companions to get over to the pit in a hurry.

The several minutes before Sheriff Anderson arrived in the rapidly gathering darkness were long enough for Milam, who did not move closer to the bodies, to once again regret getting involved. In those agonizing minutes while he waited, Milam had time to reflect on the recent events that had brought him to this sorry lot.

As a general rule, he tried always to mind his own business. But his wife was nagging him to call authorities after she read in the Sunday paper that a new Packard driven by the California women was found abandoned, fifty miles east of Van Horn.

To make casual conversation with his wife, he had briefly mentioned what he saw when he returned to his modest little house at 502 South Val Verde Street in El Paso, at the end of his run the previous Wednesday.

Now, days later, she was waving the bold newspaper headline in front of him as he tried to eat his breakfast.

Despite his wife's reaction, Milam didn't think much more about the missing women until later that morning, when the operator at one of the service stations on his delivery route raised the subject while he was gassing up his own truck. When he repeated what he had seen on Wednesday, the station operator, like his wife, insisted he call the Van Horn sheriff's office.

Milam really did not want to get entangled in other people's affairs. After all, he encountered curious occurrences on his route all the time. But he finally had to admit that this particular incident involving the new Packard seemed a bit out of the ordinary. He thought his wife and the station owner were probably right — he should do something. More troubling, in the back of his mind was the thought that he should have done something the day he saw the women and the Packard on the highway. The newspaper story described the car he had seen to a tee. The women he had seen fit the description of the missing mother and daughter too well to be coincidental.

That string of circumstances was to blame for his being stuck in the hole he found himself at the moment. Milam's search companions were too far away to observe the fear that seemed to make his naturally smallish eyes widen, as he stared at the shapeless bundles becoming dimmer in the settling gloom.

While Milam had not initially been overly concerned, many other people had, including the feds. Because kidnapping was suspected, the Justice Department at El Paso had immediately joined lawmen from three Texas counties. An FBI agent had told a reporter he believed the women "may be the victims of foul play."

From where the trembling truck driver stood, there was no "maybe" about it. There had been extremely foul play here. Even a cursory glance at the two bodies revealed terrible, bloody wounds.

When Sheriff Anderson arrived at the scene, he quickly confirmed that the women were both dead. He ordered Milam and the Van Horn man to stay with the bodies while he went back into town to spread the word that would bring lawmen from three sparsely populated and sprawling West Texas counties. The broader search in the desert and mountains along both sides of US 290, and west to the intersection of US Highway 80, had to be called off.

Twilight rapidly turned to dusk, with no reflected light from a settlement or ranch house to cast an afterglow on the gruesome scene. As Milam and Schneider waited for what seemed like an eternity, the darkness slowly deepened. Joe Schneider was a large man, too, like Milam. He was better dressed, in a leather jacket and somewhat battered, but clean, ten-gallon hat. Milam kept turning on and off the bulky hand torch Sheriff Anderson had left them but avoided casting its fading beam onto the bodies they guarded. The beefy trucker ignored Schneider's suggestion that he preserve their only source of light. After the third or fourth warning that the flashlight was about to burn out, Milam told his companion that he was not about to sit there in the desert, in total darkness, with two dead women lying only a few feet away.

9

Albert Anderson wasted no time instructing the Van Horn switchboard operator to connect him with his fellow sheriffs in the adjoining counties. The operator first put him through to Reeves County sheriff Louis Robertson at Pecos, whose office was investigating the abandoned car. Robertson also had the grim responsibility of notifying the Atlas Powder entourage at a local motel, to give Pop Frome the worst possible news about his wife and daughter.

Sheriff Chris P. Fox of El Paso County was next on the list, since the women had been stranded in El Paso for several days while their car was being repaired. They had left El Paso the previous Wednesday but had not been missed until Friday, after the abandoned car found in Reeves County was determined to belong to them.

After alerting the others, Anderson rousted his small force of three deputies and the reserve, nonpaid deputies — his reliable posse of local businessmen and ranchers who could be counted on in a community crisis. He ordered them out to the crime scene, primarily to assist in crowd control. There *would* be crowds, too. He was sure that when the telephone operator finished her assigned chores, she would call everyone in town and the surrounding ranches with news of the horrific discovery. The efficiency of the rural grapevine would take care of the rest.

To be on the safe side, Anderson placed a call to Austin to inform the night desk at Texas Ranger headquarters that the bodies of two prominent California women had been discovered in his county. This was not just another killing of a migrant worker, or even a local citizen. The status of the victims would likely make this a hotter news event than a local sheriff could handle.

With that in mind, Anderson phoned an El Paso reporter who had recently covered his last election and written a couple of favorable pieces about him. Then he called Justice of the Peace L. L. Morrow, who served as the county coroner in murder cases. Morrow, in turn, called a local physician, Dr. John Wright of Van Horn, who worked as a part-time medical examiner for Culberson County.[46]

Finally, Anderson called the El Paso office of the Federal Bureau of Investigation, since the Justice Department was initially involved in the case as a possible kidnapping. Under provisions of the Lindbergh Act passed less than four years earlier, the feds gained jurisdiction in local cases, under the presumption that missing persons had been kidnapped and possibly carried across state borders. Otherwise, local and state lawmen jealously guarded their turf whenever crimes occurred in their areas.

As expected, by the time Sheriff Anderson had finished all the official and expedient notifications and arrived back at the scene less than an hour later, the shoulder of US 80 was lined with cars and pickup trucks. There was even a wagon with its horse team tethered to the bumper of an old Ford. Unfortunately, it was Sunday evening and everybody in town was off work. Such an event would bring out every male in two counties who heard about it. It was almost an unwritten part of the job description for the town switchboard operators to dispense gossip, and no amount of scolding would prevent eavesdropping on private or official conversations. Still, when he observed mayhem at his spoiled crime scene, Anderson wished the bodies had not been discovered until the next morning, when most men would have been at work, and the womenfolk and children left at home, with no access to transportation. Few families in that part of the country could afford a second car.

The bright glow of a dozen kerosene lanterns and what looked like a small sea of cowboy hats created bobbing shadows on the hardpan desert floor, a half mile south of the roadway. The sheriff had told Milam and Schneider just to watch the bodies. He could not expect untrained civilians to control the curious crowds racing to the grizzly scene.

By the time Anderson returned, milling gawkers from all over Hudspeth and Culberson Counties had trampled the area around the corpses. The denim-clad men and a few teenage boys were already collecting souvenir rocks and whispering that the women were likely raped, because most of their clothing was torn off. Anderson also noticed girls and women in the crowd, some carrying infants. The code of the times in West Texas allowed that a murder scene like this was no fit place for females to visit, but the spectacle was already too great for such niceties to be observed.

With a sheriff's authority, he had no trouble pushing back the curiosity seekers to the edge of the lantern-lit circle surrounding the bodies.

Albert Anderson's size alone intimidated many badland miscreants and good citizens alike, even before he donned his wide-brimmed, high-peaked cowboy hat and rodeo-heeled boots. He wore a large six-shooter, slung low from his hip, in the old Western style.

After dispersing a lingering knot of spectators, he went directly to the object of their morbid curiosity. He knelt over the scantily clad body of the younger woman. She was lying face down, only feet from the corpse of a middle-aged woman. The angry sheriff was too busy to notice that the barrel tip of his six-shooter dragged in the sand when he crouched so close to the ground. It was apparent to anyone that the crime scene was ruined beyond reconstruction, with footprints now too numerous to count, everywhere except in the immediate vicinity of the corpses.

While some might consider him a hick-town sheriff, Anderson considered himself fully capable of dealing with a crime of this magnitude. He was not about to relinquish authority over this case, even if the murders had not occurred in the place where the bodies were now.

Justice of the Peace Morrow and the part-time medical examiner Dr. Wright were already on the scene hovering over the corpses when the sheriff cleared the crowd to the edge of lantern light. The doctor's macabre medical work was underway, despite the press of curious spectators.

A third person had joined them and stood nodding, as they made technical observations about the condition of the bodies.[47] The man, nattily dressed in a sporty blazer and Eastern-style riding boots, seemed to be providing expert assistance to the coroner and medical examiner as they began the unpleasant task of methodically going over the corpses. His attire, swarthy good looks, thin mustache, and overly oily, slicked-down, curly black hair would have set him apart from the locals, even if his slight East European accent did not. But he seemed to know what he was doing and deftly handed over whatever medical tool or device the probing experts called for from their forensic kits.

Sheriff Anderson, who prided himself on recognizing every automobile in Culberson County and most from neighboring Hudspeth County, focused for a moment on the man assisting in the medical examination. Had his services not been otherwise needed, he would have singled out the stranger for questioning. He was too busy at the moment but took mental note that the flashy, older-model Cadillac coupe parked on the highway amidst an assortment of more practical vehicles likely belonged to the stranger. That car was not from around Culberson County. It was a 1932 model roadster, with a yellow body and black fenders. Despite the ubiquitous layer of West Texas dust, it appeared to be sporting a fresh coat of paint.[48]

Under different circumstances, the sheriff would have asked to see the stranger's credentials. But he assumed the local coroner knew the man, or he would not have allowed him near the bodies, let alone to assist in the grim process.

After again ordering the crowd back, Anderson moved closer, to observe the doctors working over the corpses by lantern light.

The women did not die merciful deaths.[49] That was apparent from the dried blood caking the wounds on both corpses. While they were now lying peacefully, side-by-side, face down in the depression on the hardscrabble desert floor, their visible wounds told another story. The grizzled Texas lawman almost recoiled when one of the examiners turned the head of the younger woman so her face was revealed. Her dark blonde hair was matted to a badly disfigured face, caked with blood and dirt. The head itself was misshapen from some sort of massive trauma. It was apparent she had struggled, from the small trenches clawed and kicked into the hard ground beneath her right hand and feet.

Both bodies were almost nude, the younger woman wearing only panties, shoes, and socks. The mother still wore a slip, girdle, hose, and shoes. The top of her slip was torn, as were the daughter's boy shorts.

On closer inspection, Sheriff Anderson could see considerable damage inflicted on both women's faces. The bodies were marked by dried blood on cuts and abrasions over their arms, legs, and exposed parts of their torsos. But by far the most damage appeared to be to the women's heads. Examiner Morrow opined on the spot, within earshot of all close-by observers, that they appeared to have been beaten to death with a blunt instrument. "Probably a hammer," he said.

The older woman had put up a hand-to-hand struggle before dying. Her face had been battered, and one of the assailants apparently had bitten a large chunk of flesh from her left forearm. A major blow had broken her jaw.

When he rolled the body of the younger woman over, one of the medical examiners noted that her rib cage appeared to be crushed. She had suffered numerous burns on the knuckles of her right hand, which were now circular scars. The wounds were burned deep into the flesh. Her left hand was balled into a tight fist. When the examiner pried it open he found that she, too, had put up a fight. The little fist held a clump of black hair, apparently ripped from her assailant's head. In the other hand, she clutched a book of matches.

Anderson was surprised to find that the killer or killers had left behind some valuable items of jewelry. The older woman was wearing a gold wedding ring, which could be easily pawned, and a diamond-encrusted wristwatch. The younger woman had a pricey looking, French-style pendant watch around her neck and a ring with a small diamond on her left hand. The assailants would have had ample opportunity to remove these expensive items, either before or after the murders.

The sheriff agreed with the medical men in their initial conclusion that the women had been tortured for a considerable length of time before they died. Evidence on the ground indicated that whoever killed them might have lingered in the area. A crumpled pack of Lucky Strikes and numerous smoked butts were found about twenty feet from the bodies. What few impressions on the ground were not ruined by the milling spectators suggested that the older woman had been dragged from a car to the shallow pit. Her abuse might have been administered elsewhere.

Sheriff Anderson was in a hurry to get the bodies out of the desert. Local service-station owner E. N. Phillips and Jim Terrell, the principal of Van Horn High School, volunteered to drive the bodies to El Paso in a hastily commandeered van belonging to a local delivery company.[50] Arrangements were made to take the bodies to the Peak-Hagedon Undertaking Parlor in El Paso, where autopsies would be performed by that county's well-known forensic expert, Dr. Willis W. Waite. Technically, they should have been taken to nearby Van Horn for further examination, rather than transported 120 miles to another county. But the rural county seat did not have facilities or experts to conduct a full-scale autopsy. The sheriff wanted to remove the bodies as quickly as possible, in hopes the gawkers would go home.

Later that night, driver Phillips told a newspaper reporter that the Van Horn medical examiner, Dr. Wright, had confided an awful fact to him at the crime scene: the younger woman had been "ravished" by her assailant. The mother, according to Phillips's account of Dr. Wright's examination at the scene, had "probably not been criminally assaulted," even though her outer garments were removed.[51]

There was never any doubt that the murdered women were the missing California socialites Hazel Frome and her daughter Nancy. But as the bodies were taken from the crime scene for further examination, away from the morbidly curious crowd, the identity of the victims was the only fact known for sure by the Texas lawmen converging on the district.

10

By early Monday morning the awful details of the murder had been broadcast across the country through a steady stream of radio bulletins from El Paso, the state capital at Austin, and the Bay Area. A horrified public began the new week with shocking reports flashed over the newswires, each update more lurid than the last.

Once the oil-truck driver told Sheriff Anderson what he had seen on the highway near Van Horn, the local lawman felt justified in declaring that the notorious case belonged in his jurisdiction. Since the bodies were found on his turf, the jurisdiction was officially fixed by law in Culberson County. The sheriff repeated to anyone who would listen that he was now in charge of the investigation — of the most sensational crime in America!

But Anderson did not reckon with the thunderous public clamor for a quick solution to the crimes.

News of the gruesome murders of the California socialites sent shock waves through the political community at Austin, even before the bodies were removed from the desert. On Sunday night, the governor was awakened in the mansion across the street from the pink granite capitol building. Aides warned of looming public relations problems for the state, not to mention personal damage to the governor's reputation if the case was not handled properly. Texas was already branded, with some justification, as a lawless land that spawned and harbored more than its share of infamous murderers, bandits, and bank robbers.

In consultation with top advisers, the governor hastily formulated a response. He ordered Colonel H. H. Carmichael, director of the Texas Department of Public Safety (DPS), to muster the state's top law enforcement resources, including the Texas Rangers, to get to the crime scene quickly. The governor wanted the case solved and the story wrapped up before the yellow press further sullied the state's reputation.

That the rich California women were traveling without male escort out in that lonely quarter provoked disapproving commentary by authorities in Austin, as it had earlier among some citizens in communities closer to the crime scene in West Texas.

In these hard times, automobile travel around the expansive state was usually limited to necessary trips to accomplish some specific chore at hand. Otherwise, only two categories of people generally frequented these long stretches of desolate Texas highway: the very wealthy and the desperately poor. The wealthy could afford to travel for pleasure. The poor, of necessity, hitched rides across the land, usually as single, male hobos, or as families crammed into rickety trucks with everything they owned on their backs and piled atop the vehicles.

Most of the country's population was still living in rural areas or very small towns. Almost every extended family in the United States lived within short distance of the rest of its members. In urban areas, the vast majority of workers lived within walking or streetcar distance of their jobs.

Though Mada, after her marriage, had moved all the way to the other side of the country, she had only been gone a few months. Most locals saw this as a frivolous pleasure trip the women had no business taking. Truth be known, there was likely a touch of envy that the women had the financial wherewithal and independence to make such a leisurely journey.

It mattered little to the public that the mother and sisters had traveled all over the world by motorcar, railway, and steamship. It certainly did not make those reading about the murders any more sympathetic that they usually traveled without male escort. While no one was so lacking in compassion as to suggest the women got what they deserved, most observers did agree the slain women should not have been out there driving around the desert in the first place.

Still, the murders struck terror in the hearts of men and women alike, as they followed every detail in their local papers. So grizzly an act, apparently by a maniac against defenseless womenfolk — with the possibility of sexual violation — aroused the darkest fears in most Americans. Despite much tsk-tsking, the crime filled people with shock and outrage.

This type of crime hit Texans especially hard, because of the arcane, prevailing attitude regarding the role of women in society. Married and single women were still so "protected" in Texas that they did not have the full legal right to own property, whether real estate or financial accounts.

By law, land and securities held by a married woman could not be sold or traded without permission of her husband.[52]

Because of this deeply held patriarchal view about the status of the *femme sole*, Texas lawmen involved in this case felt a macho duty to their own kin to track down the killer or killers as soon as possible.

Reporters at the scene recognized the emotional value of such a sensational story and played it up, in the best tradition of the yellow journalism of the era. The lurid details from the crime scene of the younger woman being "ravished," the bite out of the older woman's arm, the nearly nude bodies in ripped undergarments, and the supposed bludgeoning by hammer led the early news reports. The unknown murderer was characterized as a "fiend."

Texas governor James V. Allred was among the first officials to react publicly. The day after the bodies were found he held a news conference in the state capital and announced a rare one-thousand-dollar reward. The governor reported that five Texas Rangers and a state crime-lab specialist had been sent to Far West Texas to assist local lawmen in the investigation. The significance of that order of magnitude could best be measured by that organization's unofficial motto: "One riot, one Ranger."

"This is a case in which the state should take a larger hand than usual, because it involves the death of citizens of another state, and because it is the second instance in which persons from other states have been killed in the same general area," the governor said.[53]

The governor's reward was quickly bolstered by a pledge of five thousand dollars by Atlas Powder Company for the arrest and conviction of the killer or killers. Additional, smaller bounty offerings increased the total to a substantial ten thousand dollars, one of the largest rewards posted at the time. The FBI had offered the same amount for the capture of the most wanted bank robber in America, John Dillinger, at the peak of his career in 1934.

The similar murder in the "same general area" referred to by the governor was a case involving another wealthy female stranger. Five years earlier, the nude body of a well-to-do Ohio housewife, Mrs. Irene DeBolt, was discovered in Culberson County. Eerily, the attractive, out-of-town woman had been found in the desert less than six miles from the spot where the Frome women were discovered.[54]

Two separate murders of prominent women passing through this single backwater county seemed unusually long odds. This strange coincidence was repeatedly mentioned in newspaper accounts of the new murders, although, from the outset, it was known they had nothing to do with one another. The DeBolt woman's killer was serving a life sentence in the Texas penitentiary.

Sheriff Anderson still winced a bit when he recalled that the "big-city" sheriff of neighboring El Paso County, Chris P. Fox, was given credit for tracking down the DeBolt murderer and solving that case, even though the body had been found in Culberson County. He did not intend to let this new case slip from his control, as he had the previous one.

Anderson chalked up that loss of face to Culberson County's paltry funding of the sheriff's office. As it turned out, the DeBolt murder had not been committed in Anderson's county anyway. After his arrest, the killer had confessed to murdering the woman in Fort Worth, several hundred miles to the east. He merely used the area near Van Horn as a dumping ground, because he thought nobody was likely to find the body anytime soon in such a barren stretch of desert. El Paso sheriff Chris Fox nevertheless became somewhat famous in national crime-fighting circles when he put together the clues and tracked down the killer, all the way to British Guiana.

Sheriff Anderson could not deny that the strange circumstances of finding the bodies of attractive, out-of-state murder victims in two cases right at his back door only added to the sensational aspects of the crime. And the added sensationalism increased the likelihood that other lawmen with bigger budgets and more resources would be trying to horn in on his turf.

The publicity wasn't going to make the job of the lawmen working the case any easier. The news reporters played up the prominence of the victims and the fact that the twenty-three-year-old daughter was a real beauty in the prime of her life. An enterprising West Coast reporter had quickly secured photographs from former classmates at the University of California, Berkeley. Soon, Nancy's dimpled, smiling face was staring from the front pages of newspapers all across the country.

The rapid dissemination of information in the case was furthered by the recent advent of new technology. The photographs taken at the desert crime scene, along with a slew of family photos of Hazel and Nancy gathered from friends in their hometown, were quickly dispatched via AP Wirephoto. The newfangled device for transmitting photographs over the wire could convey real-time images of historic or tragic events anywhere in the country within hours of the occurrence.[55]

The public was almost totally dependent on local daily newspapers for timely details of global current events. Radio broadcasters had been adding news reports to programming for years, but these reports offered only snippets of information. Radio was still primarily important to the average citizen as a source of entertainment and politics. Broadcasts by opinion leaders, from President Roosevelt's fireside chats to the screeds of America's Fascist priest Father Charles Coughlin in his weekly program, brought whole families to the living room to sit together and listen. The serious news of the day was still the domain of the newspapers, and nearly every town and hamlet of any size at all had a daily.

The transmission by wire of details of the murders, accompanied now by photographs of the victims' faces, was the kind of material that soon whipped people to frenzy. The photos of the women made them instantly and intimately famous across America, pushing every other story below the fold of the front pages for days.[56] Even then, the reporters were able to provide only the scantest details of the crime.

Investigators at the scene were already speculating that these latest murders had not been committed in Culberson County. The women had been traveling for days before they finally arrived in the area — whether dead or alive. There were plenty of places along the way to look for their murderers, and tiny Van Horn was the least likely place of all.

Sheriff Anderson tried to cling to the lead role in the investigation, believing he had already made major contributions to the case. He argued that the key witness had come to him first, and he led the successful search that discovered the bodies. Other lawmen believed there was not much more about the crime likely to be discovered in Van Horn.

Jim Milam suddenly became the most important man in Texas. While the medical team worked over the bodies at the scene, Anderson had grilled Milam for more facts about what he had seen the previous Wednesday. Interviewing the trucker was like pulling teeth from a jackass. The man volunteered nothing that was not specifically asked, and then only in the barest detail.

The trucker told the sheriff he first spotted the Fromes' gray Packard when it passed him heading east on the highway near a dairy farm, six miles west of Sierra Blanca, a tiny hamlet in Hudspeth County. He said the car was being chased.[57] That was about 1:30 p.m. central time on Wednesday, according to Milam. Sierra Blanca was 107 miles east of El Paso and 39 miles west of the location where the bodies were discovered. For the Frome car to have arrived at that point in the time elapsed since they left El Paso, the women would have had to be driving at exceedingly high speeds.

The car, with two women in front, whipped around Milam's truck going east on US 80. Tailgating the Packard was another car, described by the trucker as a "black coach or sedan, or maybe a large, dark-colored coupe." There were some white letters within a white border on the car's passenger door. The second car was driven by a man with a woman sitting very close to him, "like straddling the gearshift lever," he said.

The woman in the chase car was blonde or red-haired, according to Milam, and appeared to be wearing a bonnet, "like a Salvation Army hat tied with a ribbon under the chin." He said the black car that seemed to be following the Packard bore two license plates, one on top of the other. The top one, a 1937 Texas plate, was flapping in the wind over an older, larger license plate of a state he did not recognize. The trucker said he kept the cars in sight through the hamlet of Sierra Blanca and that the Packard never tried to stop in the town. After passing through Sierra Blanca, Milam lost sight of the two cars, which were driving much faster than his delivery truck.

An hour and a half later, at about 3:00 p.m., Milam said he saw the dark car again, about six miles east of Van Horn. This time the car was being driven by the woman in the bonnet, more slowly, at about twenty miles an hour. He saw lettering on the driver's side door. Milam claimed he did not know what the letters meant because he could not read.

Just in front of him, he saw a third car, driven by another woman. That car pulled off the road near the bridge over Wild Horse Creek. A man walked toward that car, but Milam did not know where the man had come from. All this activity made Milam curious, so he stopped a short distance down the highway to see what was happening. The man got in the third car, which turned back toward Van Horn. Satisfied that nothing was amiss, or simply not wishing to get involved, Milam continued east on US 80.

After Milam had delivered more of his cargo to customers along the highway, he was surprised when, miles further down the road, and much later in the day, the gray Packard passed him again, at a high speed. Again, it was followed closely by the smaller black car he had earlier observed following the Packard near Sierra Blanca. A man was driving the Packard this time, and the woman in the bonnet was driving the small black car. There was no sign of the other two women in either of the cars.

It was all this unusual activity on the long stretch of roadway that led Milam, finally and reluctantly, to report what he had seen to Sheriff Anderson. And it was his observation about the location that led to the discovery of the tire tracks veering off the road and, ultimately, to the bodies in the desert. So at least some parts of Milam's account proved accurate. But four days had elapsed between the incidents the trucker had observed and his leading the searchers to the bodies on Sunday, April 3. And four days lost would prove an eternity.

11

Even lawmen themselves grudgingly admit there is sometimes truth to the old saying, "Possession is nine-tenths of the law." So Sheriff Anderson should have known better than to let anyone talk him into releasing the victims' bodies to El Paso County, just because the larger neighbor boasted a forensic laboratory and full-time criminal pathologists.

His good detective work up to that point was not enough to keep the investigation under his jurisdiction. In the waning hours of Sunday, April 3, the Frome case, soon to be the most famous murder case in the Southwest, slipped from his grasp. Control of the investigation might just as well have been packaged up and loaded, along with the remains of Hazel and Nancy Frome, onto the back of the delivery truck for transport to El Paso.

El Paso authorities, alerted by their counterparts from the scene, were ready for immediate forensic processing of the two victims. The women's remains were delivered to the modern, well-equipped private funeral parlor at 1:00 a.m., Monday, where a team of pathology and legal experts was waiting.

Dr. L. P. Walter, City of El Paso public health official, and Dr. Willis W. Waite, El Paso County medical examiner and surgical pathologist, conducted the autopsies in the presence of R. D. Chitwood of the El Paso County district attorney's office and other officers. Chris Fox was also in attendance, not in any official capacity but as host county sheriff.

When the corpses were cleaned up in preparation for the examination, they revealed that the victims had suffered far worse treatment than was apparent to the men who first discovered them.

After the caked blood was washed from the victims' heads, the examiners made another surprising discovery. They had not died as a result of blunt-force trauma from a hammer, as was announced by the coroner at the scene. Each woman was killed by a single bullet to the head, fired at close range, as she knelt or lay prone on the ground. The deadly wounds, along with nonlethal general battering of the faces of both victims and other abuse, caused both forensic physicians to come to a startling early conclusion unlike any they had ever made. The mother and daughter had been methodically tortured over a period of time and then carefully and deliberately put to death — execution style. The prolonged torture of the victims and execution-style killings were the most heinous crimes either of the veteran criminologists had seen in their long careers.

As the autopsies progressed, more surprises were in store. Rather than providing new clues that might be helpful to investigators, the autopsies were to raise disturbing questions that shattered some of the early assumptions about what had happened out there in the desert, or elsewhere.

The daughter was examined first.[58]

Nancy Frome's body was brought from the crime scene exactly as it was found. The body was "clothed in suede, crepe rubber soled shoes and heavy socklets, and close fitting panties of net fabric. This being all the clothing the body had on it."

After describing the general physical features — "slender young woman, average height, weighing approximately 100 to 120 lbs." — the recitation of visible external injuries began. The report started with

eight scabs on the back of the right hand, one over each knuckle of the fingers, one above the knuckle of the first finger, and three in a row above the knuckle of the second finger. The largest of these scabs measured 12 mm in diameter and the smallest 7 mm. On the left chest 4 cm from the midline and in the fifth inter-space there was a recent scarification of the skin about 2 cm in length and 1–1/2 cm wide.

The face and head were badly disfigured. There was caked dirt mixed with dried blood in the hair and over the face. The mouth was partially open and contained considerable dirt. There were maggots in the right eye, nose, and mouth. The right eyeball was badly decomposed and shrunken. The left eyeball was intact and bloodshot. Over the right cheek bone there was a recent scarification of the skin about 5 cm in diameter. This was oval shaped.

The fingernails were dyed and well-manicured and showed no sign of injury. There were no foreign bodies under the nails.

Examination of the vagina showed no injury, and a microscopic examination of the smear test showed "no evidence of spermatozoa present."

The usual Y-shaped incision of the sternum was made, revealing, "each pleural cavity contained a considerable amount of free blood, and the lungs were partially collapsed and deeply congested." The lower lungs showed heavy hemorrhaging. "The left diaphragm was rent (the wound large enough to admit two hands). The stomach adjacent to the diaphragm was also ruptured."

Other internal organs were examined and showed no additional damage.

"On turning back the scalp, a large hemorrhage was found in the temporal muscle. There was none on the right side."

The brain was removed and carefully examined.

On sectioning the brain there was blood in both lateral ventricles. On further examination of the skull a bullet hole was found in the left temporal region. This penetrated the scalp just slightly inside the hair line at a level with the top of the ear and slightly anterior to the anterior margin of the ear. The skin around the hole dried along with blood and sealed the hole, so it was hard to detect. Inside the skull a bullet was found lying free. This was a steel-jacketed bullet of .32 caliber and very little distorted.

Anatomical Diagnosis: Bullet wound of the head, strangulation, and rupture of diaphragm and stomach.

Conclusions: The lividity... indicates that the body had been lying face downward after death. The sub-pleural hemorrhages suggest strangulation. The congestion of the lungs ... the ruptured diaphragm and stomach ... must have been the result of a severe external blow of some sort. The free blood in the pleural cavities was the result of internal injuries received before death. The scabs on the back of the right hand suggest burns inflicted before death, possibly with a lighted cigar.

The bullet on entering the skull passed laterally, slightly downward and slightly more backwards. This indicates that the muzzle of the gun was higher and slightly forward to the subject's head.

The [brain] hemorrhage suggests that this person was shot before death, though the injuries to the lungs and other internal organs would have been sufficient to cause death, but not perhaps instantly. The hemorrhage into the left temporal muscle indicates this person was shot while still alive and lived for a short while afterward.

The pathologists then turned their examination to the mother.[59]

This body was that of a plump white woman about middle age, weighing approximately 150 pounds. The clothing on the body was a corset with shoulder straps broken and the brassiere part of the corset down, and long stockings and shoes. The supporters were fastened to the stockings. The shoes were a black combination of smooth and suede leather.

On the instep of the soles were several dark specks suggesting blood spots.

There was marked lividity over the anterior surface of the body, most marked on the head and neck. The face was greatly swollen and almost black. This swelling extended down onto the neck and upper chest. The eyes, nose, and mouth were filled with maggots and blood was oozing from the nose. The hair was filled with dirt and dried blood. Dried blood and dirt were also present on other portions of the body, particularly on the left hand and arm.

The eyes were swollen shut. There were small black specks present over the surface of the body, most extensive over the arms. On the outer surface of the right forearm there was an abrasion, 4 x 6 cm, which extended through the skin and down to the muscle over 3 to 10 mm in diameter. The surface of these areas was pink in color and dried. No broken bones were found.

The internal examination followed the same procedure performed on the younger woman. Specimens of the upper portion of the vagina were "examined for spermatozoa," but none was found.

"The head was opened in the usual manner. There was a large amount of edema and blood in the scalp. Turning back the scalp, there was slight hemorrhage in the left temporal muscle."

Extensive fractures of the bones of the skull were found.

On examining the skull . . . a bullet hole was found in the left temporal region on a level with the top of the ear and slightly anterior to the ear margin. This penetrated the scalp inside the hair line, and the wound in the skin was dried, as well as being partially covered with dried blood, making it very difficult to find before the scalp was opened.

In the right temporal region there was a bullet hole surrounded by fractures of the skull. There was no hole through the skin on the right side, and the bullet was found on the floor, having dropped out while the scalp was being turned back. This bullet was badly deformed.

Because of the fragmented and mangled condition of the bullet removed from Hazel's skull, the forensic report showed only that it weighed more than the bullet removed from Nancy and, thus, was likely a .38-caliber slug.

Anatomical Diagnosis: Bullet wound of the head and superficial injuries.

Conclusions: The lividity over the anterior surface of the body indicates the body had been lying face downward after death and the head was lower than the rest of the body.

The injury on the right arm suggests a blow with a sharp weapon before death . . . the superficial injuries on the forearms may have been produced before death.

The slight hemorrhage into the left temporal muscle seems to indicate death was almost instantaneous after the shooting.

With the autopsy notes concluded on both victims, the doctors Walter and Waite tried to address some of the questions lawmen had asked about the murders.

The question has been raised as to whether either one or both of these persons were raped before death. No evidence was found to indicate that they had been, but from the condition of the bodies when found, there is no reason they should not have been, should their attackers desired to do so.

The relation of the bullet wounds in the head of Mrs. Frome shows that the bullet passed through the head in an almost straight horizontal and lateral line. This indicates that the muzzle of the gun was held on a level with the bullet hole. For the subject to be in such relation to a gun held by an individual of average height she would have to be sitting, kneeling, or lying on her side.

Small specks removed from the faces and limbs of both women were chemically examined and proven to be blood, as were the smears taken from the soles of Hazel Frome's shoes.

The interpretation of these blood findings is not easy and offers many possible solutions. First, it seems that if these persons were shot without being tortured beforehand, there would have been no possibility for blood to get over the surfaces of the bodies, for the wounds were such that they would have caused paralysis and Mrs. Frome probably died instantly.

Second, it seems that their clothing must have been removed before death, but of course it would be possible for blood to soak through the clothing or run under it. But the nature of the distribution of the blood suggests that it ran onto the bare skin. Extensive hemorrhage could have been produced by blows on the nose and face [of both women]. The condition of the faces makes it very suggestive that they had been beaten.

Third, how did the blood get onto the bottom of the soles of the shoes of Mrs. Frome? Unless the shoes had been removed, it seems it must have spattered up from a hard surface like a floor. If this was the case, it would have been impossible for such a circumstance to happen on the desert.

How long have these bodies been dead when found? This is a question that cannot be answered definitely. The state of the bodies depends, to a great extent, on the surrounding temperatures.

El Paso County sheriff Fox had anticipated that climate data would be required to make a more accurate estimate of the length of time the bodies had lain in the desert. He had secured recorded temperatures for the period between the day the women left El Paso and the day they were found. He delivered this information at the autopsy.

The recorded high and low temperatures, in degrees Fahrenheit, for Van Horn, Texas, as furnished by Fox, were as follows: March 31, maximum 76 and minimum 38; April 1, maximum 70 and minimum 40; April 2, maximum 65 and minimum 29; April 3, maximum 81 and minimum 30.

"These temperatures were taken in the shade, but out in the sun, on the desert, the daytime temperatures were probably considerably higher. The daytime temperatures were high enough for rapid post-mortem changes to take place, and at night they were low enough for good refrigeration," according to the climate report.[60]

Factoring in this information with the nature of the injuries and other forensic evidence from the autopsies, the pathologists concurred in a shocking opinion that was completely opposite from the initial theory of the crimes expounded by local lawmen.

"From experience, and from conditions that surrounded these bodies, along with the post-mortem findings, we *do not believe these persons had been dead four days.* They may have been dead three days and probably not over two days, or two and a half days," the coroners' report flatly stated.[61]

> If the above assumption is true, then it must be assumed these persons were held prisoner somewhere for a day, or possibly longer.
> The near-nude condition in which the bodies were found, and the excessive amount of cruel torture inflicted before death, seems to indicate that these persons were held captive by a sadist or sadists. After inflicting the extreme torture and perhaps ravishing these women as well, it may have been necessary to kill them to keep from being exposed. Up to the present, no other motive has been presented that seems as logical as the above.[62]

All evidence suggested this was not a simple crime of opportunity — a robbery or sexual assault. There was too much prolonged violence in it.

12

The autopsy results were eagerly awaited by a growing contingent of newspaper reporters from all over the West.

Pathologist Willis Waite, after the all-night examination, agreed to stay over, to be available for a midmorning news conference called by El Paso district attorney Roy Jackson.

Dozens of newspaper reporters had already gathered in El Paso, arriving by air or car from cities in Texas, New Mexico, Arizona, and California. They were clamoring for any bit of new information to wire or phone in about the victims, investigators, or witnesses. When nothing else was available, they interviewed any local residents they could corner.

The district attorney and the pathologist had apparently agreed that none of the more startling findings from the forensic examination would be revealed that day. The complete autopsy reports would be sealed and not released to the press until the killer or killers were arrested and brought to trial. It was not unusual to withhold the official report until it was introduced at the trial of the accused.

Dr. Waite opened the news conference by announcing that the women had been killed by gunshots, rather than beaten to death with a blunt instrument, as was stated at the crime scene and widely broadcast by the news media. He quickly added that both women were brutally tortured prior to death. He even volunteered that the severe gash on Hazel Frome's forearm might have been inflicted by a "human bite," a suggestion not specifically supported by the previous night's autopsy.

The younger woman's torture included eight cigar burns to the bone on her right hand and knuckles. He said her chest was crushed by someone jumping up and down on her prone body. The latter suggestion, likewise, was not supported by the anatomical analysis. However, her stomach was ruptured and her diaphragm badly torn from some violent, traumatic force.

Dr. Waite also emphasized that the autopsy revealed Mrs. Frome definitely was not raped, and her daughter probably also had been spared that additional indignity.

District Attorney Jackson called on his assistant, William Clayton, to discuss the gunshot evidence. Clayton told the newsmen that Nancy was killed by a .32-caliber bullet. A .38-caliber bullet killed Hazel. He displayed the lead slugs, which had been removed from the women's skulls by the physicians. Two guns suggested two gunmen were likely involved. He said the actual shootings probably took place at the recovery site, six miles east of Van Horn.[63]

After explaining the ballistics, Clayton turned it back to Jackson for the wrap-up. Oddly, the district attorney opined that the women were killed late on Wednesday, March 30, the same day they left El Paso. He ignored, and did not share with reporters, the strong conclusion of the pathologists that the women had not been dead more than three, and probably only two, days before their bodies were discovered. No one hinted at the press conference that the women might have been kidnapped, held, and tortured for several days before being taken to the discovery site and shot.

In fact, the DA embellished the story with his own scenario, suggesting that the women had been taken captive somewhere along the highway and driven to a house or other structure east of Van Horn, where they tried to escape. He described a hypothetical struggle, which he claimed was borne out by a series of tire tracks. He said one of the Frome women appeared to have deliberately driven the car off the roadway into the brush, where a wild struggle ensued, sending the car careening out of control, in circles, across the desert.

With deadlines looming, the pack of reporters had enough meaty new facts to make for screaming banner headlines in their afternoon papers. They rushed to their hotel rooms to write up the details they would read over the telephone to editors at major newspapers, or wire by Western Union to smaller dailies. The local correspondents for the Associated Press and United Press, perpetually on deadline, would take care of the rest of the nation's newspapers and radio stations by newswire.

Before leaving the press conference, photographers asked assistant district attorney Clayton to pose for a picture examining the spent slugs in the palm of his hand.

Jackson's reason for deliberately misleading the press about the possible day of the murders, and omitting any hint that the women might have been held and tortured, went unquestioned by the newsmen, who were not privy to the autopsy report. The full report *was* later provided to all law enforcement agencies involved in the investigation.

El Paso sheriff Chris Fox, however, was already familiar with the findings, having been present at the autopsy, and was immediately puzzled by the DA's departure from what he knew to be the doctors' conclusions. Possibly there was good reason for withholding some details at the outset. Frequently lawmen, at the beginning of an investigation, would not want to tip their hand and reveal too much information to the perpetrators.

The DA's distortion of the findings, which was not disputed by the pathologist at the press conference, laid the foundation for the theory that the murders were the result of highway robbery by local bad men, rather than a premeditated crime of more complex motives, possibly originating elsewhere. The first theory, unsubstantiated by science, would be given continued impetus by Weston Frome's insistence on this version, which he had propounded from the beginning, before any facts were known. The two theories, pursued by different groups of lawmen, would persist and create conflict throughout the investigation.

With the autopsies complete, Frome requested the bodies be released immediately, and DA Jackson cut through the red tape to accommodate him. Since the autopsies had been performed at the funeral home, it was a simple matter for Frome's colleague, R. K. Gottshall, to arrange for the coffins to be picked up and transported to San Francisco. Frome and Gottshall would ride as passengers on the same train taking Hazel and Nancy home for burial.

NEWSPAPER REPORTERS in baggy-kneed trousers with press ID cards jutting from their hatbands were not the only outsiders pouring into the area in the wake of the Frome murders. The case had attracted law enforcement officials from federal, state, and other local agencies. The extraordinary reward also enticed a number of private detectives and amateur sleuths to make the long trip to El Paso. So many of these visiting lawmen and other strangers suddenly showed up that the local restaurants, bars, and hotels enjoyed an unexpected miniboom in the normally depressed economy.

The FBI officially backed off the case soon after it was confirmed that, in all likelihood, it did not involve an interstate kidnapping but was rather a crime for local jurisdictions. Any void left by the FBI withdrawal was quickly filled by various law enforcement agencies vying for a piece of the action. Early in the investigation, nosing around the case were officers from all three divisions of the Texas Department of Public Safety, including criminal investigation, highway patrol, and Texas Rangers. Police officers and detectives from El Paso and other nearby cities; and sheriffs, deputies, and justices of the peace from five West Texas counties, were also in town, hoping to play some role in the case.

Detectives in Los Angeles and San Francisco participated in rounding up known criminals in their cities with any connection to El Paso, particularly those suspected of trafficking illegal drugs from Mexico. Lawmen from Arizona, New Mexico, and Colorado joined in at various times. Circumstances soon called for detectives from the East Coast to get directly involved.

After the autopsy press conference, lawmen converging on the border city were tripping over one another in their zeal to solve what was already billed as one of the biggest murder cases in history. Reporters, DPS officers, Rangers, and local lawmen questioned and requestioned the same few eyewitnesses. Anyone who had seen, or had contact with, the women during their stopover in El Paso was barraged by reporters looking for new angles to their stories. When these proved scarce, the newsmen hounded random citizens for their opinions.

False tips poured in from all over the country by letter, wire, and telephone. Authorities blamed the out-of-control conditions on the huge, ten-thousand-dollar reward.

In Texas and nearby states, it was a very bad time to be a hitchhiker or petty crook. Far beyond the city limits of El Paso and Van Horn, suspicious persons or strangers were being hauled into police stations in a flurry of arrests. Innocent transients — whose only misconduct was being forced to live in the Depression-era hobo jungles, campgrounds, or cheap motor courts that proliferated in Texas, Oklahoma, Arizona, and New Mexico — were besieged by club-wielding police squads. These down-andouters' lives became even more wretched as they came under the harsh eye of local lawmen. Scores were jailed. None proved to have any connection to the Frome murders.

The first few days after the initial press headlines, chaos reigned in most of Far West Texas, because reporters as well as lawmen simply did not know who was in charge of the investigation. The Frome women's trail crossed or touched on four states and the five huge West Texas counties of Hudspeth, Culberson, Jeff Davis, Reeves, and El Paso. The manhunt even went international, with official probes extending into Juarez and other Mexican border towns.

For lack of any better angles, much of the media frenzy was centered on the sole key witness who had been identified by authorities, the elusive Jim Milam. The more Milam was hounded by the press, the less he enjoyed his moment of fame. He was especially frightened when his photograph appeared on the front pages of newspapers. If reporters could so easily track him down for interviews, so could the killers.

Unable to avoid the news reporters and repeated interrogations by lawmen, Milam became increasingly vague about what he actually saw. Then he changed his story. Maybe he had been mistaken, and there were two men and a woman in the mystery car. There might have been two cars involved in the pursuit. Maybe it was a black coach, or maybe a dark-colored coupe. Perhaps it was not a Ford or Chevrolet but a Plymouth.[64] Finally, Milam announced he was in fear for his life and would no longer talk to anyone about the case.

"I am afraid that the murderers will kill me to keep me from telling what I know," he admitted. "They might be waiting somewhere on the highway to shoot me. I have a wife and ten children."[65]

Milam already carried a pistol in his truck because of the long hauls and late hours he spent on lonely stretches of desert highways, delivering his petroleum products to hamlets and crossroads filling stations. Now he said he would seek permission from the sheriff to carry a sawed-off shotgun.

13

Melee in the murder case, caused by scoop-starved reporters and the gaggle of rudderless lawmen converging on El Paso, disturbed local community leaders and state officials alike. The need for coordination became painfully clear before the ink was barely dry on newspaper headlines from the autopsy press conference.

Due to political sensitivities, old pols in Austin did not want to appear to be snatching the now-famous case from local authorities. Still, something had to be done to bring order to the chaos.

The El Paso County Sheriff's Office, headquartered in the City of El Paso, was obviously the best-equipped and best-staffed agency in the vicinity of the crime.

Sheriff Chris Fox headed a well-trained, experienced force of forty-two male officers and three female jail matrons and clerks. His crew of deputies and detectives at the time of the Frome case was actually two officers larger than the state's entire Ranger force. The office, and particularly Fox himself, already enjoyed an excellent reputation for modern, efficient law enforcement and an impressive list of solved crimes.

Exactly how and why Sheriff Fox assumed the most visible investigative role in the Frome murder case was never made clear, but beginning Wednesday, April 6, 1938, reporters identified him as the "coordinator" and made him the primary spokesman for updates on the gruesome crimes. His elevation to this central role would have had to be signed off by the governor's office in Austin, the only authority that could make such an extrajurisdictional decision.

Chris Fox was first elected sheriff of El Paso County in November 1932 at the age of thirty-five and reelected four years later. He was extremely popular locally and had also attained a measure of national fame as one of the best law enforcement figures in the Southwest. He had the temerity to take on complicated cases that nobody else was able to solve, many of them technically outside his jurisdiction. And he solved a good number of them.

At six-foot-one and two hundred pounds, with steel gray eyes and a cleft in his chin, the sheriff had movie-star good looks that had landed him in Los Angeles on more than one occasion, for appearances at various law enforcement events. On one such visit, in August 1937, the Los Angeles sheriff asked him to pin badges on a bevy of leggy Hollywood starlets. A photograph of the tall Texas lawman with the actresses attracted the attention of an El Paso gossip columnist, who clucked that the sheriff was drinking nothing but "a bottle of soda pop" at the swell Hollywood party.[66]

Sheriff Fox found that he identified more closely with the West Coast officers than with his fellow Texas lawmen. El Paso was actually closer to Los Angeles, with better road, rail, and air connections than it had to Houston, the state's largest city.

Chris Fox was not a typical Texas sheriff. Unlike most of the county sheriffs and Texas Rangers who clung to their cowboy hats and boots, six-shooters, and lever-action Winchester rifles, Fox dressed in expensive business suits and snap-brim fedoras, and preferred automatic pistols and Thompson submachine guns. He looked and policed more like a G-man than a frontier sheriff.[67]

While the Rangers sent in by the governor to investigate the case still towed their horses in trailers behind their cars, Fox availed himself of every modern policing technology and association he could muster. That was true of some of the Texas Rangers, too, despite the organization's facade of Western regalia and arms. A small but influential core group of the Ranger force, after it was reconstituted in 1936, aggressively pursued modernization.

Sheriff Fox was in regular contact with J. Edgar Hoover and the FBI in Washington, D.C., and coordinated investigations with G-men all along the US-Mexico border on matters of international crime. He worked with the Office of Naval Intelligence (ONI) and the army's Military Intelligence Division (MID), particularly the units at the sprawling Fort Bliss Army Post nearby.[68] Fox was frequently engaged with these federal law enforcement and intelligence agencies because of his position as the top, local law officer in the border county and El Paso's unenviable role as the US-Latin American, inland gateway for international subversives of both Communist and Fascist stripe.

But the sheriff was more interested in international car-theft rings than international spies. He maintained close personal friendships with the detectives of the quasi-private National Automobile Theft Bureau (NATB), one of the most effective nongovernment law enforcement agencies in the country.

The NATB was created in 1912 by insurance companies as a nonprofit organization devoted to reducing rapidly increasing property losses due to vehicular thefts and embezzlements. The organization maintained a centralized record of all vehicle thefts in the country. More important, it recruited a national force of former lawmen to combat car theft and embezzlement rings.

In 1936, Sheriff Fox personally spearheaded efforts resulting in an international treaty between Mexico and the United States, which allowed for the recovery of stolen American cars anywhere south of the border. That one enterprising piece of law enforcement, an uncharacteristic role for a county sheriff, practically wiped out the car-theft rings operating with impunity on both sides of the border.[69]

Chris Fox was used to the fame. He had attained a degree of stardom even before leaving high school. A muscular athlete in youth, he set sports records at El Paso High that still stood when he became sheriff. By the time he graduated in 1917, he was the school's only athlete to have earned varsity letters in football, baseball, basketball, and track in all four (freshman through senior) years. Despite his size, he was also famous for his agility; he was recorded in sports stats as the fastest offensive and defensive back in the Southwest.

He had also proved his true grit early in life when he took a break from school to volunteer as a civilian truck driver in General Blackjack Pershing's Punitive Expedition into Mexico. A garrison from Fort Bliss, located on the edge of El Paso, was ordered by President Woodrow Wilson to march into Mexico after the notorious bandit and guerilla Francisco "Pancho" Villa, in the summer of 1916. Fox drove a Model T ammunition truck in the supply convoy, trailing and eating the dust of the horse-mounted cavalry regiments.

The incursion went three hundred miles into the vast deserts of northern Mexico. Villa had drawn the retaliatory American response after his paramilitary force raided the small New Mexico town of Columbus, on

March 9, 1916. The town was practically a neighbor of El Paso, and border citizens were outraged by the invasion.

When Fox and several of his high school teammates answered the call, they did not know they were participating in the last large-scale American action using cavalry troopers on horseback. The army was rapidly modernizing. Truck transports replaced horse-drawn wagons for hauling the army's supplies and artillery. For the first time the army employed aircraft for reconnaissance and mail service. Eight biplanes were in regular service, flying above and ahead of the long dusty columns as they advanced into the rugged terrain of Mexico, in futile pursuit of the wily guerilla and his irregulars.

The civilian volunteers from El Paso were in good company. A young cavalry lieutenant named George S. Patton was among the ranks of those on the expedition.

The U.S. cavalry chased Villa's colorful band of sombrero- and bandolier-clad raiders all over north-central Mexico and engaged in several skirmishes. The brief invasion, however, was largely futile: "Pancho" escaped, to die with his boots on.

The young adventurer Fox returned from the Mexican expedition to graduate from high school in 1917. He joined the U.S. Marines shortly after the United States entered into World War I, passing up the chance at a college athletic scholarship to volunteer for service. By the end of the war, he already had a family to support.

His continued education was limited to a few courses grabbed between jobs at the local school of mining, while he worked as fleet mechanic and, later, as superintendent of the delivery fleet for the city's largest department store. In 1925, he started his own trucking company, Fox Transfer and Rigging.

Even in high school Fox had been interested in politics. He was the founder and an elected officer of the Student Council. He never lost his interest in the community and acted upon it, both as a volunteer and as a public-office holder.

Christiaan Petrus Fox ran for sheriff of El Paso County in 1932, introducing himself as, "Chris to you, kid, and everybody else." The unusual spelling of his given names derived from his mother's Dutch side of the family. Fox was the Americanized version of his paternal family's German surname, Fuch. He was never anything other than an El Pasoan, having been born in the city on December 5, 1896. He grew up, married, raised a family, and worked all his life in the border city he loved.

He launched his campaign for public office by brazenly walking into the lion's den of the longtime county sheriff, Tom Armstrong, and soliciting the votes of the startled deputies who owed their jobs to the old sheriff.[70]

"Listen, you bozos," Fox said, with one of his famous grins. "If I don't get at least fifty percent of the votes in this office there's going to be plenty of fireworks raised."[71]

He was elected in a local landslide and handily reelected in 1936.

14

It didn't take Fox long, as sheriff of El Paso County, to establish a name on both sides of the border. His no-nonsense policing methods quickly gained him the reputation of tough cop. If he was to keep the peace in the thousand-square-mile county, he had to seem as hard as the rocky desert he was sworn to protect.

Law enforcement problems in his jurisdiction were compounded by the fact that the fifty-six-mile southern boundary butted up against Mexico. The international border was a magnet for more than its share of bad men seeking to flee or enter the United States. Sheriff Fox made it clear that the lawlessness allowed by the Mexican neighbor ended at the Rio Grande, and his side of the river was a place for churchgoing, law-abiding citizens.

Just as he drew a no-trespassing line on the map, Fox kept his professional life and family life separate.

He and his wife Gladys had three children, Chris P. Jr., Ellen Antoinette (Nan), and Carolyn Florence (Posey). They frequently entertained El Paso social and business leaders and their families at buffet suppers in the tree-shaded backyard of their home at 4608 Cumberland Circle. He was a lifelong member of the El Paso Elks Lodge and the Masonic Lodge, and active in the Kiwanis Club and El Paso Chamber of Commerce. He was chairman of the annual El Paso Parade of Progress Exposition and perennial grand marshal of the parade inaugurating El Paso Rodeo Week and Western Picnic. He did dress in cowboy attire for Rodeo Week.

While Fox was considered a good family man and devoted civic leader, his real passion was law enforcement. He proved to be an uncanny sleuth, though he had no formal training or experience as a crime fighter. He certainly had not sought the elected post for the money. The job paid $5,500 a year. It was a living but far from a fortune. Coming cold into law enforcement, he had to earn his spurs before a flinty-eyed jury of peers and political opponents.

During much of his first year in office, the joke around town was, "Chris is a good fellow, but as a peace officer, he's a durned good truck driver."[72] All doubts about the sheriff's credentials were dispelled when he tracked down the murderer of the DeBolt woman, whose bludgeoned body was discovered in the desert east of Van Horn on November 7, 1933. Less than a year after he was sworn in as sheriff, Fox was credited with solving the case, with little more than a pair of silk stockings and a small cord knotted around the victim's neck for clues. That case set the high standards for law enforcement that Sheriff Fox would demand during the rest of his days wearing a badge.

When the resolution of that case, which had also garnered national media interest, appeared nowhere in sight, the affable El Paso sheriff had quietly stepped, uninvited, into the investigative void. Within a couple of weeks, he had puzzled out a solution.[73]

First, Fox was successful in identifying the stripped body as that of Mrs. Irene DeBolt by circulating a photograph of the corpse itself to police agencies in major cities and towns around the country. As a matter of good taste, photographs of dead bodies were not often published by family newspapers, but some tabloids were eager to appeal to the baser side of the reading public. Mrs. Frank Cheska of Cleveland saw the photograph, identified it as her sister, and notified her local police station, which, in turn, called the border-town sheriff.

Mrs. DeBolt had not been reported missing from her community for the simple reason that the wealthy widow had slipped off with a young lover, later identified by Sheriff Fox as Arthur C. Wilson, a handsome merchant seaman most recently working the Great Lakes shipping lanes. Though Fox issued an all-points bulletin for the sailor, he suspected he might have skipped the country because of his trade. So he broadened the bulletin to include ports of call.

Sure enough, within a few more weeks the suspect was found aboard a ship in Georgetown, British Guiana. He was arrested by British authorities, confessed to the murder, and held until money could be raised for his return to the United States. Fox raised the money and later raised an additional two thousand dollars to have witnesses brought from Cleveland to El Paso for a trial. The confessed killer, who narrowly escaped the death penalty by a jury vote of eleven to one, was sentenced to perhaps a worse fate, life in the Texas prison system.

Sheriff Fox's unusual sleuthing methods captured the attention of true-crime magazine writers at a time when cops and reporters already enjoyed fairly close relationships. Both lawmen and newsmen considered themselves crusaders in what seemed to be the losing war against an out-of-control national crime wave. The tabloid press made Fox out to be an iconic Texas lawman, much to the envy of some of his fellow officers.

One sample of the garlands thrown his way appeared in a December 1, 1933, editorial in the *El Paso Herald-Post*: "Our 'inexperienced sheriff' is entitled to public congratulations and renewed public confidence. The cleverness of his attack and dogged determination alone are worth something. It's a welcome variation from the long string of unsolved murders that have marred official records here [in the Southwest] in the last ten years."

From the DeBolt case onward, the sheriff's every major case was subject to close scrutiny by the press. While he did not chase publicity, neither did he shun it, leading other Texas lawmen to accuse him of being a glory hound. The fact was, as a border sheriff, Fox was handed more than his share of unusual cases.

One month after the DeBolt murder trial, Sheriff Fox was in the headlines again.

This time his derring-do involved the most-wanted criminal in America — the bank robber, escape artist, and cop killer, John Dillinger. After being thwarted in attempts to cross the border into Mexico at El Paso, four gang members and Dillinger himself were captured in Tucson, Arizona, in December 1933. His gang had already broken him out of jail after several previous arrests, and word was out that other gang members planned to waylay the lawmen escorting him back by airplane to stand trial in Indiana. A fuel stop and layover at El Paso were scheduled for January 29, 1934. Sheriff Fox, who was alerted that the entourage would be at the airport for several hours, was determined that if Dillinger's gang tried to break him free again, it was not going to be in his town.

When the plane's passengers disembarked at the El Paso airport, the escorting lawmen and Dillinger were surprised to see the Texas sheriff and ten of his deputies surrounding the terminal entrance, toting machine guns, automatic rifles, and pistols. The infamous criminal and his escorts ate lunch and flew off the next hour, without incident.[74]

Less than a year later, Fox once more garnered national attention. The operator of a nationwide, bucket-shop, stock swindle made the mistake of opening an office in El Paso. The scam involved con men "selling" customers securities or commodities on unauthorized exchanges. In fact, the shops never executed the orders. They were, in effect, "throwing the trade tickets in the bucket."[75] The wild parties thrown by the high roller and his slick salesmen were a little too public to go unnoticed. Fox quietly began checking out the operations of L. H. Marland & Company brokerage. His investigation led to the arrest and conviction of Marland and a dozen of his operators, and the closing of bucket shops, which were raking in a half-billion dollars a year from stock frauds across the country.[76]

The next month, Sheriff Fox was credited with solving a twelve-year-old cold case involving the brutal rape and murder of an eleven-year-old El Paso girl. A Missouri miscreant was arrested, indicted, and convicted in that case. An *El Paso Herald-Post* reporter wrote on April 27, 1935, "The long arm of the law, at least while Chris Fox is sheriff, is more than tradition. It is only another demonstration . . . that Mr. Fox is making El Paso County an excellent sheriff."

Another piece in the *Herald-Post* on the last day of 1935 chided the El Paso police force for a near-riotous New Year's Eve raid that involved kicking down doors of a men-only gambling parlor called the Knickerbockers Club. In contrast, that same night, Sheriff Fox had shut down a similar gaming operation at a joint called the Gleamland Club with "a mere whisper to the boss to close up."

The newspaper article noted, "After the mayor's brass-band tactics, the Knickerbockers reopened, while the Sheriff's whisper resulted in turning the Gleamland Club into a goat-herding outfit."

Fox was known to pursue suspects across the Rio Grande River. In 1936, the sheriff teamed with Mexican officials in Juarez to break up a so-called Yaqui Gold scheme by arresting an American shill working with a "closed-mouth" Mexican embezzler. The Mexican, posing as an Indian gold-mine owner, and the American, playing the role of a precious-metals broker, were bilking gringos and Latinos alike. The hush-hush scheme appealed to the victims' greed by involving them in smuggling bulk gold across the border from a Sonora mine, to circumvent the U.S. gold embargo. The problem with the scheme was that there was no gold mine, and there was no gold.

This incident was one of many in which Fox ignored the international border — particularly regarding the traffic in stolen cars and other contraband. He had chased suspects, with or without permission of Mexican authorities, as far away as Chihuahua City, more than two hundred miles into Mexico. The way he saw it, he was solving crimes that hurt citizens on both sides of the invisible line. It was rumored that, on occasion, some of the niceties of the law, such as extradition proceedings, were not allowed to stand in the way of nabbing criminals.

15

As designated coordinator of the Frome case, Chris Fox called the first planning meeting of lawmen from various agencies, four days after the bodies were found. He would need to muster his best diplomatic skills to overcome the jurisdictional rivalries pulling the investigation in significantly different directions. The case-hardened El Paso sheriff, who was not timid about speaking his mind, vowed to use tact in dealing with the other officers on the committee. He would quickly learn not everyone on the team was going to cooperate. His power to force a direction for the investigation was limited by the title of "coordinator." Though tacitly accepted, it did not carry the imprimatur of "leader."

Fox's appointment was especially irksome to Sheriff Anderson, who was not alone in his resentment over what some of the older career lawmen saw as grandstanding. Fox's reason for accepting responsibility for the Frome investigation was similar to his justification for his earlier meddling in the DeBolt case: the Culberson County Sheriff's Office was too understaffed and underfunded to handle a case with potential interstate, and maybe even international, ramifications. While the argument was no doubt accurate, it did not do much to soothe the bruised egos of the small-town sheriff or old hands who still viewed Fox as something of an upstart.

In the Frome case, the El Paso sheriff was forced to work closely, not only with Anderson, but also with a number of older DPS men who had spent their entire lives chasing miscreants all over the huge state. These lawmen suspected that Fox believed the El Paso district was a country unto itself and that he was lord of the fiefdom when it came to law enforcement.

Their view was not without a grain of truth.

A local-state jurisdictional dispute three years earlier still festered in the unfinished business files in Austin. In late November 1935, Fox got into a feud with agents from the Texas Liquor Board. The issue was over who was in charge of handling crimes at nightclubs, bars, and to a lesser degree, package stores. By going over the head of the chief of enforcement for the liquor board to higher authority in Austin, Fox won what, to him, was a compromise. The liquor agents' authority in El Paso would be restricted to collecting state liquor, beer, and wine taxes. These officers, who considered themselves lawmen, were thus reduced to tax collectors, similar to agents whose job it was to collect sales tax on gasoline and cigarettes. The agents were to leave crimes that occurred in bars and package stores to the local police department and sheriff's office. These rules seemed only to apply to El Paso County, way out on the tip of Texas. What Fox saw as a compromise, the liquor agents considered a usurping of their law enforcement roles.

The uneasy truce held until late January 1937, when ten state inspectors suddenly came to town to conduct unannounced raids. The raids resulted in the licenses of four El Paso bars that sold liquor by the drink being revoked. Sheriff Fox and two hundred bar operators besieged Austin, claiming the agents had violated the truce. That feud with the state was still simmering when the Frome case erupted.

More problematic was Fox's on-again, off-again relationship with the Texas Rangers. He had angrily stormed Austin in the spring of 1936, after three Rangers rode into El Paso and began searching local bars for a fugitive they believed to be in the area.[77] The visiting Rangers did not have the courtesy to let Sheriff Fox know they were operating in his bailiwick. When the sheriff began getting calls that the state officers were searching local saloons, he fired off an angry protest to Austin. As usual, the Rangers got their man and quickly left town. But feelings were hurt on both sides.

To get anything done in the Frome case, Sheriff Fox would need to work, not only with his disgruntled neighbor, Sheriff Anderson, but with the Texas Rangers as well. The Rangers were also not lacking in ego. One of the Rangers assigned to the Frome case was none other than the well-respected Pete Crawford, whom Fox had tried to run out of El Paso two years earlier.

Fox clearly wanted to assume a leadership role in the case, despite his history of jurisdictional disputes with the state officers. At a press conference, he told newsmen he had been asked to enter the case by Weston G. Frome and the chief of police at Berkeley, California, because they believed the killers had followed the women from El Paso.[78]

When Fox took over, several Rangers and DPS investigators were already working in Pecos, Van Horn, and El Paso to assist local officers with separate aspects of the case.

The first coordination meeting of the diverse elements of lawmen involved directly in the investigation was attended by half a dozen officers sent by Governor Allred. It included Texas Rangers and ranking officers from the DPS criminal investigations section. A photograph of the newly formed "team" appeared on the front page of the *El Paso Herald-Post*. It showed grim-faced Rangers wearing cowboy boots, Western-style suits, and ten-gallon hats pushed back on their heads, listening as Fox read from a document.

The Rangers were the only men in the room wearing hats. The other participants, who had left their hats on a rack in the lobby, kept their business suits buttoned up and their neckties knotted. There was not only a palpable difference in personalities but a marked difference in law enforcement style and culture as well. Disagreements over how to proceed with the investigation would soon foster open clashes between Fox and individuals from the Texas DPS, as well as neighboring Sheriff Anderson.

The state lawmen in attendance were Captain W. W. Legge, Sergeant Guy Smith, and criminal investigator Frank Ivey of the Texas Department of Public Safety; Ranger Captain W. C. Hawkins; and Rangers R. E. McWilliams, John Keller, and Frank Mills.

16

Noticeably absent at the organizational meeting was Sheriff Albert Anderson of Culberson County.

The twice-spurned lawman from the county where the bodies were discovered used a legitimate excuse for ignoring the gathering in El Paso. He said he was too busy to sit around jawing about the case in a distant location, when there was real police work to be done where the murders had actually occurred.

Sure enough, the disgruntled sheriff was about to prove his point. The day the group met for the first time, one of Anderson's search parties stumbled upon the place where the killers apparently took the Frome Packard to ransack the women's belongings. The site was thirty miles east of where the bodies were found and several hundred yards off US 80, in a spot secluded enough for a leisurely search.

Sheriff Anderson had organized a search party on his own initiative. He sent one group walking east from Van Horn, where the bodies were found. Sheriff Louis Robertson of Reeves County dispatched another group to walk the highway west from near Balmorhea, where the Packard was discovered. The two search parties, comprised of a total of one hundred deputies, volunteer civilians, soldiers, and workers from federal highway gangs, scoured the desert several hundred yards on either side of the highway. The idea was to have the groups meet up somewhere in that fifty-mile stretch of road, even if it took several days of hard walking in the rugged terrain.

A team of CCC workers in the Anderson party made the first discovery. What led them to the spot were pages of Los Angeles and San Francisco newspapers, dated the week the women left California, scattered across the desert. Pop Frome had mentioned to Anderson that both Hazel and Nancy were avid news hounds and had left home with unread San Francisco papers in their luggage. The women had apparently picked up LA papers when they stopped at the Biltmore on the first night of their trip.

The newspapers were tangled in the spiny branches of cacti and tasajillo bushes. By retracing the direction downwind from the prevailing breezes, Sheriff Anderson found tire tracks and other disturbances in the rough earth. There were signs of recent human activity at the spot, including an empty wine bottle and bloody paper tissues. Curiously, in the debris was a pair of crumpled, thin rubber gloves, like the ones used by physicians. The gloves were wrapped in a page from one of the California papers found at the desert scene.

While Sheriff Anderson was exulting in the discovery of these latest clues, two hundred miles away Sheriff Fox was setting the parameters for what he hoped would be a methodical, thorough investigation. He established his office in El Paso as the central gathering place for all evidence previously discovered and made arrangements for investigators to drop off any new clues.

A stenographer in his office was assigned to be on call for any investigator, be it local lawman, federal agent, or state officer, to transcribe notes from interrogations and interviews. Incoming tips from the public, as well as correspondence and contacts from out-of-state law enforcement agencies, would add to the collection. Fox said any officer working on the case would have access to the whole file at any time, and he would compile weekly summaries of all this information, to be typed by his clerical staff. He would provide copies to all local agencies working on the case and Berkeley police chief Jack A. Greening.

The Frome murders were designated as El Paso Sheriff's Office Case #9628.

Sheriff Fox's coordinated plan sounded good in theory. But it left out one key factor: the jurisdictional proprietorship and unspoken professional jealousies that historically hamstrung any genuine cooperation between authorities.

Some of that interagency suspicion, particularly between local lawmen and the feds and Rangers, was probably justified. In the topsy-turvy, often lawless Depression era, when G-men or Rangers came to town, it was as often to investigate the malfeasance of the local officials as it was to hunt down other criminals. Politics and politicians were also constantly intruding in criminal investigations, sometimes to help their cronies out of legal jams.

The Rangers at the table were still smarting from such big-time political interference. Only five years earlier, a Texas governor named Miriam A. "Ma" Ferguson had fired the entire Ranger force, believing its members supported her opponent. Accused of selling pardons at the rate of more than a hundred a month, that governor appointed hundreds of notoriously corrupt civilians to run the state law enforcement agency. The remainder of the governor's term was a scandal-smeared two years. Finally, the state legislature acted to restore the Rangers in a newly reorganized Department of Public Safety, removed from the direct control of any future governor. Most of the Rangers fired by Ma Ferguson were reinstated, but the bitter lessons of mixing politics and law enforcement were not forgotten.

So, while the politically savvy Rangers attending Fox's first meeting dutifully followed orders from Austin, their plans for the future conduct of the investigation were quite another matter. The only grin in the somber room that day was on the human skull of some "John Doe," retrieved in the desert long ago, and displayed now by Sheriff Fox on the credenza behind his desk.

In 1938, the Texas Rangers were in major transition. The days when a lone, tough lawman with a silver star rode into town with blazing guns to clean out the bad guys were over. A new breed of leadership was emerging from the scandals of the early thirties to bring the Rangers, sometimes kicking and screaming, into the ranks of modern law enforcement.[79] That year, the force consisted of only thirty-eight commissioned officers.

Rangers remained true to their heritage and reputation in performing their unique role as a criminal investigative force. Their job was to report to any troubled spot in the vast state, whenever local citizens found themselves in a crime wave too overwhelming for their local constabulary to handle. The mandate establishing the modern Rangers as a unit within the Department of Public Safety gave them the authority to enforce any state criminal statute. However, at the end of the day, they had to turn over the product of their labors, be it an arrested wrongdoer or evidence, to local authorities for the prosecution of the crime at hand.

Much of the Rangers' work in the thirties involved cases of gambling, prostitution, bootlegging, or drug running. Chasing cattle rustlers, a job often credited to Rangers in novels and Hollywood movies, was no longer on their agenda. The Texas and Southwestern Cattle Raisers Association hired its own special agents to handle livestock rustling, as incidents of that crime soared during the Depression.

The Texas Rangers' illustrious reputation was formed at the very beginning of the state's Anglo-American history, when settlers from the United States colonized the Tejas territory under land grants from Mexico. To protect pioneers from Indian raids, informal bands of paramilitary riders were hired by colonizer Stephen F. Austin in the 1820s to range the frontier. The force was formalized as a full-time militia when Texas seceded from Mexico to become an independent republic in 1836.

In 1845, when the Republic of Texas joined the United States, the Rangers became the state's official law enforcement agency, as well as a frontier defense against Indian bands that still waged warfare against settlers' incursions into their land. They were also responsible for arresting cattle rustlers, stagecoach and train robbers, and gunslingers. The Rangers, who fought for the Confederacy as mounted units in the Civil War, were briefly disbanded when the South was defeated. They were reactivated at the end of Reconstruction as the state's primary law enforcement agency. After 1875, when the Indians no longer threatened the Texas frontier, the force gave up the function of ranging militia but kept the Rangers name, in recognition of the historic role they had played in the state's development.

Texas experienced one type of crime that was unique to the state. Crude-oil theft was a major part of the Ranger workload. Hot-oil racketeers and drip-gasoline thieves poured into Texas in the 1930s. The oil patches like Kilgore, Mexia, and Midland attracted common criminals and hucksters from all over the country. When the lawmen weren't confiscating barrels of stolen oil, they were often called on to corral rioting roughnecks and roustabouts in the state's rowdy, Depression-era oil fields.[80]

The challenge of modernizing the state's law enforcement agency fell to a well-respected Texas lawman, Colonel H. H. Carmichael, who assumed the job as director of the Texas Department of Public Safety in 1936. Sheriff Fox maintained fairly cordial relations with Carmichael, despite the occasional disputes over jurisdictional issues.

Carmichael, in turn, passed the responsibility for updating the state's police force to a most unusual Ranger named Manuel Trazazas Gonzaullas, the first lawman in the elite force with a Spanish surname. Gonzaullas had earned the nickname "Lone Wolf" for his solo exploits in law enforcement in the Texas oil fields and along the Rio Grande River. He was born in Cadiz, Spain, and by the age of twenty was a major in the Spanish Army. He served as a U.S. Treasury agent before joining the Rangers.

Despite his nickname, Gonzaullas was anything but a lone wolf in his quest to modernize the state's law enforcement. Colonel Carmichael appointed him the first superintendent of the new Bureau of Intelligence at the same time the Rangers were made a division of the Department of Public Safety. The new head of the DPS bureau took a tour of major state police and federal law enforcement agencies on the East Coast and was impressed by the modernization of practices he saw there. One of his first acts upon returning home was to seek funding for a forensics laboratory. The crime lab was established at the DPS headquarters located at Camp Mabry, an old army post on the outskirts of Austin.

By the time of the Frome murders, and only three years after its creation, the DPS crime lab had already gained a reputation for efficiency, second only to the FBI's famed Technical Laboratory, then located in the old Southern Railway Building in Washington.[81] The Texas laboratory was not fully funded until 1937, but much of the groundwork for a modern criminology lab was provided by progressive-minded volunteers from the science and medical departments in Austin's college and university community. When he finally got state funding, Gonzaullas could quickly hire specialists in fingerprinting, ballistics, and chemical analysis. He also started a criminal records section that profiled cases by modus operandi and cross-referenced crimes and criminals from all over Texas and bordering states.

Money for modernizing the force was scarce. The state provided each Ranger with a silver badge, a Colt .45 pistol, and a Winchester rifle. They were required to buy their own white cowboy shirts, boots, and silver-belly hats.[82] In 1938, while Gonzaullas and his boss Carmichael were badgering the state politicians to fund the Bunsen burners and beakers for their new crime lab, individual Rangers still had to buy their own cars and horses. For some inexplicable reason, the state provided the trailers to haul the horses to crime scenes. The state also gave a mileage allowance. Funding to pay for newfangled gimmicks for something as unorthodox as a crime laboratory was often an uphill battle for DPS officials, appearing hat in hand before the ever backward-looking, conservative state legislature.

It was to this new crime lab that physical clues, pieces of potential evidence, and suspicious objects from the Frome murder case were sent from several West Texas counties.

Hard evidence that could point investigators in any specific direction was sparse. The lab initially received only a patch of black hair from an unidentified suspect, a bloody handkerchief, a book of matches taken from the hand of Nancy Frome, a crumpled package of Lucky Strike cigarettes, and several butts picked up at the scene where the bodies were discovered. The women's shoes and underwear were bagged at the autopsies and sent to Austin. The slugs removed from the dead women had been identified in West Texas as being fired by .32-caliber and .38-caliber pistols. They were sealed in an envelope and sent to the crime lab along with the other evidence.

An additional packet of items gathered at the scene where searchers believed the Frome car was ransacked included a wine bottle, bloody tissues, pages from San Francisco and Los Angeles newspapers, and the rubber medical gloves. No fingerprints could be lifted from any of the items.

The Austin lab was as good as any in the country, but the limited forensic science available to criminologists of the time meant that very little information could be gleaned to aid in the investigation.

Since the Frome car had been scrubbed clean after it was found by the Reeves County deputy, there was no usable evidence from inside the vehicle itself. Even the cigarette and cigar ashes were of no use after officers admitted they had smoked in the car. Only one unidentified smudge of a fingerprint had been lifted from the inside mirror by the time officers finally realized the car might be involved in a major crime.

Because the field where the bodies were found had been thoroughly trampled by spectators before evidence was gathered, that scene, too, yielded little. The desert floor at the locations where the car was found and the site where it had been ransacked was too dry and hard packed to give up any viable footprints.

Only the wisp of short, black hair taken from Nancy's hand offered even a hint to the identity of the killers. Unfortunately, no scientific method existed to analyze human hair or blood. The only thing that could be determined was that at least one of the killers was a dark-haired person, probably a male, since the strands she was clutching were short.

17

After the first flash of publicity, a dozen of Texas's best law enforcement officers had rushed to West Texas to address the challenges of the Frome murder investigation. Despite the coordinating committee, the lawmen from various jurisdictions were tripping over one another. Most of the visiting officers did not bother to check in with the coordinator's office on any regular basis, creating a situation where lawmen often covered ground someone else had already plowed. In other situations, potentially valuable leads or interviews were missed entirely because they were directed to the wrong agency.

However, within a week of the discovery of the bodies, only one Ranger was left in El Paso to work full time on the case. An old-school lawman, Ranger Frank Mills let it be known rather quickly that he preferred to work alone. He announced he was taking up permanent residence in town. When Fox offered him a desk in the sheriff's office, Mills said he would be working the case out of his hotel room. Other Rangers assigned full time to the Frome case were dispersed across the state to follow other leads.

The day after the cordial but icily formal coordination meeting, Sheriff Fox had made a point of including the visiting Texas DPS investigators in a "microscopic examination" of the Frome car. None of the investigators thought much could be learned from such a detailed inspection, since the car was cleaned up and passed through the hands of so many officers before being driven to El Paso by Sheriff Robertson of Pecos. The car, impounded at the Toltec Garage, was literally searched with magnifying glasses, but as expected, the fine combing yielded little new information.

Then, one of the Texas public-safety detectives spotted the previously ignored scrape and splotch of green paint on the right front fender of the Packard. It was obvious that the Frome car had been in a glancing collision with something painted green. DPS captain W. W. Legge said the paint very well could be from another vehicle, because it was a color popularly used on sportier cars.

Sheriff Fox called the Packard garage and asked if anyone there had noticed a scrape on the car's front right fender when it was in the shop for repairs. He was assured there was no such mark on the car when they released it.[83] All automobiles were carefully inspected, and such scrapes, however minor, were noted on the work order, as protection against customers accusing the garage of the damage. Later, Fox questioned the deputy who had the car washed the day after it was discovered. The officer said he might have noticed the scrape and green paint, but the damage was so slight, he thought nothing of it.

The new discovery was troubling. The green paint did not seem to fit any eyewitness descriptions of cars seen pursuing or parked near the Frome vehicle the Wednesday of the disappearance. Yet the damage was apparently inflicted between the time the car left the garage and when it was found abandoned in the desert.

Upon closer examination, it was determined that the green paint did, indeed, fit the color used on sports coupes. Nothing else on the roadways came to mind that would have been painted such a color. Still, no witnesses had mentioned a green car. Most of the witnesses who had seen the Packard and another car said it was a coach or small sedan. The vast majority of those cars were painted black.

One of the more credible witnesses, besides the now-wavering Jim Milam, was an unemployed oil-field hand who had a day job building a cattle stock tank at a ranch on property near where the bodies were found.[84] Bill Tripp, an oil-field roughneck from Odessa, was working on the tank at Wild Horse Creek six miles east of Van Horn on the day the women disappeared. His girlfriend, Juanita Elliott, drove out from Van Horn to pick him up that afternoon.

She stopped on the highway and blew her horn to attract his attention. As he was walking to the highway from the stock tank, he noticed a small car parked about a hundred yards off the roadway. He was sure the car was not a coupe because he saw a man and woman sitting in the backseat. He thought it was a dark blue or black sedan, probably a Ford, Plymouth, or Chevrolet. Tripp commented about the car and its occupants to Juanita. He thought it odd that a couple would be necking at that time of day, in plain sight of the highway.

Juanita said that when she was driving slowly down the same highway a short time earlier, looking for Tripp, she saw the roof of "a large, aluminum-colored" car far out in the desert. The Frome car was silver gray. She also recalled that she had twice seen a small "two-seater" driven by a woman in that same area. The woman was driving the car east at a slow speed. A short time later Juanita saw the woman again, driving the car west on the highway. She thought the woman had medium-blonde or chestnut-colored hair.

Tripp and Elliott thought nothing more of the incident until a week later, when they learned that the bodies of the Frome women were found in that same area. They then called Sheriff Anderson.

When Sheriff Fox learned of the pair's description, he confronted the original witness, Milam, with the new accounts. Suddenly, the trucker recalled that he had seen the second woman, Juanita, at about the time he witnessed the woman in the black car driving, strangely, up and down the highway east of Van Horn. Furthermore, Milam now recalled seeing another car, a dark coupe, parked on the highway in that area — something else he failed to mention in his earlier interview. So now there were at least two dark-colored cars, possibly three, sighted at about the same time — two driven by women and one parked on the side of the highway. The confusion over cars continued to grow.

As news spread across the country about the murders and witnesses' statements began to appear in the press, others came forward to report unusual sightings along US 80 on the afternoon of March 30.

Five women returning to Dallas from an Order of Eastern Star convention in El Paso called Sheriff Fox to say they had seen the Frome Packard parked on the highway a few miles east of Kent. This was in the area where the authorities believed the car was ransacked. None of their other recollections added anything new to the investigation.

An attendant at the Davis Mountain Service Station near the intersection of Routes 80 and 290, just west of where the abandoned Frome car was discovered, reported to justice of the peace J. M. Ross of Balmorhea that he observed two men driving a silver Packard at a "terrific rate of speed" on the afternoon of Wednesday, March 30. He was sure it was two men. The attendant said he watched the car turn off Highway 80 onto the Old Spanish Trail, the local name for US 290. The Frome car was discovered abandoned only a few miles from that point.

E. M. Wells, division engineer for the Texas Highway Department, called Sheriff Anderson to report that he had spotted "a large dark coupe," driven by a man with a male passenger, following closely behind a silver-colored Packard driven by a woman. This sighting was between the Davis Mountain Service Station and Balmorhea, late on that Wednesday afternoon.[85]

Pacific Greyhound bus driver Everett Harmon called Sheriff Fox to report a sighting. He recalled a dark coach with two men in the front seat and a woman in the back, following closely behind a silver-colored Packard driven by an older woman, with a younger female passenger in the front seat. According to Harmon, this occurred near Sierra Blanca, early on the afternoon of March 30. The bus driver was certain the dark car had two men in the front seat. He said the coach was a Ford, Chevrolet, or Plymouth with two license plates on the rear: one looked like a Texas plate, the other a New Mexico license tag.

Mrs. Frances B. Hammer of El Paso called Sheriff Fox with a sighting that included a new description of one of the men that other witnesses reported seeing in the dark car. She and her husband had seen two women standing outside a light-colored Packard, which was stopped on the side of the highway near Sierra Blanca on Wednesday afternoon. Mrs. Hammer asked her husband, who was drowsing in the passenger seat, if they should stop. He said they did not need to, because a smaller, black car was already stopped, and a man appeared to be helping them. There was a blonde woman in the smaller car. Mrs. Hammer said the man had "piercing black eyes, a sharp chin, and prominent nose." He was wearing a light-colored fedora, dark coat, and tan shirt.

"His eyes gave the impression of a dope fiend," Mrs. Hammer said. "I've worked as a nurse in hospitals and I know about dope."[86]

Sheriff Fox set out to track down and reinterview all the earlier witnesses. He soon found the two women who had waved to soldiers from a light-colored Packard near Balmorhea. After reading newspaper statements of the soldiers, one of the women called to tell the sheriff she and a girlfriend were in the vicinity on that afternoon and flirted with a truck full of army men. They were driving a light-colored Packard. Fox quickly determined the women had nothing to do with the case, and that the soldiers' earlier story placing the Frome women near the place where their car had been found was just another false lead.

18

A silent huddle of more than 150 onlookers stood outside Wilson and Kratzer Funeral Chapel in Richmond, California, on Thursday, April 7, waiting for a glimpse of the grieving family of the most famous murder victims to be eulogized in their area of the country in many years. Inside the chapel only fourteen close friends joined relatives of Hazel and Nancy Frome for a brief private service, conducted by the Reverend P. M. Cassidy, minister of All Souls Episcopal Church of Berkeley. Following the last rites, the bodies were taken to Sunset View Mortuary in Richmond for the entombment, attended only by the closest family members.[87]

After the services, newspaper reporters from the Bay Area and Los Angeles were afforded a short interview with Weston G. Frome, the bereaved husband and father. A reporter asked about an article that had appeared the day before in the *Los Angeles Times*. The article linked the women's slaying to two murderous bandits who had shot a cabaret owner in the head in LA, on the day Hazel and Nancy reportedly left that city for the second leg of their journey. Police said the LA killers were known to have been fleeing through Arizona for Texas, on the same route the women had taken.

Pop Frome's answer surprised the reporters. He said the story was nonsense, because his wife and daughter were not in Los Angeles at all on the evening of March 23; rather, they had stopped overnight in Bakersfield, more than a hundred miles away. He claimed the women stayed at a motor court called El Padre in that smaller city, after driving only 280 miles on the first day of their trip.

When reporters pressed for more details, Pop told them that a close family friend and local banker, George Thornton, would answer any additional questions. Frome abruptly left the mortuary, shielded from those who would follow by a husky young man in the family entourage. That man was marine lieutenant Benjamin McMakin, husband of the younger Frome daughter, Mada, who had flown in from the East Coast to take care of her father in the aftermath of the tragedy.

As far as the LA murder being linked to the women's death, the designated spokesman also pooh-poohed the idea and derided the investigation. Mr. Frome believes that "Texas authorities have as yet not unearthed a single clue as to the identity of the murderers," said Thornton.[88]

The banker told reporters that Mr. Frome was certain, from the time he learned of the disappearance, that his family had been murdered by robbers who mistook them for wealthy women because of their nice clothes and new automobile. He said any other speculation by Texas authorities and the news media about the killers' motives was merely an attempt to sensationalize the tragedy. Thornton asked journalists gathered at the funeral to respect the privacy of the Frome family members, who were staying at his home in Richmond, and refrain from following them or attempting further interviews.

When the Rangers and Sheriff Fox heard about the critical interview, they shrugged off the part suggesting Texas lawmen were somehow incompetent or deliberately sensationalizing the case. But Fox did take note of Pop Frome's assertion that the victims had not gone through Los Angeles on their way to El Paso. Several police agencies were working from the assumption that the women had been in LA, as they reconstructed their movements on the trip.

AT FIRST it looked like the state and local coordination might work well for the joint investigation. The Rangers fanned out across the vast state, employing a score of officers — half their force — to check out every cad and bounder who had crossed paths with the law. Sheriff Fox tried to wall off his domain of El Paso and Juarez for his usual methodical approach to crime solving.

The Rangers focused on the traditional bands of known evildoers operating in and from lairs within the state, with special attention to those with records of dope dealing tied to the porous Texas-Mexico border. Fox, on the other hand, quickly developed a theory that the unfortunate women might have been followed from California by their killers.

The sheriff restricted his deputies to following up on the victims' movements while in his city and nearby Juarez, hoping to find links between the women and someone they knew from the Bay Area or Los Angeles. He planned to trace their every action or deed all the way back to the doorstep of their home in Berkeley. Fox already suspected that the murders had more to do with who they were and where they came from than with the happenstance of where they ended up at the time of their disappearance.

He based his evolving theory on several factors that had surfaced early in the case. The severe nature of the torture, as revealed in the autopsy, bolstered his certainty of a motive beyond simple robbery. The pathologists' conclusion that the women had been dead only two or three days before their bodies were discovered, while they were missing for five, created a serious discrepancy with eyewitness accounts that the Packard and a second car were seen in the death field on the same day they left El Paso. The latter account led some to believe the women were snatched from the highway and taken directly to the site where they were tortured and murdered the same day.

But for the second theory to make sense, the women would have had to be held somewhere else for up to two days. After that the killers would have had to return them to the same area where the Packard had been seen earlier in the week. Or, a less likely scenario would be that they were shot elsewhere after being held for a day or two, and their bodies dumped at the scene. The clawed earth under Nancy's hand at the crime scene debunked the latter theory.

Another piece of conflicting evidence that might indicate the women were taken somewhere other than the death site also brought the account of eyewitnesses to the chase into question. The DPS criminal investigators found a discrepancy between the Packard's mileage recorded by the mechanic when the car was released in El Paso and the mileage recorded by the Reeves County deputy, before he moved the car from the site where it was abandoned. The difference was forty miles greater than the actual driving distance between those two points.[89]

While the extent of the women's wounds indicated their torment was inflicted over a period of time before they were shot, several investigators believed it all happened in a three- or four-hour period on the afternoon they disappeared. The examiners' report to the contrary, the investigators chose to ignore the possibility that Hazel and Nancy had been held and tortured for a day or two.

There was other troubling evidence that made a random robbery-murder unlikely. The killers evinced an unusual interest in the women's personal belongings. While used clothing might be worth something, most of the Frome women's things, though expensive, were well worn. Nothing in the suitcases or trunks seemed to have enough value for the killers to risk being linked to the brutal slayings, by either spending time to search them or hauling them away. Yet, the discovery of California newspapers taken from within the luggage indicated that the killers had risked the added time to go through the trunks at an exposed site not far off the highway. The perpetrators then took the bulky luggage with them, apparently not finding what they sought in the initial search in the desert. Sheriff Fox thought this behavior pointed not to common robbers but to people interested in something hidden in the women's belongings. He further reasoned that the simple robbery theory was disproved by the fact that the killers had taken some time burning Nancy's hand with a cigar, beating both women, and disrobing them; yet, they left expensive jewelry on both corpses.

"I do not believe the slayings were a chance crime," Fox told newsmen the day of the funeral. "I shall check all possible clues as to whether either woman had enemies or made acquaintances between Berkeley and El Paso who might have had a motive for torturing them, other than robbery. My belief is that revenge or hatred could have prompted such a brutal crime."[90]

Because of the brutality of the crime, a number of lawmen in Texas and elsewhere also harbored doubts the case was simply an opportunistic robbery-murder. They quickly surfaced tips and rumors that the women were not merely a mother-daughter pair on a gay cross-country vacation.

The unusually large reward, a sum of money that could have comfortably supported two families for a year, became an impediment to the investigation. The audacious ten-thousand-dollar reward prompted dozens of nutty crime theorists to contact authorities with their stories.

The Rangers received calls from all over the country regarding potential perpetrators. In the first week following the discovery of the bodies, more than 150 suspects were arrested in Texas, New Mexico, Colorado, and Arizona, and questioned about the murders. A University of California student arrested in Colorado in an unrelated murder was a prime suspect for a day. A young couple from Berkeley was detained in Austin by Rangers, when a waitress overheard the girl mention she had been at a sorority party also attended by Nancy the night before the victims left on their trip. A Southwest dragnet was spread for the mystery motorcyclist who was seen leaving the motor court in Phoenix at the same time as the Frome women.

Any criminal arrested with a .32- or .38-caliber pistol was automatically questioned in the murders.

The Los Angeles Police Department notified the Rangers that a car similar to the Frome Packard and driven by two women was believed to be involved in transporting narcotics between California and the Mexican border. It was possible the Fromes were mistaken for the women hauling the large shipments of illicit drugs and tortured by bandits to reveal where the drugs were hidden.

The grim accounts of the torture led many tipsters to report similar violent crimes all across the United States, committed by "drug-crazed" criminals and "drug fiends." Wives and girlfriends of domestic abusers turned in their own tormentors by the droves to Texas authorities.

Oddly, the Frome murders generated another, more positive, unintended consequence for law enforcement agencies in the vicinity of the women's travel route. A number of previously unsolved crimes were suddenly resolved. Criminals snared in the roundup of Frome murder suspects were eager to offer up confessions to lesser felonies that provided alibis for the more horrific killings of the California women. The reason was understandable: odds were good that any culprit accused of the murders could expect a swift trial and nearly appeal-proof execution.

One of the first such cases linked directly to the dragnet involved three fugitives who an informant told Rangers were hiding out in El Paso at the time the Frome women were waiting for their car to be repaired. The trio was identified as J. M. (Jack) Flippin, age 30, Jack Barnes, 33, and James Earl O'Brien, alias James Hood, 33. An all-points bulletin for the three men and a blonde female traveling companion was issued by the Texas Rangers on April 6.⁹¹

Two of the three suspects were identified as the bold, daylight bandits who had tied up and robbed the manager of the loan office, a block from where Hazel and Nancy were staying at the Hotel Cortez on March 29. All three were suspected in the heists of a drugstore and café in El Paso at around the same time. The three men and a blonde woman had been seen fleeing the robberies in a dark green or black coupe.

Flippin and Barnes were arrested in a Dallas suburb on April 11 by FBI agents and a posse of Dallas County sheriff's deputies, led by chief deputy Bill Decker. During interrogation, the agents told the men they were suspects in the Frome murders. The two quickly gave details of robberies they had committed in several Texas towns from El Paso to Dallas, which provided them with rock-solid alibis. While dropped as suspects in the Frome murders, the pair cleared up a string of recent robberies in Tulsa, Houston, Fort Worth, and Dallas.

The crime spree also provided an alibi that cleared the other suspects, O'Brien and the blonde. The four had fled El Paso the day before Hazel and Nancy left town and committed mayhem all along the route the Fromes would have taken.

While the hunt for the Flippin gang went on in North Texas, Rangers in South Texas were picking up reports from small-town merchants about a mysterious couple driving a dark, two-door automobile with luggage piled in the backseat. Some type of white signage appeared to be painted or fixed on the doors. However, the car was so mud splattered that none of the eyewitnesses could clarify what the sign read, or even if there really was anything painted on the doors at all.

A service-station attendant at Carrizo Springs claimed he had seen the car and, more ominously, spotted a pistol on the floorboard as he cleaned the windshield. When the woman driving the car realized he had seen the weapon, she pushed it under the front seat with the toe of her shoe.

An attendant at another station said a woman in a black car loaded with suitcases stopped for assistance. She requested air for a low tire. When told the station had no air pump, the woman sped off at an unnecessarily fast clip. A man in a light hat was asleep on the passenger side of the coupe.

Rangers Pete Crawford and Alfred Y. Allee picked up the trail of the suspect car at Eagle Pass, and a chase ensued that was to last several days and extend for two hundred miles along the border.

The mystery car had initially been spotted at Del Rio on March 31, a day after the women disappeared near Van Horn, 285 miles up the Rio Grande River. However, at the time, there was no missing-persons alert out for the Frome women, so no one paid much attention to the couple and their luggage-filled car.

A week passed before reports of the strange car and couple driving it came to the attention of the Rangers. After that, they seemed to flood in from all over the borderland.

The reports were so persistent that two additional Rangers were dispatched to Far South Texas on April 9 to backtrack the eyewitnesses' stories. The Rangers were told that the couple was acting suspiciously at every location where they appeared.[92]

"They were cruising about town as if they were looking for something," Ranger Crawford reported to Sheriff Fox.[93] He said the Del Rio witnesses were sure the car had white lettering, at least on the passenger side, and that it was filled with luggage.

By the following week, there were dozens of other sightings, as Rangers, the Texas Highway Patrol, and local officers stepped up their search of the entire lower Rio Grande. Rangers sent bulletins to local radio stations up and down the river. The car and the couple were sighted at Crystal City and Cotulla. There were reports that the female tried to sell women's clothing to ranch families in the area.

Air searches, in this instance using planes provided by the U.S. Coast Guard and private owners, were used by the DPS for the first time in a major manhunt in Texas. The use of airplanes with spotters was the idea of Rangers Crawford and Levi Duncan. The vast, flat terrain was too much to cover by automobile.

Because the Rangers' vehicles were not equipped to pick up air-to-ground radio communications, handwritten messages were dropped from the planes to Ranger-coordinated ground centers, staged along the highways. While the use of airplanes did not result in any sightings of the elusive suspects, the operation marked a new milestone in Ranger efforts at modernization, and state law enforcement officials soon made their first requests that airplanes be added to their arsenal.[94]

After the aerial search failed to produce a sighting, the car was spotted again between Rio Grande City and Roma by a couple visiting the Roma ranch owned by the famous pro-Fascist radio priest, Father Charles Coughlin. Starr County sheriff Gus Guerra went to investigate. The blonde woman and now bearded man were briefly cornered in a mesquite thicket off the paved road. As Sheriff Guerra approached, he heard gunshots, and the car made a dash to the highway. He gave chase, but the large coupe outdistanced him. When he returned to examine the spot where he had encountered the car, he found what appeared to be an overnight campsite, with a fire pit and litter obviously left by long-term campers. Several feet from the campsite he and his deputies found a handkerchief embroidered with the letter *F*. Later, Ranger Crawford collected the handkerchief and sent it to the Austin crime lab. The monogrammed handkerchief could not be positively identified as belonging to one of the Fromes.

As suddenly as the borderlands search had begun, it ended. After the third week in April, there were no more sightings of the car or its occupants. Rangers had no new leads to follow. Crawford speculated that the man and woman had probably found an unguarded river crossing and driven the car with the luggage into Mexico.

Sheriff Fox had warned that if the ill-gotten belongings of the murder victims made it across the border, the valuable evidence would be lost forever. The atmosphere along both sides of the border had grown increasingly hostile after Mexico seized the oil and mining properties of U.S. companies. There would be even less cooperation from Mexican authorities than usual.

19

After weeks of chasing down dusty roads that seemed to dead-end at the border river, the Frome-case investigators were frustrated by the lack of progress in identifying the killers. Though a number of new eyewitnesses came forward with stories about suspicious characters and automobiles similar to the ones seen chasing the women on Highway 80, oddly, none offered detailed enough descriptions to provide any solid leads. And not a single witness was certain about the make, model, or exact color of the dark car or cars.

One male suspect had been described as having unusual eyes. The female suspect was variously described as a slim redhead and a heavy-set blonde. But upon close interrogation, it turned out that not one of these witnesses was sure about the actual color of the woman's hair or any feature of her hat or the other clothes she wore. The newspapers had apparently dubbed her a blonde or redhead because it made for bolder headlines. The details about the man or men were just as sketchy and often contradictory.

Nevertheless, Sheriff Fox turned to the local newspapers and radio stations for help when he decided to issue a plea for more local citizen participation. The El Paso native believed the women's fate had been sealed in his city, if not earlier in California, and that someone locally probably knew something that could break the case wide open. He hoped his message would also be heard across the border in Juarez, although he did not count on much help from that quarter.

Local law enforcement offices, like that of the Rangers in Austin, were inundated with tips, but almost all were useless, because either they lacked evidence relevant to the case or they were from downright cranks. At times, telephone exchanges were backlogged with calls. Waiting periods on the operator-run telephone systems ran as long as two hours in some smaller towns in the region.[95]

Fox still believed responsible citizens on both sides of the border could provide valuable new information on the movements of the two women.

On April 12, the *El Paso Herald-Post* responded to the sheriff's request for public assistance by running a boldly boxed item on the front page, urging readers to come forth with anything they had noticed about the Frome women's visit to the area.

Sheriff Chris P. Fox, who previously won national recognition through his solution of several major crimes, was named coordinator of information in this case. He believes it will be through the aid of private citizens that the crime will be solved.

The sheriff has called on everyone with any information, no matter how remote, to report to him or other investigators. Especially he urges the operators of filling stations, garages, tourist camps, or hotels to report persons who might have been traveling in automobiles resembling the one in which the murderers were traveling.

The public plea for help prompted an immediate response from several area residents who earlier were reluctant to come forward, or had thought what they saw was not important.

M. K. Graham, a sales representative for the National Cash Register Company, was on the Juarez trolley on the Saturday morning the Fromes took their first trip across the border. An attractive, middle-aged woman had introduced herself and struck up a conversation. She quickly told him that she and her daughter were stranded in El Paso by car trouble and were taking advantage of the situation to shop for good prices in the Mexican markets across the border.[96]

He told the sheriff that Mrs. Frome was especially talkative. Her daughter seemed rapt in the squalid scenery after the trolley passed over the Rio Grande without being stopped by border officers at either end of the bridge. Hazel informed the sales rep that her husband held a key executive position with the biggest explosives company in the world. He seldom traveled with them, she explained, because his important work — some of it involving sensitive government contracts — kept him tied up. Graham had noticed how well dressed the women were, perhaps overdressed for shopping in the seamy, open markets of Juarez. The girl wore a fawn-colored coat, although the day was not overly chilly.

When he mentioned their somewhat excessive dress for the occasion,

Hazel assured him that she and her daughters knew their way around Mexico and often haggled over prices in similar open-air Mexican bazaars.

Shopping was especially good at the time, since most tourists had been frightened away by the political upheaval along the border. It was a buyer's market and an exciting opportunity to get imported merchandise at very low cost.

"Expensive European perfume at really good prices was their quest for the day," Graham remembered. "When I told them I called on some of the better shops in Juarez, they asked for recommendations."[97]

The salesman suggested Green's Curio Shop and the City of Paris. The last he saw of them was when they stepped off the trolley car in front of a Mexican restaurant in the shopping district.

Another, more significant, account came from a hotel maid who claimed she had held back earlier, partially due to shyness over the fact that she spoke almost no English. Maria Baca, who tidied up the Frome women's suite during their five days at the Hotel Cortez, had witnessed a peculiar scene on the morning they checked out. Hazel and Nancy had become agitated over something in a handwritten letter the older woman was reading aloud.

Detective Captain Stanley D. Shea, the chief investigator from Fox's office, had been having little luck interviewing lower-level employees at the hotel. Mexican employees were either not available for interviews or, when he did manage to corner one of them, nervously dismissive, with a "maybe later." For several key witnesses, there was no *mañana*; they simply disappeared when investigators started poking around. Since most of these employees — maids, bellhops, janitors, laundry workers, and kitchen helpers — were paid in cash at the end of each week, the hotel had no record of their home addresses. Most of them lived across the border and walked over the bridge to their jobs each day.

The detective believed the real reason these employees, including Maria Baca, were reluctant to talk to authorities was fear of getting involved with anyone in law enforcement. This fear was innate among most of the Mexican population in Texas because of the not-so-gentle treatment they or their kin had experienced with the mostly Anglo lawmen of the day.

There was one employee in particular — a young, Mexican bellhop — Shea wanted to interview about the Frome's first night at the hotel.

Investigators learned that Nancy had been suffering a severe cold and some sort of leg problem when the women arrived at the Cortez. The regular hotel physician, who had already left for the weekend, did not attend her. But a rumor persisted that the girl had seen a doctor in her room. No one in hotel management could supply a name.

The young bellhop had been singled out by the doorman as someone who had attached himself to the women from the time he first carried the luggage to their room. Since the regular concierge did not call for an outside doctor, it could have been a bellhop who recommended or even personally summoned one — perhaps even a doctor from across the border. Many of the local physicians, whose clientele consisted almost entirely of El Paso's Mexican Americans, were not licensed to practice on the U.S. side but did so anyway. The bellhop would likely have known and been in a position to contact a doctor whose practice was generally restricted to the Mexican community.

Since this young man was the first hotel employee to assist them, Nancy — who spoke fairly good Spanish, polished on her trips through Mexico — might have specifically asked for the lad whenever she wanted some small errand done around the hotel or nearby stores.

Unfortunately, the bellboy, whose real name was unknown, was absent from his job, having completely dropped out of sight about ten days after the Frome investigation began.[98] Captain Shea told Sheriff Fox the bellboy had very likely seen more of the women's activities around the hotel than anyone else on the staff, as he kept an eagle eye out for extra tips from the out-of-town guests he served.

Apparently, there were other hotel employees who had suddenly stopped showing up for work. Even those Mexican workers still on the job seemed frightened to come forward with information. Captain Shea soon learned why.

Texas Ranger Frank Mills, who was working full time on the investigation in the vicinity of El Paso, was not just questioning the hotel workers; the grim-faced lawman had actually moved into the Hotel Cortez. Texas Rangers, in particular, struck fear in the hearts of minorities. Largely because of their legendary rough methods in dealing with Mexican cattle rustlers and other borderland troublemakers in bygone eras, as well as more recent, highly publicized incidents with farm workers, the Rangers were greatly feared in the Texas-Mexican community by citizens, immigrants, and illegals alike. The proximity of a Texas Ranger, coming hard on the heels of the horrifying murder of two hotel guests, was the final straw.

But it wasn't only the Mexican population that was disturbed by Ranger Mills's activities at the Cortez. His taking up semipermanent residence in the heart of the crime scene caused the territorial Fox to hit the roof. Since Mills was not checking in with the sheriff about his activities, the prospects for a separate and conflicting investigation further irked the local lawman.

Fox telephoned and then fired off an angry letter to Colonel H. H. Carmichael at D P S headquarters in Austin, complaining about the Ranger's choice of lodging and apparent lack of cooperation.

"Unfortunately, Frank Mills takes it upon himself to register at the hotel without consulting anyone, and on top of that he informs the hired help that he is to stay there until the Frome case is solved," the sheriff wrote. "This naturally gives them the jitters, and it has upset our plans to date. We have had considerable difficulty getting information from employees and management, and we have been working very hard to gain their confidence and work things out." Fox concluded with a suggestion that the top state law enforcement officer could reassign the Ranger, noting sourly that "perhaps he [Ranger Mills] could be more benefit to the Republic of Texas in some other locality." He signed the letter to Colonel Carmichael, "Your amigo, Chris."[99]

No immediate response or action followed the sheriff's complaint to Austin. After all, it was not his first tiff with authorities in the capital city, and it would not likely be his last.

Detective Shea, using his friendliest techniques of persuasion, was finally able to assure some of the hotel employees they would be safe cooperating with him and others from the local sheriff's office. The maid, Maria Baca, was one who was convinced. She finally agreed to tell Fox and Shea her story about the strange behavior she observed the morning the Frome women left.

Maria said when she arrived to clean the suite, Nancy was embroidering a pillowcase in the sitting area. She looked up from her work to greet the maid cheerily in Spanish. Maria told the investigators that during most of their stay, the women lounged around their rooms reading or listening to the radio. The younger woman spent much of her time stitching ornate initials on bed linens, a gift for her newly married sister.

That morning started out the same, except Nancy informed the maid they would be leaving shortly to continue their journey. Mrs. Frome was not present when Baca arrived to clean the room.

At about 10:00 a.m., Mrs. Frome, who had returned to the hotel, came into the sitting room with an envelope. She opened it, removing a handwritten letter. The maid thought it was three sheets of paper in length. When Hazel began reading aloud, Nancy put down her sewing to listen. About halfway through the letter, Hazel's voice became agitated, and she told Maria to go finish cleaning the bathroom. From the bathroom the maid could hear the woman resume reading, but she could not understand a word, since it was all in English.

"Mrs. Frome read something that made her very blue and sad," Maria told the officers through an interpreter.[100] After the reading stopped, the maid came back into the main room and found the women, who had been leisurely packing earlier, suddenly in a hurry to finish. They were throwing things into their open luggage. Both appeared highly upset.

Hazel called the front desk and ordered a bellman to be sent up for their luggage. The call was logged in at 10:45 a.m.

The sheriff had the maid's interrogation notes typed up and sent to the other members of the coordinating team. He added his own summary notes about the incident to the transcript.

The source of the letter was a complete mystery. A plain, unmarked, business-type envelope with the name "Frome" inked on it had just "appeared" on the counter at the front desk sometime late on Tuesday, March 29. Questioned by officers, the night clerk, James O'Reilly, had no idea where the letter came from or who had placed it there. He said he put it in the women's key slot and handed it to Mrs. Frome when she came in with her daughter for the night. He thought she didn't seem curious about it because she just put it in her purse. The clerk told the deputies both women smelled of alcohol that night.

Apparently, Hazel forgot about the envelope until the next morning.

"We are taking further steps to check all sources from which a letter may have been delivered," the sheriff's summary read. He said his detectives "believed the letter may have contained valuable clues as to the identity of the slayers."[101]

Fox found the maid's account especially interesting, even though she could shed no light on the contents of the letter or its origin.

"We had heard so much about Nancy and Hazel being in such a terrific hurry to get on their way. They knew positively on Tuesday afternoon their car would be ready early the next morning, yet they were not finished packing this late in the morning. Something in that letter made it suddenly urgent for them to get on the road."

"It was a hurried job," the Fox report concluded. "Please note that the Fromes were supposed to be very anxious to get started on their way to Dallas and yet their car was not called for until after eleven, which was over two hours after they were notified the car was ready. Two hours in the lives of most motorists means something."[102]

All lobby personnel for both the day and the night shifts were questioned repeatedly about the mysterious letter, and not one had a clue as to how it was delivered. The sheriff's investigators surmised it must have been placed on the desk by someone who could move about the hotel unnoticed, either an employee or another guest familiar to the staff. Investigators further questioned why the women had not called the local company man or authorities, if the letter had frightened them.

The investigators also theorized that recovery of the mysterious letter that so disturbed Hazel and Nancy might have been one reason the killers seemed so eager to ransack and finally haul away all the women's bulky luggage. They apparently went to great effort and took considerable risk to search for something in the luggage only a few miles from where the bodies were later discovered. The letter became the main focus of the investigation.

After reading the sheriff's appeal for citizen help in the newspaper, E. L. Bradford reflected on the morning Hazel Frome came into his hair salon for a cut, rinse, and set. Prior to learning of the murders, he thought nothing about the stylish California woman's visit to his shop. Many wealthy guests of the better downtown hotels were sent to him by concierges and other lobby personnel. He, in turn, dutifully thanked his benefactors with little gifts, from time to time.

Bradford recognized Mrs. Frome in the front-page photographs, and the news coverage of the tragedy jogged his memory. He stopped in to see Sheriff Fox with his story.

"During the time I was cutting Mrs. Frome's hair I noticed a man standing in front of the shop," Bradford recalled.[103] His salon had a full-length glass window across the front, providing a clear view of the sidewalk and street outside. Hazel was seated in the first chair closest to the street.

"I paid no attention to the man until he came right up to the window and shielded his eyes to look inside. He repeated that two or three times." The man, who was in his mid- to late thirties, with a medium slender build, was wearing a business suit and dress hat. There was nothing unusual about his clothing.

"Mrs. Frome was well-dressed, not fancy," he recalled, "but wearing considerable jewelry, one or two nice diamond rings."

One reason Bradford had paid little attention to the man at the time was that, when the Frome woman left his salon, the man approached her. She stood talking to him for a few minutes. There seemed to be nothing amiss.

"He walked after her down the street, but did not join her," Bradford said.

The information intrigued authorities. But Bradford was unable to find anyone who looked like the stranger when he pored over mug shots of suspects and previously convicted perpetrators of violent crimes in the area.

Although the incident was not given much weight, it was the first indication the sheriff found that someone might have already been following the Frome women before they ever left El Paso.

20

The sheriff's plea for local citizens to come forward with any and all information relating to the Frome women produced more bad leads than good. A flurry of calls sent deputies chasing all sorts of tales about encounters with female strangers passing through the city during the previous few weeks. Most of them quickly proved not to have involved Nancy or Hazel.

One promising tip about the possible disposition of the women's luggage caused brief excitement when a Gladstone bag was found along the railroad tracks at Sanderson, Texas, 315 miles southeast of El Paso. An empty envelope from the Hotel Genève in Mexico City was discovered inside. Since the Fromes had stayed at that hotel the previous summer, it was assumed this was a piece of the missing luggage. The bag turned out to have been tossed from a train by a porter several weeks before the murders and had nothing to do with them.

One of the strangest pieces of information was supplied by an El Paso fortune-teller who claimed to have met with Mrs. Frome. She contacted the press with her story at the same time she called the sheriff. While the woman was willing to talk to wire-service correspondents, she would not allow them to publish her name. She said her special telepathic powers might cause the killers to track her down, if they feared she would be able to accurately describe them to police. The seer's tale caused brief excitement for editors clamoring for a new angle, and the alleged encounter between the victim and a local psychic ended up on the front page of several newspapers around the country. It was treated by the press as if it were legitimate evidence of sinister skullduggery.

The report did have uncanny resonance, particularly since the fortune-teller was aware of some facts that were not otherwise known to anyone but the investigators.

Captain Shea went for an interview in response to the newspaper account, more out of interest in the woman having spent time with Hazel in

El Paso than a belief in otherworldly intervention. The sheriff's detective knew the psychic's name but promised not to reveal it.

Mrs. Allie Gillespie claimed that on Monday, March 28, Hazel Frome visited her apartment at 1405 E. Missouri for a reading. She did not have an appointment and did not tell the soothsayer how she found her.

"Mrs. Gillespie told Mrs. Frome during the reading she could see that she had connections with the Navy, and that she had a daughter married to a naval officer," Shea's report stated.[104] "Mrs. Frome told the seer that she and another daughter, Nancy, were en route to visit that married daughter and would be traveling through Dallas and Memphis. Mrs. Frome seemed to be very nervous and asked Mrs. Gillespie if she could see any enemies around her," Shea's interview revealed. "Mrs. Gillespie told her she could see someone following her, described the man as a large dark man, not a Mexican. Two men were following her, not one. Mrs. Frome seemed to become more upset on hearing this, and she became even more nervous when Mrs. Gillespie described the man with the dark complexion. She said her reading showed that these people had been following Mrs. Frome for some time."

Reporters badgered the sheriff to identify the El Paso fortune-teller, until he finally arranged for a meeting. With promises not to print her name in the papers, Mrs. Gillespie held a press interview arranged by Fox.

"I saw enemies around her in the reading. I read the death card," she told the newsmen.

> However, not wishing to frighten her, I did not reveal this until she asked, "Do I have an enemy who would do me bodily harm?" I saw a journey from which there would be no return.
>
> I want to help police as much as I can, but I do not want to divulge my name, because I feel the killers are in or near El Paso yet. Mrs. Frome seemed only to fear for herself, not her daughter. She was very nervous and kept turning her rings, a diamond and a plain gold wedding band.[105]

The fortune-teller accurately described what Mrs. Frome was wearing that day, a description not previously mentioned in any newspaper accounts.

Fox was skeptical.

As the sheriff and his deputies sifted through countless interviews, one troubling detail kept popping up. The presence of mysterious, unidentified men on the periphery of the Frome women's activities during their stay in El Paso was mentioned time and again.

Another reluctant witness surfaced more than two weeks after the bodies were found. This person was not in fear for his life but in fear of his wife. He called Sheriff Fox and said he would come in with information only if promised complete confidentiality. He was not supposed to be in Juarez the night he saw the Frome women and was afraid his wife would read about his trip across the border in the newspaper.

El Paso offered plenty of opportunities in the way of male entertainment. In fact, the day the latest tip was received, Sheriff Fox and his deputies were distracted from the Frome case for some local house cleaning. They were out at the city dump destroying roulette wheels and slot machines confiscated in a recent raid on a so-called men's recreation club.

But for unfettered partying and even some darker vices, El Paso could not hold a candle to its smaller neighbor across the river. Juarez was known throughout the Southwest as the sin city of the border, with bordellos, dope dens, and cabarets well staffed with pliant taxi dancers. Juarez was reputedly a "bachelor's" smorgasbord of illicit temptations not openly available in the more puritanical communities in the Southwest. Much of the wide-open bawdiness of the town and its disproportionate prostitute population was supported by the ranks of young soldiers stationed at El Paso's Fort Bliss. The sprawling military reserve was the largest army base in North America at the time. Soldiers from the base were routinely issued the notorious "Pro-Kit" by the first sergeant, along with their weekend or overnight passes. The prophylactic packet, containing a tube of sulfathiazole and calomel salve, was supposed to prevent venereal disease, should the soldier disobey standing orders and fraternize with a lady of the night.

Thus, the latest witness, an otherwise respectable El Paso businessman and churchgoer, had good reason not to want his name associated with a stag night across the border. Sheriff Fox, while not approving of such activity, promised B. N. Gist complete anonymity.

What Mr. Gist had to say was not, in and of itself, particularly startling. But where it led the sheriff soon came as a complete surprise. On the evening of Monday, March 28, Gist and another El Paso man were in the

Café Juarez Lobby #2 nightclub when they were "attracted to" two well-dressed, good-looking American women seated at the next table, within easy earshot.[106] After seeing their pictures in the El Paso newspapers, Gist realized they were Mrs. Frome and her daughter Nancy.

"In a few minutes, two men came up to their table and stood talking to them, with their hats in their hands," Gist told the sheriff. "Mrs. Frome remarked that she was sure she had seen one of them before, and that she thought he was from the Pacific coast. The man asked Mrs. Frome and her daughter to come and join them at their party at the Tivoli Café across the street." The men were well dressed and spoke politely.

Fox asked if the women had accepted the invitation. Gist was unsure if they left soon after, remembering only that they finished their drinks after the men walked across the dance floor on their way out of the establishment.

With this lead in hand, Sheriff Fox and Captain Shea crossed the border for an interview with Keno Smith, floor manager of the Juarez café.

Silence was the unwritten code of nightclub operators in Juarez. It took considerable badgering before Smith finally relented and admitted he had seen the women in his place on at least one occasion.

"He stated that while Mrs. Frome and Nancy were there they were approached by two well-dressed men," the sheriff's interview notes confirmed. "The men asked them to dance."

The nightclub manager was too busy to observe if they had danced or not. Later he said he saw the men leaving without the women. Smith said the women came into his club unescorted, ordered two Mexican suppers, and stayed through at least one floorshow.

"They left by themselves," the club manager told Fox. "They were drinking sauterne wine. They ate only a little of their meal, and I asked if they did not enjoy the food. They said it was good, but just too much food for them."[107]

Fox and his deputy proceeded to nearby nightclubs but did not meet with as much success talking to the other managers or waiters. Their questioning did produce witnesses who said they had seen the women the following night, Tuesday, in the Spanish Town Café, "in the company of two men of neat appearance."[108] But that was as much as investigators could learn about the second Juarez sighting.

"We are now devoting considerable effort in determining the exact movements of the Frome women while they were in El Paso," the sheriff stated in his report to the other officers. "As strange as it may seem, this is a very difficult job."[109]

Fox and others on the case were somewhat shocked to learn that the Frome women would go unescorted into Juarez at night and particularly go to dance joints two nights in a row. Juarez not only had a reputation as a bawdy place after dark but also was considered dangerous because of the extensive criminal element drawn to border-town nightlife. The officers agreed that the women were either very naive or unusually brave.

Sheriff Fox came to the conclusion that this new information about the risky nightlife of the two socially prominent California victims threw everything he and the Rangers had thus far uncovered about them into a cocked hat.

One investigator even noted, disapprovingly, in a report about the Juarez sightings, that "Mrs. Frome liked to drink . . . liked to attract men." His report concluded, "What can you expect from one who dyes her hair and plucks her eyebrows? A woman of her age doesn't do that unless to attract men. Much talk is also being bandied about the two men they are supposed to have met in Juarez."[110]

From the new interviews and information, Fox concluded that Hazel and Nancy "apparently did not care much for the company of the White family." He pointed out that after their first outing with the local Atlas manager and his wife, the Fromes chose to be on their own, despite being stranded in an unfamiliar city.

The women's five-day layover in El Paso was suddenly not as innocent as it first seemed. The already hard slog of the investigation was now further complicated by a whole new set of problems. Chief of these was finding out who the two mystery men were and why the Frome women would allow conversation, or maybe even partying, with strangers in the dangerous border-town bistros. Perhaps the two men were not strangers at all.

It appeared from what little the club managers and staff would confide that the men were Americans, or at least not Mexicans. But as with the fuzzy descriptions of the individuals seen chasing the Packard on the road, no one was able or willing to provide specific traits of the two men seen with the women in the clubs. All claimed that their places were too dark to get a good look. Fox had observed, however, that the tables and dance floors were well enough lit for clear recognition of the women.

Many lies were being told. Investigators suspected the Mexican nightclub staff had been instructed to keep quiet about the whole incident. Whether or not it was an organized cover-up or just the usual code of silence shielding this sleazy business, the investigators did not know.

Keno Smith even slipped at one point in the interview and told the sheriff he thought he knew one of the men, that he came to the nightclub frequently. But amnesia quickly set in when the club manager realized he had said too much. All the questioning in the world would not get more out of him. Since they were across the border in Mexico and cooperation was at an all-time low between authorities in the two countries, he could not be hauled in for proper interrogation.

While Fox and his deputies were busy looking for these possible new suspects, another bit of potentially troubling information was telephoned into their office. This time Fox went to question the witness himself.

Toby Martin, owner of Martin's Travel Bureau located near the Cortez, said the two women had dropped into his business on Tuesday, the day before leaving on the next leg of their trip. They posed an unusual inquiry.

"They said they were interested in finding a companion to accompany them on their trip to Dallas," Martin told the sheriff. "They didn't want any money for the trip, just someone to ride along with them." He said the women, whom he positively identified from photographs, said they would accept "a presentable man" as a passenger, when we told them we did not have a female seeking transportation to Dallas.[111]

Evidence was beginning to confirm Fox's earlier contention that whatever happened to the Frome women probably started in his jurisdiction in El Paso, and not in remote Culberson County where the bodies were discovered.

Meanwhile, Sheriff Anderson stewed, watching his chance to help solve another widely publicized murder case — one that rightly belonged in his own county — slip from his grasp. He admitted as much to the Rangers sent to assist him in cleaning up last-minute details of the Van Horn part of the investigation.

It seemed even fate was conspiring with politics to rob him of his one chance for fame as a crime fighter. An outbreak of common measles was sweeping the Van Horn community. The tough old sheriff contracted the childhood malady and was benched at this critical phase in the investigation. On April 13, the *El Paso Herald-Post* ran a boxed sidebar deep inside its pages, noting that "a severe attack of measles has eliminated Sheriff Anderson from the search for the killers of Mrs. Hazel Frome and her daughter Nancy. He is being treated in a dark room of his home in Van Horn. Physicians say it will be at least two weeks before he will be able to rejoin the search."

21

Almost from the outset, the newspapers and some Austin officials were publicly calling the Frome murders the biggest criminal case in Texas history. The national attention turned up the pressure on the famed Texas Rangers to find a quick solution. Much was made by Governor James Allred and other politicians in the state capital about the crime-solving abilities of the elite, Stetson-crowned lawmen. To put money where his mouth was, the governor had dispatched half the Ranger force across the state to investigate all aspects of the case, or to participate in the manhunt. He hinted that he expected the case to be wrapped up in short order, having dedicated so much of the force to the job.

It was becoming evident to seasoned investigators that this crime had probably been committed by sophisticated, ruthless killers. Sheriff Fox and several of the Rangers believed the killer or killers had strong motives and the skill to professionally cover an escape without leaving any viable trace of evidence. In the alternative, they may have just been incredibly lucky. It was beyond the wildest odds that anyone could snatch two adult women driving a powerful automobile, after a high-speed chase on a major U.S. highway in broad daylight, and not be credibly identified.

It was further implausible that the assailants could hold their victims captive for hours while driving more than a hundred miles through several towns and settlements, torture and murder them just off a busy highway, leisurely ransack their belongings near another busy road, and then vanish completely with a carful of distinctively marked luggage, including two steamer trunks. Yet those seemed to be the circumstances of this case.

Lawmen — local, state, and federal — repeatedly interviewed witnesses who could not describe the number of pursuers they believed they had seen, let alone their specific features. They could not be certain of the make or color of the cars they claimed to have seen in the unusual chase.

Even normally common clues, such as the make and caliber of the death bullets, defied adequate description. The slugs removed from the skulls of the victims were proving to be a problem for the new DPS laboratory in Austin. The lead projectile from Hazel Frome's head, believed to be of .38-caliber weight, was so badly mangled it could not be further identified. The slug taken from Nancy's head was still intact. It was a .32 caliber, with clear manufacturer markings. However, it still could not be specifically identified. The lab head, "Lone Wolf" Gonzaullas, reported after ballistics analysis in Austin that it appeared to be a kind of Spanish-made ammunition not sold in North America. His technicians were not positive about that, because they had no match for the slug on file.

The Rangers themselves disagreed about several key aspects of the case. On April 10, Ranger captain Harvey Purvis told reporters at a press conference in Houston that the Frome murders had been overly sensationalized. Contrary to earlier announcements that two different caliber weapons were used, Captain Purvis claimed that only one gun, of "unidentified foreign manufacture," killed both women.

He said the massive amount of blood on the women's heads was not unusual and that Nancy probably had not been tortured at all. Purvis said Nancy had been shot "in the face," and the excessive blood resulted from a nosebleed. The eight scabs on the back of her hand were attributed by that veteran Ranger to the victim having been dragged along the ground, even though the autopsy described them as "burns inflicted . . . possibly with a lighted cigar." He said the girl's ruptured diaphragm was not caused by a major blow to the abdomen, or by being stomped while lying on the ground, but was probably caused by decomposition of the body after death. Despite the deep gash or bite mark on Hazel's arm, he claimed there was no evidence that either woman had been tortured or involved in a struggle.

Purvis seemed to make light of the massive Ranger manhunt being conducted along the state's southern border, by concluding the press interview with the statement that the slayers most likely fled east. They "might be in Houston, San Antonio, Dallas, or somewhere else in East Texas," he said.[112]

Upon reading the Ranger captain's comments seeming to debunk most of the findings to date, Sheriff Fox and other local investigators were furious about Austin's meddling in the case. Even some of the Rangers working with local lawmen in West and South Texas were perplexed by the comments and expressed concern about the direction — or lack of direction — the investigation was taking.

The cream of the law enforcement crop from a dozen agencies in several states had thrown every available resource into the notorious case, and it was getting colder rather than closer to resolution.

Discouraged by the lack of progress and the slew of unsubstantiated accounts, Sheriff Fox admitted to the *El Paso Herald-Post*, "All clues that might lead to the killers have run up against a dead end."[113]

He said investigators were going to retrace some of the evidence and reinterview some witnesses. A team would physically restage the exact trip the women were believed to have taken after their last sighting at an El Paso service station at noon, on March 30.

"The purpose . . . is to follow along the murder trail as it was run by the Frome car and the killer's car," Sheriff Fox told reporters. "We may stumble upon something important."[114]

A group of investigators set out from the Hotel Cortez to revisit the crime scene and recheck the witnesses' statements as to time and landmark descriptions. With trucker Jim Milam in tow, Sheriff Fox, Ranger Pete Crawford, and crime-scene specialist Guy Smith from the Texas DPS left El Paso on April 12 to reenact events described by witnesses along Highway 80. They retraced the entire route, stopping at places where witnesses had reported unusual activities involving the Frome Packard and the mystery car.

Smith noted key points on a topographic map of the highway — the terrain and side roads the women would have driven past on their ill-fated trip.

The caravan of officers stopped at every service station on the open highway, asking if anyone had recently changed a flat tire on a Packard. The fact that the Frome car had blown a tire at some point on the route suggested they might have called at a service station, since the tire was obviously changed using tools other than those belonging in the car. When and how the tire was fixed remained one of the more perplexing mysteries, of many.

No station operator had changed a flat on a Packard recently; so the traveling investigators concluded that someone, probably one of the killers, had used a tire repair tool from the mystery car or some other vehicle. The tire tool, then, would have to fit the Packard wheel lugs. Such a wheel lug size would likely have been found on a large car. The vehicles that chased down the women were described by eyewitnesses as smaller cars — Ford, Chevrolet, or Plymouth.

During the long drive, Sheriff Fox paid particular attention to Milam's reiteration of what he had seen at exact points, as they arrived at each spot along the road. The officers ordered Milam to stand on the roadway and show them where his truck was, where the Frome car was, and where the mystery vehicle was at the time. It was clear from the proximity of vehicles, as described by Milam, that a reasonably aware observer would have seen a lot more than the trucker claimed to remember. He should have been able to provide a clear description of the man and woman in the chase car. He also should have been able to describe accurately what he saw painted on the door of that car.

Fox already suspected the veracity of the trucker's account. Investigating Milam's background, the sheriff had learned that he was occasionally sent by his bosses to Detroit, to pick up new trucks. On those trips he would be required to read, sign, and exchange sales documents and titles. Yet Milam told investigators that because he could neither read nor write, he could not tell them what letters or words were written on the car door.[115]

Maybe the man was withholding key information out of genuine fear for his life, or maybe he had some other reason for not wanting to get more deeply involved. Either way, the sheriff concluded he was being less than truthful.

Fox clocked the time required to drive from point to point, at normal speeds, along Highway 80. These drive times were checked against witness statements regarding incidents they claimed to have observed along the route. His calculations turned up additional disparities between the hours the witnesses recalled seeing something at various locations and the normal drive times between those places. Even allowing for variations in speed, some of the sightings simply could not have occurred at the locations, as described.

He was almost certain the women left the hotel at 11:45 a.m. mountain standard time. The desk clerk noted the exact time on a log sheet when Hazel called down to have their luggage picked up. It was 10:45 a.m. A bellhop picked up the luggage and brought it to the lobby, where it sat unattended for nearly an hour.

The doorman was certain the car arrived and sat parked at the curb for almost an hour before Nancy and Hazel came down to have it loaded. He was annoyed that the Packard was partially blocking the entrance for arriving guests. For that reason, he glanced at his timepiece, noting that the women drove off at exactly 11:45 a.m. This schedule was confirmed by the service-station attendant, who said the women had their car gassed by noon and seemed in too much of a hurry to have their tires or oil checked. They told him the car was just out of the repair shop and did not need service. They left the station near downtown El Paso about ten minutes after twelve.

Sheriff Fox calculated that the distance from El Paso to the place where the Frome car was abandoned at the Y intersection of US 80 and 290 was about 210 miles. That distance could be driven in about three and a half hours, by maintaining an average speed of sixty miles an hour. A witness saw the Frome car abandoned near the Y intersection between 5:00 and 6:00 p.m., a discrepancy of two or three hours.

Another factor making it difficult to reconcile the ambiguities between eyewitness accounts and realistic scenarios was that mountain time changed to central time at the Hudspeth-Culberson County line, at the city limits of Van Horn. None of the witnesses were sure which of the time zones their watches were set to on that day. The difference of an hour mattered, but no eyewitness to the incidents on the road could be sure about the time they had occurred.

One thing became frustratingly apparent. Most of the witnesses' accounts simply could not be accurate, if the women departed El Paso at noon or later. Three separate motorists said they saw the Frome car parked beside the road with a dark car immediately behind it at about 11:00 a.m. But if it was 11:00 a.m. mountain time, it would mean the sighting was almost an hour earlier than the women left El Paso. If it was 11:00 a.m. central time, it would be *two* hours before the women left. One witness, when reexamined, even believed that he himself departed El Paso at 11:00 a.m., yet claimed he saw the Frome car and the suspect car at the same hour more than seventy miles further east on US 80.

Milam's first sighting was the Frome Packard whipping around him at high speed, followed closely by a dark coupe or coach. That was six miles west of Sierra Blanca, between 1:30 and 1:45 p.m., according to the trucker. It was 107 miles from El Paso to Sierra Blanca, so his account seemed plausible. But in that time frame the women would have been driving very fast. And there would have been little or no time for anyone to change a flat or to chase down and commandeer their car.

Most of the witnesses said they spotted the two cars parked on the side of the road somewhere between Fabens, forty-nine miles east of El Paso, and Fort Hancock, seventy-three miles east of El Paso. These accounts led investigators to believe the women had stopped for car trouble or a blown-out tire and that their killers seized them and the car at that time. However, according to Milam's account, the small car was chasing the Packard at high speed all the way through Sierra Blanca, with the mother and daughter still in charge of their vehicle.

While Sierra Blanca was a small town, it had a busy commercial center along US 80. It was the county seat as well, with a regular presence of sheriff's deputies around their headquarters. If the Fromes were in control of their car and in fear for their safety, they could have found ample help available on the main street, anytime around the noon hour or early afternoon, on a weekday. Van Horn, the next town, twenty-five miles down the road, was even larger.

Thus, the investigators reasoned, the Frome women either were taken by their attackers somewhere before reaching these two towns, or they were in no fear for their safety when they passed through them.

Witnesses to later incidents involving the women, the suspected killers, and the two cars were a little more certain about the time frame, with more agreement about what they had seen. Juanita Elliott was sure she had seen the small car driven by the woman back and forth on US 80 six miles east of Van Horn at 3:00 p.m. CST. And the oil-field hand, Bill Tripp, was sure he had seen the small car with a man and woman in the backseat and the silver-colored, larger car further out in the desert at ten or fifteen minutes after 3:00 p.m.

These times jibed with Milam's report of the same sighting at the same location, at around 3:00 p.m. However, that still left almost two hours unaccounted for, since other eyewitnesses had reported seeing the Frome women and their car west of that location on US 80, earlier in the day.

The Frome Packard, driven by a woman and followed by a "large dark coupe" with two men in it, reportedly was seen by highway engineer E. M. Wells near the Davis Mountain Service Station at the intersection of US 80 and 290 later that afternoon. Wells could not be more precise.[116]

Further on down the road, between where the bodies were dumped and the car abandoned, all witness accounts of seeing the two cars were vague, as in "late in the day," or "late afternoon." One motorist named Casey Farrington did say he stopped when he saw the silver Packard abandoned on the Balmorhea highway, just past the Y intersection. He said he was there between 5:00 and 5:30 p.m. But Fox was not comfortable with the young man's accuracy, because he claimed also to have seen the Frome car earlier, at 11:00 a.m. that day near Fabens, which was impossible by any reckoning. Two soldiers on a survey crew also reported seeing the abandoned Frome vehicle near the highway intersection but could not place a specific time on their sighting.

So the only reasonable time fix the investigators had to work with was between 3:00 and 3:15 p.m., at a location six miles east of Van Horn. This is where the bodies were found, a half mile south of US 80, four days after the women left El Paso.

At that point tire tracks were still visible exiting the north side of the highway and angling wildly into the desert. It appeared the Frome Packard had gone out of control for quite a distance. New plaster casts were taken of the best of these tracks. A car had apparently run off the highway as it proceeded east, crashing for several dozen yards in an erratic arc, and then crossing the highway again before running south into the brush. But there was no way to determine when that happened, and no witness had seen such wild maneuvers. The tire tracks were so shallow that it could not even be conclusively determined that they were laid by the Frome Packard.

The tracks ended a half mile into the desert near where the bodies were discovered on Sunday. While Fox and the DPS men were at that location, they once again pondered the horrific methods the killer or killers had used in committing the grizzly executions.

DPS investigator Guy Smith took new measurements and made a detailed forensic drawing of the site. They stooped, and probed, and examined the caliche pit as if it were a fine work of art, more out of hope than expectation of finding anything new after weeks of nearly continuous searches in the vicinity of the crime scene. Every inch of the site and several miles around it had been walked by volunteers — some areas several times.

As the shadows from the Sierra Diablo Mountains once again crept with the setting sun over the Frome death site, the desert yielded no more of its secrets. The lawmen's spirits matched the darkening gloom as they trudged toward the highway, dreading the long drive back to El Paso.

22

A sizable case file on the Frome murders was gradually being assembled at the El Paso County Sheriff's Office, despite resistance on the part of some lawmen to acknowledge that office as the center for the investigation. Nearly a month after the murders, Chris Fox was diverting considerable manpower from regular policing duties to the Frome case. He personally sifted through diverse bits of information to create some coherent order, though the investigative agencies seemed to be making very little progress.

Fox's methodical reexamination of eyewitness accounts and clues gathered from all the agencies produced previously overlooked items that proved important. One letter, among the hundreds received from across the country, had gone unnoticed in the chaotic early days of the investigation.

The handwritten letter, addressed to "Chief of Police, Pecos, Texas," was postmarked April 4, at Lagrange, Mississippi. It was penned by a Chauncey Worchester of Newburyport, Massachusetts. In it he wrote that he and his parents might have seen something unusual while traveling across West Texas on March 30.

Fox found a second letter from Worchester, this one nine pages long, sent to the "District Attorney" at Van Horn, postmarked April 9, from Washington, D.C.

The two letters had been delayed or ignored earlier because they were addressed to officials who were not directly involved in the case. Eventually, they were forwarded to specific investigators at Pecos and Van Horn. Because they were postmarked from Mississippi and Washington, D.C., neither with any apparent connection to the frantic investigations underway in Texas, they either went unread or, at best, did not receive priority attention. By this time, the lawmen were being inundated with mailed-in tips from all over the United States, most of which were filled with bogus leads or wild theories.

After Fox read the detailed account in the second letter, he quickly seized on the possibility that these tourists might have key evidence previously missed in the investigation. He immediately telephoned his contacts at FBI headquarters in Washington and asked that an agent call on Chauncey Worchester in Newburyport for an interview.

Although the case was no longer under FBI jurisdiction, a bureau man from Boston conducted a brief interview and then turned the request for more in-depth questioning over to district attorney Hugh Cregg of Newburyport. He detailed the interview in a telegram to Fox.

There could scarcely have been a more credible witness than Chauncey, who was the scion of the earliest English settlers of New England.[117] The heir to the Worchester family in America traced his forebears to the original founding fathers.

But Sheriff Fox was less interested in Worchester's past lineage than in his recent recollections. On March 30, Chauncey, along with his mother and father and a family friend, were returning from an extended vacation in the southwest United States when they claimed to have had several encounters with the Frome vehicle and a second car.

When he received the report from the initial FBI contact, Fox was not disappointed. Chauncey and his mother appeared to have good memories and an excellent description of the key mystery figure in the case. The Massachusetts family members were certain they had been privy to an up-close view of the Frome Packard and the women on the side of the road, as well as the chase car and at least one male suspect. Chauncey's father, a retired physician, could have corroborated his son's account. Unfortunately, he had died suddenly only days after returning to Massachusetts from their trip. Hester Worchester, Chauncey's mother, did vouch for the son's account, even though she was still in mourning for her husband and would not be available for interviews herself.

Chauncey said he could accurately describe what his parents saw, because they had discussed the incidents at length after the family read newspaper accounts of the women's disappearance. They first learned of the missing women when they stopped to rest at Lagrange, Mississippi. Chauncey penned his letter to Pecos from a motor inn there. He wrote the second letter, which he sent to Van Horn, when they next stopped over in Washington, D.C.

The Worchester family was motoring back home after spending all winter at their property in Arizona. They spent the first night in Deming, New

Mexico, and passed through El Paso on Route 80, sometime between 11:00 a.m. and noon on March 30.

According to the FBI telegram, they saw a young woman wearing no hat, standing beside a silver-colored Packard, with one foot on the running board. An older woman sat in the front seat of the car. Chauncey Worchester said he believed he saw "possibly two people" standing between the Packard and a smaller black sedan or coach. Mrs. Worchester said she saw another man getting out of the sedan.[118]

Mrs. Worchester, who was seated on the passenger side of the family vehicle, had stared directly at the man exiting the black car. Since Chauncey slowed down as he approached the cars on the highway, his mother claimed to have had a long look at the man's face. The telegram quoted Chauncey at some length.

> My mother got a very good look at the man. He was middle-aged, thirty-five to forty-five, with stocky build. He had a large head, a round face, and large eyes.
>
> We continued on, thinking nothing of the incident, but inside of fifty miles the same two cars passed us. The Packard was in front, followed closely by the black sedan, which was either a Ford or a Chevrolet. The younger woman of the two in the Packard was driving at an excessive rate of speed. She appeared to be driving against her will and looked very nervous, as did her companion beside her. It appeared to us there might have been a third party in the back seat of the Packard, but we cannot say positively.[119]

The first sighting took place on an isolated stretch of road where the highway passed through low, barren mountains. Later, Chauncey fingered the location on a map as between the towns of Fabens and Fort Hancock. The second sighting occurred a short distance before the Worchester family arrived in Sierra Blanca. The family stopped for lunch at a small café in that town at about one o'clock. After eating a leisurely meal and having their car serviced and gassed, they proceeded on US 80 east. Later that afternoon, Chauncey said, he saw the two cars again.

"I happened to glance in the rear mirror and saw these same two following me, just as we reached the junction of the San Antonio route. I kept to the right of the highway to let them pass, but as we arrived at the junction, the two cars took the right-hand road and were lost to sight. We proceeded on the Dallas route."[120]

At the request of Sheriff Fox, Chauncey was reinterviewed several times by the Newburyport district attorney's office and detectives from the Newburyport police department. However, the family was unable to add much to their first account. The only real additional information they provided was that the man was wearing a "soft hat, not the large Texas type."

They were extremely vague about the time of their encounters with the two cars, probably because they had crossed the time zone. Chauncey thought they had passed through El Paso at 11:00 a.m. MST and arrived at Pecos, where they again stopped for the night, at 5:00 p.m. CST. But his mother thought they went through El Paso closer to the noon hour.

What piqued Sheriff Fox's interest in the letters and subsequent interviews was the Worchesters' physical description of one of the male suspects. This new account happened to correspond to an earlier description from another motorist, which had been largely ignored until investigators examined the Worchester letters. The other motorist, Mrs. Frances Hammer of El Paso, had described seeing the Frome vehicle parked on the highway with a smaller car immediately behind it. She emphasized that the man she saw helping the women in the Packard "had piercing black eyes, a sharp chin, and wore a light color tan hat."[121]

Mrs. Hammer's description had been discounted by investigators earlier because other parts of her story were not deemed credible. Their skepticism arose from her claim that the same black car had also stalked her. By her account, the dark car, with "markings on the door that looked like the California Highway Patrol shield," followed her car, passed her, and dropped behind, only to pass her again several times. That incident took place days earlier on a stretch of lonely highway in Arizona, between Phoenix and Tucson.

In one important detail, the Worchester and Hammer descriptions of the mystery man matched. It was the man's eyes.

Mrs. Hammer, whose interview never appeared in the newspapers and thus could not have influenced the Worchesters, described the man as having "piercing black eyes" that "gave the impression of a dope fiend." The Worchesters' interviews described the suspect as having unusually "large eyes." Oddly, neither the Hammer account nor the Worchester interviews provided any additional information about the other person or persons who might have been in or around the dark car. Neither party noticed the redheaded or blonde woman the other witnesses claimed to have seen.

Such was the state of the investigation that this new and now corroborated description of a suspect with unusually large or piercing eyes was seized on by authorities. The Rangers issued a region-wide bulletin alerting law enforcement officers to notify Austin if any of their criminals had noticeably odd eyes. The new description made it into the press.

As should have been expected, Austin headquarters was flooded with tips on every bug-eyed bandit, cross-eyed killer, and gotch-eyed gambler in the West.

23

Armed with a new description, albeit not as definitive as most lawmen would have liked, Sheriff Fox sent his deputies back to places the Frome women were known to have stopped. The investigators were now asking questions regarding a man with unusual, memorable eyes.

Fox returned to the tedious chore of checking the minutiae of the women's stay in El Paso. He ordered his best detective to push harder on the hotel staff. With some effort, Captain Shea convinced the management of the hotel that its patrons' identities would be handled with discretion. A list of guests who were at the Cortez during any portion of the Fromes' five-day layover was finally forthcoming. The upper-class travelers, tourists, and businessmen who could afford to stay at the pricey hotel were fairly easy to track down, and most were quickly cleared of suspicion.

At last the list was culled to only two guests who could not be located for discreet follow-up inquiries about their recent stay.[122] The two men had registered separately, were assigned rooms on different floors, and appeared to have no relationship. Both spent more than one night, but their schedules did not mesh. None of the staff had seen them fraternizing or leaving the hotel together.

One man signed in under the name G. N. Gepge, giving his business as "mining equipment" and "New Mexico" as his only address. He was registered from March 27 through March 30. The other man was registered as Dr. Romano Trotsky of Las Cruces, New Mexico, for the nights of March 28 and 29. Trotsky listed his business as "medical doctor."

Both men were gregarious and spoke with foreign accents. In questioning lobby personnel, the sheriff's investigators discovered something else peculiar. Both boasted about being pro-tsarist Russian expatriates.

The mining man, Gepge, claimed he was a Russian count who had once served as a captain in the tsarist army.

The doctor claimed also to be of Russian nobility, the nephew of Leon Trotsky, the famous exile who, at the time, was hiding in Mexico from Soviet assassins. "Uncle Leon," bragged the doctor, was an important guest of the Mexican government, having been granted political asylum. Romano Trotsky said he had visited his uncle there.

According to the bellhops, who griped that neither of the so-called Russian aristocrats were good tippers, both Gepge and Trotsky claimed to speak several languages, but neither spoke Spanish very well. Not much else was known about their stay at the posh El Paso hotel, and no one recalled seeing either of them in the company of the Frome women.

When Sheriff Fox was unable to locate either man at the incomplete addresses they had written in the hotel registry, he became suspicious and began a relentless records search to find out more about them. Since both appeared to be foreigners, he asked the FBI in Washington to check their newly developing criminal ID files for the names the men had left.

He was particularly interested in the man calling himself Gepge, because the doorman recalled that this guest had ordered his car delivered to the hotel entrance at twelve noon on Wednesday, March 30. That was just minutes after the Frome women had their car loaded and drove away. Of further interest to Fox was the fact that Gepge did not return to the hotel until twenty-four hours later. He had been scheduled to check out the morning of March 31 but did not pick up his luggage until late in the day.

Sheriff Fox also contacted Ranger Pete Crawford in Austin and asked him to check DPS files for any records on the two.

The sheriff's own investigators in El Paso quickly picked up the trails of the men, despite the possibility they were both using assumed names.

They found that Gepge was an occasional visitor to El Paso who, when he was in town, frequented the nightclubs across the border. He was especially fond of chasing women at Lobby #2, where Hazel and Nancy had reportedly dined and encountered two men, and at the Tivoli, which was also mentioned in connection with their trips to Juarez.

The sheriff's detectives were able to piece together information about some of Gepge's recent business trips to El Paso. It seemed he was not actually in the legitimate business of mining-equipment sales; rather, he had been involved in a number of questionable deals to sell old or used equipment to junk dealers. There were rumors that some of the mining equipment he tried to sell was of less than sterling provenance. Local junk dealers even implied it might have been loot from idle mines that abounded in the region. The man had appeared periodically in El Paso over the past two years. He claimed to be from the Pacific coast.

A metal dealer said Gepge had arrived in El Paso between March 12 and 15 with a large lot of mining equipment for sale. Although that deal was scheduled to be completed on March 30, Gepge did not show up until the following day. When in town he was known to run around with the son of a local junk dealer, but on this trip he did not contact the younger man for their usual ribaldry in Juarez.

Gepge was described as a striking-looking man with fair complexion, about forty years old, with blond, curly hair and a blond moustache. He stood six feet tall and weighed about 165 pounds. None of those questioned had noticed anything unusual about his eyes, except they were very blue. Some of the contracts selling junk metal to local dealers were signed with the names Gepge, Gepe, or George. He claimed to have a wife in California and to have resided in Los Angeles, San Francisco, and Richmond.

The self-proclaimed Russian count spoke fluent Polish, Russian, and German and was described by several witnesses as "a real Casanova." He always dressed well, was "extremely handsome," and often wore fine leather gloves or carried them in his hand. One witness told the deputy he believed the man was "a queer."

Another informant told a sheriff's investigator that Gepge was "absolutely mad about women" and put on quite a show about being a "big shot" when he was trying to seduce the fairer sex.

"He has a reputation for being able to make any woman he sets out to make, regardless of her social and marital status," the investigator reported. "This was also confirmed by bellhops at several hotels in town."[123]

The sheriff's detectives concluded that this man, who in various transactions signed his last name three different ways, was probably an entirely different person, involved in some nefarious business. But they turned up no information that might have advanced the investigation.

The true identity of the second man at the Cortez who raised the sheriff's suspicions was equally elusive. However, he made the mistake of using the name "Trotsky" when he registered at the hotel. The Rangers' new criminal files in Austin made a quick, if somewhat sketchy, hit on that name.

Ranger Crawford called Fox almost immediately after the El Paso sheriff made his inquiry. Trotsky, which was an alias, was a certifiable con artist with a long record of petty misdeeds in Texas. While awaiting a report from the FBI's more extensive, and slower, records search, the Texas officers put out an all-points bulletin for Trotsky throughout New Mexico and West Texas.

Sheriff Fox, with the information compiled by his detectives and gleaned from the DPS files, issued an urgent report to all members of the investigative team on April 26, 1938. Trotsky had become a prime suspect in the Frome case.

"We are checking further the possibility of Romano or Nicholas Trotsky being a suspect in this case, and on the surface there appears to be very strong likelihood of his being involved," Sheriff Fox wrote in his report to the team. "We must not overlook the fact that he was a resident of the Hotel Cortez at the time the Fromes were there, or rather during part of that time. We also know he had a sweetie in Van Horn, and he went to Van Horn after leaving El Paso on March 28."[124]

A short time later the sheriff traced Trotsky, using one of his aliases — the last name Lukian — to an address in Las Cruces, just a few miles over the New Mexico state line, north of El Paso. He discovered the doctor had recently abandoned a wife and child there. After contacting the Las Cruces police department, Sheriff Fox's chief deputy asked the local authorities to schedule an appointment with the doctor's wife.

From an initial interview with the wife by phone, Fox learned that Lukian had lived in Richmond, California, a year or two earlier. Mrs. Lukian also revealed that she and her husband had camped out at various places in South Texas just months prior to moving to New Mexico. The sheriff passed this additional information along in a bulletin to the other investigators and told them he was going to Las Cruces to talk to her in person.

He notified other officers that the car Lukian or Trotsky was known to be driving did not match the description of the chase car in the Frome case but stated, "That is not a matter to be given too much attention, as another car could have been procured."[125]

Fox's own records check revealed that Trotsky was arrested in El Paso in 1929. "There was much comment about him in the local press as he worked himself well up into the good graces of many prominent El Pasoans, and had set himself up as an exiled Russian aristocrat," he said in his report.

"There was considerable furor when he was arrested and taken back to Minnesota on a murder charge. His criminal record is very barren, but it does not put him anywhere but right in the middle of this thing as a very likely suspect," the sheriff wrote.[126] The murder charge was brought when a patient died of complications from a back-alley procedure. He was convicted only of abortion in that case.

Hardly had the word gone out about Trotsky than Fox received a call from an H. C. Horsley, the agent in charge of the U.S. Department of Labor's division of immigration and naturalization, New Mexico district, which included El Paso. Horsley was already looking for Trotsky on a deportation order as an illegal alien. The bogus doctor was well known to immigration agents, although nobody seemed to know his real name. He had been arrested many times for petty crimes, been convicted and served time, been deported, and reappeared elsewhere in the United States under yet another name.

He almost always posed as a medical doctor, usually claiming to be an eye, nose, and throat surgeon, offering his skills to local doctors on a split-fee basis. However, there was considerable reason to believe that the doctor's real specialty was performing abortions, which were almost universally illegal in every state.

The immigration agent's bulletin warned, "His usual procedure on arriving at any locality is to contact 'certain types' of physicians and to make arrangements for doing eye, ear, nose, and throat work on a split-fee basis."[127] Whether the established local physicians participated in split fees for the illegal abortions had not been determined, probably because local lawmen were reluctant to probe too deeply into the murky secrets of local physicians, who were some of their communities' most prominent citizens.

The bulletin further said that Romano Nicholas Trotsky, aka Roy N. Anthony, Bob Luken, Dr. Romano Lukian, Roy Fox, and Dr. Alexis N. Romanoff, was last seen in the San Antonio area on April 16, 1938. He was described as about forty years old, five foot ten, weighing 162 pounds, with blue eyes, black hair, medium complexion, and sometimes wearing rimless glasses, moustache, or Van Dyke beard.[128]

Texas Ranger Crawford, who was checking with local authorities on sightings of unfamiliar automobiles in other parts of the state, was the first lawman to get a fresh lead on Trotsky's whereabouts. He picked up his possible trail near Benavides. He learned that the suspect had been hop-scotching from town to town in South Texas, seemingly desperate to collect money from local doctors for past services rendered. The Ranger obtained a statement from one doctor that Trotsky was driving a 1932 Cadillac roadster with a new yellow and black paint job. The large coupe was tagged with two plates, one a New Mexico license plate number 4371, and the second a plate reading, "Regulation Physician."

Crawford sent out his own correspondence to fellow Rangers and other Texas lawmen, advising,

> We have some information that makes us take a good deal of interest in a quack doctor who operated at Van Horn, El Paso, and Las Cruces. He practiced his rackets in Benavides. Remember that while we were trailing the suspect's car down there not long ago on the same Frome case, we found one camp about a mile east of Benavides off the highway. We visited his camp and know right where it is. It was at this time that we found a handkerchief with letter *F* in one corner (this, hanging on a cat claw bush about 50 steps from the campfire). I wish you would go to Benavides and find out all you can about the quack doctor who operated there around August–October 1937. He probably left a lot of bills behind, and find out if the same man showed up around there any time in the week I was there on the trail.... If this was the same man or you find anything hot, please write me at Marfa, and also Chris Fox at El Paso.[129]

In wrapping up all the sketchy facts about Gepge and Trotsky, Sheriff Fox was struck by the obvious. These suspects did not fit in with everything else known about the Frome women.

On the surface, it seemed peculiar that either man would even have been registered at a place like the Cortez. They were not the kind of characters to be staying at expensive hotels since both, it appeared from preliminary interviews with informants and a review of the records in Austin, were always short on cash and, in the criminal scheme of things, merely petty operators.

Sheriff Fox was well familiar with these alien types — mostly German, Ukrainian, and Russian émigrés — who frequented border towns looking for opportunities to slip into the country. They had poured out of Europe in great numbers after the war, especially after the worldwide Depression began in the late twenties. Juarez, across from his town, was teeming with these desperate men. While this motley crew of expatriate Russian revolutionary exiles served as bully boys and gofers for the more sophisticated Germans operating out of Juarez and Chihuahua City, Fox could not recall any incidents involving agents provocateurs in murder or armed robbery. Their main schemes, other than the petty scams they plied to support themselves, seemed to be limited to rabble-rousing among agrarian workers and labor unionists. They showed up at protest rallies for some sinister Fascist or Communist *cause du jour* and were the legmen handing out the propaganda material and rough-drawn picket signs.

Fox badly wanted to talk to this pair of oddball immigrants anyway.

24

A man who goes crooked is sure to be
turned in by a lady in red.

Chris Fox often began with that opening remark in his popular lectures to local high school students on the importance of being law-abiding citizens.[130] The sheriff coined this bon mot following the untimely demise of cop killer and bank robber John Dillinger, when his girlfriend turned him in to the G-men. Her red dress was the signal for the ambushing agents. Fox had had a brief personal experience with Dillinger when he and his deputies encountered him as a prisoner at the El Paso airport.

Now, years later, it seemed to have special resonance in the Frome murder case when an angry, "spurned" lady proved only too willing to freely provide information on the leading fugitive suspected in the case.

The lady in question may not have worn a red dress, but she had red hair matching her fiery wrath at being recently abandoned by her husband. The suspect, Romano Trotsky or Lukian, or whatever his name, had left his wife and young child destitute in the New Mexico farming hamlet of Las Cruces, located a short distance north of El Paso. All she knew about the case in question was that lawmen wanted to find her husband. She did too, because the man she married under the name Dr. Lukian had left her and their seventeen-month-old baby with barely enough milk in the ice box when he disappeared on March 27. She had heard little from him since, and he sent no money. Out of desperation, she had lodged an official abandonment complaint with the local police department.

After confirming that the doctor using the name Lukian was the man Trotsky they were seeking, Sheriff Fox and Captain Shea left El Paso for the twenty-five-mile drive to Las Cruces. Within a few minutes, the lawmen had crossed from Texas into New Mexico. The roadway sloped from the flat desert pan to the lip of a canyon, descending into the Rio

Grande valley. The historic little New Mexico farming center, located in the fertile, oasis-like Mesilla Valley, was well irrigated by the Rio Grande River. The location was just upstream from where the river separated El Paso and Juarez, forming the U.S.-Mexico boundary.

They stopped at the Las Cruces Police Department to pick up a detective who had set up the appointment with Lukian's wife and proceeded to an elegant old house in the slightly rundown section of town. Mrs. Lukian greeted them on the porch, appearing quite animated and happy to see them. She expressed hope that someone was finally coming to her rescue.

The woman was rather stocky, Fox guessed about five foot eight and 160 pounds. She looked about thirty years old, with a round, attractive face framed by full, reddish-blonde hair.

From the outset, it was clear she was dismayed by her predicament and accustomed to much better than her current living conditions. She immediately informed the lawmen gathered in the spacious parlor that she was from a good family and was, in fact, an accomplished classical opera singer, whose promising career had been interrupted when she met the fast-talking doctor. She had married him only to learn, too late — after the arrival of a baby boy — of his duplicitous nature.

Fox quickly discerned that the poor woman actually knew very little about her husband. But she knew enough to be hopping mad. The angry wife was Mrs. Helga Lukian, whose maiden name was Dorn. She had never heard of anyone named Dr. Romano Trotsky. While her husband Dr. Lukian had displayed some strange behaviors during their two-year marriage, Helga quickly let the questioning officers know that she was not aware of his alias or, for that matter, that her handsome and debonair spouse might have used several other names and personas as well.

When Sheriff Fox commented that the large old house with its plethora of overstuffed furnishings was nice, the woman told them her husband had left without paying any of the past-due rent, and she had no means to placate the angry landlord. Her husband had left home stone-cold broke.

At the mention of rent in arrears, Sheriff Fox wondered how the fraudulent doctor had then managed to afford staying at the pricey Cortez in El Paso. He knew the Depression-wary management at the upscale hotel would not have accepted a guest without extracting the room charges up front. Yet he had registered and paid cash for his lodging. Someone must have given the suspect money between the time he left home and when he checked into the hotel.

At the moment, Fox and his chief investigator hoped Mrs. Lukian could shed some light on where he might be now. Unfortunately, she could not; but she did want to talk about the couple's recent past. Fox later wrote a lengthy report of the interview, much of it in the wife's own words.[131]

Under the name of Romano Lukian, Trotsky had worked for the L. Williams Health Systems in Los Angeles from January 5 to August 5, 1937.

"During the last few weeks he worried me constantly with his desire to leave California, as he did not like to work hard at any time, and he was certain he could practice his own profession in either Texas or New Mexico and make a great deal more money," she lamented. "He was so anxious to leave California, and did not wish to inform his employers of his intention, that I had the impression he had reasons unknown to me for wanting to leave the state."

Mrs. Lukian said her family came to suspect that her husband was a phony, which had caused her temporary estrangement from them.

"My parents also had a bad impression, and mentioned to me several times about our hasty departure, when I personally had very good prospects to resume my profession by staying there. I also would have preferred to live near my family," she said. "However, I allowed myself to be persuaded, and we left LA after August 5 and then drove through, camping to economize, all the way to Laredo, Texas. We settled in Benavides because it was an isolated oil town, and he figured he could make quick and easy money there. Which, he did."

She said Lukian established credit all over town.

"He proceeded to get everything he could, borrowed several large sums from new friends, and left without warning about two months after his arrival," she continued.

Lukian took his wife and baby back to California, where he dumped them with her parents at Montbello on November 12 and left for the Bay Area. He claimed to have excellent prospects around Richmond, where he had lived and worked for several years. He would send for her after he got reestablished.

He was gone until after Christmas, when he showed up again at Helga's family home and told her to hurriedly pack for a move to New Mexico, where he said he was going to open a practice. She had foolishly agreed, even over the protests of her family, who by now were convinced that Lukian was not even a doctor. But she went with him anyway.

"He brought us first to Silver City, where he ran up a number of small bills on the pretext of settling there," she said. "We left, and he dropped me and the baby in El Paso in January 1938, at a boarding house. Then he took off again."

While in El Paso, Lukian went to Van Horn once a week to perform surgery for a Dr. J. P. Wright. She said he worked every Friday there and stayed over in Van Horn through the weekend. In early March, Lukian took her and the baby to Las Cruces and rented the large house they were in now. He promised the landlord he would pay several months' rent once his new practice was up and running.

"My husband told me not to make any long-term plans for a permanent home here," she said. "He repeatedly said he did not wish to be burdened with extra possessions, as we might have to leave in a hurry and not be able to take much along. His obsession and whole ambition was to somehow make a large sum of money so he could buy a ranch and raise polo ponies to sell to movie stars," the woman told the officers.

By this time she and her husband were fighting constantly.

"He said repeatedly if he could ever get out of this marriage he was going to marry some wealthy, elderly widow who could supply him with money and be no trouble to him. He claimed he was still on corresponding terms with several who were glad to do this." Helga was sobbing.

Her husband had stayed around Las Cruces the first week in March, again borrowing money from new acquaintances. He went to Van Horn on March 10, to substitute for Dr. Wright while he went on vacation. He returned to Las Cruces on March 15 and remained there until Sunday, March 27.

"During that time he was continually in an ugly, quarrelsome temper and drinking heavily, which was unusual," Helga said. "He very rarely took liquor in any form, and usually did so only in temper or to antagonize me. After his departure, I learned he had been planning all the time to leave, and had obtained as much credit as possible with that in view. He collected all the cash owing him for treatments, then went through Van Horn sometime the following week and borrowed everything possible there, saying he was on his way to Pecos.

"On April 5, he charged five dollars of gas in Kendall's Service Station in Carlsbad, New Mexico," she said. "I don't know where he is. I've heard rumors he might be in either Vaughn or Bellam."

The distraught wife offered nothing that would lead to the current whereabouts of Lukian, aka Trotsky. Furthermore, she was unable to answer any questions about her husband's stay in El Paso at the Cortez, except to say she was surprised he had the money to afford a fancy hotel. She was not even sure what type of car he might be driving, noting that he frequently showed up, inexplicably, with a different car. When he left the house on March 27, he was driving a green, 1932 Cadillac sports coupe.

Helga knew little about her husband's earlier life in the San Francisco area and had never heard him mention the names of Nancy or Hazel Frome. She said she never saw a gun in his possession. She assumed he knew how to use one, because he talked frequently about his service as an officer in the White Army during the Bolshevik Revolution.

Sheriff Fox and his deputy returned to El Paso with no information that would lead to the cad's current whereabouts.

PART II

SPIES ON
THE BORDER

25

When Sheriff Fox got back to the office after interviewing the suspect's wife, he was handed a copy of a report that cast more mystery than light on the investigation. It was from the Texas D P S crime lab and contained an F B I ballistics report sent to Superintendent Gonzaullas by J. Edgar Hoover.[132]

Under a cover letter from F B I director Hoover, the report summary stated, "Acknowledge your letter of April 12, relative to type of bullet and cartridge used in the murder of Mrs. Hazel and Nancy Frome. Cartridge case bearing the head stamping D W A : You are advised that information in the files of the F B I indicates that cartridge cases of this type were produced by the Deutsche Waffen Aktiengesellschaft of Berlin and Düsseldorf, Germany. No information is found concerning the identity of any importer of this type of ammunition in the United States."

The report provided identification only of the slug that killed Nancy Frome, noting it was the kind of ammunition manufactured for use in 7.65 mm German and Eastern European automatic weapons. The F B I lab had no better luck than the Texas lab in identifying the heavier, badly mutilated slug found in Hazel Frome's skull.

However, the slug that killed the younger woman was distinctly marked with a letter *S* stamped in the base of the lead bullet. It was identified as a type of ammunition not legally imported by arms dealers anywhere in North America. The F B I had only recently acquired a sample of this type of bullet. It was manufactured in Germany for special automatic weapons issued to Nazi elite. The F B I suggested that the peculiar ammunition might possibly be obtained south of the border.

The earlier theory that the weapon might be an old Spanish-model revolver commonly found in Mexico was now out the window. How did a slug, positively identified as a type only recently manufactured in Germany, end up in the brain of a murder victim in the middle of the vast West Texas desert? The Rangers and Sheriff Fox were no closer to identifying the murder weapons than they were at the beginning of the investigation. It now seemed, however, that at least one of the guns used in the execution-style slayings was possibly a German-made automatic, if the weapon could be assumed to match the ammunition.

An increasingly frustrated Fox notified Rangers and other investigators of his sparse findings from the interview with Helga Dorn Lukian.[133] The tearful interview had convinced him that this self-styled doctor was certainly cruel enough to have committed murder. By Fox's measure, any man capable of abandoning his wife and infant without food or a roof over their heads was capable of just about anything.

The sheriff's report to fellow lawmen on April 26 named the doctor as his chief suspect and urged that, upon his arrest, the man be made available for extensive interrogation at El Paso.

Chris Fox was not content to simply let fellow lawmen know of his interest in the man who was now his prime suspect in the Frome case. He leaked word to the local wire-service reporters, identifying the suspect by name and aliases. Since newsmen were clamoring for any tidbit to update the sensational murders, the leak was telegraphed and widely published across the country. As hoped, the publicity resulted in a flurry of calls and letters to the El Paso sheriff's office about sightings and mostly unpleasant encounters between good citizens and the con man doctor.

Meanwhile, in Culberson County, Sheriff Anderson surfaced some witnesses who definitely placed Trotsky, known there as Dr. Lukian, in Van Horn at the time of the Frome murders.

"Dr. Lukian tried to make several women in Van Horn, but seems to have had no luck," Anderson told fellow investigators. "He hung around Audrey's Beauty Shop a lot. I talked to Imogene Martin, a hairdresser, and she tells me that the doctor was there quite a bit, and that he tried to make the proprietor, Audrey. At the time she thought he was just kidding and paid no attention to him."[134]

Sheriff Fox also noted in his report that a judge in San Diego, Texas, a small South Texas town more than 650 miles from El Paso, called to say that Lukian or Trotsky had resided in his community for most of the last thirty days. He had left in a hurry, "owing a lot of people money."

"This doctor was in partnership with a local Mexican doctor," the unnamed Duval County judge told Fox. "At the time he was here, he made statements to certain people that he was in El Paso at the hotel the night they [the Frome women] were there, and that he lived in California near the Fromes."[135]

Fox told the judge to get in touch with Texas Ranger Abie Riggs, who was stationed at nearby Alice in Jim Wells County.

Ranger Riggs was unable to find any leads on the strange doctor at the county seat of San Diego. On a hunch, he drove fifteen miles over to the oil-boom camp at Benavides. That small town was enjoying a temporary respite from the Depression, with the discovery of a major pool of oil nearby. There, he struck a bonanza of information about a so-called doctor going by the name of R. Lukian.

A local doctor named Henry B. Day knew the man well from bad experiences with him the previous year, and he had seen him in town again only a few days before the Ranger arrived.

"Sometime in July 1937, a man named R. Lukian came into town claiming to be an eye, ear, nose, and throat specialist and opened a practice here," Dr. Day recalled. "He is inclined to be a little sporty and dresses very well. His wife had reddish hair, was probably in her late twenties, and had a baby with her. She claims to be a musician, or singer, or dramatist of some sort.[136]

"I had suspicions that he was not what he claimed from the start. Later, I was informed by the state medical board that he was not licensed to practice, and I have a copy of a letter to that effect," Dr. Day told the Ranger. "I showed him the letter and he left town in a hurry, in an old model Ford. After he left, I started receiving phone calls from people looking for him, from all over the place, trying to collect unpaid bills."

In early April, the doctor heard Lukian was back and ran into him in downtown Benavides. The man claimed he had been practicing medicine in California and Wichita Falls, Texas, since leaving South Texas.

"I was not surprised he had continued to operate his racket. I had tried to find out who he really was, but could find out very little. His claim to have received a medical degree from Russia could not have been true, because he is no more than thirty-five years old."

Lukian, alias Trotsky, used counterfeit documents alleging he was a member of the family of the doomed Russian dynasty, with a medical degree from the University of Petrograd.[137]

Ranger Riggs asked Dr. Day when he last saw Lukian.

"Two or three days ago he was in town asking everyone how to get to

Freer, Texas, twenty miles north of town," the doctor said. "That was obviously a cover-up for something, because there are road signs all over the place with directions to Freer. Later, I had calls from doctors in San Angelo that he had visited their offices looking for surgery work."

The Ranger ran across a chiropractor named Ed Estes, who had talked to Lukian or Trotsky only a few days before.

"I know he was in and around town until the latter part of April, because I was trying to collect money he owed me," said Estes. "He told me he'd been in Monterrey, Mexico, getting a divorce from his wife."[138]

The Ranger learned that Lukian's wife Helga had taught music in the Benavides schools for a short time in 1937 and that Lukian was hired to give eye exams to school children.

"Mrs. Lukian held a number of rehearsals at our school. She was engaged in high-class singing," principal James Momeny told the Ranger. "The couple seemed to be having much trouble between them. The last I heard, he left town to go on a singing tour with his wife last year. The first week in April of this year he came by my house and said he was opening a practice with a Doctor Duran in San Diego or San Angelo. He said his wife was where she could not bother him anymore."[139]

"He asked me what I would think about the person who would kill the Frome women," the school principal said. "I told him I thought no punishment could be severe enough. He remarked that a man must be insane to do something like that, and ought to be executed. During this last visit he seemed somewhat nervous and more fidgety than usual. This time he was driving a large yellow roadster."

Ranger Riggs suggested it might be worthwhile for his counterparts in San Angelo, 350 miles to the north, to begin checking with their medical community, in an effort to pick up the elusive doctor's trail.

26

The subject of the statewide dragnet brazenly wheeled his mud-splattered Cadillac into a parking space across the street from the county courthouse at San Angelo on Friday afternoon, April 29. This time the crafty fugitive's luck had run out. Two steely-eyed lawmen were standing by their cars parked outside the courthouse talking about the case when, to their surprise, Trotsky simply materialized before their eyes. Despite its heavy coating of dust, they immediately recognized the distinctive, old-model Cadillac sports car. A brush of the hand across a fender revealed a gleaming, new yellow and black paint job.

The veteran officers were flabbergasted that a person sought on an APB for weeks would nonchalantly park his car in view of the county sheriff's office in broad daylight, with a dozen or more cop cars parked directly across the street.

Ranger Captain W. C. Hawkins and Deputy Sheriff Jim White of Tom Green County, acting as casually as their targeted suspect, simply walked across the street and arrested Trotsky as he stepped out of his car.[140] Inside the vehicle, officers found a surgeon's kit, camping gear, bedding, and cans of food. Of special interest to investigators, the surgical kit contained medical-type rubber gloves similar to the pair found a month earlier wrapped in California papers at Balmorhea, near where the Frome car was abandoned.[141] But they found nothing directly linking Trotsky to the Frome women.

Sheriff Fox talked to the arresting officers and reminded them that when Trotsky disappeared from home, his Cadillac had been green, matching the paint in the minor dent on the Frome Packard.

The El Paso sheriff offered to travel the four hundred miles to San Angelo to join in the interrogation of Trotsky. But he was assured that the Texas DPS was sending two of its top criminal investigators from Austin, agents A. L. Barr and John Reese, to question the suspect.[142] Since he requested a hold be put on the man on a misdemeanor charge of wife and child abandonment, Fox assumed the suspect would be transferred either to his custody at El Paso or to Las Cruces, where a warrant was pending. He was satisfied that he and his chief investigator would have ample time to question him.

He soon regretted that assumption.

Fox was almost certain they "had their man" in the Frome case. At least, he believed a person directly involved in waylaying the women on the highway was in custody, and the notorious case would now wind down to a speedy conclusion.

Sheriff Anderson, who had been chafing for weeks over being quarantined with measles, saw the arrest as the chance he was waiting for, to reassume the role of lead investigator in the famous case. He announced to reporters that he was headed from Van Horn to San Angelo to take charge of the interrogation.

A local newspaper reported that the suspect had been taken to county jail to await the arrival of Anderson and federal immigration authorities, who already held warrants for illegal entry into the country.

When the questioning began, Trotsky attempted to change his history. He denied he was Dr. Lukian and that he had a wife in New Mexico. This time, he claimed to be a "Rumanian" from Belarus. He said he fled his country during the Russian Revolution after killing three Red Army soldiers, and he had entered the United States illegally from Ontario, Canada. He also denied ever claiming to be a nephew of the famous Trotskyite leader, whose name he had adopted as one of his aliases.

As with most events in the now month-old Frome case, the arrest drew large crowds of newsmen and generated headlines from coast to coast.

Reporters for the *Oakland Tribune* learned of the suspect's Bay Area connection and discovered he had recently stayed with former in-laws in Richmond, the next town over from the Frome family's Berkeley home.

One newsman soon dug up witnesses who knew the suspect under the name of Romano Trotsky, not Lukian. That man had practiced medicine as an eye, ear, nose, and throat surgeon at Vallejo and Richmond from 1932 to 1934. While there, he had married a nurse named Elsie and had one son. The couple met at a clinic in Winslow, Arizona, where both worked in 1931. The nurse divorced him in 1934, several months after he disappeared. She died a year later.

Their son was being raised by her mother, Mrs. Marie Aichinger. She told reporters that Trotsky, after years of absence from the boy's life, had suddenly surfaced in Richmond and moved in for a monthlong visit with his son. That appearance was as recent as the previous December. In fact, Mrs. Aichinger said she had just received a letter from Trotsky the day before, on April 30. In the letter he inquired about the health of his son. He requested that, in the future, she address him as Romano Lukian at General Delivery, San Antonio, Texas.[143]

The former mother-in-law told reporters that Trotsky had become well known in Bay Area social circles. He passed himself off as a member of the deposed tsarist royalty. Because of his suave good looks and European manners, he was a sought-after party guest.

He was also well known for his skills as an equestrian. At the time, it went without note that Nancy Frome was also an accomplished equestrian and habitué of local social events involving the area's "horse people." Because of the lack of communication between agencies, no one in law enforcement sought to link the murder victim and the suspect through the show-horse circles.

Newspapers in both El Paso and the Bay Area filled their front pages with articles about the peculiar fellow arrested in the case. Under the banner headline "Californian Jailed in Frome Murder Case," the *Oakland Tribune*'s May 1, Sunday edition all but declared the case solved. That story, mixing wire reports from Texas with local interviews, noted that the suspect identified as Romano Trotsky had a long record of criminal activities — from car theft and wife and child desertion to murder by illegal surgical procedure. The various stories included a litany of white-collar crimes strung out across the United States over a dozen years, including practicing without a license, impersonating a physician, and abortion.

The California newsmen became as intrigued by the doctor's questionable lifestyle and reputation as they were by his connection to the women's brutal deaths. The *Tribune* reported,

Although records elsewhere showed that he claimed to be the nephew of Leon Trotsky, the exiled Russian Communist leader, he said tonight that he was not related. He went under the names Trotsky, Nicholas, and Lukian, and lived in Richmond, California, near the Berkeley home of the Fromes.

He was questioned by Richard Martin, an official of the U.S. Border Patrol. Martin said that federal officials would make no attempt to take custody of the man until local officers completed their investigation of the Frome connection.

Lukian, or Trotsky, speaks with a slight foreign accent. He is dark complexioned, has dark hair, is about 35 years old, weighs 145 pounds, and is 5'9"tall. He told officers that he is a native of Rumania and entered the United States through Ontario, Canada.[144]

The California and Texas newspapers quoted Ranger Captain Hawkins as the first official to express doubt that Trotsky was involved in the Frome murders. "We don't have anything definite to connect this man with the Frome case," the Ranger captain told reporters.[145] The pronouncement was incredible, even considering the known bits of circumstantial evidence of the suspect's criminal record and his proximity to the women, both at the hotel in El Paso and in Van Horn, the day they vanished.

Hawkins had not been working full time on the Frome case and knew little about it. In fact, none of the veteran DPS investigators hurriedly sent to San Angelo had working knowledge of the case, yet they took over the interrogation all the same.

Though Trotsky was most certainly a crook, he did not fit the stereotype of the armed robber, dope-dealing gangster the Texas Rangers arbitrarily decided had most likely committed the heinous murders. This suspect was a con man par excellence, but the criminal files in Austin had no record of his having used firearms in the commission of a crime. That seemed to be the minimum criterion the Rangers would accept for a suspect in the Frome case.

While the arrest of Trotsky generated considerable excitement in both El Paso and the San Francisco Bay Area, the links between Trotsky and the crime began to unravel, as far as the interrogators were concerned. The Austin officers swallowed the con man's story, hook, line, and sinker. He seemed to have answers that could exonerate him for every question the Rangers and local deputies tossed his way.

The relative isolation of San Angelo, Texas, may have played some role in the short shrift given this suspect by the local officials and state police. While the county seat of twenty-five thousand was the largest of any city in the high Edwards Plateau region of the state, it was relatively out of the mainstream of current events.[146] The one investigator with familiarity about the case, Sheriff Anderson, might have salvaged something from the Trotsky interrogation, but he arrived early Sunday morning as the questioning was winding down. Once again, the Culberson County sheriff was elbowed out of a meaningful role in the case.

Meanwhile, sketchy information from the interrogation of Trotsky was given to an El Paso reporter arriving on the scene in time for the Saturday, April 30, questioning. Interviews with lawmen in San Angelo and Sheriff Fox in El Paso were carried in the *El Paso Times* on Sunday morning.

"Dr. Romano Nicholas Trotsky, a man with a dozen assumed names, was being questioned by San Angelo officers in the Frome murders," the Sunday lead article reported. "He had been sought for some time by Sheriff Fox, who earlier determined he stayed at the Hotel Cortez at the same time as the Frome women."[147] A subhead cryptically pointed out,

GLOVES CONNECTED — RUBBER HAND COVERINGS
TYPE USED BY PHYSICIANS

The article prominently featured the El Paso sheriff, even though he was not present at the interrogation in San Angelo.

"Sheriff Chris P. Fox, chief investigator in the Frome case, was advised the self-styled physician probably will be returned to El Paso for questioning. He is alleged to have left his wife and baby destitute at Las Cruces. Immigration authorities have been seeking the doctor, who has a long police record for immigration law violations. He was arrested several times in El Paso about ten years ago. He is reported to have told questioners that he went directly to San Antonio after he left Van Horn, about the time the mother and daughter were tortured and murdered." Fox was quoted as disputing this, noting witnesses had placed Trotsky in Van Horn on March 30.

"Besides the name Trotsky, the physician is also known as Roy N. Anthony, Bob Luken, Dr. Roman Lukian, and Roy Fox," the article continued. "Trotsky has boasted that he fled Russia after killing three men, and then went to Vienna where he studied medicine and surgery."

An article in the local San Angelo newspaper reported that Trotsky had practiced medicine in that community in 1929. He "carried a medical diploma from a Moscow university. He says he is a member of the White Russian Club in California. Trotsky had been of special interest because he had lived in Richmond, California, a community adjoining the home of the Frome women. Trotsky lived in Richmond and the Bay District for more than three years."[148]

TWO MEN WERE DISPATCHED to New Mexico on Sunday to check out Trotsky's alibi: an agent from the Texas DPS Criminal Investigation Division, Pat Taliafarro, and a Tom Green County deputy. The deputy said he confirmed that a Dr. Lukian had been in Monahans, Texas, and the small New Mexico towns of Hobbs, Roswell, and Artesia, on or about the times and dates he claimed.

"It may establish that Lukian [Trotsky] was not the murderer," the deputy said.[149]

Even so, southern New Mexico was geographically well connected to the Van Horn area of Texas. For anyone with a fast car, a network of lightly trafficked, flat, straight roads made for short travel times between a large part of southeastern New Mexico and the area just north of the Texas border. Artesia — the most distant New Mexico town the suspect claimed to have visited on the day the women disappeared — was 150 miles from Van Horn, a trip that could be made in a little over two hours, in a car like Trotsky was driving.

A detailed report on Trotsky's movements was filed by Agent Taliafarro.[150] During the interrogation, Trotsky had said that on March 30 he visited two doctors in Artesia, attempting to collect money they owed him. Taliafarro spoke to both. He carried with him a photograph to show the alibi witnesses, since the suspect was known to be using different names.

"At Artesia I contacted Dr. C. Cornet, and he said Trotsky was in his office between 3 and 4 p.m., Mountain Time," the agent's report stated. "Dr. H. H. Stroup said Trotsky was in his office sometime around noon."

Both men said they knew the bogus doctor from past referrals of patients for surgical work. They did not specify the nature of the surgeries he had been retained to perform.

There is no indication that the DPS agent did more than talk briefly to Trotsky's alibi witnesses at Artesia, and no other doctors that Trotsky claimed to have called on in Monahans, Texas, or Hobbs and Roswell, New Mexico, were willing to confirm his story.

The only solid evidence that Trotsky might have been in any of those towns on the day of the murders was offered by a clerk at a seedy motor inn in Roswell, 194 miles from Van Horn.

The clerk remembered Trotsky from the photograph shown him by the Texas officer. The man in the photo had come in late on the night of March 30, in a disheveled condition, and asked about room rates. He immediately began to complain about the high price for the cheapest room available. The clerk thought the man was overly loud and unduly wrought up about the paltry charge. He seemed more interested in making his presence memorable than in the price of the room. There was no receipt or record of the stay, but the clerk said Trotsky had indeed taken a room and paid in cash.

After hearing the agent's report, the officers holding Trotsky in San Angelo appeared oddly incurious about why their suspect would have protested so vehemently about the cost of a cheap motel room in Roswell, New Mexico, when, according to his own admission, he had paid substantially more for a room at the Cortez, the most expensive hotel in El Paso, only the night before.

The suspect had been in Carlsbad, New Mexico, only 116 miles from Van Horn, on March 31, a day after the women went missing. There, he engaged in activities that any investigator with knowledge of the case would have found suspicious.

The DPS agent reported that "Trotsky was in Carlsbad, New Mexico, on March 31, trying to borrow money from a doctor. He said he had a car accident. His car hit a livestock trailer and it had taken all his money to get his car repaired and painted."[151]

Trotsky claimed the minor collision with a silver-colored trailer had damaged a fender on his car. Repairs were done in Carlsbad, where his green Cadillac was painted black and yellow after the dented fender was fixed. None of the investigators at San Angelo seemed to be aware, or at least did not consider it significant, that the Frome car, which was silver gray, had a green paint smear on the front fender. The Ranger investigations all focused on the small black car or cars seen parked near, or in pursuit of, the Packard.

In Carlsbad, Taliafarro interviewed a doctor named J. L. Cavanagh, who said a man calling himself Dr. Romano Lukian came to his office about 1:30 p.m., asking to borrow some money. Since Dr. Cavanagh did not know the man, he declined. When the man persisted, using the ploy that he was a fellow physician, the Carlsbad doctor agreed to take him next door to fill his car with gasoline and oil.[152]

The attendants at Kendall Service Station in Carlsbad remembered the incident because of the newly painted yellow and black Cadillac roadster. Cavanagh signed for twenty gallons of gasoline and three quarts of oil. He gave the DPS agent the purchase receipt. It was concrete evidence that Trotsky had been in New Mexico a day after the murders supposedly happened in Van Horn. It also conflicted with what Helga Lukian had told Sheriff Fox a week earlier. She said she heard that her husband had been in Carlsbad, New Mexico, trying to charge five dollars' worth of gasoline. Helga recalled that was on April 5, not March 31.

DESPITE THE DISCREPANCIES in the alibi, and the fact that Trotsky was caught lying about having gone directly from El Paso to San Antonio on March 30, the new story about traveling all over southeastern New Mexico on that date apparently raised no eyebrows. His interrogators seemed satisfied that the alibi checked out. Inexplicably, the suspect's frequent inconsistencies and obvious lies were ignored.

None of the officers conducting the questioning in San Angelo bothered to probe into prior connections between the bogus doctor and the New Mexico physicians he used for his main alibi. The two physicians who remembered seeing him in Roswell on the date the women went missing acknowledged they had done business with a Dr. Lukian in the past, but they did not specify what kind of patient referrals were made. The DPS agent checking the suspect's alibi was unaware that his real specialty was not eye, ear, nose, and throat surgery but performing illegal abortions.

No one consulted Sheriff Fox in El Paso about the content of the brief interrogation or the efforts to validate Trotsky's alibi until well after the fact. But Culberson County sheriff Anderson, who should have been up to date on the case, went along with the Rangers' assessment that Trotsky could not have been in the area on March 30, despite the fact he personally had earlier obtained eyewitness statements, in his own town, to the contrary.

On Sunday, May 1, Anderson told reporters, "There is no evidence yet to connect the man with the Frome case."[153] He apparently was so eager to regain control of the case that he did not want to cross the Austin officials.

A short time later, the sheriff and D P S officers released the suspect into the custody of U.S. Immigration for deportation. His wife Helga dropped the desertion charges pending against him in nearby Las Cruces. "I know Dr. Lukian is vain, selfish, hot-tempered and stubborn," she told reporters, "but I do not think or believe him guilty of the crime [Frome murders]. I will stand by and help every way I can to free him of that charge."[154]

Her newfound loyalty to her irascible husband was not reciprocated. She returned, alone, to her parents' home, never to see him again. She was at least the fourth wife of the con man, and there was no record of him ever having divorced the first two. His third known marriage had ended in the wife's death.

On Monday, May 2, the phony doctor was transported by border patrol officers to San Antonio, which placed him more than five hundred miles beyond the reach of the El Paso County sheriff who had so much wanted to question him in the first place.

Sheriff Fox's prime suspect had been interrogated for less than twenty-four hours. His rambling, often cockamamie stories were good enough to convince seasoned Texas lawmen that he knew nothing about the murders. And so it was that the person most likely to have at least some direct knowledge about what had befallen Hazel and Nancy Frome slipped from the scene for good.

The only reason Sheriff Fox had not made the drive to San Angelo with his notebook full of questions was because he had been assured the suspect would be brought to El Paso for rigorous interrogation. Trotsky had once again used his devious wit to elude the authorities, this time after a brush with the most famous case in America. The escape was the most brazen to date in his outrageous criminal career, but it would be far from his last.

27

Chris Fox was furious when he learned his lead suspect had been whisked away by immigration agents without being returned to El Paso. The sheriff was already in a running feud with more than one Texas Ranger over handling of the case. Now his criticism turned toward the neighboring county sheriff, Albert Anderson. The week after Trotsky was transferred to federal custody, Fox wrote a terse letter summarizing his frustration and anger about what he deemed the lack of professionalism in the investigation.[155] He began his letter cordially enough, addressing the recipient, "My Dear Albert."

"I have been debating for some time as to whether I should write to you concerning this matter, but I feel the time has now come where I can no longer overlook what I have in mind. I might just as well lay the cards on the table so we both might get our heads together."

Then he dispensed with the pleasantries and got down to business.

"I'll be frank with you. I'm not interested in running around the country to talk to suspects. In other words, we must shape up a definite mass of corroborative testimony so that when we do get in touch with a suspect we are in a position to work on him. The way it is now, it is just a matter of what is what, and whose opinion is what."

Fox was expressing the futility of questioning suspects without solid evidentiary material on hand to compare with statements.

"In other words, Albert, I am not particularly interested in suspects. I don't give a damn about them at this time. What I want is to get things established and shaped up in the proper form so that we can travel when we do have a suspect. Trusting that all is well with you and yours, and that you know and should know I will break my neck to help you in any way I can. It has been a pleasure to do it and we will continue to do so. With kindest regards, I remain your sincere amigo."

Trotsky, alias Lukian, was given a short hearing before a San Antonio immigration magistrate on May 5. He presented an elaborate and almost comical new vitae, which he must have made up on the way over from San Angelo.

His new story that he was a professional wrestler named Romano N. Lukiancguk failed to impress the federal judge hearing his case, who rendered a verdict of illegally entering the United States and ordered him immediately deported. His fingerprints trumped his nonsensical tale and revealed him to be many, many persons — all felonious and unsavory — and none of whom the judge wanted to remain in the country.

The immigration authorities had already encountered problems deporting Trotsky several times, because the Soviets refused reentry to Russian deportees from the United States. This time, the problem was resolved somewhat outside the bounds of legality. Trotsky had previously evaded deportation by pleading he would be shot upon his return to Russia. Now he seemed almost eager to be escorted to the Texas-Mexico border by immigration officers. To facilitate his quick exit, he agreed to "return" voluntarily to Mexico, from whence he now claimed he had illegally entered the United States at Laredo, in 1935.

Because the border was so porous, Trotsky had nothing to fear from being booted out of the country. Kicked out many times before, he had simply turned around and come back at another location. Deportation was like a get-out-of-jail-free card.

Trotsky, under various assumed names and identities, had been rearrested at least nine times between 1918 and 1935, for illegal entry into the United States from points in Canada and Mexico. He must have successfully entered surreptitiously many other times, or he could not have been around to establish the breathtakingly long criminal record already amassing at the Federal Bureau of Investigation.[156]

As it was in the past, so it would be again. Trotsky was rearrested for illegal entry at Laredo, Texas, less than two weeks after being physically escorted out of the country by border patrol agents the first week in May. He was again tried before an immigration magistrate at Laredo and this time found not guilty of illegal entry. Sheriff Fox was unaware of this turn of events or even that Trotsky had once again slipped back into the United States.

In El Paso, on the day Romano Trotsky was being escorted to the border, Fox received a copy of a witness statement that had been secured by the Texas Rangers the week before Trotsky was arrested. Apparently, the Rangers weren't even sharing with each other, because the information was not available to the interrogators at San Angelo.

The transcript described an encounter between a Dr. Lukian and a schoolteacher in a South Texas barbershop. It belatedly put Trotsky squarely in the middle of the case once again. The teacher's recollections made Fox even more concerned that, because of a sloppy and uncoordinated investigation, this suspect might well have slipped from the grasp of lawmen, while having more than a little guilty knowledge of the women's disappearance, if not collusion in the actual killings.

The teacher's statement offered a chilling account of a conversation he had with Trotsky, whom he knew as Dr. Lukian, in Benavides, on April 11.[157]

Andy Edwards said he was waiting in a downtown barbershop in Benavides when Lukian came in for a shave and haircut. The doctor immediately, and without prompting, brought up the Frome murders. "Dr. Lukian said he had been in California doing some post-graduate course work and was returning through that part of the country at the time of the murders," Edwards revealed. "He said he was visiting the doctor who was called to examine the bodies, and accompanied him to the scene."

The man described, loud enough for everyone in the shop to hear, the condition of the corpses in nauseating detail, right down to how they were positioned, and the wounds inflicted on them.

"He said worms were crawling out of their mouths, and described how their clothes were ripped off, and other gruesome details," the teacher said. "This was on April 11, but I had seen him around town the day before. He was driving an older model Cadillac with a good new paint job. He asked me if things he had in his car might be stolen, and finally went out and got a small leather satchel like doctors carry, and brought it in, and watched it all the time he was there."

The interview transcript was only one of a dozen telegrams, letters, and calls about Trotsky that Sheriff Fox's office received as a result of the nationwide publicity on the suspect's arrest in the Frome murders. It seemed the man was notorious all over America. But by the time the communiqués started flooding in, the object of the great hue and cry had long since been released. Fox was certain Trotsky was now out of his reach somewhere deep in Mexico.

Hard on the heels of the interview with the schoolteacher, the sheriff received another report about the cold-blooded nature of the suspect. FBI agent R. E. Vatrelli, stationed in New York, had been contacted by a doctor who was Trotsky's supervisor in 1925, at a Ford Motor Company medical facility at the Green Island Plant in Troy, New York. "Trotsky worked as a first-aid man and, under my supervision, performed a number of tonsillectomies and other minor surgeries," Dr. Ferdinand Schmitter said. "He started borrowing money and left suddenly in 1926, after pocketing money he collected for another doctor in the area."[158]

Dr. Schmitter said he later received letters from Trotsky, which explained his reason for disappearing. "He was dodging immigration officials who wanted to deport him to Russia. He also wrote that he was trying to get away from a woman who was suing him for breach of promise. Trotsky was a very smooth, cold-blooded individual and is capable of committing murders such as those in Texas," the former employer told the New York FBI agent.

Chris Fox was doing a slow burn. He was deeply disappointed, not just because the suspect had been prematurely released, but also because his fellow lawmen had done it without extending the professional courtesy of giving his office a crack at him. Trotsky — or whatever his name — was obviously a skilled liar, and he seemed to have a long list of physicians of questionable repute willing to cover for him. Fox had made it plain that he at least wanted a shot at breaking down the man's alibi. Plus, it was the El Paso sheriff's detectives who had unearthed the suspect in the first place. Since Fox had specifically requested that Trotsky be brought to El Paso for further interrogation before being handed over to immigration authorities, this clearly was an intentional snub.

The sheriff was a proud man. He did not want his rivals to have the satisfaction of seeing just how angry he was. The professional slight prompted him to downplay the importance of the bogus doctor, in a face-saving statement to newsmen that seemed to backtrack on his earlier pronouncements about how significant this suspect might be. "His records show that he's too smart to have become mixed up with anything like the Frome case," Fox told an International News Service reporter.[159]

He had no idea how right he was about the renegade doctor's intellectual prowess. Notwithstanding the fact that the con man devoted all his substantial cunning to unsavory enterprises, he had talked his way out of many tight squeaks with the law. At the time of the arrest, Sheriff Fox, the Texas Rangers, and other local lawmen knew only of the thin list of crimes on file in the Texas Department of Public Safety's new records section. Most of the crimes on his rap sheet in Austin were relatively petty, including obtaining and selling property by fraud, car theft, practicing medicine without a license, and performing illegal medical procedures.

Along with the letters and telegrams from citizens who described being ripped off by Trotsky, an important official organization entered the fray, with more serious information about his criminal life. A heavy airmail packet arrived at the sheriff's office, several days after Trotsky slipped from Fox's grasp. Unsolicited, the Bureau of Investigation of the American Medical Association (AMA) in Chicago had sent files on Trotsky containing complaints of its doctor-members from across the nation, newspaper articles, major alert bulletins, and other incriminating documents. A copy of an extensive report about Trotsky's illicit activities published in the association's journal was also included, along with official reports from AMA investigators and law enforcement agencies in the United States and Mexico. The cover letter, dated May 4, 1938, and personally addressed to Sheriff Fox, asked that the AMA be kept apprised of developments about the doctor's role in the Frome murder case.

A second sizable packet came in the mail a few days later, from the Federal Bureau of Investigation. This was in response to a request for information that Fox had made to the Justice Department after his interview with the suspect's wife Helga, in April.

A quick scan of the two files by Fox and his investigators revealed an astounding criminal record for a man who had, incongruously, managed to remain almost invisible to local authorities while engaged in criminal rampages all around them. The man was a true medical mountebank.

The AMA record of complaints, arrests, and convictions of Trotsky under his many aliases dated back to 1925 and spanned the nation from New York to California, with stops in Minnesota, Idaho, Oklahoma, New Mexico, Nevada, Arizona, numerous towns in Texas, and across the border into Mexico. The FBI file provided additional details on the federal charges that resulted from his nefarious deeds.

28

A man forty years old would have to work very hard to amass a more reprehensible record than this person with more than thirty aliases, most frequently known as Romano Trotsky. The notorious con man claimed nearly as many birthdates as fake identities, ranging from 1897 to 1904, which meant he could have been anywhere from thirty-four to forty-one years of age when he was arrested as a suspect in the Frome murders. Yet he was already one of the most prolific white-collar criminals of his era. His tawdry criminal career spanned twenty years, much of that time as an itinerant abortionist using the guise of an eye, ear, nose, and throat surgeon working with licensed physicians.

Sheriff Fox pieced together the man's modus operandi from the expanded files provided by the FBI and AMA.[160] Trotsky usually arrived in a smaller town or satellite of a larger city and rented a house or commercial space for an office. He presented himself as an eye, ear, nose, and throat surgeon. He would immediately set out to establish credit and borrow money from local community leaders who wanted to see a new doctor in their area. After setting himself up in the town, he then traveled the region, contacting general-practice physicians to offer his surgical skills to their regular patients. He did perform some minor throat and eye surgeries from time to time. He also clandestinely made "certain kinds of doctors," as one AMA investigator characterized them, aware that he was available to perform abortions.

Trotsky lined up hometown doctors who could put him in contact with potential patients needing the illegal operation. The licensed doctors made the appointments, collected the money, and later paid Trotsky a fee for the procedure. Often, the doctors were in arrears because the patients paid in installments, so Trotsky was forever hitting up doctors for past-due payments. Since it was a racket to begin with, collections had to be made under the table. He could not sue for back payment and could not complain in public. But he could, and did, pester the deviant doctors incessantly. Needless to say, once they had conspired to use his services, they were somewhat under his thumb.

Almost all doctors of the day refused to have anything to do with abortions, not necessarily as a matter of conscience, but because the procedure was illegal in every state. The only exceptions were for the protection of the life or health of the mother. A few states permitted termination of a pregnancy resulting from rape or incest. Trotsky had to be careful which doctors he approached. To their credit, a great majority of those he contacted called their state medical association or the AMA's Bureau of Investigation. For that reason, Trotsky constantly changed his base of operations and his pseudo identity, frequently moving across state lines when it got really hot for him. Still, he was apprehended and charged with illegally practicing medicine or performing illegal operations a surprising number of times, and he served any number of short sentences in local jails.

From these calls by local physicians, the AMA investigators began to track the elusive fraud. The file catalogued over a decade of illicit practice under at least thirty-five assumed names.[161]

When questioned by local authorities, Trotsky produced an impressive-looking document printed in the Cyrillic alphabet and embossed with the double eagle seal of the tsarist Imperial Military Medical Academy. He variously claimed it was his diploma for graduation from medical colleges at either Petrograd or Moscow, or an actual pre-Soviet Russian license to practice medicine.[162]

Trotsky would explain that his application with a state's board of medical examiners for his license to practice was taking a little longer than usual because of the red tape created by the change in governments in Russia. Since almost no one could read Cyrillic Russian, this audaciously phony document fooled many local doctors, who were perhaps not interested in questioning it too closely in the first place. The document was, in reality, a copy of an elaborately printed official 1905 Act, establishing new qualifications for doctors to practice medicine in tsarist Russia. It was issued by the Imperial Military Medical Academy and thus bore that institution's official seal. Neither his name nor the name of any other individual appeared on the document, but since it was all in Russian, no one seemed to notice that minor omission.

The bogus doctor's second specialty was car theft, by fraud. Whenever possible, Trotsky drove a Cadillac automobile, which he always acquired on credit and for which he rarely made payments. He was an exceptionally persuasive talker, with a brazenness that allowed him to argue away most doubts. Sheriff Fox learned just how bold this con man was from a lengthy newspaper clipping in the packet provided by the AMA.

A key element of Trotsky's fraudulent routine was to present his story to the local newspaper in whatever town he was trying to establish his next scam. If he succeeded in getting a favorable feature story, he parlayed the article as part of his credentials to local doctors.

The article that struck Sheriff Fox as proof his suspect was no ordinary crook appeared above the fold on the front page of the January 18, 1934, edition of the *Oakland Tribune*, along with a photograph of the man and his then wife, Elsie Trotsky, née Aichinger. The headline read,

NEPHEW OF TROTSKY IS VISITOR HERE — FEARS COMMUNISTS

"Being the nephew of Leon Trotsky is almost as dangerous as being Trotsky himself," the item began. "Dr. R. N. Trotsky, 37-year-old physician of Twin Falls, Idaho, who came here two weeks ago for a vacation, is returning home today for a rest, after having spent the entire fortnight dodging recognition, even to the extent of having all his mail sent him through a secret Oakland address."

The article said the prominent physician and his wife were staying at the home of her mother, a Richmond-area socialite.

"It isn't pleasant to be shot at," Trotsky remarked. "That's why I try to avoid publicity whenever I can."

The phony doctor told the reporter that Red assassins had made several attempts on his life, most recently on the train ride from Idaho to the Bay Area, two weeks before the interview.

He claimed to have been born into a family of tsarist military officers from the Odessa region of Russia. His family enrolled him in military school at the age of twelve. He said he was a former captain in the White Russian army and was sent to Japan to train imperial army cavalrymen prior to the Russian Revolution.

In a weird aside to the interview, Trotsky said that, in 1932, he received a coded telegram from the commanding general of the Japanese army, addressed to Count R. N. Trotsky, offering him a commission in the Japanese army. The ever-scheming Trotsky might have had a reason for inserting this yarn in his newspaper interview. He had devoted a great deal of time attempting to ingratiate himself with the large White Russian community of immigrants that had settled in the United States after the Russian Revolution. While he claimed at various times to be a nephew of the former Red Army revolutionary leader Leon Trotsky, he also boasted of being Russian aristocracy. He risked contradiction by also claiming to be from a branch of the family that actively fought against the Reds. He said his father, a tsarist general, had married a Russian noblewoman and was anointed a count by the tsar himself.

Trotsky told the reporter a different version of the story. In this account, he had graduated as a doctor from the Imperial Military Medical Academy the year the revolution began and was immediately sent to a White Russian army unit fighting the Bolshevik army. He said he fled Russia after the Reds took over, and his entire family, except for his Communist Uncle Leon, was slaughtered. He also told the reporter that Stalin was still interested in having him exterminated and sent agents after him whenever Red spies discovered his whereabouts. That was why he was always on the move, changing addresses and aliases.

"If Germany reinstates the crown and Russia once again becomes a monarchy," he said, he would return to Russia to reclaim his family's vast estates. Trotsky was parroting a well-worn party line widely used by the White Russian diaspora of the day to justify its Fascist and pro-Hitler leanings.

He further predicted that war between the Soviets and Japan was "inevitable," probably within a year, and that the United States should take the side of Japan when that war broke out. But he feared the nation would instead go to war against Japan before long. He himself, he assured the reporter, was well known in Japan and could play a role in preventing such a war.

It must have been a slow news day. The reporter either bought the story completely or found it compelling enough not to bother checking any of the claims of the well-groomed physician.

Trotsky likely intended to use the article from a major California newspaper to help establish his credentials. He could add it to his bogus Russian certification to enhance his biography, as he set about practicing medicine in the San Francisco area. It had the desired effect. He was soon dispensing his illegal services there, moving from town to town around the Bay. He continued to work gullible or craven doctors and their patients, on and off, for the next three years, borrowing money from local merchants whenever he could.

He also seemed to think the story would help establish his bona fides with local lawmen, if he impressed on them that he was an anti-Soviet freedom fighter, active in the circles of the White Russian organization in the Bay Area. Trotsky claimed to be one of the founding members of the Bay Area branch of the Russian Club.

None of the lawmen involved with his questioning in the Frome case were particularly taken with his heroic claims or club affiliations. The doctor's claims about his anti-Red past and association with a Fascist organization might have merited deeper scrutiny at a later date; but at the time of the Frome murders, most local lawmen were not interested in foreign intrigues.

29

Sheriff Fox was burning the midnight oil, poring over the thick files on Trotsky from the FBI and the American Medical Association. It was clear that the man of many aliases was a master at escaping punishment through the skillful use of guile. His long trail of repeat offenses proved he was a career criminal without a conscience; but he had managed to escape any serious jail time for nearly two decades of continuous felonious conduct. He would barely be released from one jail term before he was at it again.

Yet, in the whole sordid list of Trotsky's criminal activity, there was no indication he had any penchant for the kind of violence wrought against the Frome women. He was never convicted of using firearms in any of his crimes, preferring instead to use his glib tongue and oily good looks to prey upon his victims.

Then Fox came upon a file on an obscure, four-year-old case out of Arizona that showed Trotsky at least knew how to use a gun.

The AMA file revealed a 1934 Nogales, Arizona, case against Trotsky in which he had coerced local doctors to cover for his unlawful practice and serve as alibi witnesses to help him beat abortion charges. The doctors were so deeply ensnared in his schemes that coming to his defense put their own, legitimate medical licenses in jeopardy. Still, they doggedly covered for the con man's illegal activities.

In that case, Trotsky was flagrantly running an abortion ring under the guise of an eye, ear, nose, and throat surgery practice. The initial investigation was launched by the Arizona Board of Medical Examiners. The case was referred to the FBI as a federal matter when a doctor with the U.S. Public Health Service stepped up to vouch for Trotsky's credentials.

The investigation soon revealed that Trotsky was performing the illegal operations in cooperation with a Dr. W. F. Chenowitz, whom the FBI identified as "a well-known abortionist" and a good friend of a doctor from the Public Health Service.[163] The government doctor accused of facilitating Trotsky's and Chenowitz's criminal activities was identified as Dr. Glenn L. Harker.

A synopsis of the investigation stated that the public health service physician "allowed Romano N. Trotsky to use his office for the illegal practice of medicine, knowing that Trotsky was not a licensed practitioner, and that Trotsky had a criminal record; further, subject made bond for Trotsky when Trotsky was arrested."[164]

The FBI found that Chenowitz and Harker refused to cooperate with the Arizona medical examiner's orders to cease abetting the illegal activities, which allowed Trotsky to practice for several months in early 1934.

"Dr. Harker was very foolish in appearing as a witness for Trotsky after he knew Trotsky was making a laughing stock of him," the FBI reported. Harker was accused of lying to investigators by telling them that Trotsky was working as an intern in his U.S. Public Health Service Hospital in Nogales.

The investigation concluded that, because these doctors continued to support Trotsky — including making bond for him on several occasions, even after they were presented evidence of his criminal background — "any statements they made would not be reliable."

There were other examples in the AMA file of Trotsky's successful use of gullible physicians in the furtherance of his schemes. Sheriff Fox determined that Trotsky's pattern of co-opting doctors as alibi witnesses was clearly analogous to his ploy in the Frome case.

During the Nogales investigation, the FBI also found that Trotsky had used a firearm at one point, but on himself, not a victim. Apparently, in an attempt to gain sympathy from the court, Trotsky concocted a story that two men, "probably Soviet agents," had kidnapped him, taken him into the desert, and tried to kill him. He claimed he escaped after the men made him kneel and began shooting at him. As evidence, Trotsky showed up at an emergency room with a minor gunshot wound in his arm and bullet holes in the sleeve of his suit coat and shirt.

An investigation by Nogales police chief J. J. Lowe concluded the story was made up and that Trotsky had actually inflicted the wound on himself. This report also provided Sheriff Fox with proof Trotsky could use a gun, even if not in the commission of a violent crime, and was somewhat skilled in the use of firearms.

Trotsky's breathtaking audacity was exhibited in the Nogales case when he persuaded his then wife Elsie to pen a letter for his signature to FBI director J. Edgar Hoover. The last thing a person with such a notorious reputation might be expected to do was yank the chain of the top cop in the land. But the con man did exactly that.

The letter was written on stationery of the Bowman Hotel in Nogales. Although Trotsky acknowledged that the FBI "undoubtedly" had a file on him, he asked Hoover personally to help him "in a very vital" situation.[165]

"I am trying to live honestly," Trotsky wrote the director. "However, this seems impossible as these records are concerned. Wherever I go, these records are made public. I come from good Russian people, was educated in one of Russia's finest universities, am married to an American girl, and have a twenty-month-old son," Trotsky said. "We ask for the chance of supporting this little family to keep them in comfort and live honestly and happily. I would appreciate anything you can do to help me regarding these records."

Surprisingly, Hoover answered the letter on December 12, 1934. Not surprisingly, he refused to expunge the record. The FBI "cannot assist you regarding a record of your previous difficulties," he wrote.

Sheriff Fox, who had belatedly received copies of the massive file, wished he had seen it before the suspect was allowed to disappear into the immigration system.

Of even greater interest to the El Paso sheriff was a three-page magazine article about Trotsky that appeared in the *Journal of the American Medical Association* (*JAMA*), which clearly established that R. N. Trotsky — or this man of many aliases — was, in actuality, a hardened career criminal.

"Undoubtedly, the secret of this criminal's ability to get away with crimes, from petty swindling to abortion, lies in the fact that he is good-looking, makes a good appearance, has brains, and, more and above all, colossal assurance and impudence," said the article.[166] Prior to that conclusion, the article detailed an almost unbelievable litany of criminal activities from the files of the AMA and FBI, dating back to 1921.

If, as he often claimed, Trotsky had illegally entered the United States from Canada in 1920 after fleeing Russia, his records revealed that his criminal career began almost immediately after he crossed the border. Trotsky seemed always to operate just below the surface of full exposure by limiting his crimes to rather petty offenses. And he usually beat a hasty retreat after each scheme was discovered by local officials. In case after case, he was given light sentences and fines or probation. Time and again, he was let off with a slap on the wrist, after promising local authorities he would leave the area and never return. In many cases, he agreed to voluntarily leave the country. After one conviction for performing an illegal surgery, he promised a California judge that he would not return to the Los Angeles area for "at least two years."

Thus, in the best tradition of the royals of old, the ersatz Russian count agreed to a modern version of self-imposed exile, to spare himself more severe punishment. Still, Trotsky's unsavory biography in the *JAMA* article read like a felony fairytale.

"R. N. Trotsky, alias Ray Anthony, alias Bob Lukan, alias Romano Trotsky, is a Russian born in 1894, height 5'8", weight 162 pounds, with a medium-dark complexion, blue eyes, and black hair," the article began. "The story that follows gives another interesting example of how a persistent and smooth-working impostor can continue to ply his trade, despite the fact that the man is a deportable alien with a criminal record."[167]

The article first detailed his "Government Record" beginning in 1921, with a charge of selling mortgaged property in Minneapolis. In 1923, he was convicted of writing bad checks. Sometime before 1927, he assumed the false identity of a physician. He was convicted of murder in Minnesota for the death of a girl during an illegal abortion and sentenced to a four-year term in prison, for which he served one year.

After release from prison, he moved to warmer climes and was next arrested and convicted of illegally acquiring a Cadillac under false pretenses and taking it to Austin, Texas. In 1928, he was convicted of car theft under the federal Dyer Act and sent to the U.S. Penitentiary at Leavenworth for a year.

He returned to Texas from the federal prison and made his first appearance in El Paso. At Beaumont Veterans Hospital at Fort Bliss, under the assumed identity of an army doctor, he charged medical instruments from Southwestern Surgical Supply Company. With these purloined instruments he disappeared, to surface again as a Dr. McCormick in Albany, New York. After acquiring a Cadillac from a local dealership without making any payments, he showed up in Chicago as Dr. Romano Trotzky, a slight variation of his earlier alias. After borrowing money to set up a practice, he once again promptly left town in a new Cadillac.

In 1929, he was arrested again in Minnesota for abortion and sentenced to another four-year term in the Stillwater, Minnesota, prison. After serving three years, he next appeared as a doctor in San Angelo, Texas. He was sentenced to eighteen months in jail there. Upon his release, he went to Twin Falls, Idaho, where he was arrested for practicing without a license. He was sentenced to four months in prison and fined one hundred dollars.

More importantly, this latest conviction for medical crimes caught the attention of the AMA's Bureau of Investigation. The national medical association realized a serious career criminal posing as a doctor was loose in the land. When AMA investigators discovered that dozens of the complaints filed with them regarding fraudulent doctors all matched one man, the dossier of Dr. R. N. Trotsky was compiled. It contained complaints from doctors about a man practicing without a license under the names Romano Douglas Anthony, Romano Makorski Lukangok, Bob Anthony, McCormick, and "Trotzky."

The imposter had worked at the Ford Motor Company Hospital in Detroit and at the Manhattan Eye and Ear Hospital in New York City. In Ponca City, Oklahoma, a Dr. Trotsky, who claimed to be a Russian physician, practiced at the local hospital, pending licensing by the state. He soon left town after obtaining a new car — a Cadillac — from a local dealer, without making payment. In Wichita Falls, Texas, "Dr. Roy Anthony practiced for three months and left town after running up numerous bills and securing a mortgaged car."[168] There were other reports of a mysterious doctor who drove a Cadillac, appearing in Louisiana to borrow heavily from local businessmen.

He had attempted to open a practice in Winslow, Arizona, but was fingered as a fake by a sharp local doctor when he claimed he had once practiced medicine at Leavenworth, Kansas, where, in fact, he had only resided as an inmate in the federal prison. He next appeared as Dr. R. N. Trotzky in Flagstaff, Arizona, where he was charged with murder and acquitted in the death of a patient on whom he performed an illegal abortion in August 1932.

He left Arizona for Idaho. When he was caught practicing without a medical license in Twin Falls, he jumped bail and was recaptured hiding out in Boise. Returned to Twin Falls for trial, he was sentenced to four months in county jail by Judge W. A. Babcock, who was furnished a brief of his criminal record by the Idaho state's attorney.

"I am sorry it is impossible under the law dealing with this offense to remove this defendant farther from society because of his past record as a menace to society," Judge Babcock intoned at sentencing. "Reports from the United States Department of Justice show that he has been convicted and served time at least twice for other and more serious crimes."[169]

Once out of jail in Idaho, he returned to the Bay Area, where he conned the Oakland news reporter into the yarn about being chased and shot at by Soviet agents on the train from Idaho.

On his trip to the Bay Area, in 1934, he plied his illicit practice and was active in the White Russian organization without attracting the attention of authorities. That all changed when he moved to Nogales, Arizona. He was soon the target of investigation by both the AMA and the FBI.

The AMA investigation followed Trotsky into Mexico after his conviction for practicing medicine without a license in the Nogales case in December 1934. He served a short term in a local jail and, once again, was escorted out of the country. As it turned out, the ne'er-do-well Russian was soon in trouble with Mexican authorities, too.

Sheriff Fox found information about a curious incident in Mexico in the AMA packet. Trotsky was arrested in August 1935 in Mexico City as an illegal alien, after participating in radical political activities.

A front-page newspaper article in *El Dia* about his arrest depicted him in the uniform of the Mexican Fascist Gold Shirts organization.[170] The uniform was in the style made popular by Nazi SS and SA officers in Germany, featuring jodhpurs, riding boots, and a military tunic. It was also the uniform, worn with the trademark Sam Browne belt, of the marching columns of the German-American Bund and other American Fascist groups. The Bund was an organization of pro-Hitler Americans of German descent and recent German émigrés, founded in March 1936, to promote Nazism in the United States. The Mexico cohort of the pro-Hitler organization was also built on a large base of German immigrants who had attempted to establish Volkish colonies in Mexico and South America from the turn of the century onward.[171]

The Gold Shirts were a violent paramilitary party with ties to the American-based Silver Shirts, a pro-Fascist organization founded by a Hitler worshiper named William Dudley Pelley. The Silver Shirts, organized in 1933, were also allied with the All Russian National Revolutionary Party.

Trotsky professed to be an early member of the West Coast chapter of that Russian Fascist group, headquartered in the Bay Area.

Trotsky told the Mexico City reporter that there was a misunderstanding about his involvement in a paramilitary group. He said he treated wounded Cossack troops who were under the command of his late father in Russia during the revolution, but he had not been involved in politics since that time.

"We spoke to Romano Trotsky about his political ideas and he indicated that he had none, that he does not share those of his uncle Leon," the article reported. "He has not seen his uncle in many years. He assured us that he has not received any help from Leon Trotsky. Dr. Trotsky came to Mexico with the intention of remaining in the country and hopes to ask General Cardenas to permit him to devote himself to his profession and to have his diploma in sanitation revalidated," the report said. "He says he has never offered difficulties to anyone and hopes that the Mexican authorities will allow him to establish himself in this country. He maintains that he will never go back to Russia alive; they will only be able to deport him dead. For him to return to his native country would be a sentence of certain death."[172]

Ten days later, a second article appeared in *El Dia,* while Trotsky remained in custody of the Mexico police.

Readers will probably recall that in our edition of August 3, we published different photographs and information referring to an individual who claimed to be a nephew of Leon Trotsky and also a physician, and that he came to this country to settle here and to practice his profession," the article read. "Well, MR. Trotsky is NOT a physician, nor is he a nephew of Leon Trotsky or anything to that effect, but he is a jail bird that has unfinished business with the Department of Justice of the United States.[173]

The article said the American Medical Association had given the newspaper a large file of "bulletins from around the world" that told of the man's practicing medicine illegally.

The story provided extensive details of Trotsky's record in the United States. It did not tell what the Mexican government did with Trotsky, but he must have been kicked back across the border, because he soon showed up again in the Bay Area, illegally practicing medicine.

Once again using the name Lukian, he was reported by the AMA operating in several cities in the San Francisco Bay and Los Angeles areas, from 1935 to 1937. He then made his appearance at Las Cruces, New Mexico, and became a suspect in the Frome murders the following year.

THE FROME MURDERS reached a two-month anniversary as Sheriff Fox pondered the files on Trotsky, albeit too late to matter, since the suspect had already been released before the material from the AMA and FBI arrived. Whether or not the extraordinary criminal records would have mattered in the current case would never be known. Trotsky had taken to ground until things cooled down.

At the time, the sheriff thought Trotsky was forever out of reach in Mexico. After all, what criminal would willingly come back into a country where he was a prime suspect for heinous murders? The mysterious second man from the Hotel Cortez, the debonair Russian junk dealer Gepge, or whatever his real name, never turned up for questioning at all.

Trotsky's California connections interested the sheriff more than anything else he learned from the belated report of the interrogation. Everything kept pointing to the women's home base. Now Trotsky's connection to that area convinced him that his earlier hunch was correct: the solution to the case would be found on the West Coast.

A letter to Fox from the San Francisco agent for the American Medical Association and the California Board of Medical Examiners cinched it for the sheriff. It was imperative that he make a trip to the West Coast if this case was ever going anywhere.

Special Agent T. P. Hunter wrote Fox and Berkeley police chief Jack Greening that the AMA and state medical investigators had been seeking Trotsky for years. He said the doctor was especially active in the most recent past in the San Francisco Bay Area.[174]

It seemed too much of a coincidence that the criminal imposter's activities were concentrated not only in California but also at one time in the Frome family's backyard, on the east side of the bay.

Fox had ample reason to take off for the coast. As intrigued as he was about the con man's California career, he was even more curious about the California man who seemed so oddly uncooperative regarding the brutal murders of his own wife and daughter.

30

Sheriff Chris Fox considered himself a modern cop when it came to adopting the latest techniques of law enforcement, but in 1938, very little advancement had been made in scientific forensics. So, like his Texas Ranger counterparts, he relied heavily on past experience, knowledge of criminal behavior, and gut instinct. And his "gut" was telling him that this case simply did not bear the earmarks of banditry gone wrong.

The likelihood that the women were taken captive and not just hijacked on the side of the road, the brutal torture, and the execution-style killing all cried out for attention beyond a routine case of murder during the act of robbery. Fox was certain the motive, whatever it was, specifically targeted the Fromes. Thus, he reasoned that the chain of events leading up to the slayings in the Texas desert almost certainly originated near their home in California. The women were not in El Paso long enough to have attracted such enmity.

Most Rangers and Sheriff Anderson still thought the women were merely victims of one or more of the common criminals afoot in the badlands of Texas. Those lawmen's positions had hardened. The murders were a result of either highway robbery or mistaken identity in a drug-running operation. Sheriff Fox was the most vocal advocate for a premeditated plot originating in California.

Early in the investigation, Fox had asked an old friend, C. F. Cline of the National Automobile Theft Bureau in San Francisco, to do some off-the-record snooping on the Frome family around their home in the Bay Area. In a subsequent exchange of correspondence, Cline, a former police detective himself, agreed with Fox that there was a more sinister motive in play. "It would appear that the motivator of this murder was not for sexual gain, and in the extent of the abuse and torture, particularly the daughter having been stomped on and the mother's arm bitten, the case differs a great deal from other murder cases I have worked in which robbery was the motive," Investigator Cline wrote. "Therefore, I am bold enough to make the deduction that possibly a grudge or deliberate destruction was the motive."[175]

Fox had come to the same conclusion within days of the discovery of the bodies, even though he and his deputies diligently checked every local lead possible.

With those leads exhausted, the sheriff decided to take the unusual step of drawing on scarce funds from his always tight budget to carry his investigation to the women's home base. His attempts to get Weston Frome to cooperate during his brief visit in El Paso immediately after the murders had proved unsatisfactory. Fox thought it understandable at the time, due to the man's grief. But lately, he was not so sure. His efforts, early on, to get answers through the Berkeley police investigators were also stonewalled.

A month after the murders, Fox called Jack A. Greening, chief of police at Berkeley, and informed him that he was turning his attention to a theory of a more complex motive. He said this theory was leading his investigation to the victims' background and lifestyle in California. Fox asked Chief Greening to arrange a meeting with Frome when there would be plenty of time for an in-depth interview, which had not been possible or appropriate when the man was in El Paso. Attempts by Fox to get the executive on the telephone had been unsuccessful.

Thinking he had a confirmed meeting, Fox flew to California the second week in May. After spending the night in a hotel near the San Francisco airport, he called on Chief Greening. He was unpleasantly surprised to find that, despite his having an appointment, Frome did not show. He had suddenly left the Bay Area on a previously unscheduled business trip. The Texas lawman was stood up, for no apparent good reason, and without so much as an apology.

Frome's arrogant insult not only angered Sheriff Fox but also made him even more suspicious that the executive was intentionally hiding what might be the key to the murders. He found this conduct unfathomable and told California officers so.

Chief Greening tried to placate Fox by assigning one of his top men to the case. He asked Detective O. M. Thompson to assist the Texas sheriff with whatever he needed. But Fox soon found that the cooperation of the Berkeley police was not much better than Frome's. And he again expressed his displeasure directly to Greening.

"To be perfectly frank with you, I do not appreciate the fact that Frome had to leave town about twenty-four hours before I got here," Fox complained. "I feel that he could have just as easily waited, as his trip was not of sufficient importance that it could not have been postponed. I do not intend to be unreasonable with this man, but I feel the time must come when we stop beating around the bush and worrying about his sentiments and feelings on the matter, and have him get down on the line and answer our questions."[176]

Detective Thompson had already questioned most of the people Sheriff Fox intended to reinterview on his visit to the San Francisco area; instead of helping set up meetings, he gave Fox a copy of his reports. Fox suspected he might be a relative of the Berkeley city manager with the same last name who pulled the purse strings at the police department.

Once he reviewed the statements, the sheriff was quick to express disappointment. He wanted interviews with George Thornton, president of Mechanics Bank where the Fromes had banked for years; Dr. U. S. Abbott, the family physician; and Berkeley city manager Hollis Thompson, Pop Frome's close personal friend and fellow Elk member. These interviews conducted by Detective Thompson, ostensibly using questions supplied by Fox, were unsatisfactory to the sheriff.

"They have let their hair down, partially, but have lied gloriously," Fox told Greening. "This is most natural, however, when you stop to think that they were intimate friends."[177]

After getting the runaround from Detective Thompson, the sheriff pointed out to Chief Greening that by deliberately avoiding him, Frome was causing authorities in Texas to be even more curious about circumstances in California leading up to the murders.

"If it were not for certain questions that are still hanging fire, I would be inclined to think we could prove the killings of Nancy and Hazel Frome were entirely of a local matter [in El Paso]," Sheriff Fox told Greening.[178] The sheriff said those items hanging fire would be very simple for Frome and "his pals" in Berkeley to address. But by refusing to cooperate, what might be explained simply was now becoming extremely suspicious.

Among the lingering questions Fox hoped to clear up in interviews in California were the discrepancies regarding the women's travel route prior to arriving in El Paso and the possible California connections between the women and the two mystery men they had been seen with in Juarez. At least one of those men was likely from the Bay Area, because Mrs. Frome was overheard in a cabaret saying she knew him from California. The sheriff still thought one of them may have been the elusive doctor Trotsky.

Fox was interested in finding any direct links between the women and Trotsky while he lived in California. In particular, he now wanted to know if Nancy's former fiancé, Dr. William Crawford, an ophthalmologist, was ever associated with the bogus doctor. After all, Trotsky had used his practice as an eye surgeon as cover for other illegal activities in the Bay Area for years. Since his modus operandi was calling on legitimate local doctors to offer his "surgical skills" to their patients, Fox thought Dr. Crawford might have run across him.

The sheriff learned that Crawford had married and, like Frome and friends, was unwilling to talk about his own associations. He did say he had never met Trotsky, or even heard of him, other than what he had read about the charlatan in the Oakland papers since the murders.

Fox was doubly interested in why Pop Frome continued to insist that his wife and daughter had stayed the first night of their trip at the El Padre Auto Courts in Bakersfield, when there was concrete evidence they had spent that night at the Biltmore Hotel in Los Angeles. Also, there were lingering questions about why the women took the longer, southern route along the U.S.-Mexico border, rather than driving straight across the middle of the country on the newly completed highway system. Explanations offered through Detective Thompson did not satisfy the dogged Texas sheriff.

Culled from the blizzard of tips were a number of anonymous ones that seemed to have come from persons with some real knowledge of the Frome family's activities. Perhaps they were sent in by tipsters who valued their privacy more than a potential reward.

Fox was working on one such tip that Mrs. Frome wanted to accompany Nancy on the trip and go by car because she had made plans to rendezvous with someone on the Mexican border. "It will be necessary to get further information concerning the reasons Hazel and Nancy wanted to take the southern route," Fox insisted.[179]

He continued to argue with Thompson, even after the Berkeley detective said Frome and friends knew nothing more about anything on the list of questions Fox submitted, specifically about the women's choice of travel routes. "Our informant tells us that Mrs. Frome wanted to come through the border route in order that she could contact somebody in Mexico," said Fox.[180] This, too, went ignored by Detective Thompson.

The sheriff was also troubled by tips he had received that another hotel in faraway Mexico City, the Hotel Genève, was somehow involved in the Frome case. He wanted to talk to someone familiar with the mother and sisters' travels in Mexico in 1937. What was the significance, if any, of their lengthy stay in Mexico that year? Fox had learned from his contacts in the FBI that Hotel Genève was a well-known gathering place for Europeans, particularly German diplomats, journalists, and businessmen suspected of intrigue against American oil interests south of the border. The sheriff wanted to know why they had chosen that particular hotel and why they stayed there for such an extended period.[181]

He peevishly told Berkeley investigators that just because Pop Frome and his cronies did not believe these angles were important, it did not mean everyone should simply drop this line of questioning. Since when did material witnesses in a major murder case dictate which police questions were relevant and which were not? "Don't get the idea that I am trying to stir up a lot of scandal and dirt, or anything like that, but it's because the Mexican border angle and the men the women met in Juarez are going to play a large part in the scheme of things," the sheriff explained.[182]

What might have looked to Berkeley authorities like a fishing expedition into the Fromes' private lives was far from it to Sheriff Fox. He wanted more from family doctor U. S. Abbott, to clear up loose ends about a report that Nancy had been ailing on the trip and might have sought medical attention in El Paso.

"To date we have received no more definitive information regarding our tip that Nancy received treatment while in El Paso," Fox complained. "The informant in San Francisco attempted to get this information, but the persons contacted refused to talk."[183] He was referring to attempts to interview Dr. Abbott about Nancy's health history around the time of the trip. Once again, the bogus doctor Trotsky, who was known to be at the Hotel Cortez during the women's visit, could somehow have been involved.

The sheriff's interest in the family's financial situation, and the reason he wanted to talk to Frome's banker, was spurred by another anonymous tip that Hazel was desperate for money and might have been serving as a courier to deliver something to someone in Mexico. While narcotics were mentioned more than once, particularly by the Rangers, Fox was also curious about exactly what type of explosives Frome was selling and to whom.

"Could they have met someone in Juarez who would have paid them money to bring something across for them?" the sheriff asked Chief Greening. "From my tips I am of the opinion that the more money they had the more they liked it."[184] Fox reasoned that Mrs. Frome insisted on accompanying Nancy, and particularly in taking the longer route along the Mexican border, for some financial reason.

But neither the family doctor nor the personal banker would agree to meet with him, further fueling his suspicions that the Frome women's trip was something other than a visit to Mada on the East Coast. The Texas sheriff had no jurisdiction in California that would have empowered him to compel these men to be interrogated against their will.

Finally, Sheriff Fox threw up his hands on trying to get anything directly out of Frome or his friends. They were too well connected in the immediate Bay Area. It became apparent that, even if Chief Greening and his detectives wanted to cooperate fully, they were under pressure from city manager Hollis Thompson not to do so.

Chris Fox was angry and shot off another letter to Greening.

There is no good reason to continue to place our good friends on the spot, such as yourself and Inspector Thompson. I note that you and Detective Thompson believe Frome has been sincere in his previous statements to you. I am sorry I have been unable to concur with you on that . . . when it comes to covering up his own tracks and saving his own hide.

Now Jack, I was not born yesterday, and no one is more thoroughly impressed with the fact that I am just an ordinary country cop than myself. But I know exactly the spot you are in, and I think enough of you and your boys that I do not wish to embarrass you or to inconvenience you. It would not be fair of me to do so.

Furthermore, it would not assist one iota in the investigation of this case for me to continue to place you all at a disadvantage. You boys have to live in Berkeley and work under the direction of your superiors, and for that reason I am discontinuing any further personal investigation through you.

I like you and your boys tremendously, and have always appreciated the courtesies extended to me. I only regret that I have not been able to reciprocate.

However, that day may come. It has been my policy and the policy of this department when we work on a case of this nature to try to find out as much as possible concerning the background of the deceased and his or her relatives. So should you ever have the occasion to talk to Mr. Weston G. Frome again, you tell him that he was not singled out because of his great prominence in the community, or because of his exalted position that he holds in the Elks Club.[185]

During the early days of the investigation, Sheriff Fox was led to believe that Frome was little more than a glorified salesman, albeit for one of America's largest explosives manufacturing companies. On his Berkeley trip, Fox discovered that the secretive executive held a far more important role than he had, at first, let Texas officials know.

This, like so many things about Weston Frome, struck the sheriff as odd, since most people tended to exaggerate the importance of their positions, not play them down.

Hazel (*left*)
and Nancy
Frome.
Wide World
Photos

The entrance to
the Hotel Cortez
looks just as it did
when the Frome
women took refuge
there in 1938.
Photo by author

These images of Hazel (*left*) and Nancy Frome appeared on front pages of newspapers around the world, following their murders in March 1938. *El Paso Times* Collection, di_08908, The Dolph Briscoe Center for American History, The University of Texas at Austin

Nancy, in sombrero, and Hazel Frome made several trips across the border to Juarez, Mexico, while stranded by car trouble in El Paso. *El Paso Herald-Post* records, MS749, University of Texas at El Paso Library, Special Collections Department

WEST TEXAS HOTEL COMPANY OWNERS AND OPERATORS

Hotel Cortez
"Un hogar simpático"
El Paso

Fri. night
March 25

Al dear,

Just a note before I go to bed. Excuse the terribly large paper but beggars can't be choosers.

We arrived here tonight with car trouble and still aren't sure what time tomorrow we'll get away tomorrow. We want to leave early as Dallas is 650 miles and we want to get as close as possible. So far we have had quite a few detours the flood in Calif. took out so many bridges and made lots of the road impassable. After we left L.A. it began to get warmer until now I'm really practically roasting. Of course, it isn't like the summers here — but just to help things along Mom won't let me wear a coach dress because of my cold so I've been

wearing that cute grey number plus my brown coat.

Tonight we splurged and took ourselves to see "Bluebeard's Eighth Wife." It was cute but it was so hot and stuffy in the show — and the place was fully of many "smelly" Mexicans.

South Carolina still seems miles away and I'm getting more impatient every minute. As we have figured now we will get in sometime Tues — we hope early in the afternoon.

My "scotch blood" is coming out now that we're in Texas where cigarettes are 18¢ a pkg. and of course we arrived without any. We're practically ready to give up smoking.

Do write and have fun.

Lots of love,
Nancy

Nancy Frome's letter, written from El Paso to a sorority sister, just days before her death. Courtesy Alison Knope

Sheriff Anderson (center) examines the Frome murder scene, while trucker Milam (left) and others look on. *El Paso Times* Collection, di_08909, The Dolph Briscoe Center for American History, The University of Texas at Austin

The El Paso County Sheriff's Office was the best-staffed law enforcement agency in West Texas. Courtesy of W. H. Peterson III

El Paso Sheriff Chris P. Fox spent years trying to solve the
Frome murders. Allen G. Falby papers, MS149, University of Texas
at El Paso Library, Special Collections Department

Sheriff Chris P. Fox
believed the motive for
the murders originated
in the Bay Area. Allen
G. Falby papers, MS149,
University of Texas at
El Paso Library, Special
Collections Department

The Frome-murder investigators included local lawmen, Texas DPS agents, and Rangers. Sheriff Fox (*seated left*) was the early coordinator of the investigation. *El Paso Herald-Post* Collection, di_08906, The Dolph Briscoe Center for American History, The University of Texas at Austin

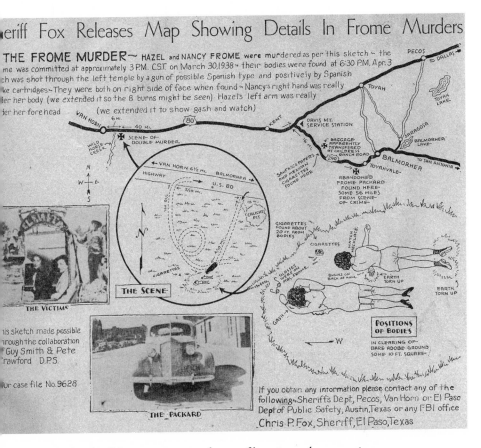

Forensic sketch of the crime scene and map of locations where eyewitnesses reported unusual incidents on US 80, drawn by a DPS criminal investigator. *El Paso Times* Collection, di_08907, The Dolph Briscoe Center for American History, The University of Texas at Austin

Desert site of the murders east of Van Horn, in dusky gloom, taken at the same time of day that the bodies were discovered. The Sierra Diablo Mountains are on the horizon. Photo by the author

One-time prime suspect Trotsky used more than thirty known aliases and had many bogus trades. Here he claims to be a professional wrestler. Courtesy of American Medical Association Archives

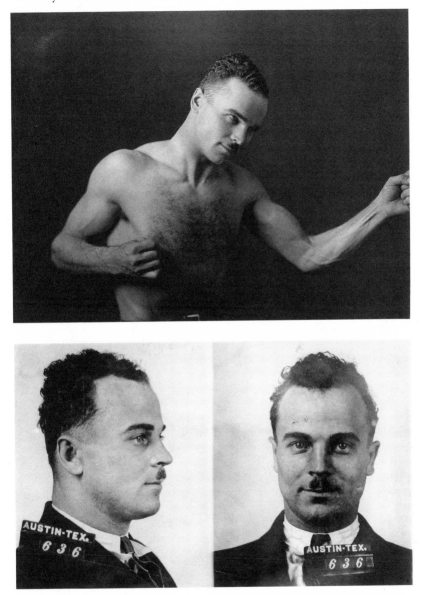

Convicted dozens of times for performing illegal abortions and other offenses, Trotsky's criminal record covered many years and two-dozen states. Courtesy of American Medical Association Archives

El Paso doctor Wolfgang Ebell, arrested for Nazi espionage in 1941, led from federal court by a U.S. marshal. Nancy Hamilton papers, MS314, University of Texas at El Paso Library, Special Collections Department

31

Weston G. Frome was as secretive about the projects and products of his company as he was evasive about his job title and description, and to an inquisitive cop like Chris Fox, that was like waving a red cape in front of an angry bull.

The sheriff was a practical man, not given to paranoia, but he was baffled by the hush-hush behavior of the husband and father of the victims. Never in his experience had he seen a surviving family member so uncooperative in a murder investigation.

Fox intended to find out why the executive deliberately avoided interviews and dodged questions about the family's personal affairs and his own business dealings. The Texas lawman had learned, while in the Bay Area, that Frome was not simply involved in sales for Atlas but wore many other hats, both at the regional and corporate level.

Frome's title was assistant general manager for explosives for the national corporation, as well as western regional sales manager. Fox learned that Frome also held the title of plant manager for a secretive explosives manufacturing installation at nearby Giant, California.[186] That plant, with an annual manufacturing capacity of nearly two million kegs of blasting powder and 108 million pounds of dynamite, was the direct supplier of explosives for Atlas's vast western region.

Frome was, in actuality, the top executive officer for the huge Atlas Powder Company for the entire western United States. That region also encompassed Latin America and U.S. installations on islands and atolls in the Pacific Ocean. His frequent absences on business may have lent an air of suspicion to his activities, but the nature of his work did require a high level of secrecy.

Many of the company's contracts called for providing massive amounts of explosives for government construction projects run by the U.S. Army Corps of Engineers. In order to make technical decisions on the amount of explosives required, Frome and his subordinates were privy to construction blueprints. Some of these projects were military installations located in the Hawaiian Islands and at far-flung bases across the Pacific, all the way to the Philippines. Atlas dynamite made in California and sold by Frome was used in the construction of dozens of fortifications, airfields, and naval facilities. Details of these military projects were secret.

The U.S. Navy Pacific headquarters at Pearl Harbor was among them.

WESTON FROME had devoted part of 1937 to setting up the wholly owned subsidiary Atlas de Mexico, S.A., headquartered in Mexico City.[187] On the Mexico projects, he worked closely with Harold White, the district manager who had helped Hazel and Nancy when they arrived in El Paso with car trouble.

Frome personally spent a considerable amount of his time in Los Angeles. Some of Atlas's biggest contracts were with construction firms rebuilding the harbors and ports there, as well as other water-purification works, dams, and canals to serve that sprawling metropolis. These projects, particularly the harbor installations and adjacent naval base in the Los Angeles basin, could be considered vulnerable to sabotage if the country faced a hostile foreign adversary. Even then, the cloak-and-dagger atmosphere surrounding Pop Frome seemed excessive, since Atlas Powder Company was just a supplier and not a prime contractor.

In 1937, the year before the murders, Frome and his top salesmen were acquiring major new contracts to provide the explosives for one of the largest federally funded waterworks developments in the history of the United States — the Central Valley Project. This Depression-era public works project, run by the Bureau of Reclamation, called for the construction of several great dams on a number of rivers in the western United States, which would ultimately bring water to California growers and the cities of Southern California.[188]

When Sheriff Fox was in California conducting his investigation, Frome and his team were busy filling orders for construction explosives for two of these dams, the Friant Dam on the San Joaquin River and the Shasta Dam on the Sacramento River. They were working with a longtime business associate named Hans Wilhelm Rohl, who was one of the largest heavy-construction contractors on the West Coast. Rohl, not so coincidentally, also kept a suite of rooms at the Biltmore Hotel, even though he had a permanent residence in Los Angeles.

The business relationship between Rohl and Atlas was mutually beneficial and highly lucrative for both concerns. Rohl's government contracts could not have been easily completed without ready access to a large, customized source of explosives; and Atlas could not have remained as profitable during the Depression without these huge orders.

THE AMOUNT OF TIME Weston Frome spent in LA, and his repeated insistence that the women never stopped there on their ill-fated trip, whetted Fox's interest in expanding his quest for information from the Bay Area to the sprawling metropolis to the south.

He was not acting on gut instinct alone. A cryptic note he received from an agent of the Federal Bureau of Investigation while he was in San Francisco served as added impetus to his already growing suspicions.

"You may want to stop in Los Angeles to ascertain the identity and present location of persons involved in this matter," hinted FBI agent R. H. Colvin of the bureau's office in El Paso. "It is suggested that you contact Lieutenant L. J. Hurst of the Los Angeles Police Department." The terse note concluded, "I will expect you to treat this as extremely confidential and to use it with discretion."[189]

Since the FBI was not investigating the Frome murders, Fox assumed this meant the bureau had come across information about the case while pursuing something else involving federal malfeasance or national security. As a result of his close working relationships with military intelligence units as well as the FBI, Fox was vaguely aware that off-the-record activity involving the clandestine services was going on. Like most local lawmen, he felt the less he knew about it the better, especially since much of this activity was being conducted without proper congressional authority.

Because El Paso was strategically located at both interstate and international junctions, Sheriff Fox was required to work more closely with the feds than most other local sheriffs would have been.

The Los Angeles detective mentioned in the note, Lieutenant L. J. Hurst, also worked with the FBI from time to time on local coordination of investigations normally beyond the scope of duties for police authorities.

Likewise, the LA police department and El Paso Sheriff's Office frequently worked together, most recently on coordinating arrests of border hopping, fugitive felons, and investigation of interstate and international car-theft rings.

Fortunately, Sheriff Fox had nurtured personal relationships with his peers in the law enforcement establishment in Los Angeles. His LA connections weren't all business either.

The tall, good-looking Texas lawman had made numerous appearances in recent years for various charities and Western movie premieres. His activities as an El Paso booster brought him in close touch with movie producers. And he never visited Hollywood to solicit movie shoots in his Texas county without paying courtesy calls to the Los Angeles city and county offices of fellow lawmen.

These carefully nurtured work and personal relationships were about to bear fruit in an unexpected way that would lead Sheriff Fox in a new direction in the Frome case.

32

Despite Chris Fox's close association with individual FBI agents, and the occasional work he had done with the bureau on other cases, he was completely unaware of a large-scale investigation centered on possible subversive activities in the West Coast construction industry.

Coincidentally, that investigation also involved the Biltmore Hotel in Los Angeles, although it had nothing to do with the Frome women's stay there on the first night of their trip.

Since mid-1937, the bureau had been interested in Nazi activities emanating from the German consulates at San Francisco and Los Angeles. In the process of surveilling foreign agents hiding behind diplomatic cover, the G-men had come across a number of American citizens whose association with the Nazis brought them under scrutiny.

The initial target of the FBI's surveillance had been a debonair ex-actor posing as a purveyor of fine wines to the elites of Hollywood. Werner Plack was actually an agent on the staff of the German consul general George Gyssling, in the Los Angeles diplomatic offices. Both men were on the FBI's watch list of prime suspects in a West Coast Nazi espionage ring.[190]

While most suspected Nazi subversives kept a low profile, Plack sought the limelight. He was a fixture on the Hollywood nightclub scene and was dating the movie starlet Peggy Joyce. The brazen spy made no effort to hide his loyalty to Hitler. In an incident at a club in Beverly Hills, Plack gave the stiff-arm Nazi salute and shouted, "Heil Hitler!" A screenwriter named Sy Bartlett took offense and punched out the German agent, breaking his nose.

Gossip columnist Louella Parsons frequently included the flamboyant doings of the German wine purveyor in her columns. "Peggy Joyce and Werner Plack, at a night spot, continuing as Hollywood's most consistent twosome," she wrote in a February 27, 1938, column. That tidbit was followed by, "Errol Flynn smuggled his favorite dog, Arno, on the set, and the canine did him dirt and spoiled a scene by barking."[191]

The famed Hollywood nightclubs the Trocadero, Brown Derby, and

Coconut Grove were the scenes of wild celebration, far removed from the oppressive economic malaise gripping the rest of the country. Nazi spies, sympathizers, and isolationists mingled with movie stars and moguls, corporate titans, and wannabes, with little regard for conditions at home or gathering war clouds abroad.

The FBI didn't care how hard Plack partied. But they did care who he partied with. The ribald lifestyle of the Nazi playboy led the FBI to American associates and friends, who soon became subjects of interest in the surveillance file the bureau was building for Washington. They included construction executives and army engineers responsible for most of the government projects — both military and civilian — on the West Coast and in the Pacific. A top executive in the group drew special attention. He was the influential construction contractor Wilhelm Rohl.

One particular incident in the summer of 1938 merited the attention of FBI agents monitoring Plack's activities. At a night spot called the Swing Club, the Nazi agent, in the company of the construction executive, made a grand entrance that stopped the music.

An informant offered the following account: "They ran a little floor show at The Swing Club, and the floor show was going on when, all of the sudden, the orchestra leader stopped the music. He stopped the music and he stopped the floor show. The music changed and all the girls in the floor show, including the band, started to sing, 'Here comes Bill, here comes Bill, here comes Bill Rohl now.' With him were Werner Plack and one other man I never remember having seen before."

The close association between the two Germans, Plack and Rohl, generated interest at the bureau after any number of such sightings were reported. Finally, FBI agents were able to enlist the help of a housekeeper in the Rohl home, who provided information that Plack also visited there.[192]

Rohl was the founding owner of a heavy-construction company that bore his name. During the Depression years, he performed work on dozens of government-funded waterfront and highway projects throughout the western United States and Pacific region. He became a multimillionaire on government building contracts that were aimed at providing jobs to alleviate the suffering of massive unemployment, while creating a new infrastructure for the nation.

In building the highways, dams, breakwaters, channels, and waterfronts of the West Coast from the late 1920s forward, Rohl and his construction partners were among the largest users of explosives manufactured and sold by the Atlas Powder Company. During that time, Atlas Powder's profit center for the sales of high explosives gradually shifted from mining operations to heavy construction. Because of the changing economy, Rohl and his associates, and Frome and his salesmen, were drawn into countless deals of mutual benefit. Thousands of kegs of high explosives and boxes of dynamite were required to blast the rock from quarries on Catalina Island and at a site near Riverside. Rock from both quarries was used at Long Beach Harbor for the Port of Los Angeles improvement projects, supervised by the Army Corps of Engineers.

This work was nearing completion in 1937–38 by one of Rohl's construction consortiums. The miles of breakwaters forming the inner basin at the Port of Los Angeles, Long Beach, required thousands of tons of rock, and Rohl owned the barges and tug boats required to haul the loads. The project changed the oceanfront south of the metropolis, creating seawalls and new islands, and making the Long Beach port one of the finest on the West Coast.

The Atlas Powder Company was supplying much of the explosives for this project, as well as for the two major dams under construction at the same time. Weston Frome assigned the contracts to one of his key sales project managers, Eugene F. Daley. He still kept himself in the loop on all major contracts.[193] Daley was one of the Frome associates that Sheriff Fox had tried unsuccessfully to interview.

PARTIES THROWN by the Nazi Plack, which began openly at Hollywood nightclubs, sometimes led the revelers back to the Biltmore Hotel, where they ended up in Rohl's private suites. The surveillance of Plack led the FBI to open dossiers on the construction millionaire, along with his friends and business associates, although most of these men were of little or no interest to the bureau.

Wilhelm Rohl, like Plack, was German born, but he had lived in the States for so long that almost everyone assumed he was a naturalized citizen. He had entered the United States in 1913 from Chile, where he claimed to have been a mining engineer.[194] Born in Lubeck, Germany, on September

29, 1886, he said he left Germany for South America to avoid being drafted into the kaiser's army on the eve of World War I. He settled in Sacramento in 1916 and fathered four children with a common-law wife.

Rohl clawed his way up in the construction industry, starting with ownership of one dump truck used in hauling for mining operations in central California. He made a brief trip to Germany to visit relatives in 1924 and stayed in England until 1925. He returned from the European visit with enough cash to start his own construction enterprise, H. W. Rohl Company. His first major breakthrough was a 1932 contract to build a segment of the Pan-American Highway from Laredo, Texas, through Monterrey, Mexico, to Mexico City.

From that successful project, Rohl went on to make millions through construction consortiums with mostly government-funded, Depression-era projects all over California and Colorado. He ultimately landed defense contracts all along the West Coast to Alaska, throughout the Rockies from Arizona to Canada, and into the Pacific islands. These contracts required the use of tremendous amounts of blasting materials, supplied by Atlas Powder and its competitors.

Throughout the impressive expansion of his business, Rohl kept one small detail from his government clients. In all those years, he had never bothered to become a naturalized American citizen, even though he had entered the United States legally on a permanent residence permit.

A large, gregarious man, the fifty-two-year-old engineer was no more or less rowdy than many of his construction-industry peers, in a field famous for its rough-and-tumble characters. While some informants depicted him as simply a "hail fellow well met," others held darker opinions.

"Hans Wilhelm Rohl was arrogant, boastful, and aggressively pro-German," an FBI informant averred, in one sworn statement collected by the bureau. "He claimed to be a nephew of the managing director of the Hamburg-American and North German Lloyd Steamship companies, and bragged of close acquaintance with all visiting German diplomats and persons of high rank."[195]

By 1938, American intelligence agents had ample evidence that much of the spying activity aimed at the United States, particularly in the major cities on the East Coast, was being conducted by personnel arriving by, or working on, German cruise ships operating out of German ports.

Rohl's vocal sentiment about Germany's rapid new economic growth under the dictator Adolf Hitler would not have been, in and of itself, a reason to arouse much alarm. Many prominent Americans, not the least of them the aviation hero Charles Lindbergh, were making public speeches of admiration for Hitler and in support of Germany against the British and French policies in Europe.

Rohl's views and his close association with the known Nazi agent Plack never resulted in the loss of any government contracts.

Construction moguls and suppliers, Army Corps of Engineers brass, and movie stars made up the male contingent at Plack and Rohl's lavish parties. Among the guests, almost certainly, were Pop Frome and his top salesmen from Atlas Powder, as major suppliers of explosives to Rohl and the associated consortiums. The proximity was just too overwhelming to be a coincidence, since Frome, on behalf of his company, also kept a suite of rooms at the Biltmore throughout most of 1937 and into early 1938.

At the Biltmore, the parties really cut loose. The FBI had, by this time, recruited a number of willing informants from the staff at the luxurious hotel. The construction millionaire Rohl leased several rooms at the hotel, including his own Apartment Z, a permanent suite with a panoramic view of the Los Angeles skyline.

Hotel employees told the bureau that Rohl used the other rooms he permanently rented for what he called "dinner parties." While food may have been available at these soirees, their primary purpose was to entertain, in grand style, army officers and business associates.[196]

"The liquor was brought up there by the case," one employee told the FBI. "During the course of the evening there were about twenty young girls, who kept coming in and out of the apartments. The girls appeared to be cheap, commercial party girls. They had parties on a great many occasions. The same cheap-looking party girls appeared in and out on every occasion."

Hotel maids frequently cleaned up the various rooms on the ninth floor, where the beds were messed up with lipstick stains, bobby pins, and other items. The maids told the FBI that there were always at least four or five girls with the older men attending the parties at the fancy suites. The girls were described as young, "good-time partygoers." Some of them were identified as show girls and dancers who came with the construction men to the parties directly from the nightclubs in Hollywood and Beverly Hills.

While some of the straight-laced G-men conducting the investigation were shocked by the conduct they uncovered, they were instructed to record only the activities of the main targets in official reports. The names of other army officers and civilian executives attending the orgies were sent to Washington, to be kept in a separate file personally maintained by Director J. Edgar Hoover.

Other prying eyes, such as the henchmen of the gadfly spy Plack, were just as likely to have kept dossiers on these big shots for more nefarious purposes, like blackmailing them into trading secrets for silence.

Because of the sensitivity of snooping on prominent Americans, Hoover and his field men would not readily share the names of the executives caught in these unseemly goings-on with a local sheriff or police department. While the behavior of construction-industry executives and some of the army engineers who were supervising their work might be considered poor judgment, the activities did not constitute a violation of federal law per se. The bureau's interest at the moment was in espionage activities of the man Plack and his contacts, not moral turpitude, and not the Frome murder case.

Nonetheless, the private affairs of other important figures associated with the activities were noted. It was one such association that prompted the FBI tip to the Texas sheriff that sent him to Los Angeles.

33

When he arrived in Los Angeles, Sheriff Fox headed directly to the Central Division of the LAPD at First and Hill Streets. On his way, he passed the entrance to the imposing Biltmore Hotel at 506 South Grand Avenue. The hotel was only five blocks from his destination at police headquarters.

After entering the nineteenth-century building known as Old Central, he asked for, and was escorted to, the office of Detective Lieutenant L. J. Hurst. The lieutenant was expecting Fox, with whom he had actually worked cases in the past.

The name Weston G. Frome had come up during a joint FBI–LAPD surveillance of activities at the Biltmore Hotel. This prompted the city detectives to start a separate file on notable local participants. Hurst had suggested the bureau might also want to drop a hint to Fox, the coordinator of the Frome case in El Paso, regarding that one name the stakeout had uncovered. The bureau, not wanting to be involved in handing over information to a local official, threw it back to the lieutenant to follow through himself.

Hurst first showed Sheriff Fox hotel records proving that Hazel and Nancy Frome had stayed at the Biltmore on Wednesday, March 23, the first night of their cross-country trip. According to the records, Weston G. Frome had checked into the hotel the following Sunday and had stayed there through March 30, the day his wife and daughter left El Paso for the drive to Dallas.

With the routine business out of the way, the Los Angeles detective leaned in toward Sheriff Fox, as if to emphasize the importance of what he was about to say. He briefly explained that the hotel was the site of frequent drinking bashes thrown for government-contracting officials and big wheels in the public-works construction business.

This was not news to Fox. He was aware from several sources that Mr. Frome entertained quite a bit in the course of doing business. That lifestyle was described to him as normal for a person in Frome's position who "had to do a lot of entertaining, drinking, and partying in order to obtain large contracts."[197] But this was something more.

Without going into details or naming other attendees, Hurst revealed that the parties involved bringing in showgirls to entertain the brass. Some of these women were prostitutes. The detective's account was all business. He told Fox only what he needed to know and did not describe the orgies.

Hurst stated, almost matter-of-factly, that Weston Frome was one of the construction big shots who attended. And as a result of the parties, Frome had struck up an ongoing relationship with one of the Hollywood showgirls.

The El Paso lawman knew it would do no good to ask why the LAPD was interested in the Atlas Powder Company executive, and Hurst was clearly not willing to expound on why the hotel was being watched in the first place.

Fox vented about Frome's frustrating denial that his wife and daughter had stopped in Los Angeles on the first night of their trip and wondered if this was the reason. Hurst nodded and said he might be able to shed even more light on that lingering question. He pulled several typewritten sheets from a file marked for "official use only" and glanced at them briefly before sliding them across the desk. He told the sheriff he could make notes while he was there, but the issue was too sensitive for the LAPD to provide copies of the excerpted pages.

The pages were full of names and dates. It took a few minutes for Fox to read through the information and let it sink in. With all his previous suspicions, he had not predicted this.

Weston G. Frome, for a period of more than two years, and until very recently, had been the target and paying victim of sexual blackmail.

The Frome blackmail revelation complicated an already perplexing part of the case for Sheriff Fox. Was the blackmail somehow connected to the murders? Was Pop Frome's ham-handed effort to keep his private life secret, with the collusion between Atlas executives and Berkeley city officials, a deliberate cover-up? Or had the powerful executives simply duped the local police department? The sheriff's relationship with the city officers had already soured with his persistent pursuit of information about the Frome family. But this new angle had to be fully investigated. In the sheriff's experience, blackmail was often the handmaiden of murder.

In this case, the middle-aged father and husband had been paying a Hollywood showgirl and professional dancer from one to two hundred dollars a month in hush money for a sexual affair. LAPD records also showed the girl had been arrested several years earlier for prostitution.[198] This revelation had apparently been a spinoff from what was usual business practice in the construction industry. It started in Los Angeles, in a setting of upscale nightclubs and hotel parties, where liquor flowed freely and young girls were paid to entertain older, wealthy men. Even for a jaded border-town sheriff, and certainly for an American public comprised largely of church-going Protestants, the excuse that it was just business as usual would be a dubious one.

The fling did not end with the Hollywood parties. The file revealed that the woman and her boyfriend had followed Frome to San Francisco. According to a police informant, Frome was still seen with the dancer from time to time, at least through the end of 1937, in both San Francisco and Los Angeles. All the while he was paying her "blackmail" money. Since he continued to see her, Sheriff Fox surmised that, at least for a time, the money might have been more for upkeep than blackmail.

According to the report, the girl, identified as Jane Levy, was now twenty-eight years old; the affair began when she was twenty-five. Her accomplice, a man identified only as Robert, was a suspected pimp. She was married to a man named Carl Levy. Police records named Robert and Carl as members of a large criminal gang headed by a German hoodlum named Herman F. Schmiedling. The Schmiedling gang had connections in both Los Angeles and San Francisco, and was believed to be involved in a number of rackets in both cities. It was considered a dangerous bunch, since among its list of alleged crimes was armed robbery.

The fact that the Nazi consulates also employed just this sort of German gang to carry out the dirty work of missions was not known by local police at the time.

Sheriff Fox was astounded that the closed-mouth, prominent executive would have an ongoing involvement with such unsavory criminals. The police report did not indicate that the blackmail scheme itself was the subject of the investigation. Rather, Frome had come under scrutiny, quite by accident, because of something else the FBI and Los Angeles police were investigating at the Biltmore Hotel. The detective assured Fox that the LAPD was not pursuing any current case involving Frome. Since there was no complaining witness at the moment, a blackmail case against the German gang was not on the Los Angeles detective's agenda either.

FOX HEADED BACK to El Paso, not quite sure what to do with this troubling bit of new information. This blackmail angle was too germane to the case to be ignored.

Even though he had decided to wash his hands of the Berkeley police department and Pop Frome, the sheriff felt compelled to pursue this new lead, no matter where it took him, no matter whose feathers got ruffled. Deciding to let the chips fall where they may, he contacted Berkeley police chief Greening.

"My investigation in Los Angeles disclosed that Frome was being black-mailed by one Jane Levy and her boyfriend or husband, Robert. I would much prefer that he would tell you the whole story, because that would obviate my having to put it in a letter," Sheriff Fox telexed the police chief. "But if he should not see fit to do so, then I will give you all the details, and you can draw your own conclusions. My only point in wanting to ask him about this Jane Levy and her husband is that, when a man has been blackmailed it is highly possible that there may have been others, and possibly of a very recent date, and probably still smoldering. He probably was not a very discreet man, since both of the Levys have police records which show that their main line of accomplishment was that of robbery."[199]

Three days later the police chief responded:

Mr. Frome flatly denied ever having been blackmailed by a woman named Jane Levy or her husband. Inspector Thompson had a long talk with Mr. Frome at his home on the evening of May 26, and he stated that, while he did have a past, he had racked his brain repeatedly and could not come up with anything that would have the slightest bearing on this case. He flatly denied that any woman or man had ever blackmailed him or attempted to blackmail Nancy. He stated that because of his position with Atlas Powder Company, he frequently had to do a lot of entertaining and that he fre-quented nightclubs there [in Los Angeles]. He told our inspector that he spent considerable money, and that at times he did considerable drinking.

So far as any affair with a woman is concerned, or having placed himself in a compromising position where anyone would attempt to blackmail him, or where he might have acquired the enmity of any person, he did not believe this was possible.

He feels he would have [told us] all the details of his past life, even though some incidents possibly might be things he is not proud of, if there was the remotest chance that they would have a bearing on this case or aid in any manner in bringing it to a successful conclusion.

He would have to have absolute guarantee of public privacy, and it wouldn't be in the newspapers. Mr. Frome said if you have anything specific he would be glad to answer it, but he didn't think anything would serve a purpose that would be the result of fishing.

But short of your having specific information, he does not feel that any good purpose would be served by disclosing information that would really be the result of fishing or which might be misconstrued if falling into improper hands. He feels many details have appeared in newspapers that served no good purpose because they did not appear to be related [to the murders]. Regarding the feeling that he ducked out on you shortly before you arrived in Berkeley, he says this is not the case, and I really believe his absence while you were here was not intentional.

Inspector Thompson is continuing to work on the confidential information, and while he may not feel that all the information he may obtain should go into the letter, I hope you may have the confidence in us to take our word for it when we assume that any information we may gain has a bearing on the case. Unless these assurances can be given Mr. Frome I am afraid he may refuse to talk altogether. If there is any information now in your possession which puts a local Berkeley complexion on this case, please let us know in detail at once.

I really believe Mr. Frome is sincere in his statement that he knows nothing which might have a bearing on the case, and the only possibility is that he may not be able to place the correct value from a police standpoint on certain incidents in his life. It has been agreed that his attorney, who is a close personal friend, will inform us, so that we can take whatever action we may see fit.[200]

The sheriff's response to this denial was swift.

34

Chris Fox took some pleasure in seeing the businessman who had so rudely ignored his past requests squirm under the heat of the new line of questioning about the blackmail. More than that, he was angered by the continued lack of cooperation from both Frome and the Berkeley police. He fired off a letter to Chief Greening, threatening to shut the department out of his investigation.

"I have your confidential letter of May 28, giving the result of Inspector Thompson's visit with Weston G. Frome. It would be well for me to predict the balance of the letter and all future letters as they are related to Mr. Frome, so that as far as we are concerned he does not exist."[201]

The Texas sheriff's response clearly displayed his ire over what he considered Frome's outrageous lack of cooperation. His anger extended to the Berkeley police department's mollycoddling of the man. Fox was, with the sharp tone of his complaint against Pop Frome, putting the Berkeley officers on notice that he was going to proceed with his investigation without Frome or them. His letter continued,

> His [Frome's] statement that he had never been blackmailed by a woman named Jane Levy or her husband and pimp is a deliberate lie. So you can see that, if the man would state an untruth about things of that kind, there is no reason for us worrying about him further. We are no longer interested in having him tell us anything. Mr. Frome states that if we have any specific information regarding persons who are alleged to have blackmailed him he would be glad to answer it. Since he denied knowing Bob or Jane there is no reason for us to worry about it any longer. If this gentleman would not only realize that practically all the inconvenience he has been subject to has been a result of his own actions, I think he would take a different slant on this thing.
>
> When you stop to think there has not been one single officer connected with the investigation of this case who has ever had one word from Mr.

Weston G. Frome, either directly or indirectly, it makes us wonder just how interested he might be [in seeing the murders solved]. As to the newspaper articles, it might be well for Mr. Frome to go back through his own memory and check to see just how many of those articles that were unpleasant to him have been the direct result of his own conversations with newspaper people and other individuals, because of his unnatural and peculiar actions.

Yes Frome did duck out on me. That is alright, and I am sure we will both be able to survive our mutual disappointment in not meeting.

I think it is no longer necessary for Inspector Thompson to continue to work any confidential information. I notice that you feel Mr. Frome is sincere in his statement, and I am very sorry that I am unable to concur, as our information has been substantiated.[202]

Fox concluded in his response to the Berkeley police chief that he felt Frome was "covering his own tracks or saving his own hide."

PRESSURE WAS BEING APPLIED on the El Paso County sheriff by officials in Austin, but this time it came from politicians and not his fellow officers in the Texas Rangers. Someone in the Bay Area or somewhere else in California had mentioned the aggressive inquiry into Frome's private life to a higher-up at the state capital. Word came down to the sheriff that he should let up on the California executive.

Fox sent an even angrier telex to Greening on May 31, in which the sheriff once again vowed to end further inquiries in the Bay Area.

I have come to the conclusion that it would be best for all concerned for me to discontinue any further investigation or request for information in Berkeley. We may have asked questions that were embarrassing from the standpoint that it made it difficult for you to obtain the information without sticking your neck out. It was just because Mr. Frome has assumed the most difficult attitude for you in Berkeley.[203]

While the riled-up sheriff may have promised not to go through the Berkeley police department in the future, he made no such promise about continuing his general investigation in California. Soon he was calling on fellow lawmen in the California Bureau of Investigation, as well as continuing his inquiries through the investigators in the car-theft bureau. Two could play the pressure game, and the West Texas sheriff was not intimidated by the bigwigs in Austin and California.

As it happened, in less than a week, the Berkeley police department was forced to eat crow. Weston Frome's attorney advised Detective Thompson that they wanted to set the record straight. Indeed, the Atlas executive *was* once the subject of blackmail.

Fox had an admission that Frome was clearly lying about an affair and subsequent blackmail involving a young Hollywood dancer over a number of years. And he had a sheepish mea culpa from the Berkeley police. "Inspector Thompson is still in the process of working out some confidential leads, and we will notify you as soon as they are completed," Chief Greening wrote to Sheriff Fox on June 3.[204]

The letter nonchalantly reversed all the earlier claims and assurances about Frome. Greening had been humiliated by the powerful executive and his corporate connections at city hall.

"I will state that Frome, through his attorney, has admitted the affair with a Jane Levy or Levey, though she was known to him as Jane Sherrill," the contrite correspondence read. "However, he [Frome] maintains there is no connection between this woman and this case."

Sheriff Fox wasn't buying that conclusion for a minute. Frome had been too uncooperative from the beginning and, more specifically, had worked too hard to hide this affair for there not to be some connection. However, Fox was not yet sure how the blackmail cover-up fit into the case.

Frome's damning admission about the blackmail bought the sheriff some time and silenced his critics in Austin. It also gave ammunition to his controversial theory that the murders might have their origins on the West Coast.

The same day Fox received the letter with the tacit confession, Chief Greening telephoned him with an update, which Fox documented for his files. "Inspector Thompson has completed his investigation on the movements of Jane Levy or Levey, alias Jane Sherrill. Her maiden name is Scherenzel. He has been able to establish definitely that the woman and her boyfriend or husband were in San Francisco on May 30 of this year. He was able to locate these people with the assistance of Mr. Frome. However, the investigation was conducted absolutely independently of Mr. Frome and his associates." Fox's notes included a physical description of Jane. She was described as "an attractive brunette, 5'5" and weighing 128 pounds."[205]

In later correspondence, the Berkeley police chief described the black-mailers' association with a loose-knit gang of characters, mostly with German surnames, such as Schmiedling and Zitzelberger. At the time, the only significance the Berkeley detectives placed on the gang involvement was that its members seemed to have plenty of money for cars and apartments, with no visible means of legitimate support. In fact, one landlord told of finding an uncashed money order for a large amount left behind in one of the apartments vacated by members of the group.

Although it turned out the girl and others in the gang were German Americans, there was no mention of them being involved in subversive activities. Certainly there was no reason to suspect the gang might have been working as agents for a foreign government. They appeared to be common criminals who just happened to be of German descent.

The lack of cross-referencing and coordination of information between law enforcement agencies in Texas and California was now beginning to take a heavy toll on assessment of evidence in the case. There was also zero coordination of the local murder case with the FBI's fledgling investigation of foreign espionage in California. A comparison of names in the separate local and federal investigations would have revealed some interesting matches, even at this early stage.

35

In spite of his recent success, or perhaps partially because of it, the El Paso sheriff was powerless to prevent the Frome murder investigation from slipping out of his control. His treatment by fellow Texas officers over the suspect Trotsky and the apparent political pressure from Austin to back off Weston Frome were early warning signs.

Fox turned to old law enforcement friends, in an unusually candid moment of frustration, to predict that the murders would never be solved, due to petty jurisdictional feuds.

He complained to M. L. Britt, a longtime friend at the National Automobile Theft Bureau, in a long personal letter, dated July 30, 1938:

> You know Bill, you and Jim can probably realize it better than other people, but I have had a terrific amount of headaches on the case, because several agencies involved in the investigation . . . don't seem to have the earnest desire to get in there and pitch, and dig up the dope like it is. They take too much for granted and are not willing to follow through. I know in the bottom of my heart that they have not worked the oil field district, and it should have been worked.[206]
>
> But by golly there is just so much a fellow can do, and then he breaks down and has to admit he is worn out.
>
> I still suggest there is something down there in that part of the country that could throw this case back in our laps, but we are not magicians and not able to read fortunes from the fish bowl. If they [the Rangers] could just stop worrying so damn much about who is going to get credit or discredit, do something, check things instead of running around the country wanting to talk to suspects, we could get along a lot better, and in a hurry, at that.[207]

Fox complained again about Ranger Frank Mills, this time for chasing off to Phoenix to get a list of seventy-five cars mistaken for the Frome Packard, and then taking off to Albuquerque and Los Angeles to check on each one of them.

"Ranger Mills could have just as easily turned the list over to you boys at the Auto Theft Bureau and had the answers right away," he wrote.[208]

Fox also sent a letter complaining about the "great car chase" and "false leads," directly to Ranger Mills, who was still lodging at the Hotel Cortez.

> Every day or two some person comes to the department and states they have talked to you about some matter in the Frome case that I am not in a position to discuss because I have never had the pleasure of knowing what you are doing.
>
> It would indeed be a shame, a rank shame, if either you or I as individuals were to be in possession of some information and threw it aside only to find sometime later, that if we had coordinated our effort, it would have been an important lead. I have been told that you are the lone wolf sort of investigator and believe in keeping everything to yourself in the form of a secret, and it is unbecoming of me to be critical of this peculiarity.
>
> But I think that in a case of this kind, when this department has been carrying its fair share of the load, that you should discuss these matters with us so we won't make suckers out of ourselves. Why not cut all the deep-secret stuff and super-sleuth business, and come in here and lay your cards on the table, and tell us what you want, and what you have, and what you think about it?[209]

Since the feud with Ranger Mills had been running for months, Sheriff Fox did not sign this letter with his usual "Your amigo." And, in a measure sure to keep the pot boiling, he forwarded a copy to Colonel H. H. Carmichael, chief of Rangers, at the Austin headquarters.

A week later, he turned his ire toward another agency, in a tersely written letter to a Lieutenant Lyons, Coast Guard Air Patrol, U.S. Customs, El Paso:

> "Dear Lieutenant, during the past several days it has come to me that you have been hauling investigators around in your airplane. I understand that at any time if it would be of benefit to the investigation I would not hesitate to call upon you. But just for the sake of riding around the country in an airplane to satisfy curiosity, it is not my idea of something that should be done. I hope you do not believe this is the wish of this department that certain people be flown around the country to talk to this person or that person. I wish you would correct it. We are a business organization."[210]

Apparently, Lieutenant Lyons was ferrying Ranger Mills around West Texas and New Mexico, and Fox had not been informed in advance of the trips. The sheriff also learned that two Rangers had gone to San Francisco and interviewed Pop Frome, the third week in July. Fox was not told of the interview and not sent a copy of the transcripts. He was bitterly disappointed to be shut out in such a way, because he believed that, had he been able to brief the Rangers, they could have been more effective in clearing up some of the lingering questions about the blackmail. As it turned out, the Rangers were not interested in the blackmail when they questioned Mr. Frome, and they made no attempt to find out more about the German gang that had most likely set up the scheme.

During that same time period, Texas Ranger Pete Crawford and DPS criminal investigator John Reese chased down another lead connecting the Frome case to Los Angeles. They received a tip that a Packard similar to the Frome vehicle, driven by two women, had left the West Coast with a load of drugs destined for Houston. This car had been targeted by hijackers in Texas. Like so many others, the tip turned out to be bogus.

The theory that the Frome women were the victims of mistaken identity had been high on the Rangers' list throughout the case. The Texas lawmen remained convinced that the murders had been committed by common criminals. Sheriff Fox, with his theory of a more complex plot, had antagonized too many people in high places, in both Berkeley and Austin. Clearly, by midsummer, leads worked by his officers flowed one way, from his office to other investigators. Nothing from the others was being sent to him.

Fox was not left wondering about his status for long. The other shoe dropped on July 23, 1938, in a brusque letter from Culberson County sheriff Albert Anderson at Van Horn: "We have now set up facilities in my offices to handle all matters relating to the Frome case, and I would appreciate your sending such data as you have in your files at your earliest convenience. It is possible that some of the highway patrolmen will be coming this way in the near future and you can send your records by them."[211]

Fox picked up the telephone and called Austin. He was unable to get through to Colonel Carmichael at DPS headquarters, but an assistant confirmed that the case coordination was being returned to Sheriff Anderson in Van Horn. Since the bodies had been found in Culberson County, by law the jurisdiction resided there as well.

The El Paso sheriff knew that Anderson's tiny office and staff had no way of handling such a massive case and that this was a calculated move by the Rangers to take full control of the Frome investigation. He guessed that his own troubles with some of the Rangers, as well as with Anderson and the Berkeley officials, had finally led to his being removed as coordinator. But since the murders had apparently occurred in Culberson County's jurisdiction and in Anderson's bailiwick, there was technically nothing he could do.

Chris Fox, who had reigned unchallenged as the top lawman in the El Paso territory for years, was not used to being ignored. But he was too much the politician to let his fellow officers know how deeply he was stung by the rebuke.

He wrote a letter to Sheriff Anderson on August 3, treating the transfer of authority as if it were a routine matter. "It is unquestionably the best thing for all concerned that you have moved the headquarters for the investigation back to Van Horn, where you can have it under your complete jurisdiction and direct it in your own liking, and to the end that the best results may be obtained," he wrote. "You know, the old saying that too many cooks spoil the broth applies to police work, as well as any other activity. And again, you cannot forget that there still exists a certain amount of professional jealousy among some police officers. I am happy to say that is not generally the case anymore, but nevertheless it still exists."[212]

Despite harboring misgivings about the inadequacy of Sheriff Anderson's resources to deal with the case, Fox sent most of the voluminous files he had amassed to Van Horn.

But he did not wash his hands of the matter, as his correspondence suggested. He had his clerical staff meticulously type up, with multiple carbons, a copy of every original document in the files. By then, sheriff's office case 9628 consisted of six books, including more than a thousand pages of case notes and reports originating in the El Paso office, and hundreds of letters and reports from informants and other law enforcement agencies.

In his transmittal letter with the files, Fox was still attempting to guide the investigation, urging Anderson to pursue a broader course than just questioning known professional criminals. And he again chided other investigating officers, a habit that rubbed some the wrong way and may have been a factor in his ultimate removal as coordinator.

"I have always contended that we have never done enough pick-and-shovel work in this case," the sheriff's cover letter said. "By that I mean getting in and doing the old digging that gets the information developed. You will realize, and so do I, that we are woefully lacking in facts, and have spent too much time looking for suspects and interrogating would-be suspects. You cannot successfully conduct the interrogating of a suspect unless you are supplied with facts to support your investigation."[213]

This last comment was a direct rebuke for the mishandling of the prime suspect, Trotsky, who was freed and disappeared after only the briefest interrogation and on the word of the flimsiest alibi witnesses.

A SHORT TIME LATER, a major event at Ranger headquarters in Austin was about to further impact the Frome murder case. On September 24, 1938, H. H. Carmichael, director of the Department of Public Safety, suffered a heart attack and died. Two days later a highly respected, professional lawman, Homer Garrison Jr., was named DPS director and Ranger chief, with the honorary title "Colonel," which went with the posts. While Garrison would continue to provide resources to the Frome investigation, he made it clear that the infamous case was just one of many the Rangers were trying to solve. It was not to have priority attention, and manpower would no longer be limitless.

Garrison had risen through the ranks, from highway patrolman in 1930 to assistant director in 1935. Like Fox, he was a forward-looking lawman in every respect and continued the modernization of the state's top investigative body. But the Frome case was suddenly downgraded, and the thinly spread state resources were reallocated accordingly.

Sheriff Fox greeted the new DPS chief as if nothing but the best camaraderie had ever existed between his office and the Rangers. Of course, Garrison was well aware of past, often rancorous, exchanges between Fox and other authorities, having served as assistant director of the Texas DPS for years.

Still, the sheriff could not help but remind the new Ranger boss that he was dissatisfied with how the state investigators were running the case. In a letter to Garrison dated October 31, Fox casually noted that, from time to time information comes through this office and I try to send it on to you in Austin.

I had rather not send it on to Van Horn to your man at that point, because I have never heard anything from your boys since Pete Crawford and John Reese went to California, and it was decided to transfer the headquarters for the case from El Paso to Van Horn. Subsequently, I heard from Sheriff Anderson that you had sent a clerk to Van Horn, and he was compiling the data there, and I sent what data I had in the way of loose information, letters, and so on.

To say that our interest in this case will lag is wrong, because we will never lack interest, even though it might be easy to stay low and leave it alone. However, if we all get that idea, the case will never be brought to its conclusion.

I am of firm conviction that it can be unraveled and have expressed myself freely along those lines many times. But I have not had anyone to back me up in the matter. Please don't get the idea in your head that I am trying to run your business or tell you what to do. All I am trying to do is find out what is going on, and if you think it is possible, I will lend a helping hand.[214]

Ten days later the new Ranger chief responded politely, while making it clear that the state investigators had no intention of bringing the El Paso sheriff back into a lead role. His brief reply read,

Dear Chris, I appreciate your letter of Oct. 31 in regard to the Frome case, and you are advised that it seems at this time there has been nothing new that has been uncovered in our investigation. We have run down several leads recently, but as usual they seem to terminate without leading us anywhere at all. We are still working and will continue to do so until this case is solved. However, there seems to be nothing to report at this time. I assure you, Sheriff, that when we receive any information that looks like anything at all, we will be glad to let you in on it.[215]

Less than a week after Colonel Garrison assumed the top law spot in Texas, news headlines of another sort further changed the course of the Frome case. On October 1, Hitler ordered the Nazi army to advance into the ethnic German enclave of Czechoslovakia, following the British-French betrayal of the Czech people at the Munich Pact conference. A week later, headlines revealed another pogrom against the Jews of Germany when Nazi storm troopers went on a rampage that became known as Kristallnacht, the Night of Broken Glass. Soon thereafter, all Jews in Germany were ordered to wear a yellow Star of David badge on their outer clothing at all times.

The American public was forced to try harder than ever to ignore what was happening in Europe. Closer to home, there were other distractions. That month DuPont announced the invention of nylon and launched a marketing campaign to sell a new women's hosiery to be made from that marvelous synthetic fiber. Who needed silk from Asia anymore? Al Capp, the most famous cartoonist in America, created Sadie Hawkins Day in the L'il Abner comic strip. Sadie Hawkins Day, in the parlance of the popular satirical cartoon, was supposed to be the one day that unmarried females, who in reality had no individual legal rights at the time, were granted the opportunity to chase down and propose marriage to single men.

A sizable part of the American population temporarily panicked when twenty-three-year-old dramatist Orson Welles perpetrated an enormous radio hoax by broadcasting an hour-long account of a Martian invasion of Princeton, New Jersey, on Halloween eve, 1938. The fake news report on CBS Radio's Mercury Theatre on the Air proved the power of radio over people's thoughts and emotions. The live broadcast caused an outcry for more federal regulation of the media.

By the end of 1938, the average American, as well as most of the press corps and many of the investigating lawmen, were losing interest in the sensational murder of the California socialites in the far away West Texas desert.

The seemingly congenial transfer of the coordinating authority and humble offer to be of assistance to the case whenever asked was a polite facade. Chris Fox had no intention of giving up his own pursuit of a resolution in the Frome murders.

36

Ostensibly under new direction by Sheriff Anderson, the Frome murder case quickly dropped from the front pages of the nation's newspapers. When the story did briefly resurface, it sometimes read like a tale out of *Alice's Adventures in Wonderland*.

The investigation did not exactly fall down the rabbit hole, but a parade of odd characters and peculiar twists and turns added a distinct patina of fantasy.

Someone in the new control center in Van Horn got the idea to return to the nearby death site to begin excavating the burrows of desert rats, in search of new clues. The theory was that the pack rats might have carried items of interest back to their nests.

The sheriff's deputies, sweating as they dug up the rodent nests under the desert sun, unearthed only one thing of interest: a book of Golden Bear matches. The discovery was momentarily considered a promising new lead because the matches were manufactured in San Francisco. However, any significance of this new "clue" quickly vanished when the match maker informed the Rangers that the product was widely sold all over the West, including Texas.[216] Berkeley police chief Jack Greening wrote a note to Texas Ranger Pete Crawford expressing regret that the rat burrows had not been explored earlier in the investigation. The delay had provided ample time for the critters to gnaw up any potential evidence they might have carried there.

With Sheriff Anderson merely a figurehead lead investigator, the Frome murder case was now clearly under the exclusive control of the Texas Rangers. The sheriff of a county with a total population of about 1,600, half of whom were Mexican *vaqueros* and laborers, never would have had enough clout in Austin to have prevailed in the struggle for jurisdiction. And he didn't have the material means or manpower to manage such a far-reaching, complex case. What Anderson *could* provide was the appearance that the politically sensitive case was under local control, while giving full rein to Austin.

Sheriff Fox had been effectively muzzled, and Sheriff Anderson, too, seemed to disappear from public, or at least news media, view.

While Anderson and his deputies were futilely searching for new evidence beneath the desert floor, the Rangers were casting a wider net. The Rangers' list of usual suspects, bad men — and women, too — were rounded up for questioning throughout Texas, across several western states, and in Mexico. The ten thousand dollars in posted rewards was a fortune during the Depression and continued to generate all sorts of tips. Most of them were outrageously implausible, furnished by desperately hungry, wannabe sleuths.

Ranger Frank Mills went to Las Cruces to run down one such bogus tip that the suspect chase car was seen roaming the streets of that nearby town. The car with the white markings on the door turned out to be a taxi belonging to the City Cab Company, whose logo did not resemble the descriptions the witnesses had provided of the sign on the side of one of the chase cars.

Sheriff Fox received a complaint from the cab company about Ranger Mills's interrogation of employees and forwarded the complaint, along with a pointed angry reply, to Sheriff Anderson, whom he noted was now supposed to be in charge. "We trust that the foregoing may be of interest to those who read it . . . it would be better for them to give it to Mr. Mills, since he is apparently conducting a one-man investigation of the Frome case."[217]

It was not lost on Fox that the return of the murder case to Anderson's jurisdiction was nothing more than a ploy by state authorities to remove him from any role in the case and place the Texas Rangers firmly in control.

Though the Department of Public Safety assigned four lawmen and a secretary to a makeshift headquarters in the Culberson County courthouse, the command center for the ongoing investigation would, in reality, be at Ranger headquarters in Austin. Obviously, the state was not going to waste manpower by allowing four Rangers to loiter around Van Horn.

In April 1939, Texas Ranger Pete Crawford was dispatched from his base in Marfa on a more substantial lead, this time across the border into Mexico.

Juarez police chief Edmundo Herrera had received a tip from underworld sources about two men and a married couple acting suspiciously in the border town across from El Paso. The quartet was arrested, and after they had been interrogated for more than fifteen hours, the Rangers were notified. One of the men arrested was a Mexican saloon worker who had been involved in narcotics cases in the past. The second man was believed to be one of the American men seen by witnesses talking to Hazel and Nancy at a Juarez nightclub shortly before they disappeared.

Ranger Crawford drove to Juarez on April 2 and participated in further questioning of the four. Sheriff Fox learned of the arrests through a Juarez newspaper. The article quoted Herrera as saying one of the men had worked as a bellboy at a hotel in El Paso. But before Fox could get a crack at him, to determine if it was the long-sought Cortez employee who had catered to the Frome women, the four suspects were released. They quickly vanished into the sanctuary of interior Mexico.

Crawford had determined to his satisfaction that these suspects knew nothing about the murders. A brief note in local newspapers on April 13 announced their release.[218]

EVEN THOUGH PUBLICITY had waned, the Texas Rangers remained obsessed with solving the case, not just because of its sensational aspects and notoriety but also because it had become a matter of professional pride. In addition to the Rangers and local sheriffs, the case had attracted a large number of private detectives and even retired police officers.

A tragic event involving a former lawman who was privately working on the case occurred the day after the announcement that the arrested parties in Juarez had been released.

Former FBI agent John K. Wren had come out of retirement at age 67 to devote full time to solving the case. Wren, who had retired from the bureau in 1932 after sixteen years as a federal agent, quietly entered the investigation as a volunteer shortly after the murders. He may have literally worked himself to death.[219]

On April 14, he was in the El Paso office of assistant district attorney Harold Long discussing some of his findings when he simply dropped dead. Sitting across from the attorney, Wren slumped over in his chair and died instantly. He was considered an ace criminal investigator and had solved some of the most baffling crimes in the Southwest while working for the bureau. Any secrets about the case that he might have uncovered to that point went with him to the grave.

The continuing investigation was neither confined to Texas nor of interest solely to Texas lawmen. In 1939, Joseph A. Manning, San Francisco district supervisor of the Treasury Department's Bureau of Narcotics, was investigating a crime ring on the West Coast when he stumbled across something that led him to inquire about the Frome murders. He shared the information with Sheriff Fox.

Along with agents from the Chicago district, Manning's narcs were tracking a gang believed to be involved in a well-organized, nationwide narcotics trade. The agents uncovered information in San Francisco that the German gang leader was in some way connected to the Frome murders. The gang reportedly secured narcotics in San Francisco and transported the dope for distribution in Chicago. It was headed by a Bund leader named Carl Rettick, who was alleged to have connections with another Bund gang in New York.[220]

Sheriff Fox sent the Manning information to Ranger headquarters in Austin. The Rangers cross-referenced the narcotics connections with known cases involving illicit drug operations between Texas and the West Coast. They concluded this gang was not involved in the local drug trade or in the Frome murders. At least they found no Texas angle to the case and did not seem interested in exploring possible connections at the San Francisco end.

It was not the first tip Sheriff Fox received from the West Coast that hinted at an angle connecting the murders to various German underground elements. However, at the time, there was little to suggest that any organized German espionage operations in the United States could possibly have an interest in two gadabout socialites from the Bay Area.

Still, there was the beginning of a new awareness that foreign agents with bad intentions had infiltrated America. A Hollywood movie, widely attended in the United States and Europe, packed theaters with shocked audiences. *Confessions of a Nazi Spy*, starring Edward G. Robinson as a spy-busting FBI agent, was released in April 1939 by Warner Bros. and created an international uproar. The German chargé d'affaires in Washington formally protested directly to President Roosevelt. The anti-Nazi film caused riots by Fascist sympathizers throughout the United States, movie theater seats were slashed during showings of the film, and a Warner Bros. theater was burned to the ground in Milwaukee. Across the ocean in Poland, anti-Jewish mobs actually hanged several movie theater owners for showing the film.[221]

AMERICANS WERE FINDING it more difficult to ignore the disturbing news from abroad, where political conditions were rapidly deteriorating. By early 1939, there were ominous threats of renewed global war.

American Fascist clubs and organizations, some operating in the shadows and others quite public, proliferated throughout the 1930s. The FBI listed more than 750 of these clubs by the end of the decade.[222] Despite claims that there were hundreds of thousands of members in these organizations, the bureau believed the paid-up, card-carrying Bund membership never really exceeded twenty-five thousand at any one time. But what the German-American Bund lacked in numbers, it made up for in noisy demonstrations.

The actual spies among the Bund membership were implants by the Abwehr; the rank and file was entrusted only with propaganda and troublemaking. Meanwhile, Nazi agents infiltrated American industrial plants doing defense work for companies like General Electric, Carl L. Norden Company, and Sperry Gyroscope. These spies did enjoy a high degree of success in stealing U.S. secrets, such as the Norden Bombsight.[223] This top-secret device enabled the U.S. Army Air Corps to conduct precision targeting by high-altitude bombers.

Most of the Bund members were recruited from the ranks of disgruntled Germans forced to emigrate between 1924 and 1933, because they were either fleeing prosecution for participating in the Nazi-led Beer Hall Putsch or simply starving to death in the worldwide Depression. Some of the approximately 430,000 Germans who entered the United States in this period returned voluntarily to Germany after Hitler seized power.[224] There had long been more benign German American marching and singing clubs, but the Fascist organizations were unique to the desperation of the Depression and were largely the creation of the Nazi Party after Hitler rose to power.

A zealous cadre of twenty thousand German American citizens parading in storm trooper uniforms and jackboots could gain a lot of attention, as they did in a Washington's Birthday Rally in New York City in 1939.

In San Francisco, a similar Bund rally caused riots in the streets when World War I veterans from the American Legion confronted demonstrators in a downtown square during one of the torch-lit marches. Sheriff Fox, who had mostly experienced labor strife with Reds in local agrarian and mining unions, happened to be in town on police business. Even though he was no longer in charge of the case, he still pursued any leads that came his way, particularly about Pop Frome. On the occasion of this trip to the Bay Area, Fox was physically caught in the brawl between the uniformed Bund marchers and the vets.

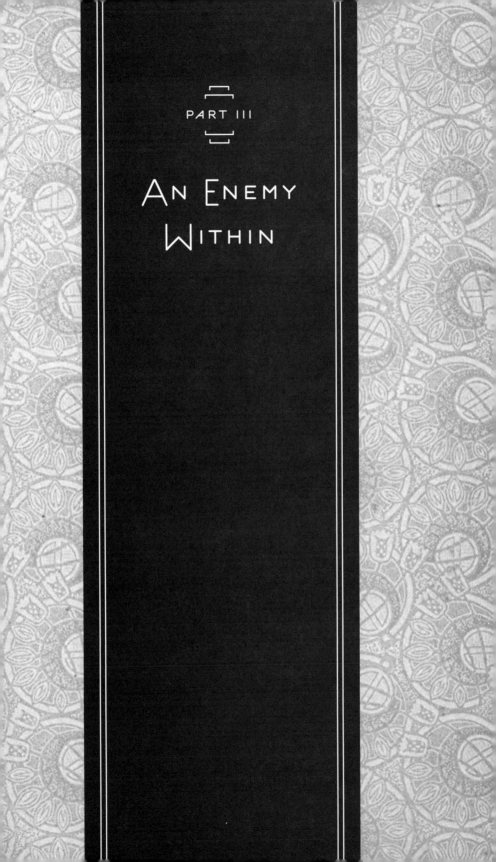

PART III

An Enemy
Within

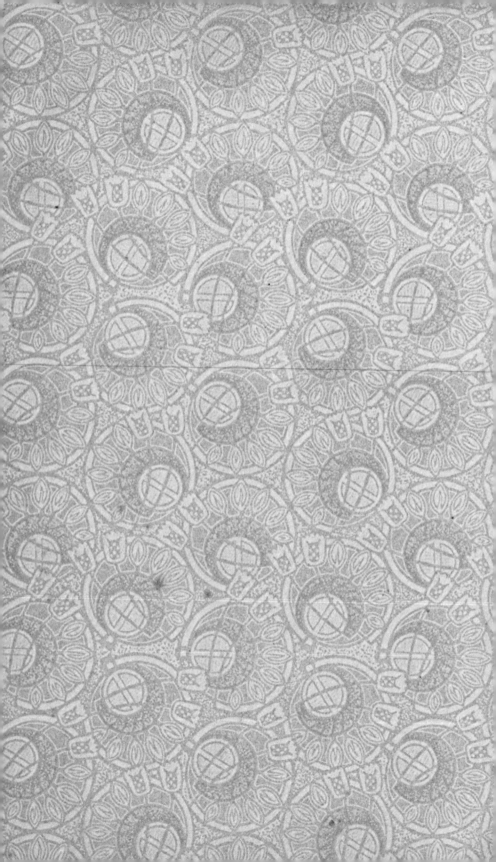

37

Nazi sycophants like Joseph Goebbels convinced Hitler that America's Achilles' heel was the loyal Teutonic blood flowing in the veins of a third of its citizens.[225] The Nazi leaders were smug in their assurances to the führer that these ethnic German Americans would, at the very least, prevent the United States from entering the fight against the fatherland. A small, though vocally powerful, clique of isolationist, anti-Roosevelt senators and congressmen, along with such notable public figures as flying ace Charles Lindbergh, further abetted the Nazi myth that America would not again actively join in the defense of former World War I allies Britain and France.

The Germans may have had a reasonable basis for their prediction. Americans were more concerned with surviving the grinding poverty of the seemingly endless Depression, then in its ninth year. A public opinion poll conducted in 1938 by George Gallup found that 97 percent of Americans wanted the United States to stay out of the wars in Europe and Asia.[226]

Germany's military intelligence leaders, such as Admiral Wilhelm Canaris at the Abwehr, did not rely on rhetoric about hypothetical blood ties alone, however. From the early 1930s, they began infiltrating propagandists, spies, and saboteurs into Teutonic fraternal and social organizations, ethnic communities, and the American society at large. The mission of these agents was to prepare the German American communities to rise up and overthrow the "Jew-controlled Roosevelt government." Failing that goal, their assignment was to steal the military-industrial knowledge of the nation. Finally, if all else failed and it came to war, these enemy aliens were prepared to sabotage the nation's defense industries and fortifications on its coasts and borders.[227]

When spies or Nazi sympathizers could not be successfully infiltrated into the plants, individual employees — from assembly-line workers to administrative personnel — were subjected to surveillance, threats, blackmail, and intimidation to force them to become sources of information. Persons with German surnames or with families still in the fatherland were especially vulnerable to these brazen tactics.

A subsidiary organization within the Nazi Party was the nexus of the spy apparatus. The Ausland-Organization (AO) compiled and maintained the names and addresses of tens of thousands of important German American families, with hopes of recruiting or coercing some of them into the Nazi world crusade. Fortunately, this effort to intimidate and compromise Americans just because they had German surnames failed miserably.

Unbeknownst to officials, even in the highest U.S. counterespionage circles, a momentous decision made five months before the Frome murders had set in motion a campaign of covert aggression that specifically targeted American companies like Atlas Powder.

On the evening of November 5, 1937, Hitler told a small gathering of his generals and party officials in Berlin that Nazi Germany must prepare for total war.[228]

From that date forward, German sleeper agents, who had been clandestinely placed in major U.S. industrial centers to steal technology, were ordered to go fully operational. The war that Hitler planned to launch to gain territory for his promised thousand-year Reich was intended to be limited to England, France, and Russia. But the American industrial complex, which was the main supplier for the Allies, as it had been in the early years of the last world war, was designated as a primary target for espionage.

Soon after Hitler's November decision, orders went out from the German intelligence organization — the Abwehr — to activate the sleeper cells. The spy operations in America were directed from a dozen consulates in key cities and from the German embassy in Washington, D.C.

GERMAN SUBVERSIVE ACTIVITIES on the East Coast, and to a lesser extent in the industrial belt of the Midwest, began to appear in newspaper headlines, from the mid-1930s onward. There were frequent reports of German-American Bund brawls at torchlight parades, the occasional arrest of an industrial spy, and even announcements that G-men had busted up a spy ring or two.

Little or nothing was reported about espionage in the western United States or on the U.S.-Mexico border. But the absence of headlines did not mean an absence of German or Japanese spy activity. In fact, it could be argued that the Axis's operations in the west were just better concealed from federal agents and the press, because an efficient German spy network had flourished there, from shortly after Hitler came to power.

Taking the helm of the Germans' western operations was a rabid Nazi from Hitler's original inner circle. Baron Manfred Freiherr von Killinger was named consul general in San Francisco in June 1937. He was sent to San Francisco to take charge of and invigorate the already existing, clandestine Nazi spy network in the western United States. His mandate covered all German espionage activities from the Pacific Northwest on the Canadian border, through Mexico, to terminal points at German embassies in Brazil and Argentina. Spies operating out of the large Los Angeles consulate also answered to the San Francisco headquarters.

This major underground pipeline connecting San Francisco to South America via Chihuahua City, Monterrey, and Mexico City in Mexico passed through a critical chokepoint at El Paso, Texas.[229]

In addition to placing trained spies in strategic jobs in German-owned companies and the consulates, the baron recruited a hardcore group of German American "gangsters" and White Russian criminals to do the dirty work. These locals already had the dark skills necessary to perform criminal assignments like burglaries, blackmail, and strong-arm assaults.[230]

Von Killinger had neither the grace nor tact generally required of a diplomat and was thus immediately unpopular in the business community he was supposed to charm. But the "baron" had other credentials of value to his true mission. His main experience, prior to assuming the post in the United States, was as an officer in the Nazi storm troopers. Identified early on by the FBI as the "most ruthless" of the consular spies sent to the United States, his assignment appeared to be for the sole purpose of espionage, not trade and commerce development.

While he had been born to an aristocratic family in Baden-Württemberg, it is not clear how he acquired the royal title of baron. A World War I officer and Nazi Party organizer, his real reputation was earned through a willingness to carry out murderous orders as a leader of death squads during Hitler's bloody rise to power.

After establishing himself in San Francisco, Baron von Killinger immediately set about bolstering the existing Nazi spy network operating under diplomatic cover in the German consulate, just as other spy rings operated from consulates in other American cities. His network was responsible for clandestine operations throughout states west of the Mississippi River.[231]

The spy ring had a double mission. It served as both a link in the international spy network established by the Abwehr and, because of its location on the West Coast, an espionage surrogate for Nazi Germany's main ally, the empire of Japan. Through the consulate, the Japanese employed local German, White Russian, or other East European immigrant hoodlums to carry out the tasks their own agents could not perform because of innate prejudice against Asians on the West Coast.[232]

The consular offices were also a primary source of support for the German-American Bund activities in the United States, at least from the mid-1930s. Von Killinger, a personal friend of Nazi Gestapo chief Heinrich Himmler, was one of the principal architects of the Bund's propaganda operations.[233] Fritz Kuhn, leader of the American Bund, confessed to a secret relationship between his organization and the German diplomatic corps, in hearings before the House Un-American Activities Committee, in September 1937.

The nationwide network was coordinated out of the German embassy in Washington, D.C., and personally directed by the Germany ambassador Hans Dieckhoff. Von Killinger was his chief agent on the West Coast.

"Von Killinger is the kind of consul we want everywhere," Kuhn testified. "The consul offered financial aid to the Bund for purposes of Nazi propaganda broadcasts on the West Coast and other Bund activities."[234]

Upon his arrival in San Francisco, von Killinger found that what little Japanese spying was being done on the West Coast was dependent on a White Russian Fascist leader named Count Anastase Andreyevich Vonsiatsky, who claimed to be a member of the deposed Russian royal family.

Count Vonsiatsky had already established a thriving pro-Fascist network of Russian and Ukrainian toughs working with the German Bund in the Bay Area and White Russian clubs throughout the Midwestern and Northeastern United States. These bully boys were available to do everything from street rioting to physical assaults, so the clandestine German spies could carry on their more important mission without exposure.

The so-called Russian Club in San Francisco was, in fact, one of the numerous cells of the count's worldwide Russian National Revolutionary Labor and Workers Peasant Party of Fascists. One of its early members was the onetime prime suspect in the Frome murder case, Romano Trotsky.

38

The self-proclaimed member of the ex-tsar's family who played such a large role in the Frome investigation, Romano Trotsky, was never more than a minion in the White Russian Fascist organization. Despite his claims of having served the imperial Japanese cause, there was no evidence that the pretender had any ideology other than his own enrichment.

The self-proclaimed count, Anastase Vonsiatsky, was another matter altogether. He affiliated himself and his organization with any anti-Soviet cause or group that might assist in the demise of the Red Russians. The White Russian Fascist leader had been on the payroll of the Japanese for years by the time he joined in the unholy conspiracy with von Killinger. The German spy apparatus, in turn, viewed the gregarious Russian as a useful tool. The newly invigorated Nazi organization quickly assumed command of all Axis espionage on the West Coast.

The next step for the new Nazi spymaster was to acquire a secure, permanent operations center for the West Coast network. At about the time of the Frome murders, von Killinger brazenly purchased an imposing edifice in San Francisco's posh Pacific Heights district.

Conspicuous for a spy nest, the fortresslike Whittier Mansion was one of the first structures in California built to withstand earthquakes. Erected in 1896, the fourteen-thousand-square-foot, four-story mansion was thought to be impervious to outside eavesdropping devices because of its thick stone walls set on a steel frame. The severe-looking Romanesque structure with turrets at each corner offered unobstructed views of San Francisco Bay, with all its busy naval and commercial maritime traffic conveniently sailing under the Golden Gate Bridge in plain sight.

Except for its presence atop a high overlook, the new German consulate made a perfect spy's nest. The huge price paid for it in 1938 — about forty-five thousand dollars — by a cash-strapped Germany, was an indication of just how important the San Francisco espionage outpost was to that country.

Baron von Killinger's invigoration of a West Coast spy operation was, from the outset, closely coordinated with the spy agency of the empire of Japan to meet the intelligence needs of that Axis ally.

Coincidentally, with the activation of the Nazis' expanded U.S. operations in 1937, Count Vonsiatsky was beefing up his own espionage network on behalf of his friends in the Imperial Japanese Army, particularly its intelligence efforts against the U.S. Navy. When the Russian married a wealthy American heiress in 1922, he acquired control of her vast family estate in Connecticut and set up his headquarters there. He used his fake identity of former Russian count not only to woo the older woman but also to claim leadership rights among the diaspora of eastern Europeans ousted by the Russian Revolution.

The count also held a leadership position in White Russian organizations in Japanese-occupied Manchuria, where skirmishes between the Japanese and Soviet armies were already taking place. His Russian Revolutionary Party was formed in the early 1930s.[235] There was a strategic branch of the White Russian organization in the Bay Area from the beginning.

AFTER AN EARLIER, aggressive expansion on the West Coast, a strange thing happened, in late 1938, in the German consular services. The Germans suddenly went quiet. At the peak of activities to mobilize the West Coast spy network, Baron von Killinger was inexplicably, and without public announcement, recalled to Berlin in November. No reason was given for his removal, either in Berlin or at the local consulate in San Francisco.

His recall came seven months after the Frome murders, at a time when Texas investigators — including Chris Fox and, later, two Rangers — had been on well-publicized visits to the Bay Area, looking for links to the crime. The Nazi baron was given no new assignments of note for more than a year after his recall.

Perhaps von Killinger's sudden recall to Germany was merely coincidental to the Frome case queries; however, it came after Fox and the Rangers did extensive snooping for information on Pop Frome's business and social activities.[236] As a result of the sheriff uncovering the Frome blackmail by the German gang, Berkeley detectives had begun asking questions about its members' activities in San Francisco.

In an even odder twist, von Killinger was not immediately replaced in the San Francisco post. Four months passed before Hitler's personal friend and aide-de-camp, Captain Fritz Wiedemann, was sent to fill the position.[237]

The appointment of a second high-ranking Nazi insider to what might be considered a relatively symbolic post further suggests how important the San Francisco consulate was to the Germans' espionage scheme on the West Coast. The captain, who was Hitler's company commander in World War I, was at the side of the führer when the decision was made to launch the next world war. Wiedemann was also with Hitler when he marched into Prague, Czechoslovakia, on March 15, 1939, shortly before being dispatched to his new post as San Francisco consul general. He was one of the chief negotiators and principal contact men between the Germans and the British, leading up to the Munich betrayal of the Czech people.

It is highly significant that an official of such status in Hitler's inner circle would be shuffled off to the outpost at San Francisco, just a few months before Germany launched total war in Europe — unless, of course, the Nazis considered the position of huge strategic importance in the joint German-Japanese spy operation against the Americans.

The congenial Captain Wiedemann was everything the dour and secretive Baron von Killinger was not, and the new diplomat was soon insinuating himself into Bay Area business and social circles at every opportunity.

He played on his close personal relationship with Hitler in a dozen interviews with local newspaper reporters.

"Hitler was my dispatch runner [in World War I]. I have known him since that time," Wiedemann told reporters at the press conference he held upon his arrival in San Francisco. "These stories that I saved his life during the war — they are entirely wrong. I only wish I had."[238]

Captain Wiedemann took some San Francisco social circles by storm, or at least, with his impressive credentials, the debonair diplomat tried to fit into the Bay Area's high society. At first he succeeded and was constantly mentioned in the local press, mostly the society pages but occasionally the front pages as well. The consul's lavish parties were the talk of the town, with such luminaries as Hollywood film idol Errol Flynn in attendance.

Wiedemann soon ensconced an old girlfriend, the German princess by marriage Stephanie von Hohenlohe, in quarters at the fortresslike consulate.[239] Her son Franz was enrolled in studies at nearby Stanford University in Palo Alto, as a freshman. But the princess was shortly kicked out of the United States by the State Department for allegedly engaging in unspecified spying activities.

Another frequent guest at Wiedemann's soirees was the famous aviatrix Laura Ingalls. The talented Miss Ingalls was also an actress and frequently shared the stage with Colonel Charles Lindbergh in delivering pro-Germany speeches. She was also a paid agent of the Gestapo, convicted of spying in 1941.[240]

Rumors circulated that Wiedemann's assignment on the West Coast was merely a prelude to greater things in his future and that he was slated to become the next German ambassador in Washington.

Still, he was not accepted with open arms. Shortly after he arrived, one thousand naturalized German citizens in the anti-Nazi German-American League on the West Coast petitioned President Roosevelt to have Wiedemann thrown out of the country.[241] That organization of loyal American Germans, whose membership numbered in the tens of thousands in branch clubs in seventeen U.S. cities, suspected Wiedemann was really a Nazi plant and nothing more than another master spy.

In fact, that is exactly what Wiedemann was, along with his fellow consuls across the country, all sent to serve as coordinators and paymasters for the Nazi spy networks blooming in the dark underground of America.

Most San Franciscans, like most Americans, remained adamant that the United States never again be involved in foreign affairs beyond its ocean defenses. A few days after Hitler's invasion of Poland and the Allied declaration of war in September 1939, President Roosevelt was still proclaiming U.S. neutrality. The American leader would soon be issuing orders for a "limited national emergency."[242]

39

Atlas Powder Company and Hercules Powder Company, another spinoff of DuPont in the explosives and chemicals field, became early prime targets for Nazi penetration.[243] Prior to his assignment as San Francisco consul, Hitler's aide-de-camp Captain Fritz Wiedemann was personally sent to the United States on a "vacation." His real purpose was to speed up spying activities against America's industrial colossus. He told one of the top spies in America at the time, Guenther Gustav Rumrich, that it was of vital interest to the German war effort to place agents in affiliated companies of DuPont chemical and Bethlehem Steel and their suppliers' plants across the country.[244]

Even though Atlas and Hercules were technically independent companies, both maintained their headquarters virtually across the street from DuPont in Wilmington, Delaware. And both were rife with incestuous cross-breeding in top management with the former parent company.

The high explosives manufactured at the Giant, California, plant and the western-region, military, construction contracts administered by Frome from his Montgomery Street headquarters came under the scope of espionage efforts being run from the San Francisco consulate. That spy network had tentacles capable of monitoring a target's every move, from its headquarters on the East Coast to its operations in the Pacific region. Atlas Powder was just such a Nazi target.

Atlas developed new blasting powder, gelatins, and other chemical compounds, which made it one of the preeminent explosives suppliers in the world. But the company studiously avoided publicly revealing the military applications of its products, whether to protect trade secrets or at the behest of U.S. or foreign-government military customers.

Throughout the 1930s, Atlas made a point of denying, in its annual reports, that the company was involved in defense work. So secret was the company's contribution to the national defense effort that Atlas, along with other chemical and explosive firms, did not even report this lucrative share of the business to stockholders. For example, its 1938 annual report to Moody's *Manual of Investments* included this disclaimer: "The company does not manufacture rifle or ordinance powders, and its only connection with war work was through the manufacture and sales on a large scale in 1915–1918 of acids and chemicals, which were used in the manufacture of munitions."[245]

Such feeble protestations would not dissuade the Nazi spy apparatus from pursuing Atlas Powder's secrets. The Germans knew exactly what the American powder companies were working on: for years they had participated in numerous, profitable joint ventures with IG Farben, the German munitions and chemical monopoly.

Even had the disclaimers been true, which they were not, German agents could not have ignored Atlas Powder as a prime target of interest. In the lead up to World War I, Atlas was the largest supplier of explosives to the British and French, annually providing thirty-seven million pounds of ammonium nitrate and tons of explosive acids and nitro cotton. Atlas was America's largest supplier of the material used in Amatol, the primary detonating chemical in munitions. When America entered World War I, Atlas had fifteen plants manufacturing explosives material for the U.S. government; in 1918, the company contracted to build a single plant with the capacity to manufacture one hundred million tons of ammonium nitrate.[246]

In the 1930s, Atlas Powder Company and Hercules Powder Company were still very much in the business of developing and supplying high explosives chemicals and components for use by government arsenals in all types of munitions. Atlas developed and acquired numerous patents for everything from smokeless powder used in artillery shells and small-arms ammunition to super-high-explosive chemicals invented in its research laboratories across the country, including the facility at Giant, California.

Early in the murder investigation, Sheriff Fox had determined that Weston Frome downplayed both his position in the company and Atlas Powder's key role in America's defense industry. He had stumbled across this well-kept secret while digging into the family background for clues to the motive for the murders. Once again, his connections with fellow law enforcement agencies on the West Coast gained him unique access to inside information.

"It may be well to note at this time that Mr. Frome holds the dual position of sales manager of the Pacific Coast Division of Atlas Powder Company and is also general manager of their plant at Giant, California," the sheriff noted in his file, after his first investigative trip to California in May 1938. "Atlas Powder Company is a very large concern, with headquarters in Wilmington, Delaware. It manufactures dynamite that is used in mining and construction work, and also is a large manufacturer of ammunition [explosives] used in bombs and torpedoes."[247]

German intelligence apparently knew more about the business of DuPont's spin-off explosives operations — Atlas Powder and Hercules Powder — than most of the companies' shareholders. These companies were specifically mentioned in a number of Nazi documents read by the FBI and scrutinized by British intelligence in transatlantic intercepts of diplomatic pouches. The German espionage hit list named Atlas and Hercules among the priority U.S. corporations targeted for penetration from the very beginning of the massive espionage and sabotage campaign launched against the United States and other countries in the early 1930s.[248]

These explosives companies — along with American manufacturers of motor vehicles, airplanes and navigational instruments, chemicals, electronic instruments, and utilities — were the primary assignments for German agents. Early efforts to place agents were generally successful, especially on the East Coast and in the industrial Midwest, because of the large number of recently arriving ethnic German, Italian, and Eastern European workers holding the lower-paying line jobs in plants in those areas of the country.

Atlas Powder's plant at Giant, California, on the bay across from San Francisco, was harder to penetrate. Japanese and German sleeper agents simply did not fit into the workforce there, because most of the lower-level jobs were filled by workers of Chinese origin. The American-born Chinese workers were not easily recruited through the usual methods of blackmail or intimidation by either German or Japanese agents operating on the West Coast. Thus, the foreign espionage apparatus on the West Coast was desperate to get a toehold at Atlas, and at Hercules, which had its main plant down the coast at Santa Cruz.

The Atlas manufacturing plant at Giant was conveniently located a stone's throw from the sprawling Mare Island Naval Depot at Vallejo, California. That ammunition facility had provided the primary assembly and storage operations for all U.S. naval ordnance in the Pacific since the mid-1930s. It is inconceivable that a major explosives manufacturing plant like Atlas's San Francisco Bay complex would be situated next door to, and not be an integral part of, the naval armaments assembly operation.

Furthermore, Atlas's public denial that it was involved in munitions and military armaments was clearly a cover-up for its vital national defense role. During the late Depression era, the manufacture of arms and materiel for the looming war in Europe was just too tempting a profit center to be ignored by any American company with the capacity to compete.

At one point in the late 1930s, it was leaked to the press that Atlas Powder Company had sent sixty thousand aerial bombs through Germany, to be used by Franco's Nazi-sponsored Nationalist forces.[249] Even President Roosevelt reluctantly admitted in April 1938 that U.S. companies were supplying the Fascist forces and that American-made bombs were raining down on the cities of Spain. Roosevelt declared, however, "It is all perfectly legal."[250]

IN 1937–38, Weston G. Frome was in double jeopardy of being a target of any secret Nazi espionage network operating in America. He was of full-blooded German heritage with a well-recognized German name, and he was a high-level executive in an industry of specific interest to German industrialists who were rebuilding that country's war machine. The Nazi Ausland Organization most certainly had a dossier on Frome and his family at headquarters in Berlin. German and Japanese agents, now established in the Bay Area, would have seen a well-placed figure like Frome, with access to industrial secrets, as a prize candidate for recruitment.[251]

The rest of the family — his wife Hazel, a first-generation Norwegian American, and his daughters, Nancy and Mada, thoroughly modern American girls — could not be willingly compromised. The women, who knew little or nothing about Pop's business, could have served only as leverage, if no other means was found to recruit the explosives-company executive. Employing such coercive methods was certainly not beyond the odious spymaster Baron von Killinger and his ilk.

In fact, during the rise of National Socialism, Hitler himself specifically sanctioned using children in the families of German industrialists to bend them to the will of the party. At a dinner at his mountain fortress, Wolf's

Lair, he boasted to a group of confidants that "when we wanted to lay siege to an industrialist, we attacked him through his children."[252]

Pop Frome's ancestral homeland and his Teutonic blood played no role in any part of his work or social life. He never belonged to one of the German Volk groups. Nothing in his lifestyle indicated that he might harbor nostalgia for his German roots, let alone ambivalence about his current loyalties to his country or, especially, to his company. The only fraternal order to which he belonged was the Benevolent and Protective Order of Elks. He seldom attended lodge meetings, spending more time with his Elk brothers on social occasions than at rituals or business meetings.

The Atlas executive, already two generations removed from the fatherland, was like most others in that large German American ethnic group of more than twenty million.[253] The vast majority were beyond the enticements of the Abwehr; in fact, many had already dropped the dual term and considered themselves simply Americans.

Nevertheless, because Frome was a German American holding such a key position in a defense-related industry, he was certain to have been singled out early by the Nazi ring operating from the San Francisco consulate. One German spy in particular, Werner Plack, was well positioned to recognize the executive's importance and possible vulnerability. Plack frequented the bacchanals thrown for big contractors and army engineers at Hollywood nightclubs and the LA Biltmore Hotel. He was a close chum of the construction mogul Wilhelm Rohl, who sponsored the parties.

Even if Plack did not instigate Frome's meeting with the German showgirl who later blackmailed him, he would have easily learned of the liaison. Since the girl was part of a gang of German criminals, it is also likely that Plack knew of the original petty blackmail. It was only a short leap from blackmail for cash to coercion for industrial secrets.

Blackmail was not an unusual tactic for the spy rings operating out of the German consulates. The professional spies, some of whom were also members of Himmler's Gestapo, used bribes, threats to family still in the fatherland, misplaced loyalty, and any other means to compromise men like Weston Frome.

It did not work on the stubborn executive. Even if he was not immune to intimidation by blackmail out of patriotism to America, his loyalty to the company was a powerful counterweight to such threats. While he was obviously willing to pay chump change from his expense account to keep the showgirl and her gang quiet, it is unlikely he could have been forced to compromise his company's secrets.

Regardless of the stakes, Frome would not risk sullying the corporate image by answering the most basic questions about his job or his private life. This was likely the main reason he went to such lengths to keep Sheriff Fox from investigating the blackmail and was so persistent in dodging inquiries about the Biltmore Hotel. The conduct that so frustrated Fox was designed not to thwart the murder investigation but rather to prevent any company-related activities from being leaked to the press.

In Frome's situation, any attempt to raise the sexual blackmail ante from cash payments to trade in company secrets would have been too high a price for him to pay.

If the sheriff was frustrated by Frome's recalcitrance, the San Francisco spies were outraged. Several months before the murders, he had inexplicably stopped paying blackmail to the German gang, according to his attorney's communiqué with the Berkeley police department.

He was unyielding in the face of criticism or coercion. After proof of the blackmail became incontrovertible, Frome remained adamant that it had nothing to do with the murder case. Sheriff Fox thought Frome's assurances in the matter should not even have been considered. Any criminal investigator worth his salt could not ignore a blackmail angle in a murder case. Blackmail would certainly be a potential motive for murder, all the more so if the target had recently and arbitrarily stopped paying his tormentors.

Nevertheless, with the exception of Sheriff Fox's dogged but futile insistence that the sex scandal be fully explored, the subject of Frome's blackmail was dropped. Any further explanation of the blackmail was simply never pursued by Berkeley detectives once Sheriff Fox was removed from the lead role. The Texas Rangers apparently were not interested in the blackmail angle either, after they took over, although Fox had fully briefed the DPS officers about his discovery. Such a complicated scenario just did not fit their theory that the murders were a case of highway robbery gone wrong.

Without question, the sheriff's investigation had been thwarted by roadblocks the Bay Area executive and his underlings put up to withhold key information that might have linked the murders to Pop's activities.

Had the Berkeley police department probed deeper, or had Frome himself cooperated with Fox's inquiries into the blackmail angle, the sheriff might well have unearthed a connection between the women's murders and a botched espionage scheme. And if the crime investigators had been made aware of information the G-men were beginning to amass on Nazi activities, the Frome murder case could have taken a different course, one that probably would have produced some results.

40

Even though Chris Fox had formally ceded his central role in the murder investigation to his fellow Texas lawmen, he was quietly pursuing his own theory about the case, outside official channels.

With the El Paso sheriff no longer around to push the theory of a more sinister motive than simple highway robbery, the investigation bogged down in Texas. It turned into a relentless slog of questioning miscreants arrested for other crimes, following up on old tips that were clearly irrelevant when they came in, and discovering leads were still worthless when they were visited again. Newspapers reported that more than one thousand suspects had been detained, interrogated, and cleared in the murders during the first eighteen months.

Having the investigation centered in remote Van Horn became the farce Fox had anticipated, with poor telephone and postal service and no regular air transportation. Investigators would be forced to drive hundreds of miles just to check out the flimsiest of tips or to meet with Sheriff Anderson, the titular head of the case.

Despite being muscled out by the Texas Rangers, and the resistance he had encountered from the Berkeley police department, Fox was still determined to solve the murders. He was more certain than ever that the answers were to be found on the West Coast, not in El Paso or nearby Culberson County. He again turned to old allies and found considerable cooperation from investigators at the Pacific coast headquarters of the National Automobile Theft Bureau in San Francisco.

Sheriff Fox's longtime working relationship with the NATB agents, as well as his contacts in the California state police, meant he still had some extraordinary resources on the West Coast. As 1939 came to a close, he was working with NATB agents C. F. Cline, M. L. Britt, and W. E. Shoppe, and was in regular touch with Owen Kessel, chief of special investigations at the California Bureau of Investigation (CBI).

Welcoming a break from chasing car thieves, Cline, Shoppe, and Britt gladly, but unofficially, joined Fox's private hunt for clues regarding the Frome family's connections in California. The auto-theft detectives, who all came from the ranks of local and state police agencies, maintained extensive contacts in law enforcement circles throughout the Bay Area.

Fox trusted these men enough to share his frustrations about the cold shoulder he had received from the Berkeley police and the Texas Rangers, and especially the stonewalling husband and father of the victims. Most of the sheriff's new work on the case was conducted by correspondence and phone calls, since he could no longer justify taking expensive trips. From December 1939 through March 1940, Fox pursued, almost by proxy, his theory that the Frome murders were orchestrated from the West Coast.

Through phone calls and letters to his contacts, Fox summarized some of the most baffling aspects of the case and points he thought needed to be further pursued. He found his California friends eager to follow up on his suggestions. In one letter to the NATB officers he wrote,

> To make a long story short, I am going to repeat myself, telling you boys again that I cannot help but feel there is something rotten in Denmark, relative to this Frome case. I have tried my level best to keep my mind open, in order that I may not become prejudiced or get into rut of thought. However, it is difficult to do when you take into consideration the many so far unexplained, peculiar angles revolving around W. G. Frome and his wife and daughter, and the immediate family background. Despite the tremendous handicap at being so far removed from Berkeley, and the veil of mystery that seems to surround the actions of Hollis Thompson, Jack Greening, and Gottshall [who accompanied the bereaved executive on his trip to El Paso to claim the bodies], I think we have done pretty well. However, doing pretty well is not going to get this particular case wound up between now and the time the Pacific Ocean goes dry.[254]

The sheriff told the agents of the strong suspicions raised by Pop Frome's continuing insistence that his wife and daughter stayed the first night of their trip in Bakersfield, California, more than one hundred miles from Los Angeles. He suggested that Frome's diversionary tactics regarding the LA Biltmore warranted further probing.

"I am willing to make allowances for an ordinary mistake," he wrote.

But Frome and his assistant, Eugene Daley, who was Frome's point man on the huge Rohl construction account, continued "going out of their way" to deny the facts and insist the women went straight to Bakersfield, even after being presented with the evidence. "This simply doesn't make any sense."

The second point the sheriff offered as proof that the motive for the murders was most likely centered in California involved the way the women were taken on the highway and the methodical nature of the torture they endured. Fox said he believed they were specifically targeted by one or more persons who knew them. He opined that the theory of most officers involved in the case — that they were randomly waylaid by common criminals when they had a tire blowout — was "flatly wrong."

"No one observed the Frome car with a flat tire," the sheriff told CBI chief Kessel. "Witnesses observed the Frome car stopped on the side of the road and the black car in back of it."[255] But none of the people who saw the Fromes along with one or two men and a woman beside the highway had observed anything to do with a flat tire, and that included the Worchester family, whom everyone deemed to be the most reliable witnesses.

"Upon paying close attention, none of them can say the car had a flat tire at the time, nor was there anything in the action and movements on the part of either the occupants of the black car or the Packard to that end."

Fox said it was obvious to him that the flat tire on the Packard was caused later, when the assailants took it into the rugged brush and thorny desert where the victims' luggage was ransacked.

He said he now believed the women were deliberately stalked and forced off the highway on a lonely stretch of road when no witnesses were around. That would have been easy, since there are long segments of the highway where a motorist can see for miles in both directions.

Fox suggested a second, as yet unidentified, green vehicle may have actually bumped the Frome Packard at some point. He noted that a green paint smear and minor damage to the right front fender received little attention in the original investigation, even though it was known that the damage occurred after the women picked up their car and drove out of El Paso on the ill-fated day.[256]

Fox referred to a newspaper article in which a Bay Area private detective asserted that a green-colored car was key to solving the case. The article from the *San Francisco Call Bulletin*, dated March 26, 1940, read in part,

"W. S. Bennett, an independent investigator, said, 'I have been convinced there is a solution to the murders and I recently found that I am on the right track. A green paint smear was found on the abandoned Frome car.' He believes it indicated the women were first forced off the road by a green automobile the day of the murders."[257]

The sheriff reminded the NATB agents that the mysterious Dr. Trotsky owned a heavy green car at the time of the killings, which he hurriedly had repainted yellow and black, after some fender damage was repaired.

He again raised the possibility that there might have been more than one pursuit car involved in forcing the women off the highway and that other witnesses said there were two men and a woman in these chase vehicles. In addition to the small black coupe with two license plates seen by several witnesses, there was a report of a "large, dark-colored coupe bearing yellow license plates" in close pursuit of a silver Packard on the highway that morning.[258]

Fox pointed out that both mother and daughter were experienced drivers and their Packard was one of the heaviest cars in America. It thus might have taken more than one small Ford or Plymouth sedan to overtake and force the larger car off the road.

The sheriff also wrote to the NATB officers that the odometer on the Frome car indicated an extra forty miles had been put on the Packard the day the women disappeared. He thought the assailants might have taken them to some place off the straight route between where witnesses first observed their car parked by US 80 and where their bodies were found near Van Horn.

Fox also reached out for help from his sources in other states. "There are a number of things in this case that sound screwy to me, and I can't get them out of my head and resign myself to dropping the case," he told NATB agent Harry Hooper in the bureau's Phoenix office.

The absolute lack of frankness on the part of Mr. Frome and the various angles we have developed . . . do not allow me to keep an open mind about things. I know that a good policeman does not allow himself to become prejudiced. Yet I cannot disregard this angle until somebody conclusively shows that there was not something dirty along the line.

I still feel that Weston G. Frome knows what happened to Hazel and

Nancy Frome, though he may not know who did it or what it was all about, he does know what happened to them. I am sure.[259]

On April 23, 1940, the sheriff received a lengthy report from NATB agent M. L. Britt of the San Francisco office. The report seemed to exonerate Eugene Daley, Frome's top deputy in LA, from any duplicity in the case, noting that the Atlas employee had only been Frome's assistant for a short time prior to the murders. It shed no new light on the question of why Frome was trying to divert attention from the Biltmore Hotel in Los Angeles, other than the fact that Frome, Daley, and other Atlas executives frequented the hotel.

Britt reported that one of his agents had recently followed Pop Frome into a bar at the Palace Hotel near his headquarters office on Montgomery Street after work, and they struck up a conversation. The agent was unsuccessful in getting anything of value out of Frome, learning only that he felt he had been bullied by investigators and unfairly harassed by news reporters ever since the murders.

Oddly, Britt's report hinted at a "possible new angle" to be investigated: Atlas Powder Company might be involved in work that was sensitive in nature. "If it proves to be necessary for any further information, we could possibly obtain it through the local office of the U.S. Naval Intelligence Service, as they undoubtedly would have someone who could get that dope from the DuPont people at Wilmington, Delaware."[260]

At that time Sheriff Fox and his contacts on the West Coast were careful not to put anything in writing that might hint the Frome murders were in any way connected to foreigners, although there were more and more indications that these lawmen were already doing work with the FBI on various espionage activities in their jurisdictions.

At the end of March 1940, the Texas Department of Public Safety was forced, by budget constraints as well as lack of new leads, to pull back most of its Rangers and close its four-man, special-case unit. Newly assigned Ranger Hugh J. Pharies, a former highway patrolman who had recently joined the elite investigators, was left as the sole Ranger working full time on the case. He would work out of Austin. The twenty-nine-year-old Ranger notified Fox of the assignment and strongly urged the older lawman to remain in close touch.

Upon receiving word that the Rangers were lowering their profile, Sheriff Fox dispatched what he described as a final report to Austin. He seemed despondent that the case had been reduced to such low priority. In a personal and confidential note to the master case file in his office, Fox appended a commentary:

> This department has never been fully satisfied with the development in this case as pertains to Berkeley, California, and the Frome family. Whether it will ever be possible to get a full, frank manifestation of interest or replies to intelligence or direct questions from Mr. Frome is unknown. My office will continue to investigate this case until it is solved, or as long as I am able to carry on.
>
> Concluding, it is hoped that no individual or agency will become selfish and try to develop information alone without consulting other interested persons, because it would spoil the splendid efforts of the wholesome and sincere cooperation that has existed so far among all agencies in connection with this particular case.[261]

Chris Fox obviously had an eye to history, because there is no way he believed, after his experiences with other agencies in Austin and Berkeley, that interagency efforts had been marked by "wholesome and sincere cooperation."

He signed and dated the summary note March 23, 1940, exactly two years from the day Hazel and Nancy Frome left their Berkeley home to begin their ill-fated journey.

41

On May 21, 1940, Roosevelt quietly but formally authorized the FBI to conduct warrantless electronic surveillance of aliens suspected of subversive or espionage activities in the United States. It was a closely kept secret that the bureau was already employing illegal eavesdropping techniques and break-ins and, with the cooperation of the post office, opening mail. The new directive not only allowed for taps of telephone conversations and Western Union transmissions but also authorized the FBI to enter public buildings and private residences to set up electronic bugs. The president told J. Edgar Hoover that he hoped the new power would be used "mostly" against noncitizens suspected of spying and other subversive activities.[262]

A week later, top officials of the FBI, Military Intelligence Division (MID), and Office of Naval Intelligence (ONI) met to formally divvy up counterespionage responsibilities within the country. The bureau would be in complete control of the clandestine civilian operation, ferreting out threats to America's defense industry, while the army and navy intelligence agencies would concentrate on protecting military secrets and installations.

For two years before these official steps were taken, the bureau had battled the growing subversive threat with one hand tied behind its back, risking censure or even legal action for running unauthorized counterespionage operations. The legality of much of the work from 1937 through 1939 was questionable.

Growing concerns about subversives from both Communist and Fascist front groups prompted President Roosevelt and attorney general Homer Cummings to authorize FBI director Hoover to set up a comprehensive, domestic counterespionage branch within the bureau.[263]

In authorizing the FBI to establish a domestic intelligence structure within the existing agency and budget, Cummings issued a secret directive that noted, "Additional legislation is not required," and the plan "should be handled in strictest confidence." The need for secrecy was further justified: "It is believed imperative that it proceed with the utmost degree of secrecy, in order to avoid criticism or objections which might be raised to such an expansion by either ill-informed persons or individuals having some ulterior motive."[264]

The president's advisers, particularly his military experts, were alarmed at what the navy and army intelligence officers were finding in the homeland. With regard to Nazi activities, military intelligence reports sent to Roosevelt warned of a definite indication of foreign espionage in the United States and that an "emergency" already existed. Nazi cells were identified that "would probably attempt to cripple our war effort through sabotage."[265]

Finally, the brazen aggressiveness of the subversive groups became so obvious that even the staunchest isolationists could no longer deny something had to be done. Congress bestirred itself to defend national security. It passed the Alien Registration Act of 1940, commonly known as the Smith Act, in June of that year. This legislation not only required foreign nationals to register but also included a strong provision, introduced by Representative Howard Smith of Virginia, that made it illegal to advocate the overthrow of the U.S. government.

The Smith Act finally codified some of what the FBI had already been doing since Roosevelt had secretly given the bureau authority to investigate domestic espionage activities two years earlier. By the end of 1940, the FBI was investigating two hundred and fifty active cases of suspected espionage, an increase from only thirty-five such investigations in 1938.

The new authority allowed the bureau to carry out clandestine snooping on aliens residing in the United States. Handling subversives among the population that had emigrated from Axis lands and become U.S. citizens was more problematic. These Nazi sympathizers still enjoyed the constitutional protections from warrantless arrest or search and seizure of any other citizen, despite their anti-American activities. A large number of German immigrants had taken advantage of these protections by becoming U.S. citizens at the urging of the Nazi government, and some of these were active Nazi agents.

The FBI was authorized to hire only 150 additional agents to carry out these greatly expanded duties. The bureau had fewer than one thousand active field agents to cover the entire country, and most were concentrated in the heavily industrialized areas of the Northeast, upper Midwest, and

West Coast. Hoover needed help. He even called on such trusted civilian organizations as the American Legion to provide eyes and ears on the ground in some areas. Realistically, the FBI director knew his manpower limitations. He reached out to a select few, local law enforcement agencies, headed by trusted, longtime friends of the bureau, for assistance in implementing the new counterintelligence powers.

Even though the near-border centers of Juarez and Chihuahua City were known to be hotbeds of both Fascist and Communist activities, the hard-pressed FBI had just two regular agents stationed in El Paso. While these agents watched for spies operating along the porous border, they still had responsibility for day-to-day crime fighting in West Texas and New Mexico, a huge area that had always been a magnet for organized criminal activities.

Sheriff Fox's relationship with Hoover had long been on a first-name basis. Fox addressed J. Edgar as "John," and the stoic director referred to the sheriff as "Chris," in their many exchanges of telephone and written messages. It was therefore a natural fit for Fox to be one of the first local lawmen recruited.

As with most of his commitments, Fox soon exceeded the expectations of the FBI. Early in 1940, his undercover operatives busted a gang using a local union for cover of subversive activities on both sides of the border.[266] The sheriff arrested six suspected foreign agents and a local union boss named Frank Sener for inciting agriculture and smelting workers to commit violence against their El Paso–area employers. These alleged subversives were handed over to the House Un-American Activities Committee headed by Representative Martin Dies Jr. Fox had worked with the Texas Democratic congressman on anti-Communist cases in the past and became a key witness in the current case. The alien organizer Sener was transferred to immigration authorities for immediate deportation to Austria.

Before the end of 1940, a half dozen of Fox's detectives were working counterintelligence, while the FBI delayed staffing up its El Paso office. As the sheriff was being drawn into the web of espionage on the border, there is no record that he sensed or imagined how close he still was to answers in the Frome case. The two areas of investigation were too separated at that point, by urgent new priorities and the passage of time, for anyone to connect the dots.

Meanwhile, the FBI was taking a new interest in an old nemesis of the sheriff, the chameleonlike Romano Trotsky. The sheriff, working in El Paso, did not know Trotsky was back in the States and was unaware of the FBI's encounter.

Trotsky surfaced this time in Nevada, in June 1940. For his new scam he assumed the identity of Prince Alexis N. Romanoff.[267] A postal inspector at Reno was notified by a clerk that a man had registered a letter addressed to "Soviet Dictator Joseph Stalin." The letter was intercepted and copied before it was forwarded. In it, the man calling himself Romanoff professed support for the Communist tyrant and warned him that Hitler could not be trusted.

Upon further investigation, agents learned from the man's landlady that he was receiving large quantities of mail from people with German surnames, as well as several German-American Bund publications. The FBI quickly determined that the man, who claimed to be a Russian prince related to the late tsar, was actually the elusive criminal who most often used the name Trotsky among his three dozen or more other aliases. Agents were certain Trotsky knew the letter would be perused and was apparently attempting to establish anti-Fascist credentials.

Trotsky was turned over to local authorities in Reno when it was discovered he was wanted for questioning in the case of a patient named H. J. White, who had died in Nevada shortly after an operation. The Russian was identified as the physician who performed the surgery. After being jailed for two days, he was cleared of negligent homicide for lack of evidence, but he was quickly rearrested and again turned over to immigration officials. The letter to Stalin and discovery of his communications with pro-Hitler elements from other U.S. cities caused the FBI and the ONI to start a new criminal file on Trotsky. For the first time the charge of "espionage" was entered on his already long and growing rap sheet.

Trotsky was held until September 20 before being released by the U.S. Immigration Service. He was now under surveillance by the FBI as a potential national security risk, and his activities in Nevada soon led investigators to a "subversive organization" operating throughout the western states under the cover name International Legion of Vigilantes.[268] The organization's so-called reading groups were suspected of being either Fascist or Communist clubs, but the FBI found no connection with known Red Party or Nazi Bund organizations. It seemed Trotsky was attempting to form his own little cells, most likely to exploit them for extra cash, rather than furtherance of the cause.

IT WAS ANOTHER, far more sinister, plot that embroiled Sheriff Fox and his deputies in international intrigue.[269] The FBI had been tailing the flamboyant Fascist leader Count Anastase Vonsiatsky on well-publicized trips around the country to conduct White Russian meetings and attend German-American Bund rallies. He had been observed meeting with a Japanese female spy aboard a ship in San Francisco Bay and had left the ship shortly before the woman was arrested. Count Vonsiatsky, who often appeared in uniform with a Russian Fascist adaptation of the Hitler swastika armband, frequently hosted known and suspected German and Japanese agents at his fortresslike estate near Thompson, Connecticut.

While shadowing Vonsiatsky, the FBI learned of an important upcoming meeting of spies. A known Nazi espionage agent and Chicago Bund leader, Dr. Otto Willumeit, paid a visit to the two-hundred-acre Connecticut estate. Willumeit was a licensed physician who had received a medical degree from the University of Bonn. Immediately after this visit, FBI agents observed that Vonsiatsky was driven by his chauffeur to Washington, D.C., where he spent several hours at the Japanese embassy.

When he left the embassy he was driven to Union Station, where he purchased a ticket to Chicago. FBI agents were close on his heels the entire time. In Chicago, Count Vonsiatsky was met at the train station and taken to Willumeit's residence for an overnight stay.

Another FBI agent, using the new wiretap authority, intercepted a telegram from the Japanese embassy to Vonsiatsky, at Willumeit's home address. The telegram read, "Be ready for arrival of Kunze at Bismarck Hotel. Chicago. Tomorrow morning. He will have name of contact in El Paso."[270]

The "Kunze" mentioned was Gerhard Wilhelm Kunze, newly named head of the German-American Bund and a suspected Nazi agent. His German-born wife had recently gone home to the fatherland with their children. The FBI had been tracking Kunze's activities ever since the native-born German American returned to the States from an extended stay in Germany in 1939. He was targeted because of his activities as the chief propagandist of the Bund and his promotion to the top leadership, following the conviction of former Bund leader Fritz Kuhn for embezzling funds from his own organization.

FBI agents arranged with a desk clerk at the Bismarck Hotel to use a room adjoining the one reserved for "Mr. G. W. Kunze," where they set up tape-recording equipment after bugging the arriving guest's room. The Bismarck, an aging, twenty-two-story building at 171 West Randolph Street, covered one full city block in downtown Chicago. With entrances on all four sides, it was a good place to conduct private meetings. However, since the agents already knew their target's name and some of the people he was going to meet, they could focus on a specific room, rather than having to cover all four entrances to the hotel.

Shortly after Kunze checked in, his visitors, Vonsiatsky and Willumeit, arrived. A lengthy meeting ensued, all recorded by the eavesdropping feds next door. Most of the conversation concerned reports on various industrial plants on the East Coast and in the Chicago area, where spies or potential saboteurs had been successfully inserted. The discussion moved on to the difficulty agents were experiencing in getting the information collected from these spies out of the country without FBI and British MI-5 intercept. Ironically, the eavesdroppers overheard the spies bemoaning the illegality of G-men and British agents intercepting diplomatic mail pouches.

Kunze boasted that was not a problem because he had established a conduit through a person who was above suspicion. While on a recent visit to the fatherland, the Abwehr had given him the name of a deep-cover agent on the U.S.-Mexico border. The man was capable of moving people and large volumes of material from the West Coast, across the border, to agents in Mexico via a well-established underground railroad, terminating in Brazil. From that South American country there was a secure route directly back to Germany by Deutsche Lufthansa, the German flag air carrier.

Kunze kept referring to this pipeline's key agent as "Wolf." The FBI's surveillance of letters, telephone calls, and diplomatic correspondence had occasionally picked up references to a "Wolf," but no one in the bureau had been able to connect the code word to a specific person or organization. He said his Texas asset had been running agents and information in and out of the country for both Japanese and German consulate fronts for several years, without the slightest suspicion.

Finally, the Russian count, seeming somewhat irritated that the German would only refer to his source by code name, bluntly asked who the agent was and why he was so well situated. Kunze did not hesitate to brag further about his valuable connection.

"His name is Dr. Ebell — Wolfgang Ebell. He is a physician in El Paso, Texas."[271] The name was entirely new to the FBI analysts. But if Wolfgang Ebell was the mysterious "Wolf," this was an important piece of information for the fledgling counterespionage offensive of the FBI. The agents were surprised to hear Kunze give it up so easily.

Naturally, the FBI wanted to know more about this Wolf. FBI director Hoover had just the man down on the border, a man he trusted to produce reliable results in a hurry and to assist his own understaffed office there in placing the Nazi spy under scrutiny. If anyone outside the agency could put a quick patch on this hole in the FBI net, it was Sheriff Chris Fox, with his crew in El Paso.

42

The Frome murders were headed for the cold-case files as the second anniversary neared when a spark of renewed interest was lit by the appointment of the eager, young Texas Ranger Hugh J. Pharies to the investigation.

Pharies was one of the new breed of college-educated Rangers recruited by Colonel Homer Garrison in his ongoing program to change the elite state investigative group from its Wild West image to a modern crime-fighting force. Notwithstanding his enthusiasm for the assignment, Pharies probably got the job because the veteran officers had already figured the case would never be solved.

The new guy in town was anything but the stereotypical Texas Ranger. He took some good-natured ribbing from the veterans over his fedoras, wingtip shoes, and business suits. He gave in a bit by getting himself a narrow-brim, Western hat and a pair of boots with walking heels.

Despite the sore spots remaining between some of the state lawmen and the El Paso sheriff, the young Ranger sought out Chris Fox for his thoughts on the case. He methodically reviewed every clue in the sheriff's files and the voluminous files at DPS headquarters in Austin. Weighing all the theories and arguments, he came up with an approach he hoped might put renewed momentum into the stalled investigation.

Fox welcomed the Ranger and his fresh approach with cautious optimism. He did not hesitate to share his controversial opinions about the case with the newcomer. He told Pharies that he thought Pop Frome knew "what happened to the women — if not who did it — what happened and why."[272] He suggested it was a shame some lawman couldn't be planted to get with him in a bar while he was drinking and "loosen him up." He believed Frome had some compelling reason, more personally important than solving the murders of his wife and daughter, making him uncooperative.

After fully backgrounding himself in conversations with Rangers who had been working the case, Pharies took his concerns to the top man in state law enforcement. He told Colonel Garrison he was "veering more and more away" from the theory most prevalent among state investigators that the Frome murders were a case of mistaken identity in a dope hijacking gone awry.[273]

He pointed to the mysterious letter, addressed only to "Frome," which was hand delivered sometime during the night before they left El Paso. The letter had apparently spurred the state of high agitation observed by the hotel maid. Pharies surfaced old clues, previously ignored. Three unidentified telephone calls were patched through to Mrs. Frome by the Cortez switchboard operator the morning they left El Paso, and a period of forty-five minutes to one hour was unaccounted for, when Hazel was gone from the hotel just prior to their hurried packing and departure. He also noted the women's seemingly fearful attempt at the tourist office to secure a passenger for the next leg of their trip.

Pharies said these and other incidents from the time they left home until they left El Paso caused him to suspect that the Frome women knew their killers and were afraid of them.

"These unexplained incidents make me anxious to talk to Weston G. Frome again," Pharies told Garrison.[274] Two Rangers had met briefly with Frome in California, but nothing of importance had come of it. The DPS chief concurred, and he used his considerable powers of persuasion to convince Pop Frome to agree to an on-the-record interview.

Ranger Pharies dropped a note about his plans to Sheriff Fox. He said he was trying to schedule a trip to San Francisco to interview the recalcitrant husband and father of the murder victims.

"In reading your last section of summary I was extremely interested in the information from the LAPD, confirming that the women stayed at the Biltmore Hotel in Los Angeles, and not at a motel in Bakersfield, as Mr. Frome insists," Pharies wrote.[275]

This issue had caused one of Fox's primary conflicts with the husband during the early investigation. The sheriff's dogged insistence that the key to the murders would be found in California was also the major reason for his split with the Rangers over the direction of the case.

Surprisingly, the new Ranger seemed to be taking the sheriff's side in the dispute. He told Fox, "I think you and I are alone in our belief that there is something, somewhere here that is not quite on the up and up, on the part of the old gentleman. I just can't get this out of my mind, and still feel it might be well to go out there and do some quiet checking."[276] Pharies said he believed too many questions were still unanswered to let it pass without another go at wheedling, or even bullying, Frome into cooperation.

When the young investigator got to California on November 15, 1940, the Atlas executive could not, this time, slip away on some pretext of urgent business. Pop Frome was hospitalized in Richmond, recuperating from minor surgery. The Ranger greeted Frome, who was lying in bed in a hospital gown. He politely asked the older man if he was up for a few questions. Frome reluctantly agreed, saying he just wanted his role in the investigation to be over, so he could get back to some semblance of normal life.

Not that he had been wearing a black armband of bereavement during the more than two years since his wife and daughter's deaths. He had, in the interim, advanced his business position rather successfully and was about to secure for Atlas Powder one of the fattest contracts for blasting powder in the history of his company. Likewise, he had not put his social life on hold. He was currently dating the widow of one of his closest friends in Berkeley.

It was 2:00 p.m. when Ranger Pharies began the interview. His "few questions" turned into a four-hour grilling. The interview began pleasantly enough, with the lawman going over routine information about the family — Hazel, Nancy, and Mada.

"It may seem to you, Mr. Frome, that you have answered many of these questions before, but we want to make sure the earlier information we have is correct."[277] Pharies started at the beginning, by verifying the women's dates and places of birth.

After the first hour, in which Frome was relaxed and talkative, the Ranger's questions became more pointed, and Pop became noticeably less cooperative. He seemed to tense every time Pharies approached the subject of Atlas Powder Company and Frome's position there.

"In California, what is your position?" he asked.

Frome was finally forthcoming and confirmed what he had previously tried to conceal about his job. He was assistant general manager of the Giant Division of Atlas Powder Company nationally, and he headed all Atlas operations in eleven western states, Alaska, Hawaii, the Philippine islands, the Pacific Ocean islands, and Central and South America.

"What is your salary?" asked Pharies.

"I would not want to say, but it is a sizable salary. The Atlas Powder

Company would not want me to put that out, but I will tell you it is a sizable sum," Frome said, with a touch of annoyance.

The Ranger continued to probe. "Is Atlas a large concern?"

"Atlas Powder Company is a very large concern, with headquarters in Wilmington, Delaware. It manufactures dynamite that is used in mining and commercial construction."

"Your company is also a large manufacturer of ammunition, that is, explosives for bombs and torpedoes?" Pharies asked. Frome scowled and did not respond. He was clearly nervous about this area of query, according to the interview notes.

Pharies pressed on. "Do you have to travel in your work?"

"Yes, I am out forty percent of the time. This is what I do: I'll go down into Mexico and pick up a salesman and go with him. I'll go into Arizona, Utah, Colorado, with a salesman," said Frome.

"Do you have salesmen working out of your headquarters in San Francisco?"

"Yes, and we have a man in New Mexico, a man in Arizona, a man in Colorado, three men in Utah, a man in Wyoming, a man in Nevada, a man in Montana, two men in Los Angeles, three men working in California, and two technicians on projects in the Pacific in our San Francisco office, and fourteen men working the Pacific Northwest and Alaska in the Seattle office."

"Had Nancy ever gone out with any of your salesmen?" asked Pharies.

"No."

"Had any of your salesmen ever wanted to go out with her?"

"No."

"Do you think if there was a favorable way to make some money easily that Mrs. Frome or Nancy would have been inclined to do anything a little irregular?" Pharies watched his subject closely for any physical response.

"No!" said Frome, sharply.

"We have information they went to nightclubs in Juarez," ventured Pharies. "Could this have been possible, causing someone to feel they were fair game for a holdup?"

"I would say this," replied Frome. "I think they would go into a nightclub. Nancy, Mada, and her mother have been all over Europe, around the world, all through Alaska and Canada. Driving back and forth, one coast to the other, three times. In 1937, they went all through Mexico. They were always out for a good time and were capable of taking care of themselves. As far as going to a nightclub and taking a drink, they would do that, sure. All the times they were in Europe, they were never molested, not once."

"Had they ever been involved in an emergency due to some indiscretion?" asked Pharies.

"No," said Frome. "The only thing was, Nancy was engaged and she broke off with Bill Crawford." The Ranger thought the insertion of the name and breakup with an old fiancé, which had occurred almost a year before the ill-fated, cross-country trip, was a bit odd.

"Did they drink heavily?" he asked.

"No, not heavily. They could always take care of themselves. Nancy never drank that she showed her liquor. She would take a couple of highballs and quit. Mrs. Frome would get quite happy." Frome said his wife was inclined to talk too much when she had a few drinks and admitted she might boast a little about the family's fortunes and her husband's important position.

"Did either of them have any phobias?" Pharies asked.

"What do you mean *phobias*?"

"I mean were they particularly afraid of anything, or have dread of anything. For example, in El Paso Mrs. Frome went to a fortune-teller. Why do you think she would do that?"

"If she went to a fortune-teller at all I imagine it would have been on account of Nancy's engagement being broken," said Frome. There it was again, an unsolicited mention of the long-ago split.

"Was Mrs. Frome worried about anything when she left?" Pharies asked.

"She was very upset about Nancy's engagement. That is why they took the trip," said Frome. Pharies knew from the files that the reason given for the trip at the time of the murders was a visit to the younger daughter, Mada, on the East Coast, not because Nancy was pining over a broken engagement.

"Now, Mr. Frome, Nancy was a good-looking girl. Do you think if some nicely appearing man saw her and her mother in a bar having a drink and tried to make conversation, she would talk and drink with him?"

"She might pass the day with him, make some crack at him, but not dance with him," Frome said.

The Ranger knew there were unconfirmed reports that the Frome women were in the presence of two men in Juarez nightclubs. "Do you think Mrs. Frome would dance with a stranger?" asked Pharies.

"No."

"What was Nancy's chief pastime?"

"She was a very good horse rider," said Frome. She rode horses very well. She was a good swimmer. They used to go to Colorado Springs quite a bit. At home she would fool around on the piano, and she did quite a bit of reading. Now Mada would do more sewing. Nancy would sew too, but in the country she would go horseback riding or swimming."

"Was she fond of dancing?" Pharies asked.

"Very much," said Frome.

"Was Nancy very interested in men? In a romantic way?"

"You might say so. Nancy was always out to have a good time. Dancing, that's all."

"How long did she go with Bill Crawford? When did they break up?"

"Two or three years," said Frome. "They broke up in the summer of 1937. She did not see him after that. She sent the ring back. Dr. Crawford married some local girl from Richmond and has a practice in San Francisco."

"They went into Mexico in 1937, did they not? How long were they there?" asked the Ranger.

"They went in May," Frome replied. "They were down there for three months. They drove and went off the road someplace they could not go by automobile. Nancy and Mada rode horses and Mrs. Frome rode in a donkey cart."

Pharies asked if either of the girls became romantically involved with anyone while in Mexico. Frome said they were just having a good time with some of the ranchers' sons where they visited, including two brothers that Mada and Nancy dated while they attended university. Frome told the Ranger that he and Mada had only recently looked through photos of the trip and talked about what a good time the women had in Mexico.

"Now, what they had figured to do was go to South Carolina and come back the southern way and back into Mexico on their return trip," Frome added. He said they told him they might be gone as long as four months.

Pressed on why they selected the southern route along the border on the way out, instead of going straight across the country, Frome said a more northerly route was never discussed.

The interrogator was more interested in working in his next series of questions than in the women's choice of cross-country routes. He wanted to approach the touchy subject of the Biltmore Hotel, which Sheriff Fox had found so troubling.

"Did the women go to Los Angeles often?"

At the mention of the Southern California city, Pop seemed to stiffen. "No, they did not go to Los Angeles very often," he replied tersely. "The whole family was there for the Rose Bowl. During their college years the girls went down and stayed at the Delta sorority house when there were football games."

The Ranger had the dates and times of the family's stay at the hotel during the 1938 Rose Bowl game. He also had the other dates when the women had stayed there without Pop. Frome was still stubbornly omitting any connection to the Biltmore Hotel.

"Did Mrs. Frome or the girls have friends in Los Angeles?" Pharies asked.

"None of them had made a trip down there since January 5, 1938," Frome said, emphatically.

"You know we have information that on that last trip they went to Los Angeles and stayed at a fancy hotel," Pharies probed.

"The last trip, they went to Bakersfield and on to Phoenix," Pop Frome replied evenly. Short of asking him why he was lying, the Ranger had no way to continue this line of questioning. It was clear the business executive had no intention of talking about Los Angeles or the Biltmore Hotel.

The young Ranger returned to more comfortable topics. "When they packed and left you were at the office?" Pharies asked.

"Yes, they got away about 10:30 that morning and stayed the first night in a motor inn at Bakersfield, and the second night in Phoenix." Frome gratuitously made the point again that the women did not spend the night at the ritzy hotel in Los Angeles.

"Now, Mr. Frome I want you to tell me this. What do you think they would have done in El Paso if they thought someone was after them or they were in danger?" Pharies asked.

"They would have gone to Harold White, our company man there, right away, if they thought they were in danger or someone was after them. Had they thought anyone was following them they would have put their car at 120. Nancy was the scardest thing in the world. She would have tried to outrun someone."

"They are supposed to have received an anonymous letter the morning they left, the source of which we have not been able to trace. Do you have any idea who this could have been from?" asked Pharies.

"If they had received anything of which they were suspicious, anyone was after them or after their money, they would have gone to the law, or Harold White, or someone. There was no one more scared than Nancy," said Frome. "I tried getting her accustomed to staying at home alone at night when we went out. No sir, she would not stay in the house alone at all. Mrs. Frome, if she was in a hurry to do something, appeared to be excited, always. Maybe that is what the maid noticed. I think I told Ranger Pete Crawford the same thing when I heard about the letter."

"Toby's Travel Bureau told me they went by the travel bureau as they were leaving El Paso and tried to get another passenger. Did they ever take passengers from travel bureaus?"

Frome was agitated now. "That is absolutely untrue, absolutely untrue, *absolutely untrue.* They never tried to get a passenger. Nancy would not stand for a passenger in the car!"

Pharies pressed on. "Toby identified the women and said they wanted some presentable man to go with them on the Dallas leg of their trip. They offered a free ride. In your opinion could they have been possibly afraid and wanted a man along for protection?"

"I still think, as I told Chris Fox, and I have not changed it a bit, they were followed out of El Paso and run off the road, and that is all there is to it!"

"For robbery?" asked Pharies.

"Yes! That is all!" snapped Frome.[278]

43

The Ranger may have been young compared to some of the grizzled professionals on the force, but he had the advantage of having recently been trained in interrogation techniques at the new FBI Police Training School.[279]

The gentleman in the hospital bed was trying mightily to mislead, if not deliberately lie. Pharies had already caught him in several "mistakes" but did not correct them, in order to keep the subject engaged and assure him the interview was going well.

Since the man was becoming agitated, Pharies suggested a brief recess and offered to refill the water pitcher. When he declined, the Ranger asked him if he wanted something else to drink before continuing. He was about to open a line of questioning that might prove key to discovering if Frome was deliberately withholding information about some motive other than robbery, a motive closer to home. Frome seemed impatient to get the interview over and indicated he just wanted to proceed.

"If someone had tried to stop them on the highway, what would they have done? For example, if some strange man had pulled across the road in front of them?" Pharies asked.[280]

"They would have tried to beat him to it and stepped on the gas," said Frome.

"When Nancy saw this man was in earnest, what would she have done?"

"I think my wife would have fought them off, but I have argued that with her many a time. On a holdup, she said she would have fought them off. I don't know what Nancy would have done."

"Mr. Frome, what significance, if any, do you attach that both of them were lying on their faces?" asked Pharies.

"I do not see anything significant about that. Of course it's Pete's [Ranger Crawford] idea, and I listened to him quite a bit, that those burns on Nancy were for identification. Pete's idea is a dope ring. I don't know. It might be that."

Frome told the Ranger that deputies at the scene said Nancy fought hard and had some black hair in her hand. "This black hair looked like straight black hair from an Indian," Frome said.

"Mr. Frome, you think the scene [where the bodies were discovered] was laid?"

"I think it was laid. They were followed to El Paso, and followed out from El Paso, and laid at the spot. I think they were followed from Juarez. Mrs. Frome still had her glasses on her, and Nancy still had the matches in her hand."

"Do you think after the murderers killed them they put the matches back in Nancy's hand, and put Mrs. Frome's glasses back on her?" the Ranger asked.

"I don't know. I see no point in their taking their dresses off and taking all their baggage," said Frome.

"Why do you think they left jewelry on Mrs. Frome and Nancy?"

Frome surmised that perhaps the killers were afraid the jewelry might be identified.

"Why do you think Nancy was tortured like she was?"

"I don't know. Nancy was tortured the way she was . . . the torture of Nancy to me, I think sometimes Pete's theory of the job was right: they were torturing her to make her tell, and that's the only thing I know."

"I would be fairly convinced of that if those burns were not in a perfect pattern," Ranger Pharies added.

Frome continued to speculate. "The only thing to me is that the way they tortured Nancy, Pete's theory might be right. Here you have two well-dressed women go to Juarez. I've gone to Juarez just to see what it's like. It is a terrible place. They have a good-looking car. Good-looking rings. Someone in Juarez said follow them and get some money."

The Ranger did not point out that the women never took their car into Juarez and left their jewelry in the safe at the Hotel Cortez on trips across the border.

At this point Pharies was hoping to get to some of the more controversial subjects in the investigation. He noticed Frome appeared worn out but planned to push him harder. That would not be easy, since the young Ranger knew he was dealing with a powerful business executive, who could just as easily have kicked him out of the hospital room as answer another question.

Since the family name was German, a number of tipsters had suggested there might be a Nazi spy angle in the case.[281]

Rumors had circulated for some time that the women were actually German agents trying to reach Galveston with a carload of military secrets, to be transported by steamship to Germany. The women had traveled extensively in Germany and other European countries in 1936 and could have been recruited by agents. That imaginative theory was quickly dispelled when investigators examined closely the almost frivolous social connections enjoyed by both Nancy and her mother.

Ranger Pharies approached the issue as a casual aside to his regular questioning. "Along the way, the theory has been advanced that Mrs. Frome and Nancy were carrying some kind of government secret. There is nothing to that, is there?" asked Pharies. He watched Frome closely for his response. The man almost came out of his hospital bed.

"No! Christ, *no!*" Pop was visibly shaken by the question. "They learned more about the explosives business from the wives of my associates than they did from me!"

Ranger Pharies had not suggested the executive leaked secrets to his family. Frome's answer seemed unduly defensive.

"The theory was that they were carrying the formula for you from one plant to another." The Ranger pushed further on this angle.

"No! There is nothing to that!"

Frome indicated he was tiring from the long interview, which at this point had lasted almost four hours. And he was clearly overreacting to any questions about his business dealings.

"You don't know anyone who would want to get revenge on either one of them, for any reason? Maybe something they had nothing to do with?"

"No!"

"They were just two normal women, neither of them ever having been mixed up in anything?" asked Pharies.

"Not a thing in the world," said Frome.

"I've been told that when you first heard they were missing your first words were, 'They've been murdered.' Is that true?"

"I did not say that," Frome responded. He launched into a lengthy reconstruction of how he had learned they were missing and his subsequent flight to El Paso to help search for his wife and daughter.

"Also this — you said that if the murderers of the women were ever found you wanted to talk to them first?" asked Pharies.

"I made this request. I said if they had been raped, I hoped that they would keep it out of the papers. They said they were unable to do that, and I said okay."

"There is one other point that we are curious about. When you were down there [in Texas] you told someone, DA Roy Jackson or someone, that if you were him you would not go to much trouble to run it down."

"Not true, absolutely not true!" Frome insisted.

"There has been a lot of comment about your drinking on that trip, both arriving by airplane having had a lot to drink, and getting drunk on the train back to California." The Ranger expected to get very little more from the interview.

"Any man in a position like that needs a drink, right then and there!" The interview was over, as far as Frome was concerned.

"Will you tell Colonel Garrison I'll do anything to help," Frome said with finality in a tone that an overbearing boss might use to dismiss an underling. He told the Ranger if he wanted anything else, to "just make out a questionnaire in writing."[282]

44

Chris Fox had little time to sit around licking his wounds after his ego-bruising ouster from the central role in the Frome murder case in late 1938. He had new challenges even more pressing than solving a two-year-old murder, albeit the most sensational one in years.

As the London Blitz and Battle of Britain raged, and the very existence of democracy in Europe hung in the balance, a thin line of government men led by J. Edgar Hoover's FBI was already secretly fighting the next world war in the American homeland. Sheriff Fox was one of the first and few local lawmen recruited to augment Hoover's small force of G-men.[283]

In this latest clandestine campaign against Nazi espionage agents, the sheriff's office was positioned — ready, willing, and able — to supplement the two-man FBI office at El Paso until new agents could be hired and trained. The local sheriff's office had worked closely with the bureau in the past and was now trusted to help track the spy operating under the code name "Wolf."

Fox was surprised that the spy identified in the FBI eavesdropping operation in Chicago was an unassuming local doctor. He secretly put his most trusted plainclothes detectives on the counterespionage detail, as this type of work was outside his authorization and the county taxpayers' idea of what the local sheriff should be doing with the personnel and resources in his charge. Even the FBI was still operating on shaky legal ground when it came to the surveillance of American citizens. Technically, the El Paso doctor Wolfgang Ebell was a naturalized citizen, having sworn allegiance to the United States in 1939, almost a decade after legally entering the country.

Once Wolf's identity was positively established, considerable information about the man was available. The suspected spy turned forty years old around the time he first came to the attention of the bureau. He had been a model citizen, with not even a speeding ticket on his official records.

DR. WOLFGANG EBELL had crossed the border at El Paso aboard the El Paso Electric Railway trolley on September 18, 1930, and declared his intention of becoming a permanent resident. Thus, the Immigration and Naturalization Service already had a file of basic information on him when the FBI first identified him as a possible espionage agent.[284] Because he was an educated and skilled professional, immigration officials were never reluctant to grant him permanent residency.

These were exactly the credentials the Abwehr was looking for as well. The seemingly soft-spoken Nazi doctor was one of the first overseas recruits from the German diaspora after Hitler seized power in January 1933. The Nazi spy chief, Admiral Wilhelm Canaris, who spoke fluent Spanish, had developed a special affinity for Mexico, which he saw as the wide-open backdoor for espionage activities against the United States. Long before America became a primary target of the Abwehr, and many years before war was declared, the German spy organization secretly launched a unilateral espionage campaign.[285] By the time the Nazis seized power, Germany's overseas spying had already begun. Men like Ebell were being silently posted at key locations to establish pipelines into North America for espionage, propaganda, and ultimately, sabotage operations.

Ebell's selection by the Nazi spy chiefs was no accident. He had the perfect pedigree for a sleeper agent. He was born on July 28, 1899, to Helene Doetsch and Max Ebell in the city of Zabern, in the Alsace-Lorraine borderlands between Germany and France. The German population of that border region had historic reasons to hate the Western Allies, particularly the French. The area had changed hands many times between Germany and France over centuries of war.

The newly created German empire retook the area from France in the Franco-Prussian War in 1871. The Ebell family was of Germanic stock and spoke an Alsatian dialect of German. Zabern, Germany, where Wolfgang was born, became Saverne, France, after 1919, when the French reannexed the region as a share of the war booty extracted from the Germans at the end of World War I.

At the time of Ebell's birth, the wealthy iron and coal region of the Rhine Valley area was populated almost exclusively by Germans. But when this region became part of France, forcefully ceded with all its industrial and mineral wealth to the victors as World War I reparations, French authorities took over government functions and began moving in French families. Thousands of German families, especially if fathers and sons had served in the military, were forced or chose to flee across the frontier to the German Rhineland states.[286]

The young Ebell, who enlisted as a private in the war in 1917 at the age of eighteen, earned a battlefield commission as a lieutenant in 1918. Shortly thereafter, he was seriously wounded and mustered out of the army, to return to a defeated and devastated homeland. From that time, the Alsace-Lorraine area produced some of the earliest and most fanatical supporters of Hitler's new National Socialist German Workers' Party (NSDAP), commonly known as the Nazi Party.

On his application to enter America, the doctor had omitted that the Ebells were among the first of the disgruntled army veterans to join the radical Nazi movement and become members of the party. Ebell and his father, a former sergeant in the German army during the war, were early members of the Freikorps of German veterans, which provided the nucleus of the brown-shirted Nazi storm troopers of the *Sturmabteilung* (SA). Both son and father joined the Nazi Party being formed by Adolph Hitler during the turbulent 1920s. His father became a Gestapo officer in a small German city immediately after Hitler was named chancellor of Germany. Wolfgang's only sister married a Nazi-leaning colonel named Littuit. He was on the German SS General Staff and was in charge of the Military Communications Board in Berlin.[287]

Soon after arriving in the United States, Ebell applied for, and was granted, a license to practice general medicine. He presented the necessary medical-school diploma and résumé to the local medical society and applied for a license with the American Medical Association. After his war service, Ebell had graduated from the prestigious Albert Ludwig University of Freiburg, one of the oldest universities in Germany, founded in 1457. He earned a doctorate of medicine degree in 1924. Curiously, his records with the El Paso medical society noted that, because he lacked minimum surgical training, he was denied certification at the El Paso hospital. Almost any physician, however crude his skill with the scalpel, was allowed to practice at the local hospital.

Like many professionals at that time, Ebell had left Germany because he was unable to make a living as a doctor, due to the chaotic economic turmoil left by the war. Only one in three university graduates was able to find a job in Germany in the years following World War I; a third of the university-trained doctors worked as clerks.[288] He immigrated to Cuba in 1927. His father remained in the German Ruhr and was promoted to a regional command post in the Gestapo after Hitler's rise to power.

Ebell soon found the pickings slim in Cuba, too, and moved to Mexico, where he eked out a subsistence as a salesman and doctor to the peasantry in Vera Cruz and Monterrey, before moving to the United States in 1930. Ebell was fluent in both Spanish and English. He married another German immigrant named Kaethe while working in Monterrey, Mexico, but the marriage was annulled in 1937. Immediately after the annulment, he wed a young Mexican American woman named Raquel, who worked for him as a nurse in El Paso. The ceremony was conducted across the border in Juarez.[289]

Ebell's mother, Helene, came to El Paso for an extended visit with her son in 1937. When she returned to Germany the following year, she served as a courier, taking with her materials that included geographical maps and photographs of defense perimeters at nearby Fort Bliss army base, and blueprints of the U.S. Army's advanced antiaircraft guns. Ebell had quietly amassed the trove from operatives in his network but never exposed himself personally by lurking with a camera around the big local military base. At Fort Bliss, advanced weapons were being tested and artillerymen were being trained to fire them.[290] No one would think to search the luggage of a matronly German lady returning from a visit with her son. Helene Doetsch Ebell rounded out the perfect family of Hitler worshipers.

After his mother had visited for a year, Ebell literally sent her packing back to Germany with a load of army intelligence material stuffed into the liners of her luggage. He was so proud of her spy work that he later bragged about her cunning to a fellow Nazi agent.

45

The usually furtive doctor let his Teutonic pride in Hitler's startling military successes in Eastern Europe get the better of him, in the autumn of 1939. He came very close to blowing his carefully laid undercover identity when he threw a tantrum with, of all people, a newspaper reporter.

The incident began rather innocently when Betty Luther, a reporter for the *El Paso Herald-Post*, ran into Ebell at an El Paso coffee shop frequented by local journalists.[291]

She was sitting next to the doctor at the counter when she casually mentioned the Nazi army's astounding sweep across the Polish country-side. The reporter had known Ebell for several years and recognized him by sight as a local doctor who had practiced general medicine in the city since entering the United States. Prior to this chance encounter, most of their brief conversations had been about Mexico, not Germany.

Betty Luther later testified to the details of her meeting with Ebell. "He impressed me with his keen understanding of the Mexican people," she said. "I liked the man for his knowledgeable conversations about interior Mexico. I knew he had divorced his German wife and married a Mexican girl. But I recently had heard rumors that he used his marriage to set up a 'Fifth Column' in Mexico."[292]

In this casual encounter at the coffee shop, Luther sought out the German's observations about the Nazi army's rapid victory over Poland. Ebell agreed to talk about the Polish invasion in an interview, after establishing that he was *not* a member of the German-American Bund, merely a German-born American citizen trying to adjust to his new home. He told the reporter the only connection he maintained with his former homeland was through the local German cultural society, which met occasionally for folk dancing and home-country music.

The reporter had no reason to question Ebell further about the German club because, unlike the East Coast and Midwest of the country, there had been little or no Bund activity in Texas. The Bund had tried but failed miserably to establish cells in the German communities in the state.

"We attempted to organize four Bund posts in Texas, but found the German-American people there unsympathetic," according to Bund leader Fritz Kuhn's testimony before a Congressional panel.[293]

The very failure to win support from the local German Americans in Texas had forced the Nazis to assign professional spies to maintain the open channel between Mexico and the United States. This critical North American pipeline was manned from the beginning by sleeper agents placed in the border communities of Texas and Mexico.

Betty Luther arranged to visit the doctor in his downtown office for an interview. Very quickly, Ebell let his true colors show through his carefully crafted facade of newly adopted American patriotism. The reporter, with pencil and notepad in hand, again said she had heard he was a leader in some sort of Nazi organization, if not the Bund, some other group. Ebell vehemently denied it, and the interview got off to a bad start.

"His face changed as if a mask fell over it. I thought he was the ugliest little man I'd ever seen," said Luther. "His already unusually large eyes bulged. He was a very peculiar looking man anyway, and his rage did not help his looks."[294]

She said Ebell seemed to realize he was on the edge of losing control and calmed himself down. He began defending Germany and telling her of the hardships suffered by the people because of the Versailles Treaty.

"You Americans don't know what hard times are," Ebell said. "You don't know how to conserve, how to make do."

"But aren't you now an American, too?" she asked.

He reluctantly acknowledged that he was now an American citizen and suddenly ended the interview. The reporter went back to her editor without a story. But the encounter raised her suspicions.

Later, she met with a sergeant in G-2 Section (military intelligence) at Fort Bliss. She told him of her suspicions and rumors she had heard that the immigrant doctor might not be the peaceful citizen he appeared. The sergeant told the reporter not to worry, that military intelligence was aware of Ebell. He apparently brushed off the reporter's tip, because there was no record that the information was passed on to intelligence officers. Likewise, there was no mention of Ebell in other military intel files for another year.

America's almost reverential admiration for doctors provided good cover. But the healing profession was a different matter in Nazi Germany, where doctors and lawyers made up a large cadre of Hitler's earliest support-ers, through membership in the Nazi legal and medical leagues. Although membership was not required to practice in Germany, more than half the German doctors voluntarily enlisted in the Nazi Physicians League. More than forty-six thousand German physicians joined the Nazi Party.[295]

WHEN THE FBI discovered the El Paso spy connection and brought Sheriff Fox and his men into the investigation, all that was known about Ebell was the seemingly innocuous material in his official application for citizenship. There were no criminal complaints against him. The only thing Fox previously had on him was a request for information from the American Medical Association regarding rumors that Ebell, several years earlier, might have been a facilitator of abortions. The AMA had received reports that, for some years, Ebell was arranging for the procedure to be performed at his office by an unnamed, itinerate abortionist who traveled throughout the Southwest performing the illegal operation.[296]

The complaint originated with a former nurse Ebell had fired when she refused to stop shopping at an El Paso department store owned by a Jewish family.

Sheriff Fox, like most local lawmen of the day, rarely investigated abor-tion complaints unless they involved the death of a patient or were brought by some local, big-shot bluenose. In this instance, he made a note to file and did not further respond to the AMA inquiry.

The FBI's request that his office look into the espionage charges *did* get his immediate attention. Fox and his men, along with the two local FBI agents, wasted no time in building a dossier on Dr. Ebell. To all outward appearances, the physician was living quietly and providing general medical care to lower-class, working families in El Paso and Juarez, as he had for more than a decade.

Usually dressed in a business suit, starched white shirt, tie, and felt fedora, the inconspicuous physician blended easily into the El Paso com-munity soon after coming to town. He was a bit under average height at five foot seven and weighed 160 pounds. He wore his blond hair in a close-cropped military style. His mild-mannered demeanor seemed somewhat dissonant with the three long scars on the left side of his forehead. They were combat wounds suffered as a German infantry officer in World War I.[297]

Ebell, as a foreigner out of favor with local doctors but certified for general practice, was relegated to serving a clientele comprised mostly of local Mexican Americans, Mexicans across the border in Juarez, a few working-class Anglos, and itinerants who fell ill when passing through town. In the pecking order of El Paso's medical society, this meant he was barely considered a fellow physician.

Anti-Mexican bias against both legal and illegal workers in the country reached new heights when jobs became scarce during the Depression. El Paso, with its location on the border, became one of the main centers for the United States' cruel, massive deportation policy known as the Mexican Repatriation.[298] By 1940, there were hard feelings on both sides of the border. While most local physicians would treat Anglo and Mexican patients, there remained distinct ethnic barriers. Many needy patients were shuffled off to a few doctors working on the fringe of the local medical society or across the border to Mexico-licensed doctors and native shamans.

Ebell kept his office in the heart of downtown El Paso, conveniently close to the main bridge spanning the international border. In 1939, he moved his home to a semirural area in the Lower Valley section of El Paso known as the Ysleta neighborhood. This community, a dozen miles from the heart of the city, had enjoyed recent growth when the nearby Zaragoza International Bridge to Mexico opened in 1938. But it was still a relatively isolated area. Few travelers between the United States and Mexico used the new Rio Grande crossing point, preferring the more frequented international bridges in the heart of El Paso–Juarez. In fact, travel was so light at the new bridge that the crossing often went unmonitored by either Mexican or American customs agents, making it a convenient route for a man who might not want his comings and goings too closely observed.

Had anyone made a connection between Ebell and the three-year-old Frome murders, they might have recalled that his former home was at 1518 North Kansas Street, only a few blocks from the Hotel Cortez. Even after his move to Ysleta, he kept his office on the sixth floor of the Abdou Building at 111 N. Mesa, one block from the hotel.

To make ends meet he worked part time as an assistant at the Hummel Clinical Lab, which was also located in the Abdou Building. Ebell frequently made the rounds of other El Paso doctors' offices, picking up medical specimens to be processed at the lab. To collect these patients' tests he used the lab's vehicle, which like most delivery vehicles, was clearly marked with a sign on the door, so it could be left double-parked while the courier hurried into the offices for the pickups.

Money was always a problem for a doctor allowed to practice only on the fringes of the medical community, so he was ever eager to earn extra fees for doing medical work shunned by other, more prominent physicians. An example of this less desirable practice was being available at night and on weekends to treat injured or ailing businessmen and tourists visiting at the nearby, downtown hotels.

These luxury hotels, like the Cortez where the Frome women stayed, contracted with consulting physicians to be available during normal working hours. Such appointments were with prestigious local doctors who were not eager to be on call at night or on weekends. When Nancy Frome needed a physician late in the day of her arrival at the hotel, she had to rely on the referral by someone on the staff. Ebell's home and office were both nearby.[299]

Eight years after entering the country, Wolfgang Ebell finally became a citizen of the United States, but it did not improve his financial position. His practice languished because of the clannishness of the doctors who controlled the local medical association and hospital admittance to practice. Instead of attempting to move up into the city fathers' clubs, Ebell joined the Mexican Optimist Club. He remained a somewhat embittered outsider, with limited prospects for improving his income.

So the doctor was always "in" for the extra, after-hours work shunned by his medical peers. Cash tips to carefully chosen Mexican bellhops, many of whose families he treated, ensured calls to his home or office whenever hotel guests needed attention at night or on weekends.[300]

46

By early 1941, international events overshadowed almost everything else on the front pages of the newspapers. Sheriff Fox and his select deputies were now dedicating significant time to assisting the FBI with the hush-hush surveillance in their own backyard. The only Texas Ranger assigned full time to the Frome case unexpectedly left the force to join the feds in the rapidly expanding counterespionage endeavor. In effect, the Frome murder case was stalled, with not enough new angles to justify even part-time, regular manpower.

Ranger Hugh Pharies was recruited by J. Edgar Hoover shortly after returning from his in-depth interview with Pop Frome. After completing a basic refresher course, he was assigned to spy-chasing activities in the Philadelphia area. While the young former Ranger threw himself into his new duties, he wrote Fox a somewhat apologetic letter about leaving the Frome case cold.

"To me, that will always be the most interesting case I have ever known," Pharies said. "Even here, when I handle anyone who has ever been in that section of the country, I always question them about the Frome case. I would really appreciate your keeping me posted of any important developments in the case. I had rather know just what happened out there in the desert that day than most anything I know of."[301]

Pharies suggested Fox get acquainted with a new FBI agent assigned to El Paso, with whom he had gone through training at the academy. He said he had heard through the grapevine about Fox's valuable cooperation on top-secret work of interest to Director Hoover.

After Pharies left for the federal police job, the manpower-strapped Texas Rangers did not designate a replacement. It was the first time in the almost three years since the Frome women were slain that the Rangers did not have at least one full-time investigator assigned to the case. There was no one at the El Paso Sheriff's Office on it full time either.

Sheriff Albert Anderson, who had fought so hard to have the case returned to his jurisdiction in Culberson County, never had the means to devote to it. He was forced to use his meager resources to chase cattle rustlers and miscreant drifters off his vast range. No one had ever whole-heartedly championed the investigation in the victims' hometown, at least partially due to the political intervention on behalf of Weston Frome.

WHEN FOX AND HIS MEN joined the feds to begin surveillance of the German doctor Wolfgang Ebell, the last thing on the minds of any of the newly minted, counterespionage snoops was the possibility of a connection between the spies and the murders of Hazel and Nancy Frome. The federal agents working with the local sheriff certainly had no interest in the old murders. And while Hazel and Nancy remained on the sheriff's mind, they were not on his agenda. He concentrated any spare time and resources he could muster on his new challenge — defending the national security.

In his usual, methodical approach to any investigation, Sheriff Fox set up details for around-the-clock shadowing of the suspected Nazi agent. Plainclothes detectives from his office began recording license-plate numbers of cars appearing at the doctor's suburban home. Detectives discreetly tailed the doctor as he made his rounds in the city and on his frequent trips across the border. They noted the meetings he attended and the people he visited. His office was watched. His associates were identified. As in the Frome case, Fox and his investigators quickly built a huge file on the target, and regularly supplied reports to the El Paso office of the FBI.

A persona soon emerged that was far different from that of the seemingly well-assimilated German immigrant doctor. Ebell's only previously known public activities included weekly attendance at his service-club luncheon in a downtown café and a German American social club that met at the Log Cabin Tavern, 2217 East Texas Street, for a Saturday night dance and songfest. Of late, however, Ebell had abandoned these social activities for more private gatherings in his own home. He was also observed to be spending more time in Juarez and taking frequent trips deeper into Mexico.

Soon after discovering Ebell was an active Nazi agent, the FBI learned he had been practicing the dark arts of espionage in America since at least 1933. He was either dispatched or specifically recruited to establish a major conduit between North America and Germany.

An arrested Nazi agent revealed under interrogation that Ebell was the linchpin in a Nazi transit chain from the West Coast of the United States to Germany.[302]

Ebell's bosses were the San Francisco consuls — Baron Manfred von Killinger and, later, his replacement, Captain Fritz Wiedemann, in the United States — although, from time to time, he passed items to and from the German consulates in Chicago and New Orleans. He was not to conduct covert spying himself or commit any overt acts of sabotage or propaganda. His mission required him to maintain a low profile as a respectable local doctor, so he could keep the international pipeline open between the obscure, border backwater of El Paso, Texas, and Juarez, Mexico.

In 1933, Ebell had been contacted by Abwehr agents from Mexico and ordered to activate the underground courier route that channeled military and industrial secrets gathered by spies working from German consulates in San Francisco and Los Angeles. The material was moved through El Paso to Juarez, and through Monterrey or Chihuahua City to Mexico City. Then it was moved into South America and packaged with other material for final delivery to Germany.

From that time forward, Ebell came to know and work with a large number of Nazi espionage agents and couriers, many of whom actually stayed at his home when in transit. Some agents sent from California handed off material for Ebell to keep until other agents could arrive in Juarez for the exchange. He set up drop houses across the border, where exchanges took place, and also maintained at least one drop through the General Post Office in Juarez.[303]

While not a master spy himself, Ebell had a number of German nationals working as agents, both in nearby border towns and in El Paso–Juarez, available if he needed help in carrying out his mission. It did not appear that he made assignments; rather, that he was a facilitator for spies already assigned to missions. Ebell was also a source for equipment and funds needed by agents arriving along the circuitous route from Germany to the United States. On at least one occasion after the war started in Europe, he provided a safe house for German prisoners of war who had escaped from British detention camps in Canada and made their way across the United States, en route to South America.[304]

His primary contact in Mexico was the German consul in Chihuahua

City, 235 miles south of El Paso. Consul S. Walter Schmiedehaus was the closest thing to an immediate supervisor the El Paso doctor had, although Ebell usually operated by his own wits.

Initially, Ebell had only occasionally moved material and people sent by the Abwehr at spy headquarters in Germany. As America gradually clamped down on imperial Japanese activities on the West Coast, the German consulates — and thus, Ebell — began assisting the new Axis allies by working with Japanese military intelligence.

The El Paso pipeline between the West Coast and Mexico was given additional responsibility to move information of particular interest to the Japanese to coastal cities in Mexico. Japanese merchant ships were increasingly being searched in America's western ports. Information redirected to Mexico was much less likely to be intercepted. There, German and Japanese agents gathered material to be transferred to Japanese merchant ships or, in the case of priority information, taken directly by boat to rendezvous with Japanese submarines.

The previous routine cooperation in the traffic of secret information, which had begun on November 25, 1936, with the signing of the Anti-Comintern Pact between Japan and Germany, suddenly took on a dramatic urgency. The Axis partners signed an agreement to coordinate all foreign intelligence activities in America on January 30, 1941. Of particular importance to the wicked alliance were the Nazi agents working on the West Coast, where the Japanese had a special interest in the U.S. Navy's fleet operations and the U.S. Army's coastal-defense installations.

47

A direct link between Dr. Ebell and the San Francisco consulate was proven beyond a doubt when a bungling German spy, sent on a mission from Mexico to the United States, was arrested in early 1940 by police in San Antonio, Texas, on a misdemeanor driving offense. The German quickly admitted to a stunned cop that he was on an espionage mission.

To the delight of the interrogating agents, the inept spy readily spilled the beans after only the merest suggestion that he might be hanged as a foreign agent. He knew who his contacts were to be in the States and was only too eager to name names, in order to avoid the gallows.

The captured man told the authorities that consular Juan Cran of the German legation in Monterrey had instructed him to make his way through Texas to a Dr. Wolfgang Ebell in El Paso, where he would be given more cash to get to San Francisco. Once there, he was to report directly to German consul Fritz Wiedemann for espionage assignments in the Bay Area.[305]

At about this time, another Nazi doctor-spy named Hermann F. Erben was being given sanctuary in the San Francisco consulate.[306] The German diplomats protected Erben, who was facing several international warrants. U.S. intelligence agents were waiting outside to arrest him. The FBI only later learned that Erben had been smuggled onto actor Errol Flynn's eighty-foot, blue-water luxury yacht, the *Sirocco*, and surreptitiously sailed to a Pacific seaport in Mexico.[307]

The two-way link between Ebell in El Paso and agents in Mexico was again proven by a clandestine, and at the time legally questionable, operation run by army intelligence. The military attaché at the American embassy received a tip from an informant that a powerful shortwave radio was en route from Mexico City to unknown spies in the United States. The secret Nazi radio set was being routed through a Dr. Wolfgang Ebell at a mail drop in Juarez. Thanks to this tip, the FBI was waiting and seized the equipment. The only thing Ebell and his cohorts in Mexico knew was that the radio never arrived.[308]

By then, the FBI's surveillance of Ebell in El Paso was going full throttle, with G-men assigned alongside Sheriff Fox's deputies.

With secret authorization by President Roosevelt, the bureau began to eavesdrop on telephone calls, intercept and screen mail, and even enter business offices and homes of American citizens, as well as suspected alien agents. While Ebell was a naturalized citizen, the president's mandate left some wiggle room, by stating that the clandestine telephone and mail taps and break-ins should be used only against aliens "wherever possible."

In Ebell's case, the FBI authorized Sheriff Fox to provide personnel as "confidential informants," to pose as patients or visitors at Ebell's downtown office and residence.[309]

The sheriff also sent his most trusted deputies to stage stealthy break-ins when the locations were vacant. Nothing was disturbed or removed, but important evidence of Ebell's espionage activities was found at both places. While there was not enough proof to warrant an immediate arrest, the intruding deputies were astounded by the arrogance of the doctor-spy.

The first thing a deputy noticed on entering the inner sanctum of Ebell's downtown office was a framed photograph of Adolph Hitler that appeared to have been personally autographed by the führer himself. The most important find, however, was a small metal file box containing alphabetized cards with the names, addresses, phone numbers, and notations on forty-four men and women in the immediate vicinity of El Paso and Juarez, whom Ebell had identified as Nazi sympathizers or collaborators. Some of the cards indicated "radio" by the names, and the FBI paid special attention to those. All the people on the cards had German surnames, except a few of the women, whose married names were not German.[310] However, the bureau was skeptical about such a large number of local citizens, German or not, being active espionage agents. They assumed Ebell's files contained mostly sympathizers who might be used in the future for some purpose other than spying.

The deputy, without disturbing the order of the cards, carefully copied the list for the FBI. It included bank officers and clerks, building contractors and carpenters, a bookbinder and a watchmaker, several retail merchants, and the wives of a border patrolman and a federal customs officer. The names of two known German agents and a Japanese doctor who resided in Juarez were also in the file.

Before leaving the doctor's office, the deputy also made a note that Ebell had a pistol in his desk drawer, an item not usually kept in a doctor's office. He didn't note the type of pistol in his report.

He also came across a medical device in the office that could be used to send shortwave signals. The device, labeled "Electro-Surgical-Radical-1-SW-12," was manufactured by H. G. Fischer & Company in Chicago. The FBI had already determined these shortwave devices were commonly purchased by German agents and easily converted into long-distance radios, to transmit or receive coded telegraphic messages or establish voice contact. The FBI soon learned that Ebell had purchased large numbers of these devices, as well as electrodes and electrosurgical spare parts from the Chicago manufacturer, over a period of years.[311]

Another counterespionage agent broke into Ebell's home in the El Paso suburb twelve miles east of town. This snoop found more damning evidence that the doctor was an ardent Nazi. There were numerous letters addressed to Ebell and other German names, believed to be Ebell's code names. The letters were addressed to General Delivery at the Main Post Office in Juarez, along with two residential mail drops in that city. Ebell had established clandestine communication links in Juarez and was receiving a high volume of packages and larger-sized envelopes. There were postmarks from Germany, Chile, Argentina, Brazil, and several Mexican locations, including Monterrey, Mexico City, and Chihuahua City. Through Sheriff Fox's connections in the Juarez postmaster's office, this mail was soon being monitored before delivery. Ebell's mail to both his office at the Abdou Building and his home at Route 1, Box 2360, El Paso, was likewise being scrutinized.[312]

The deputy also found a number of maps, including what appeared to be a U.S. military map of Mexico, and detailed, government topographical maps of the U.S.-Mexico border in the vicinity of West Texas and New Mexico. One of these maps featured a hand-drawn circle around the sprawling Fort Bliss Army Base on the outskirts of El Paso.

The nervous deputy-cum-burglar was careful not to move any item from its place in the home office. He focused the beam of his flashlight on a large desk. Inside one drawer was a polished wooden box. Opening the hinged lid he found a trove of unusual objects. They were not on most lists of suspicious contraband but revealed a lot about Ebell's present loyalties and longtime affiliations. In the silk-lined box were a number of Nazi medals, two well-cared-for letters, and an official-looking citation with an embossed Nazi swastika.[313] The deputy, who could read and write some German, made notes of the inscriptions on the medals. He hurriedly copied parts of the letters and citation for a more complete translation by a linguistics professor at the nearby Texas College of Mines and Metallurgy. The professor often assisted the El Paso sheriff's office with translations.

One of the letters was dated December 2, 1931, from the German "Fichte-Bund," thanking Ebell for his help in distributing propaganda material to other German organizations throughout America. The second letter, dated October 31, 1935, came from the German consulate in Chihuahua City and also thanked Ebell for assisting the fatherland. The official citation appeared to have accompanied a medal sent to Ebell for outstanding service to the Nazi cause. It was from the office of the German Minister of Foreign Affairs. It stated that the honor was being bestowed by the Nazi Party for "information from Texas" that will help Germany in the "reconstruction of the fatherland." The citation was dated October 25, 1933, which corresponded with the date on the largest medal in the box.

The deputy immediately recognized another medal. The distinctive Teutonic cross was the famed Blue Max, the highest imperial German decoration for bravery in World War I. Ebell was given the award for his outstanding bravery as an army officer in that war. He had attached the medal to a gold chain, to be worn with formal attire.

The next medal identified the bearer as a member of the German veterans' organization, the Freikorps. A membership number was on the back.

The final medal was the most interesting. It was a round, apparently sterling-silver emblem depicting a raised swastika, encircled with an inscription in German, which read, "You have conquered!" On the reverse was the name of the issuing authority — the Nazi Party — and the date, 1934.

The deputy studying the medals and other items in the doctor's home did not know the significance of what he had discovered. This last medal from the Nazi Party was a coveted recognition for services rendered to Hitler's new Third Reich. It usually came with a more tangible expression of appreciation, a specially made automatic pistol manufactured for, and bestowed with honors on, civilian members of the National Socialist Labor Party for meritorious service. The special Nazi pistol was manufactured exclusively by the Carl Walther & Sons arms factory in Germany. It was a smaller-gauge replica of the German Wehrmacht Works standard 9 mm service automatic issued as a sidearm to German military officers.[314]

The special Nazi Party version was a 7.65 mm Walther PP. It used a type of ammunition that was not available for sale in the Americas. The 7.65 mm cartridge was made in Germany by the Deutsche Waffen Aktiengesellschaft of Berlin and Düsseldorf, Germany. It could be identified by the letter *S* stamped in the base of the lead bullet, but the deputy had no way of seeing that embossed marking on the slug.

The deputy sheriff cut short his clandestine survey of the suspected spy's private study and hurriedly prepared to wrap up, before the doctor and his wife returned home. He observed that there was an automatic with Nazi symbols etched on the barrel in Ebell's desk but did not further describe the weapon in his report.[315]

48

It was during this troubled twilight of peace, in the late spring of 1941, that Sheriff Fox and the Rangers rekindled peace themselves. Perhaps the ominous threat of greater external enemies looming on the horizon put their petty differences in perspective.

Chris Fox and Texas DPS director Homer Garrison exchanged a series of friendly telephone and mail communiqués that were obviously aimed at healing the rift between the El Paso sheriff's office and the Rangers in Austin. Although they chatted about the job, and particularly the Frome case, the only hint of the sheriff's secret cooperation with the FBI was one veiled reference. Fox mentioned that he was "in the big middle of some work," not in the normal duties of a local lawman, "that made him feel as low as the bottom of the ocean."

Referring to a phone call from Garrison the previous day, Fox wrote on April 30, 1941, "I'm going to get by there [Austin] in the course of the next few days and tell you what it is all about, but until that time I want you to know how deeply I have appreciated your friendship and how much it has meant to me during these years."[316]

The sheriff and the top Ranger expressed mutual angst over the fact that the Frome murders remained unsolved. Fox wrote to Garrison,

Sometimes I become thoroughly disgusted with myself about this case, but I know in my own heart that when the answer comes I will be butting my head against a stone wall for having been so damn dumb. I cannot help but think the solution is somewhere that so far has remained untouched, and that in the final analysis it will be or should be very simple.

When you stop to think about it, there is nothing new or startling about this case. It is just one more case involving dual homicides. It has happened before and it will happen again.

Of course, I realize that many things were against us, among them the fact that Jim Milam had to be illiterate and couldn't read the sign on the car door. High winds on the day of the killing, and for days after, blew away evidence. And what wasn't blown away Sheriff Albert Anderson was unable to uncover because he was unable to keep half the population of Culberson County from assembling on the scene of the crime.

And not forgetting our mutual friend, Frank [Ranger Mills], who scared off all the Mexican help at Hotel Cortez before we could properly learn what they knew. But in fairness to Frank, none of the rest of us have shown any great skill, so I guess we should stop being so critical of him.[317]

Fox signed the letter, "Your sincerest Amigo."

Director Garrison responded a few days later, expressing his own frustration at not having solved the now three-year-old case. He didn't mention that he had no regular DPS investigator currently assigned to it.

"I, too, have the same opinions about this case that you do and very often spend much time trying to figure out some new angle," Garrison wrote. "But I always come back to the original starting point with nothing new. I am confident this case will be worked out. How or when I wish I knew. Any new information we get I assure you we will send you. It's been quite a while since this department has been graced by your presence, so we hope it will not be long before you come in the door that always has the latch string hanging on the outside for you."[318]

Just how far down the list of investigative priorities the Frome case had dropped was apparent in a series of articles written by a *Dallas Morning News* reporter named Felix McKnight. The articles recited the history of the Rangers and noted that their ranks would soon be substantially increased from thirty-one to forty-six. The reporter also noted that, while machine guns and hand grenades had been added to the Rangers' arsenal, they still hauled their trusted horses in trailers behind their V-8s. Buried on the last page of the last article was this notation: "Incidentally, the department still works unceasingly on the fiendish slayings of Mrs. Weston Frome and her daughter Nancy on the desert near Van Horn in May of 1938."[319] The actual murders had occurred in March, not May.

Nevertheless, the Rangers did assign investigators to the Frome case if they received new leads. One such incident occurred in March 1941. Rangers quickly debunked any connection to an Odessa murder case involving a .32-caliber automatic used by a disgruntled girlfriend to kill her philandering lover, a minor-league baseball player. Isabelle Messmer was a New Jersey jail escapee who fit the description of a woman seen driving the car in chase with the Frome Packard on the day Hazel and Nancy went missing. When arrested for the Odessa murder, Messmer was found to have photographs of the Frome crime scene. The Rangers eliminated the gun as a ballistic match and saw nothing unusual about the photographs, since half of Culberson County had taken snapshots at the scene where the bodies were discovered.[320]

Later that year, Sheriff Albert Anderson surprised everyone by announcing that the case had been solved with the arrest in Los Angeles of a truck driver named Charles Hatfield; his wife Bonnie, of Bakersfield; and a material witness, Mrs. Wood Butler of Mexia, Texas. Sheriff Fox somewhat skeptically reminded the press that Hatfield and his gang had been arrested and eliminated as suspects in the Frome murders years before. The flurry of erroneous headlines that ran through several months of 1941, claiming the case was solved, would disappear with a Ranger's announcement on New Year's Day 1942, that the three suspects could not be connected to the Frome killings.[321]

Fox had been contacted by an associate in Dallas, congratulating him on the solution of the case with the arrests of the Hatfields. He quickly responded that it was just another false lead among the hundreds already exhausted during the years of investigation.

"The Frome case, as it now stands, is still rather uncertain, despite this latest outburst in the papers," Chris Fox wrote Dallas postal inspector C. W. B. Long. "The Hatfields were put through the mill a month or two after the murders and were emphatically cleared by members of the Famous Texas Rangers. Unfortunately, however, no definite motive has ever been established. But as long as there are tongues in the heads of men there can be no such thing as a perfect crime."[322]

Sheriff Fox, all but giving up on the Frome case, was now deeply involved in secret national security issues. America's porous southern flank had never looked so defenseless.

49

It is not often that local lawmen are caught up in the intrigue of chasing spies, but El Paso County's strategic location on the U.S.-Mexico border placed Sheriff Fox and his deputies on the front lines of an undeclared war.

When Fox reported to the FBI the out-of-town license plates seen at Ebell's home, the federal agents often came back with matches to German-American Bund leaders or suspected Nazi agents from Chicago, Philadelphia, and several cities in New Jersey. Among these was Gerhard Wilhelm Kunze, the German-American Bund leader who, by this time, had been identified by the FBI as an active Abwehr agent. Kunze was among the most frequent visitors to the home in Ysleta, along with another top Bund official named George Froboese.[323] These two Nazi agents traveled extensively around the country and almost always ended up in El Paso.

Deputies followed discreetly, as Ebell escorted these shadowy figures across the nearby international bridge to Juarez for meetings with other Germans. Fox was under strict orders not to intercept or interfere with anything his men saw in El Paso and Juarez. The FBI found that the mere surveillance of the El Paso go-between was producing a trove of intelligence on activities of other Nazi spies from Texas to California, as well as identification of Nazi agents previously unknown to the bureau.

If Sheriff Fox hoped for a quid pro quo from FBI director Hoover, he was disappointed. On several occasions, the sheriff's suggestions that the bureau might get involved in the Frome case were gently rebuffed in notes from Hoover himself, reminding Fox that the FBI had no jurisdiction in a local murder case.

In one instance, during the spring of 1941, Fox seemed close to making a connection between the Frome murders and the subversive activities of the German doctor.

At the peak of his deputies' surveillance of the Ysleta residence and subtle questioning of the doctor's associates, Fox came across thirdhand information about a potential link between the Frome case and the spy case.

A nurse in another doctor's office was told by one of her friends who had once worked for Ebell that she had information relating to the murders. A lawman friend of Fox's knew the nurse in question.

The sheriff contacted game warden W. B. Stubblefield, a longtime resident of Ysleta, asking that the official help track down Ebell's former employee.

"I would like very much, if you can do so, to get in touch with a young lady who lives in Ysleta and works for Dr. Brown R. Randall, to help us locate Mrs. Betty Holbert, the wife of Jack Holbert," Sheriff Fox wrote.[324]

It was possible Mrs. Holbert could identify at least one of the men the Frome women were seen dancing with or talking to in Juarez, several days before their disappearance. The former Ebell employee Fox was seeking was married to a mining engineer working in Torreon, Mexico.

"Mrs. Holbert is supposed to have seen Hazel and Nancy Frome in Juarez with two men during the time immediately before their deaths," the sheriff continued. "I expected Mrs. Holbert would be coming back this way sometime this spring, but our contact has not heard from her. Could you check your source [the nurse in Ysleta] and determine how we might contact her?"

As it turned out, the game warden did not know how to reach either woman, and nothing came of this inquiry.

FAR REMOVED from the local sheriff's work watching the spy for Hoover in El Paso, FBI counterespionage operations were rapidly coming to a critical juncture. A massive amount of information that would have a profound impact on all German and Japanese subversive operations on both coasts and in the heartland had been slowly accumulated in Washington, D.C. The bureau was preparing to spring a trap.

The complex Axis spiderweb began to come unraveled prematurely when a gruesome car-pedestrian accident killed a high-level Nazi agent in New York City.[325]

Ulrich von der Osten had entered the United States at San Francisco on March 16, 1941, aboard a freighter from Hawaii. He was traveling on a Spanish passport under the name Julio Lopez Lido, as a businessman from Shanghai, China. Von der Osten immediately went from the port to the

German consulate in San Francisco, where he was greeted at the front door by none other than Captain Fritz Wiedemann himself. The FBI realized they had a high-ranking person in their sights, but the man disappeared into the diplomatic walls and was not seen leaving. He next appeared two weeks later as a corpse with a nearly severed head, after foolishly jaywalking in front of a New York City taxicab. From receipts found in his pockets, the New York police traced the dead man's tracks back to the Hotel Taft. What the cops found in his room caused them to immediately summon the FBI.

In a briefcase in the hotel room, agents found detailed sketches of defense installations under construction at the U.S. Naval Base at Pearl Harbor and the nearby U.S. Army Air Corps' Hickham Field. The work was being performed as part of a project awarded to a consortium headed by the California contractor Wilhelm Rohl.[326] A cryptic note at the bottom of the large envelope containing the professionally drawn blueprints and topographic maps read, "Our yellow friends will be very interested in this information."

With this, the bureau had rock-solid evidence of the importance of the San Francisco consulate in the scheme of things. But they did not know where, when, and from whom the copied work papers on the key Pacific defense installations originated. The spy, posing as a Spanish businessman, was likely only the courier. He had been within hours of making off to Germany with the plans.

U.S. authorities were horrified by how potentially devastating such detailed plans could be in the hands of the Axis. It was time for intelligence officials to stop watching and start busting up the spy networks.

In June 1941, agents of the Federal Bureau of Investigation swooped down on a network of three dozen German agents operating under the spymaster Frederick Joubert "Fritz" Duquesne on the East Coast. The New York–centered ring relied on dispatching its bulk stolen secrets through the German embassy. Smaller bites of intelligence were relayed by shortwave radio to submarines prowling off the East Coast. An FBI mole and German American named William Sebold had been trained as a radio operator by the Abwehr and sent to America in 1939.[327]

Over a two-year period, Nazi agents in the Duquesne ring had penetrated many of the defense-related American companies in the Northeast. Duquesne had personally secured specifications of a new aerial bomb developed for the war department at a former DuPont plant in Wilmington, Delaware. It was the second major espionage ring to be busted by the FBI, following the 1938 cracking of the Guenther Gustav Rumrich spy ring. In the Rumrich case, Nazi spy handler Wiedemann had specifically directed espionage efforts against DuPont's spin-off munitions and explosive businesses, the Atlas and Hercules Powder companies.

When all members of the Duquesne gang were finally rounded up across New York, New Jersey, and Illinois and charged with espionage, FBI director Hoover, in a rare radio interview with Walter Winchell, called the bust "the greatest spy roundup in U.S. history."[328] The arrests provided the proof needed to shut down the vital links that enabled the networks to operate. Both the Duquesne and Rumrich spy rings operated with the full support of the German consulates established in American cities, coast to coast.

Almost simultaneously with the bust-up of the huge East Coast spy ring, the bureau provided intelligence to President Roosevelt that justified a dramatic open assault on all Nazi spy networks operating across the United States.

The president ordered the U.S. State Department to cancel diplomatic cover for all German consulates on June 16, 1941, citing "activities of an improper and unwarranted character."[329] All German personnel from these twenty-four spy centers were ordered out of the country by July 10.

Cutting off the consulates meant the Germans lost their main source of cover for agents and method for conveying secrets out of the country, and the Japanese lost their only source of intelligence on America's West Coast defenses. It also immediately ended the funding sources for the rest of the spy rings still undetected or still allowed by the FBI to keep operating under ever closer scrutiny.

The FBI had, by this time, gathered enough intelligence on the illegal activities of the German spy network operating out of San Francisco to tip a *New York Times* reporter that Consul Wiedemann, in his short tenure, had paid out more than five million dollars to Nazi agents operating in the western United States.[330]

Hitler's personal friend and former army captain Fritz Wiedemann and the entire entourage of the German consulates in San Francisco and Los Angeles, as well as other well-placed German business executives, were booted out of the country. The German diplomatic personnel were not exactly placed under arrest, but they were assembled in the San Francisco consulate building to await the next Axis-friendly ship out of the United States. State and local police, along with federal agents, massed outside the building under the pretext of providing protection from angry Americans for the Germans, as well as a few Italians and some Japanese citizens inside.

Among those high-ranking Germans awaiting ouster behind the diplomatic shield was Werner Plack, the Hollywood wine salesman who had worked so diligently a few years earlier to insinuate himself into the high-rolling circles of U.S. defense contractors with partying headquarters at the Biltmore Hotel.

Upon arrival of the first Japanese ship at San Francisco, Wiedemann and the rest were rounded up under heavy guard and driven in a caravan to the port. The Japanese steamer was bound for Tokyo. The debonair spymaster would be assigned to another hornet's nest of espionage, but with far fewer comforts than his San Francisco posting. Wiedemann was named consul at Shanghai, where he was placed in charge of intelligence coordination between Berlin and the Imperial Japanese Army occupying China.

With the deportation of German diplomats and the FBI bust-up of the New York ring, the obscure border outpost run by the German doctor Ebell became the central and last asset for the few remaining Nazi operators in North America. The main funding source had dried up with the consulates closing, and those agents in the tattered networks went into panic mode. Ebell and his henchmen were still unaware they were under round-the-clock surveillance by the FBI and Sheriff Fox's men and their counterparts in Chicago, Philadelphia, and — oddly enough — a small town in New England.

Anastase Vonsiatsky, a member of the Ebell cabal, maintained his headquarters at Thompson, Connecticut, and it, too, was now under twenty-four-hour watch.

Meanwhile, although not a target of the FBI's grand purge of Nazi spies, one of Vonsiatsky's former White Russian Fascist club members was caught up in the bureau's house cleaning as well. That man was Romano Trotsky.

Any espionage ventures he might have been involved in were nipped in the bud by FBI agents. Trotsky, who had recently been run out of California after serving a monthlong jail sentence for illegal practice of medicine, was under surveillance as a potential spy. He had temporarily changed his professional disguise and now operated as an equestrian instructor.

The Bureau of Investigation of the American Medical Association was also trying to have the phony doctor declared a habitual criminal and bring him to trial in cases still pending against him in other states. Most of those cases involved practicing without a license and performing illegal abortions.[331]

Trotsky, operating under the false front as Prince Alexis N. Romanoff, told his landlady that he was being pursued for extermination by Soviet agents. He failed to return to his boarding house one evening in early March 1941.

On March 15, a self-styled Russian prince showed up in Tijuana, Mexico, dragging a two-foot-long chain attached to him by handcuffs. He told Mexican authorities he had been kidnapped in Reno a week earlier and taken to the desert in Mexico to be killed. He claimed he had escaped.

The Mexicans, who did not want anything to do with this weirdo, dumped him off with U.S. immigration authorities at Chula Vista, California. The FBI quickly determined that the ersatz Russian royal was actually the notorious con man best known by the name Romano Trotsky.

As usual, the man was ready with a fantastic tale of intrigue, including a dramatic account of his kidnapping.

He claimed he had been lured to the horse stables early one morning by a stranger who wanted to have his horse boarded there. Instead, the stranger and another man pulled a gun on him, put it to his head, and forced him onto the back floorboard of their car. A lengthy ordeal ensued, in which he was forced to live on slices of oranges fed to him one piece at a time. He said the Soviet agents forced him to shave his Van Dyke beard and took him to Mexico.

"If I should attempt to do anything or let out a peep they said they would blow my brains out," Trotsky told the incredulous border patrol agents.[332] He said when the kidnappers had a change of heart about shooting him, they left him chained in the desert to die, without food or water. He was, however, able to get to his feet and wandered through the desert until he saw the lights of Tijuana.

No one believed his story this time. He was transferred to a federal lockup in San Diego, pending transfer to Nevada authorities to stand trial on remaining charges of illegal medical practice. While his wild tale was discredited on the spot, no one thought to further investigate what his real mission in Mexico was. The fact that he had been under surveillance as a potential espionage agent did not come up. The U.S. Justice Department also had charges of repeated illegal entry into the United States pending against him. The Nevada authorities gladly turned him over to the feds for trial on those charges.

On June 17, 1941, a federal jury in the Southern District of California convicted Trotsky of illegal entry and sentenced him to two years in federal prison. He was transferred to the McNeil Island prison near Seattle to begin serving the sentence on June 26, with no provision for early release. From all available records, the criminal career of the man most commonly known as Trotsky was effectively ended.[333]

50

The Frome murder investigation suffered another major setback in the summer of 1941, one that almost guaranteed the case would not be solved. El Paso sheriff Chris P. Fox suddenly gave up his illustrious career in law enforcement. With that, Texas lost one of its most progressive and effective lawmen. But the victims Nancy and Hazel Frome lost even more — the most devoted remaining advocate for justice in their cruel murders.

Even though the veteran sheriff had been removed from the official coordinating role in the case, he had remained a behind-the-scenes force in keeping the investigation alive, right up until the day he announced his resignation.

He quit law enforcement to assume one of the most influential, paid leadership positions available in his hometown. El Paso civic leaders unexpectedly offered him the job of executive vice president and general manager of the El Paso Chamber of Commerce. In the day, that high-paying post was one of the most influential positions any city had to offer someone not born to wealth and privilege.

While it appeared Fox made his decision quickly, his first letter to a fellow lawman on the subject revealed his personal struggle.

"You can well realize that it was a most difficult decision for me to make, that of leaving the world of police fraternity and engaging again in business life," Fox wrote to FBI director Hoover. "My years as a police officer have been most happy, and if I have reached any degree of competency or success, it has been as a result of the untiring and devoted efforts and cooperation on the part of my friends, . . . my friends naturally being brother police officers. Although I may be leaving this particular 'game' I will always remain a 'copper' at heart," Fox concluded. He signed it, as usual, "Your Amigo."[334]

A second letter about his major career change lamented its effect on the Frome investigation. He wrote to one of his favorite former Texas Rangers, Hugh J. Pharies, now an FBI agent working counterespionage in

Philadelphia: "The Frome case is just about in the same spot it was when you left months ago. I am still vitally interested in that case. I know you are also, and you may rest assured that, should anything develop of interest, I will advise you at once."[335]

He attempted to justify his decision to leave law enforcement in his letter to the younger career lawman. "The Board of Directors of the El Paso Chamber of Commerce honored me by tendering this position," Fox wrote. He explained that he accepted the job for personal, financial, and family reasons. "I enjoyed my years as a police officer greatly, because I not only was able to get a little work done, but also made many friends and enjoyed associations that can only come to those who make a career in law enforcement."

Without being specific, the letter alluded to the clandestine work his office was doing for the FBI in the spy case and assured the agent that his successor would continue that work.

The ex-sheriff was also keenly aware of the possibility of America becoming ensnared by the rapidly spreading war in Europe. In a letter to Herbert S. Bursley, a friend and the consul in charge of the antismuggling division of the U.S. State Department, Fox wrote, "I can only say it looks inevitable now that we are going to have to nail this fellow Hitler's ears back."[336]

Sheriff Fox and his deputies were, of course, already involved in that effort in their round-the-clock surveillance of the borderland Nazi spy network.

With the abrupt and unexpected ouster of German consuls and the effective isolation of the German embassy in Washington, D.C., the remaining Nazi spies in North America were adrift — cut off from leadership, funds, and secure travel arrangements.

The closing of the spy headquarters in the German consulate in Chicago under the direct control of Consul Krause Wichmann virtually shut down all spy operations in the industrial Midwest.[337] The last major Nazi operations on the East Coast had been smashed by FBI arrests in the huge Duquesne spy sweep.

Only the thin pipeline into and out of the country through El Paso, Texas, remained open. The importance of Wolfgang Ebell's operation greatly increased. German espionage operators and their White Russian and Ukrainian Fascist allies desperately clung to this last source for moving their trove of stolen secrets. More importantly, the Nazi pipeline through El Paso was rapidly becoming their only escape hatch, as American G-men closed the trap. Nazi agents still at large realized they needed to make plans to leave the country.

War with America looked inevitable. Hitler's legions swung the seemingly invincible Nazi war machine from conquered western Europe to the East, in the massive invasion of the Soviet Union called Operation Barbarossa, on June 22, 1941.

But while Nazis were celebrating Hitler's success in Europe, things were not going well for the few remaining German spies operating in the Americas. The FBI's tightening encirclement prompted a second clandestine gathering of Fascist spy leaders at the Bismarck Hotel in Chicago, in early July. This meeting was called by the Russian Fascist leader Anastase Vonsiatsky, after a telephone conference with the free-ranging Abwehr agent Gerhard Kunze. The frantic telephone call to the Russian's fortified compound on his wealthy wife's estate at Thompson, Connecticut, was monitored by the FBI. The G-men had devised an even bolder scheme than wiretaps to find out what the Nazi agents were planning.

Vonsiatsky called his Midwest contact man, the Chicago Bund leader and German spy Otto Willumeit, to make arrangements for a meeting in late July.

Around the same time, another of Vonsiatsky's contacts, a highly respected Lutheran minister in Philadelphia named Kurt E. B. Molzahn, called the Russian to make an important introduction. Molzahn told Vonsiatsky that a well-connected Nazi agent from South America had just arrived in the area and needed to meet with him. Vonsiatsky's arrogance would not allow him to decline such a request. He invited the new spy, an Eastern Orthodox priest named Aleksi Pelypenko, to his headquarters. Even better, from the Fascist leader's point of view, Father Pelypenko, who claimed to have been sent to the United States directly from a top Nazi official in Argentina, was a native Ukrainian and spoke Vonsiatsky's beloved Russian tongue, as well as German and several other East European languages.

Reverend Molzahn, a forty-six-year-old minister who had served the Old Zion Lutheran congregation in the City of Brotherly Love since 1929, was actually a former German army officer, a dedicated admirer of the Fascist cause, and active facilitator for the German embassy in Washington, D.C.[338]

His brother-in-law was the head of the Gestapo in the German province of Schleswig-Holstein. The reverend had run any number of errands between the German diplomats and their American Bund and White Russian allies. Vonsiatsky had no reason to suspect anything different when Father Pelypenko was introduced by an equally unsuspecting Reverend Molzahn. But there *was* a difference. Father Pelypenko was a cleverly placed, confidential informant for the FBI.[339]

Vonsiatsky was so taken with the Ukrainian priest's radical zeal that he invited him to attend the emergency meeting in Chicago.

Before going to Chicago, Count Vonsiatsky drove to San Francisco with a large cache of secret documents on naval defense installations in Alaska that his Ukrainian Fascist agents had gathered. He was to deliver the material to a Japanese agent named Madam Takita, arriving on the freighter *Tatuta Maru*. But authorities refused to allow the ship to enter the U.S. port. Since the German consulate had already been closed down, there was no place to drop his valuable cargo. Vonsiatsky returned east with the illicit booty in his car, undelivered. He stopped at Chicago for the meeting.

The meeting at the Bismarck Hotel had been called primarily to develop plans for the last remaining Nazi spies to escape from the United States. A secondary, but urgent, purpose was to address the critical money shortages created by the closing of the pipelines through the consulates.

Willumeit, Vonsiatsky, and Kunze were already at the hotel when the FBI double agent, Pelypenko, arrived. They were joined by Wolfgang Ebell, who arrived in Chicago by train from El Paso.[340]

Pelypenko got an earful for the FBI, which also had agents listening in from an adjoining room at the Bismarck. As with the previous Chicago meeting, the FBI had bugged the meeting room well before the spies convened.

After hearing Kunze's lament about the shortage of money, the Russian count said he would provide emergency funding for a last-ditch effort to gather military intelligence on naval defense installations, which the Japanese had been urgently requesting. He offered to give additional funds for Kunze and Willumeit to travel into Mexico, where they could rendezvous with a Japanese submarine with the bundle of intelligence material already gathered by the Russian Fascist agents on the coast. The trip would also present the opportunity for the German agents to gather new information while en route. The funds were to pay for a whirlwind tour of specific port and air defenses around Puget Sound, San Francisco Bay, and others along the Pacific coast. In addition to taking photographs of any changes being made to defense installations, the agents would gather up all intelligence still in the hands of spies they would contact on this trip.

Kunze announced he was not going to return to the United States from Mexico but intended to join his wife, who was now living with her family in Germany, and remain there. He planned to renounce his American citizenship and become a citizen of Germany.

Vonsiatsky gave Kunze an envelope containing $2,800 in cash. He told the group gathered in the hotel room that there would be more to come from his wife's sizable inheritance, if needed later.[341]

In return for the money, Vonsiatsky asked Kunze to report his assistance to the Nazi bosses upon his return to Germany. As he took his leave, the Russian Fascist said he hoped to receive a top leadership position in Russia after the German armies annihilated Stalin's Soviets.

The FBI made no arrests at the time, perhaps hoping, if they waited, to root out the last remaining members of the spy network as the two agents toured the West.

51

The pressure was now on the remaining cohort of spies to shut down operations in the United States and start making good on escape plans. Kunze informed Ebell that he and Willumeit would conclude the final, grand tour of the western states in El Paso. Once they arrived, they would use the El Paso pipeline to smuggle their trove of secrets and themselves into Mexico and, finally, back to the fatherland.

The trip took on new urgency when, in rapid order, President Roosevelt made moves that appeared to be propelling the country toward war. The day Kunze and Willumeit set out on the last spying expedition, U.S. troops were debarking at ports in Danish Iceland and Greenland, at the invitation of local government officials, despite the fact that the Germans occupying Copenhagen ruled under a puppet Nazi government.

On the same day Japan took Indochina from the Vichy French, the American president announced an embargo on all U.S. oil and petroleum products to Japan.

The next day, August 1, Roosevelt declared gasoline rationing for the entire United States, a serious hardship for anyone trying to traverse the vast stretches of West Texas from the isolated city of El Paso.

Still, many American leaders did not believe Hitler's aggression in Europe and Emperor Hirohito's aggression in Asia threatened the national interest, or that it justified getting the country into the fight. Charles Lindbergh thundered at an America First rally that "the British, the Jewish, and Roosevelt" were all "pressing the country toward war."[342]

Mass deportation of German Jews to concentration camps in Poland began shortly thereafter, but it would still be some time before Americans acknowledged these deportations were occurring.

Kunze and Willumeit surreptitiously continued the grand espionage tour of the West Coast into the autumn, unhindered and unnoticed by existing security around the military bases. The spies had quickly lost their FBI tails after leaving Chicago and dropped completely out of sight.

Ebell, who had returned to El Paso after the Chicago meeting, had, to all appearances, settled back into the normal routine of a hometown doctor. He even paid a visit to the El Paso FBI office, on the pretext of inquiring whether or not it was all right for him, as a German American, to make charitable contributions to Germany at the time.[343] Ebell was boldly testing the waters to see if he or his group had attracted the feds' attention. The brazenness of the Kunze-Vonsiatsky-Ebell spy clique never failed to astound the FBI agents directly involved in tracking them.

The men in this last vestige of a spy cell ridiculed the U.S. counterespionage efforts and held them in the highest disdain. Perhaps not without reason, since there had been no move by Hoover's men to arrest any of them. They figured that they, too, would have already been arrested if the operation was compromised.

The FBI special agent in charge (SAC) of the El Paso office was Delf A. "Jelly" Bryce. He wanted to go ahead and pick up the arrogant doctor, but the Justice Department felt the case for espionage was still too weak to authorize the arrest of an American citizen.[344]

Bryce feared the spy might try to make a run for it. The local deputies assisting the bureau had come across information that Ebell was telling some of his patients they might soon have to find another doctor, as he was anticipating an extended trip away from the area in the not-too-distant future. The Justice Department attorney advised SAC Bryce to try to get the sheriff's office to arrest Ebell on some local charge, if it appeared he was at risk of fleeing into Mexico before a proper case for espionage could be compiled against him.

Prior to losing contact with Willumeit and Kunze, FBI agents had learned of growing tensions between them. The touring pair did not get along well from the beginning. Willumeit, an educated and imperious sort, loathed the crude former truck driver who had risen to the top of the Bund and held a higher rank with the Abwehr masters in Germany.

"Kunze and Dr. Willumeit, during the trip, are not getting along amiably together," an FBI agent reported. "The principal cause of the friction between the two men is the fact that Kunze insisted on mixing love affairs into the official business with which they were concerned."[345]

Despite their petty rifts, they finished the mission. On November 8, 1941, at 7:00 p.m., a 1940 Ford sedan bearing New York license plate number C9246 pulled up to Ebell's residence with three road-weary occupants. The men entered Ebell's home carrying several suitcases. An El Paso deputy sheriff on watch called the local FBI office to report the car and its license number, which they soon determined was registered to Kunze.[346] From the deputy's description of the men, the Abwehr agent Kunze and Chicago Bund leader Willumeit were quickly identified. The third man, a rough-looking character with several days' growth of beard, was not immediately known.[347] He was obviously a German agent, picked up somewhere on the West Coast.

Later, the deputy, joined by FBI agents, watched as Willumeit stormed out of the doctor's house when an El Paso taxi cab arrived. One of the agents followed the cab, which delivered Willumeit to the downtown station to catch a train headed for Chicago. The unidentified third man was picked up by a car with a Mexico license plate. Another agent followed it as far as the international bridge, where it drove off into Mexico. That left Ebell and Kunze at the Ysleta residence.

Shortly after, Ebell and Kunze loaded several suitcases into the backseat of the doctor's sedan. Then an odd thing happened. Ebell opened the car trunk, Kunze climbed in, and Ebell slammed it closed. He drove with his special cargo across the Zaragoza Bridge into Mexico. Incredibly, no one stopped Ebell as he drove slowly past the customs station at the south end of the bridge, despite prior information that the spies were about to bolt to Mexico with what had to be a large quantity of defense and industrial secrets.

FBI agents following at a safe distance crossed into Mexico behind the doctor's vehicle. The car stopped on a deserted side road at the outskirts of Juarez, where Ebell opened the trunk to let Kunze join him in the front seat of the sedan.

The FBI tail followed Ebell and Kunze to a German brewery in Juarez where another known Nazi agent named Fernando Goeldner joined them.[348] They held a lengthy meeting, with several other suspected agents arriving on the scene. Following the meeting, Ebell, Kunze, and Goeldner left in Ebell's car and drove to Chihuahua City. Agents tailing the car had trouble staying out of sight during the drive of more than two hundred miles across the sometimes flat, treeless desert.

Once in Chihuahua City, the spies drove straight to the German consulate, where they were greeted and housed by Consul General Walter Schmiedehaus. FBI agents and their Mexican federal counterparts observed a flurry of activity at the consulate for the next several days. Then Ebell and Kunze left the diplomatic sanctuary for another road trip, this time driving to a small town a few kilometers from Vera Cruz on the Gulf of Mexico. Throughout this activity, the observing agents noticed that the spies from North America were lugging around a lot of heavy baggage, which the feds assumed was more than just their personal clothing.[349] Ebell and Kunze then split up, with Kunze taking a train to Mexico City and the doctor driving back alone toward El Paso.

A few days later, FBI monitors intercepted and copied an airmail letter from Kunze in Mexico City to German agent Goeldner in Juarez. "My Dear Ferinand [sic], All your mail arrived and I thank you and Wolfgang heartily for your trouble. The soap melted, as was to be expected under the circumstances. Nevertheless, I am glad and grateful to be enjoying gracious hospitality."[350]

Kunze thought he had slipped undetected into Mexico and began openly to make arrangements for his final escape. Not so openly, German agents in Mexico communicated with a Japanese submarine cruising off the Pacific coast, to arrange for the agent's final getaway with the valuable collection of what was later learned to be U.S. defense-installation films and other intelligence data.

Kunze wrote, "I have not yet heard of the Yankees knowing that I have been out of the country. Caution is demanded. In the next few days I expect to be obliged to call upon your friendly assistance once more in correspondence matters. Until then heartiest greeting to you, Wolfgang, and his family. Heil Hitler! Your Wilhelm K."[351]

Ebell returned from delivering his human cargo and intelligence treasures to Mexico. Since no arrest had been made, he assumed his pipeline from the United States to Mexico had proved, once again, to be fully effective.

The Nazi physician-spy arrived back in El Paso on November 28, 1941.

52

On Sunday morning, December 7, 1941, Americans painfully learned what the rest of the world already knew: ignoring tyrants would not make them go away.

A goodly number of the churchgoing residents of El Paso heard that the Japanese were bombing the U.S. naval base at Pearl Harbor, Hawaii, from broadcasts on their car radios while driving home from Sunday services. The city's largest radio news station, KROD, owned by the *El Paso Times* publisher Dorrance D. Roderick, broke into a local minister's regular sermon to air the CBS news bulletin at 12:25 p.m. mountain standard time. An Associated Press bulletin was dispatched on the newswires at the city's two daily newspapers three minutes earlier. Within minutes, most affiliated radio stations across the country had suspended normal broadcasts to air live accounts of the Japanese air raids.

Mada McMakin, the still-grieving sister and daughter of the Frome victims, heard the terrifying news at around 11:30 p.m. Pacific time. By then, many of the great battleships and cruisers of the fleet were already aflame or in smoldering ruins, sunk in the shallow waters. But it was not the Pearl Harbor bulletins that agonized Mada the most. It was the follow-up bulletins that a similar attack was underway against U.S. bases around Manila Bay in the Philippines. Mada, now living near her father in California, had good reason, at least temporarily, to forget her grief over the still-unsolved murders. Her husband, Captain Benjamin McMakin, had recently assumed command of Company F, First Separate Marine Battalion at Cavite Sangley Point Naval Station, near the entrance to Manila Bay.[352]

Within days, the War Department was canceling contracts with civilian construction firms and mobilizing a force of one hundred thousand Seabees that would take over most defense construction throughout the Pacific Theater of War. The volunteers who joined these battalions came from the ranks of the American construction industry; many were too old to serve in regular combat units.

These volunteers represented only a small number of the Americans who immediately began to enlist in all branches of service. The ranks of local U.S. law enforcement agencies, including the Texas Rangers and the El Paso Sheriff's Office, were nearly decimated by the flight of their youngest officers to the recruiting stations.

Chris P. Fox's son, Chris junior, was among those hundreds of thousands of volunteers. He took a leave from his engineering position with a West Texas oil company to accept a commission as an army infantry officer. The former sheriff told friends he would have joined up, too, if he weren't so old. He had to settle for the less heroic, but critically important, position as director of the El Paso region selective service, where he was to spend the rest of the war as volunteer head of the civilian draft board.

PATRIOTIC AMERICANS were not the only ones shocked by the Japanese attack on Pearl Harbor. The Abwehr spy Gerhard Kunze was caught by surprise as well. After spending some time in Mexico City with Nazi agents, he had been smuggled to the Pacific coast of Mexico, where he was to make connection with a Japanese submarine.

The expected submarine never showed up, probably because the U.S. Navy and Coast Guard immediately extended patrols down the coast into Mexican waters. Kunze was stranded in Mexico with his illicit loot. The day after the Pearl Harbor attack, he penned a letter to his co-conspirator and benefactor, Wolfgang Ebell, in El Paso. That letter was seized at the drop box being monitored by the FBI in Juarez.

The content of the letter, which began "Dear Wolf," was both philosophical and urgent: "Roosevelt has the war at last. It will cost him his head. The unexpected declaration of war has made my trip to Japan late. I will have to keep going. Please send the enclosed letter by Air Mail from El Paso after you have read it. I want you to scratch out your return address. Be very careful when you bring this letter over the border. If a reply comes, please ship money-order from Juarez in Kurt's [unknown co-conspirator] name to Mexico City. He will then keep on forwarding the thing. Heil Hitler! Your Wilhelm K."[353]

The enclosed letter, also carefully opened and read by agents, was addressed to Anastase Vonsiatsky at Thompson, Connecticut. Kunze had addressed the Russian Fascist as "My dear Andreievish!" The letter to Vonsiatsky read,

Roosevelt finally has what he thinks he wanted, but before long he will have "it" in the neck. If the Japanese war had waited a few weeks more, I'd have been in Japan! As it is, I shall have gone on in another direction by the time this letter reaches you.

The Atlantic crossing by air, which I originally had in mind, would cost $2,600 more than I have now and would require months of waiting. Another method of travel, the only one left open, will require about $1,000 more than I have. There can be no going back for me anymore, and the farther away I go, the more difficult it will become to send me money. Please send what you can to: "Dr. Wolfgang Ebell at 111 N. Mesa, El Paso, Texas."

He is my very good friend and I have asked him to forward money or mail intended for me to another address (please do not use my name on money orders or letters, but only his). Do not write much, as his mail may be censored. I am being very careful with my money and still have about two-thirds of the travel sum I originally took along. I shall certainly save what I can of whatever money you send me. Your Wilhelm Gerhardevich.[354]

The FBI copied the letters and put them back in Ebell's box. They were picked up the next day by another agent working for Ebell and delivered over the border to the doctor. Kunze and his protectors in Mexico were being squeezed by the Mexican federal police, who were finally working closely with FBI agents stationed in key locations south of the border. The Germans' financial pipelines for espionage activities in North America were choked off in Central America, as they had been a few weeks earlier in the United States. Without the money from Berlin, the Nazi agents quickly discovered their Mexican hosts were not so hospitable after all.

Kunze made his way to the Gulf Coast of southern Mexico after hiding out for a time at the ranch of a German Mexican family. He arrived in the fishing village of Boca del Rio, just south of Vera Cruz, and began preparing to escape Mexico by surface craft. Using forged papers provided by the German embassy in Mexico under the name Alfonso Graf Cabiebes, he acquired a twenty-five-foot launch.[355] The spy eluded the Mexican agents tailing him for the FBI and dropped completely out of sight while stocking the small motor launch with gasoline, canned food, and water for an extended sea voyage. During this time he again tried to make arrangements to be picked up, far off shore in the Gulf of Mexico, by one of the handful of German U-boats that were harassing American shipping in the area. But he was prepared to cross the Pacific Ocean to the Azores in the small motor launch if necessary.

Meanwhile, Ebell was less fortunate in slipping across the border into Mexico, using the pipeline he so successfully ran for years. Hitler had followed Japan's declaration of war two days after Pearl Harbor by declaring Germany to be at war with the United States as well. Suspected German spies, even those with U.S. citizenship, were suddenly classified as enemy agents and, for the first time, became completely legal targets of American wrath.

The U.S.-Mexico border was immediately closed at all regular crossing points, from the Pacific Ocean to the Gulf of Mexico.

Ebell's escape route was blocked by FBI agents and El Paso deputies. Within hours after the attack on Pearl Harbor, the U.S.-Mexico border, all along the Rio Grande in the El Paso area, was sealed by horse-mounted soldiers from nearby Fort Bliss.

Appropriately, the uniformed and armed riders were a reassuring vestige of the Old West for anxious citizens who spotted them patrolling for miles in all directions from El Paso. These patrols, supplied by the First Cavalry Division, were the last horse-mounted troops ever used by the U.S. Army.[356]

53

Chris Fox, who had ruefully left law enforcement only a few months before U.S. entry into the war, was undoubtedly chomping at the bit to get back into the action. He even tried to join the Texas Department of Public Safety in any capacity as a peace officer, without pay, for the duration of the war.

Though no longer at the center of the action, Fox, as always, stepped up when he recognized a need. As chairman of the El Paso regional draft board and sponsor of war-bond drives, he served as one of the top civilian leaders supporting the war effort on the border.

Ironically, at the same time he was feeling regret over leaving the sheriff's office, he received an important communiqué from a former colleague, suggesting a possible connection between the current counterespionage cases and the unsolved Frome murders.

The arrest of a suspected German spy in California led to a curious bit of intelligence. Fox's old friend, Division Chief C. H. Stone of the California Bureau of Investigation (CBI), called from Sacramento. The California crime bureau was assisting the FBI in keeping track of suspected Nazi agents. The CBI had long been one of the state agencies asked to cooperate most closely with the bureau. That cooperation went back a long way. The modern criminal identification method adopted by the FBI had been designed by the California agency and expanded to a nationwide system by J. Edgar Hoover's men.

When the German spy was arrested shortly after the Pearl Harbor attack, Chief Stone was informed by one of his detectives that the suspect was trying to make a deal with a bit of information on the Frome case. The man had heard secondhand talk about an operation that had gone awry several years earlier in El Paso, requiring the kidnap and murder of a bellhop. The story was that the bellhop had provided special services to the Frome women during their stay at the Hotel Cortez, in the days prior to their disappearance and murder in the desert. The employee, who was not named by the informant, had allegedly been grabbed by Nazi agents, taken into Mexico, and killed.

Fox and his deputies had searched for such a hotel employee shortly after the murders and actually picked up similar rumors about the possibility of foul play. Because they were unable to run it down, the ex-sheriff now expressed some doubt about the story.

"The information relative to the porter at the Hotel Cortez having been taken out into the weeds, hijacked, and killed is somewhat far-fetched," Fox wrote, in response to his old friend. "By that I mean there was never any record presented that leads us to believe that such was the case."[357]

But he was also quick to leave the possibility open. "However, there are many people working at the Hotel Cortez and many of them naturally worked there at the time Hazel and Nancy Frome stayed there," he wrote. "It is possible that some porter, busboy, or some other male employee of the place who worked in a position that did not make him conspicuous has been killed. His killing could have been accomplished after he had left the employ of the hotel, or even while he was working there for that matter, and no one need have known of his having been done away with. I want to pass this information on to Captain Stanley Shea of the Sheriff's Office and see that he works on it and checks carefully. Either he or I will advise you as to the outcome of this investigation."[358]

No record of the disposition of this tip ever appeared in the Sheriff's Office Case File 9628. But during the chaotic first days following the attack on Pearl Harbor, law enforcement officers at all levels of local, state, and federal government were forced to abandon many leads in pending criminal cases. Certainly it would be understandable that an obscure new lead in a long-cold case would be subsumed by the national crisis.

The sudden drain of able-bodied officers from law enforcement agencies in Texas, as elsewhere, meant that many unsolved cases were moved to the back burner — most never to be actively reopened.[359]

It became nearly impossible for law enforcement agencies to allocate scarce manpower and other resources to anything except major, current criminal cases. A three-year-old unsolved homicide case, even one as sensational and brutal as the murders of Hazel and Nancy Frome, was no longer on anyone's list of priorities.

From the moment America was forced into the war, attitudes changed as well, with daily news of overwhelming death and destruction becoming nearly commonplace. At a time when all the country's resources were shifted to the life-and-death struggle to win World War II, genocide would soon supersede homicide in the American lexicon. The violent deaths of two California women in the desert near El Paso would become an infinitesimal statistic.

54

As days passed after the Japanese surprise attack without any sign that he was suspected of spying, the smug Wolfgang Ebell must have enjoyed the thought that the inept Americans were not aware of his still-intact underground railroad.

Behind the scenes, the Nazi doctor was very much in the crosshairs of the FBI, even though his status as a naturalized citizen had delayed a move against his operation. It was ten days after the attack before the Justice Department approved the local FBI agent's request for an arrest warrant. Far from inept, special agent Jelly Bryce, heading the El Paso FBI team, had requested the warrant the day after Pearl Harbor, as evidence mounted that the spy might be planning to flee. In the interim, Ebell and key members of his ring in El Paso and across the border in Juarez had been under constant watch while the legal issues were sorted out.

Finally, a federal arrest warrant charging the Nazi doctor with espionage came through.

"A warrant was issued this morning [by the Justice Department] for the arrest of Dr. Wolfgang Ebell," FBI legal counsel D. M. Ladd reported in a memo to his supervisor, E. A. Tamm, in Washington.[360] Agent Bryce was notified by phone on December 17 that he was cleared to make the arrest of the El Paso master spy and to search and seize evidence at the doctor's home and office.

"Bryce inquired as to what publicity could be given out concerning the matter at this time, and I told him to give only a brief statement based on limited facts," the FBI lawyer wrote.

The telephoned authorization for the arrest was followed immediately by a confidential teletype confirmation from the FBI office in El Paso to Director J. Edgar Hoover. It stated, in part, "This subject [Ebell] is beyond any doubt the leading Nazi agent in this division, and plans are being made to cause his apprehension at his home near El Paso tonight."[361]

On Wednesday night, ten days after the Japanese sneak attack, the FBI and local authorities, including deputies from the El Paso sheriff's office, surrounded Ebell's house in the quiet Rio Grande River valley suburb of Ysleta. At exactly 9:00 p.m., the net closed when lawmen kicked in the front door of the doctor's modest home.

The raiders were perhaps a bit more zealous than necessary in their enforcement of the warrant. Graphic images of the smoldering U.S. fleet were freshly impressed upon their minds by the front-page photographs that were saturating the newspapers as they were finally allowed to take action. The Axis spies, traitors, and sympathizers still in the country in the immediate aftermath of Pearl Harbor bore the brunt of American fury for their henchmen who had already fled.

As G-men swarmed the residence, other agents and deputies broke into the doctor's downtown office on the sixth floor of the Abdou Building, a block away from the ritzy Hotel Cortez. Military maps, Nazi medals, and two guns were seized as evidence. The feds knew what they would find in Ebell's home and office because the sheriff's deputies had already catalogued these items in stealthy break-ins, several months earlier. The Nazi doctor's arrogance had prevented him from disposing of the incriminating cache of records and correspondence with his spymasters that he had amassed over the years.

Faced with the ferocity of the angry arresting officers, the doctor, who had once boasted, "Hitler will rule the world," meekly surrendered, without so much as a whimper of protest.

A Japanese doctor named Sadakayu Furugochi was also arrested by the FBI in El Paso that night. He was accused only of being in contact with enemy agents and was not formally linked to the Ebell ring.[362]

Several Nazi agents in Mexico who had been observed in prior contacts with Ebell were arrested by Mexican authorities. When word spread of the roundup, other agents and their lackeys fled deeper into Mexico, attempting to escape to South America. Fernando Goeldner, the chief Juarez contact who had helped the fleeing Abwehr agent Kunze, and whose name the German so badly botched in several letters as "Ferinand," was one of the successful escapees. SAC Bryce was particularly angered at losing this agent, as he had hoped through interrogating him to track down Kunze's Mexico hiding place.[363]

Cross-border legal problems and the long delays had prevented the FBI from moving immediately on the arrest, and their Mexican counterparts had somehow let the important spy escape. However, the Mexican federal agents did capture another valued Nazi asset, Alois Schill Hepp, working in the Ebell ring in Mexico. The forty-year-old veteran Abwehr spy was arrested at Casas Grandes and returned to Juarez for interrogation by Mexican brigadier general Jaime Quiñones.[364]

Across the country, federal agents were conducting similar sweeps in Chicago, Philadelphia, and Thompson, Connecticut, arresting other men who were associated with the El Paso doctor during the long months of passive surveillance.

Ebell was taken to the El Paso county jail and booked on espionage charges. Bail was set at the extremely high sum of fifty thousand dollars. Immediately, an additional action was filed against the doctor by the Bureau of Immigration and Naturalization, to begin proceedings to revoke his naturalized citizenship and have him declared an enemy alien. Pending these proceedings, Ebell was classified in custodial "Group A — Individual, believed to be the most dangerous and who, in all probability, should be interned in event of war."[365]

After the doctor's citizenship was revoked, a presidential warrant signed by the U.S. attorney general, Francis Biddle, was issued against him. It charged that Ebell, as an enemy agent, was an imminent internal security risk.[366]

Although the El Paso newspapers on December 18 carried front-page articles on the arrest of Ebell and other alleged agents in Juarez, the FBI and local authorities were releasing few details. More sweeping operations were underway on both sides of the U.S.-Mexico border, and the bureau did not want to warn other Axis agents and sympathizers.

At one point, when the conservatively dressed German doctor was being transported to a federal courthouse hearing, a reporter noticed the man had peculiarly large eyes. He referred in his story to the accused spy as the "pop-eyed El Paso physician."[367]

Witnesses had used similar terms in describing the distinctive eyes of one of the suspects in the Frome murder case, three years before. At that time, rumors that the case might in some way involve Nazi spies had gone unchecked. Now, an all-new team of G-men failed to make other connections as well. No one in the espionage investigation was aware of the fact that a special Nazi automatic confiscated from Ebell's house was similar to one of the pistols used in the murders, or that the arrested spy earned some of his livelihood as a substitute doctor at El Paso's upscale hotels. These coincidences went unnoticed in the rushed bedlam of the mission at hand.

Shortly after his U.S. citizenship was revoked by a federal magistrate in El Paso, Wolfgang Ebell, chained between FBI agents, was flown to Hartford, Connecticut, to stand trial with other arrested spies. He was indicted along with his fellow conspirators, who all faced federal espionage charges. Also indicted were Otto Willumeit of Chicago, Anastase Vonsiatsky of Thompson, Connecticut, Kurt Molzahn of Philadelphia, and Gerhard Kunze, who was still at large somewhere in Mexico.[368]

The five men came to be known in the popular press as the Vonsiatsky Espionage Ring, so named for the more flamboyant antics of the White Russian Fascist leader. The massive amount of evidence gathered by the FBI investigation suggested that the gang could more appropriately have been called the Ebell Spy Ring, since Ebell's organization was the main pipeline for the movement of spies and stolen secrets for much of the western United States in the last days before Pearl Harbor.

The arrest of the El Paso doctor was only the beginning of the sweep for alleged Nazi spies and supporters on both sides of the U.S.-Mexico border and in cities and towns throughout the American West. FBI raids on pro-Nazi organizations were occurring simultaneously across the United States.

In Houston, seventy Axis aliens suspected of either spying or aiding spies were rounded up. In El Paso and Juarez, two dozen were arrested from names in the card files found in Ebell's office. In Far West Texas, FBI agents, sheriffs' deputies, and Texas Rangers raided homes and businesses, arresting twenty suspected sleeper saboteurs in the oil-field towns of Odessa, Midland, Wink, Stanton, and Monahans.[369]

Gradually, the size and scope of the raids and number of arrests became too large to be ignored, even by a cooperating news media, and stories began dribbling out in the local and national press. The Mexican government announced the arrest of more than two hundred Axis agents, including a dozen sexy German and Italian female spies, whose job was to coax defense secrets from U.S. and Mexican army officers. The female spies operated out of bordellos in border towns like Juarez, across from U.S. military bases.

The arrests were not limited to the West. In New York City alone, 158 German aliens and Bundists were arrested in one night. Throughout the country, within seventy-two hours of the Japanese attack, more than 3,800 Germans suspected of subversive activities were taken into custody by government agents heading up joint operations with local lawmen.[370]

In all, more than 11,500 German immigrants or naturalized German Americans were rounded up in the weeks after Pearl Harbor. Very few of these would ever be charged with anything. Several hundred were charged with draft dodging or failure to register as agents of a foreign government. The others were mostly dealt with outside the judicial system by simply declaring them to be aliens from enemy countries. These were placed in internment camps without benefit of legal hearings for the duration of the war. The internees included more than four thousand German-surnamed residents shipped from fifteen Latin American countries, who were on FBI lists of persons or families suspected of aiding German agents. The largest internment camps in North America for Germans and a few other aliens from European Axis countries were established at Kenedy, Seagoville, and Crystal City, Texas.

Once the United States was at war, less than a score of actual espionage cases were made against German spies like the Ebell group and a few hardcore members of the German-American Bund and White Russian Fascist organizations, who worked as bully boys, arsonists, or saboteurs in industrial plants at the direction of the actual spies.

Wherever possible, the FBI encouraged local law enforcement agencies to have persons who were suspected of actually aiding and abetting Axis spy networks tried for common crimes. The type of charges brought in local jurisdictions were for crimes alleged to have been committed on behalf of their spymasters, such as burglary, armed robbery, assault, and even murder or manslaughter.

The principal federal crime charged against the members of the Ebell ring was espionage. The cases were brought for indictment by the Justice Department under the 1917 antispy laws enacted at the beginning of World War I, primarily to punish acts of sabotage. Since America was now at war, the old act applied, and the FBI no longer had to tiptoe around the legal fine points of civil rights and privacy that they had previously violated in shadowing and eavesdropping on many naturalized American citizens. As a result of months of diligent surveillance by federal agents and cooperating local lawmen, and the sweeping raids, the FBI had plenty of hard evidence to present to judges and juries.

The sheer volume of contraband seized in raids on the homes and businesses of German aliens in El Paso and the surrounding area created quite a public stir, when the bureau finally allowed newsmen to have a look at it. A delivery truck was required to haul the confiscated contraband to a government warehouse at the edge of Fort Bliss. The FBI, bowing to pressure from a news media that had cooperated by withholding stories about the roundup of aliens, called a news conference in early 1942, months after most of the raids were conducted. Astonished reporters and photographers were given access to the property seized from suspected German agents and enablers in the earlier raids. The media, and thus the public, were at last given a tangible glimpse into the broad scope of subversive activities that had been ongoing in America for years.

The cache included scores of shortwave radio senders and receivers; sixty-five semiautomatic rifles and German and Japanese military-style, bolt-action rifles; dozens of pistols, daggers, and swords; film and movie cameras; rolls of undeveloped film; reels of exposed movie film of military and border facilities; and military and aerial maps. Some explosives and a huge amount of ammunition were also displayed. There were detailed drawings of U.S. warships, including several that now lay burned out at the bottom of Pearl Harbor.

The material seized in the raids was carefully bagged and placed in a conference room for newsmen to inspect and photograph. The pictures were subsequently wired around the country. Prominent at the front of the stacks of weapons in the FBI display was an automatic pistol of the military style being manufactured in Germany. It was similar in appearance to the 7.65 mm automatics awarded German civilians for outstanding service to the Nazi Party. The distinctive weapon fired the same type of German-made bullet used to execute Nancy Frome. The now-indicted Ebell had received such recognition for his service as a spy. Neither the owner of that particular weapon nor the owners of the other contraband were identified in the published photographs.[371]

IN MID-1942, in Hartford, Connecticut, the five top members of the Ebell spy ring, including Gerhard Kunze, were brought to trial. Thomas J. Dodd, who was later to gain fame as a prosecutor in the Nuremburg Trials of Nazi war criminals, headed the federal team against the Ebell ring.

Prior to the beginning of the trial, Kunze was tracked down in a joint manhunt by Mexican agents and special unit agents from the FBI. He was arrested on June 30, as he prepared to flee Mexico in a small motor launch. Mexican agents deposited Kunze at the U.S. border at Brownsville, Texas, and he soon joined his fellow conspirators in Connecticut.

Faced with a massive amount of evidence, and the possibility that a panel of angry citizens would throw the book at them in a jury trial, Vonsiatsky, Ebell, Kunze, and Willumeit each pled guilty to one count of espionage. Vonsiatsky and Willumeit were given five-year sentences. Ebell was given a seven-year sentence; Kunze got fifteen. Molzahn, who pled not guilty to espionage, was found guilty by a jury and sentenced to ten years in prison.

Wolfgang Ebell watched from his cell at Seagoville, Texas, as Hitler's thousand-year Reich crumbled to dust and the beloved fatherland was reduced to rubble. His spymaster, Baron Manfred von Killinger, suffered the worst fate of the West Coast spies. He blew his own brains out, rather than fall captive to the vengeful Red Army slaughtering and raping its way to Berlin.

The spy ring, which once thrived from the Bay Area to Latin America through the portal at El Paso, was never linked by authorities to the torture-murders of Hazel and Nancy Frome, but no key Nazi ringleader in that espionage scheme escaped punishment for what they had done.

A HAUNTING LEGACY

Unsolved murders take on a life of their own. What would be a closed chapter if the mystery were solved becomes the stuff of conspiracy theories, ghost stories, and legends. When the murder is particularly brutal, and the victim especially beautiful, the images continue to haunt, long after the deed is done.

Almost eight decades later, the Frome story is still being told. On the seventy-fifth anniversary, Steven Finacom of the Berkeley Historical Society wrote a column for the *San Jose Mercury News*, harking back to the tragedy that befell the Bay Area mother and daughter in 1938 and the coverage a local paper gave to it.[372] Since then, the country has experienced incalculable loss, from World War II through the protracted war on terrorism, including the assassination of a president and hundreds of thousands of other individual murders. Despite the innumerable headlines from all the intervening history, the killing of Hazel and Nancy Frome continues to be covered in print publications and on the Internet.

Occasionally, a curious soul who has read of the case will stop at Van Horn, Texas, to ask where the murders took place. There is no historical marker, no memorial there. Since the day the bodies were discovered, the interstate highway has been built. Motorists speeding by on the road east of town do not realize they have passed within a few feet of the death site.

Yet, even those who have never heard of the Fromes may fall prey to the tricks the desert plays on the mind. The bleak terrain of the great Chihuahuan Desert, the largest on the North American continent, lends itself to myth and mystery. It is host to the eerie Marfa ghost lights, which have been seen by locals for generations. Old-timers prospecting for ore tell of seeing apparitions of the dreaded war chief Victorio, roaming the nearby Sierra Diablo foothills where his Apache band made its last stand.

The extremes of climate give rise to strange phenomena. When the sun beats down and the ground heats up, the air currents create dust devils, swirling soil and sand across the land like dervishes.

On crisp spring nights, the desert is bathed in silver moon glow. A small zephyr can raise a single vortex, causing a tall, slender yucca plant to tremble and sway. Its pale, white blooms will seem to wave, while all that surrounds it stands perfectly still. A weary traveler, driving on that long stretch of highway, may see a fair-skinned woman beckoning from the roadside, a ghostly girl pleading to be rescued, as Nancy might have done, with her last breath, at this very place, on her last day.

EPILOGUE

The Hazel and Nancy Frome murder case was acknowledged by officials of the Texas Department of Public Safety as the most costly murder investigation in the history of the state. It is still often referred to as the biggest unsolved mystery in the American Southwest.

This dubious distinction was first awarded the Frome double murders in an in-depth retrospective, written fifteen years after the crime by Dawson Duncan, a reporter for the *Dallas Morning News*. The lengthy article appeared in newspapers across America and for a brief moment revived interest in the case, which was all but forgotten during the long years of World War II.

"Texas's costliest, most intensive, and most complex crime-detection project — to find the Frome murderer — will be fifteen years old March 30, and the end is not in sight," Duncan wrote, in 1953.[373] "Results so far: Dozens of criminals wanted for other offenses jailed. The most complete murder investigation file in the history of the Department of Public Safety developed. The double murder still not solved."

Twenty-one years after the murders, Texas public safety director Homer Garrison described the case as "the state's most exhaustive murder investigation."[374] It comprises the largest case files in the department, with more than 2,500 interview transcripts alone.

"There are several theories of the case," Garrison said. "Some think they [the Frome women] were mistaken for dope or counterfeit-money runners and were tortured to make them talk. Others think they were killed after being robbed. They were tortured. There's no doubt about that. Somebody wanted information. The husband and father said he felt robbery was the only motive. But if it was robbery alone, why did the killers pass up Mrs. Frome's diamond-encrusted wristwatch and gold ring and necklace? Why was the spare tire slashed in the killers' search of the car?"[375]

Chris Fox, the former sheriff who coordinated the early months of the investigation, was interviewed by the reporter for the same article. He still maintained his strong belief that the women's murder had its roots and motive in California.

By this time Fox had been out of law enforcement for nearly two decades and was a highly successful banking executive in his hometown of El Paso. Yet he still had a keen interest in the unsolved murders, as did many of the original lawmen involved in the investigation. After leaving the job as sheriff, Fox continued to correspond with local, state, and federal law enforcement officers, sharing tips and ideas.

One of the oddest of these was a contact with a counterespionage agent in the Office of Naval Intelligence at the height of World War II. That agent, who signed his letters simply "Joe," had run across a German agent named Francisco Lugo with a Mexican wife, hiding under an assumed persona as a rancher living twelve kilometers south of Nuevo Laredo.[376]

The ONI agent told the former sheriff he was investigating a case that was similar to the Frome murders. Lugo was involved with an Axis group that had murdered an American man from California, his Mexican wife, and a maid on the border. The victim's car was taken, along with luggage and personal belongings, to be searched later. The agent asked Fox what he should do with the information. Fox referred him to the El Paso sheriff's detective, Captain Shea, who was still working on the case, as time permitted.

Fox remained interested in the Frome murders, as a civilian, for the rest of his life, until his death in March 1984, as evidenced by an extensive file of clippings on the case left in his personal papers in the archives at the University of Texas at El Paso.

The former sheriff went on to become one of the most successful banking executives and prominent civic leaders in El Paso. He was often referred to as "Mr. El Paso," a title conferred on him by his business peers.

He and his family, however, suffered a major tragedy shared by thousands of American families during the Second World War. Shortly before the Nazis surrendered to end the war in Europe, Fox's son, Chris junior, was killed in a German artillery barrage on the front lines. First Lieutenant Fox died leading his company, part of the 273rd Infantry Regiment attacking the Siegfried Line in western Germany, on February 27, 1945.[377] V-E Day was declared on May 8. The death-hardened former sheriff was devastated by the tragedy, so near the end of the war.

Fox wrote a close friend that, on learning of his son's death, he, too, would have wished for his life to end, except that he felt it his obligation to stay strong for his wife and daughters: "It was not fair that Gladys and the girls would have had more of a burden to carry."[378]

The onetime lead investigator in the case was not the only person close to the Frome murders to pay a tragic price in the war against Fascism.

Mada McMakin learned that her husband, marine captain Benjamin McMakin, was in the thick of the first days of defense against the Japanese invasion of the Philippines. He was the commander of a marine company guarding the mouth of Manila Bay. The battalion was ordered to move to the naval base at Mariveles on the Bataan Peninsula, where heavy fighting was already underway.

On Christmas Day, 1941, Captain McMakin's unit was fighting its way through the jungles to the naval station when he was wounded. He remained in command of his marines during the successful mission to destroy all assets at the naval base that could be of use to the invading Japanese.[379] He led his unit in the fierce fighting at Corregidor until all American forces were ordered to surrender to the Japanese in late February 1942. Promoted in absentia to major, McMakin survived the infamous Bataan Death March and nearly two years as a prisoner of war in one of the barbaric Japanese concentration camps. He did not, however, survive the war. He was one of the hundreds of American POWs killed aboard the *Oryoku Maru*, the "hell ship" taking prisoners to Japan from Luzon.[380] U.S. war planes mistook the freighter, which was not marked as a prisoner ship, for a troop transport, and sank it on December 15, 1944.

History was not yet done with Mada. The widow married another marine officer in 1948, Colonel Robert A. McGill. Her new husband was trapped at the Chosin Reservoir in North Korea when the Chinese army poured over the border in massive waves in December 1950. Colonel McGill was awarded the Legion of Merit for his role in successfully extracting the division while under constant fire by the Chinese, in a forced march across the peninsula in severe winter conditions.

After the war, Mada and her husband eventually settled in Tucson, Arizona. The long-suffering sister of Nancy and daughter of Hazel Frome died in March 2001, having never come to peace with the terrible, unsolved murders of her beloved family members.[381]

Weston G. Frome's penchant for secrecy served him well in corporate

America, and his career prospered at the former DuPont explosives company. Named general manager of Atlas Powder Company, he took over operations at the international headquarters in Wilmington, Delaware, in November 1945. Two years later, he was named a corporate vice president and member of the board of directors. After retiring in 1956, he returned to California, where he lived in the fashionable Bay Area community of Walnut Creek until his death in July 1973.[382]

Playboy and onetime spy Werner Plack returned to Germany to become the Nazi radio minister and was captured by American forces at the end of the war.[383]

Wolfgang Ebell served the full seven years of his prison sentence. His American wife petitioned President Harry S. Truman, near the end of his term, to allow her husband to remain in the United States, a request the president promptly denied. Ebell was deported aboard the SS *Marine Tiger*, which sailed for Germany from New York City on December 5, 1947.

Ebell disappeared into the chaos of his war-ravaged fatherland so completely that, when his wife divorced him on December 7, 1951, the tenth anniversary of Pearl Harbor, he could not be located by authorities for the service of divorce papers.

Baron Manfred von Killinger, the ruthless Nazi consul general at San Francisco between 1936 and 1939, who established the German espionage network in the western United States, returned to the fatherland to administer the Holocaust in Romania, earning him the title "the Butcher of Bucharest." He committed suicide on September 2, 1944, rather than be captured by the advancing Red Army.[384] His San Francisco replacement, Captain Fritz Wiedemann, was captured in Tientsin, China, where he served as intelligence coordinator between the German and Japanese legations, and returned to Germany to stand trial as a Nazi leader. His wartime activities were deemed so minor that he was fined only six hundred dollars and allowed to retire to his family estate in Bavaria. Evidence was presented at his trial in Passau, Germany, that Wiedemann had helped dozens of Jews escape the clutches of the Gestapo while he was a diplomat in China.[385]

Romano Nicholas Trotsky, the onetime prime suspect and subject of an international manhunt in the Frome murder case, served the early war years in the federal prison on McNeil Island in Washington's Puget Sound. The bogus doctor, whom the FBI ultimately calculated had used as many as thirty-five different aliases, served out his term and was released to the custody of immigration authorities for another deportation, supposedly to nearby Canada. Trotsky had slipped back into the country after previous deportations at least nine times and been arrested on each of those occasions.[386]

He resurfaced in the FBI files in March 1958, under the name Alexis Nicholas Romanoff, in an internal security advisory. This time he had appeared at an immigration office in Arizona seeking a permanent residency card, claiming he was the son of the last Russian tsar. He was even using the title "crown prince" of Russia.[387]

The FBI advised the immigration office it would be unwise to have any official correspondence with Trotsky, "either orally or in writing," lest it be used to his advantage, either in a book or in legal proceedings.

Trotsky brazenly wrote a personal letter to FBI director J. Edgar Hoover on March 7, 1958, requesting that the bureau allow him to come to Washington, D.C., to take a lie detector test about his true identity as heir to the Russian throne.[388] Though Hoover ignored the letter, he opened a new file on Trotsky.

It seems the master chameleon had finally found his "wealthy widow" and married her. With the new wife's fortune, Trotsky established himself as the owner of a stable of registered palomino horses and opened a polo training academy in northern Arizona. He claimed a federal judge had granted him temporary asylum because he would be killed if forced to return to the Soviet Union.

Thwarted in his efforts to get a legitimate permanent residency visa himself, in 1960 he and his wife's influential friends and family convinced a prominent U.S. senator to sponsor a special bill to have the U.S. Congress grant him American citizenship.

Despite sterling credentials as an organized-crime fighter, Senator C. Estes Kefauver (D-TN) sponsored legislation to grant U.S. citizenship to Alexis N. Romanoff.[389] Kefauver had run as the Democratic Party's vice presidential nominee on the ticket with Adlai Stevenson against Eisenhower-Nixon in 1956. Fortunately, the special bill was brought to the attention of the Immigration and Naturalization Service. Shortly before its passage, the applicant's entire record was produced, to the amazement and embarrassment of the prestigious senator, and the bill was quickly withdrawn.

Trotsky, however, remained in the United States, living out his years as a respected citizen in a major southwestern American city, until his death from rheumatic fever in 1986. The identity of this rakish character continued to baffle the experts for two more decades.

In 1993, a Russian geneticist and forensic expert named Pavel Ivanov announced that he was trying to determine if the now-dead Arizona man who claimed his name was Alexis N. Romanoff was, in fact, the son of Tsar Nicholas II. Rumors persisted that when the tsar was massacred with his family by the Bolsheviks in 1918, his son Alexei and a daughter had been spared. Trotsky's widow, who believed her late husband was indeed named Romanoff, produced body tissue that was preserved at the time of his death and cremation. After a brief flurry of interest in the DNA tests by the press, the story quietly disappeared.

A decade and a half later, DNA tests done on bone fragments found in Russia in 2007 proved conclusively that Alexei and his sister were murdered with the rest of the family. Whoever Romano Trotsky — the man with three dozen aliases — was, he was not the tsar's son, Alexei Romanov, just as he was not the nephew of the late Communist revolutionary Leon Trotsky.

The Frome murder investigation, unfortunately, came to no such neat conclusion.

In September 1970, Texas Ranger captain Alfred Y. Allee, in charge of the Carrizo Springs district on the Texas-Mexico border, told newsmen at his retirement party that he believed the DPS was on the brink of solving the Frome murders. The old Ranger, who was among the dozen original investigators on the case, based his hopeful statement on some new information provided by a relative of one of the earliest suspects. The relative of the alleged participant in a gang that purportedly killed the Frome women said one of the members was still alive and living in California.

Captain Allee called in a young Ranger who was considered one of the top sleuths in the elite state law enforcement agency, an FBI-trained officer named H. Joaquin Jackson. After spending days at headquarters reviewing the massive cold-case file, Jackson went to Dallas to interview the relative. The man claimed the murders had been kept a family secret. The tale was whispered about a distant relative who had confessed to his kin on his deathbed that he and several other hoodlum associates of the day had been involved in killing the women.

The reopened investigation took Ranger Jackson to Los Angeles, after he had walked the murder site and reviewed every scrap of information still in the files of lawmen in El Paso and Culberson County. Working with detectives of the Los Angeles Police Department, the Ranger tracked down the only living member of the gang once suspected and cleared of the murders years before. The man, who was in poor health in a nursing home, denied any knowledge of the case and volunteered to take a lie-detector test. The test results were inconclusive, but the examiner chalked that up to his advanced age and poor physical condition.

The cold case went nowhere, much to the consternation of Ranger Jackson, who invested weeks checking out what now appeared to be just the same old rumor that had bedeviled investigators thirty years earlier.

Jackson returned to Texas to later write in his own memoirs, "It's my opinion that all the witnesses and suspects in this case are deceased."[390]

Despite the best training and modern techniques that are currently available to the Texas Rangers, the Frome investigation never returned to priority status for Texas lawmen after World War II. Ranger Jackson noted about the case that "all the training in the world will not be able to overcome bad clues, the calendar, or circumstances that just favor the criminal."[391]

But the case remained in the Texas Department of Public Safety's unsolved crimes section through the turn of the century. It was considered an "open case" in August 1992, when I requested access to conduct research for *Fetch the Devil* on specific aspects of the investigation, in the three file drawers maintained at Ranger headquarters.

"It is technically an open case, and even though it is very old, the Frome matter must still be considered an ongoing investigation," the Department of Public Safety responded, in denying the request.

My second request under the Texas Open Records Act, made in December 1995, drew a similar denial of access, along with this comment: "Though the Frome case is still considered open, since there is no statute of limitations on murder, it is not actively being investigated. No Ranger is presently assigned to the case, given its age and the lack of any new evidence."

My third request, made on September 29, 2006, under provisions of the Texas Open Records Act, to examine the case files for historic research purposes, drew an even more disappointing response. I requested access to the case files to clarify and further explore a list of specific questions that arose from the review of other sources, including federal government files released under the Freedom of Information Act.

The state files were gone.

"A thorough search of D P S files has found no records responsive to your request," an assistant general counsel of the Texas Department of Public Safety replied. "The age of these records puts them well outside the agency's normal retention period."

Subsequent telephone inquiries to the legal office at D P S confirmed that the Frome murder case files maintained by the Texas Rangers had been shredded, with no record of the disposal date on file. The spokesman for the Rangers pointed out that "a lot of people are disposing of old files when they pass their retention date."

Retired Ranger Joaquin Jackson, the last lawman to investigate the baffling case, was interviewed for the living history project of the Texas Ranger museum at Waco, Texas, in September 2008. The former lawman was asked by interviewers Nancy and Eddie Ray about his recollections of the most important cases he had worked. He immediately cited the Frome women's murders.

Of all the thousands of leads and theories about the case over the years, the veteran Ranger singled out the seldom-mentioned angle of a Nazi espionage connection to the murders as the most troubling aspect of the mystery. "There was even a lot of intrigue later that the case had something to do with spying. There were a lot of Germans [agents] on the Mexican border at the time of the murders," Jackson recalled.[392]

Jackson wrote a fitting conclusion to the case in his 2008 book *One Ranger Returns*. "It is frustrating to give your best professional effort to a case and still come away empty-handed. The truth is, though, it doesn't take a perfect crime to foil the lawmen who investigate it," retired Ranger Jackson observed. "It only takes time — time for suspects to vanish and witnesses to die and the trail of evidence to grow cold."[393]

The case that fascinated and horrified much of the nation for years, the murders of Nancy and Hazel Frome in 1938, is still, almost eight decades later, the biggest unsolved mystery in the Southwest. Officially, it will likely remain so.

CODA

Author's Theory of the Frome Murders

In the American criminal justice system, the three primary elements popularly considered necessary for a conviction are *means*, *motive*, and *opportunity*.

By triangulating information from several archival sources, most of which has never been made public before and is presented in this book for the first time, I developed a scenario and plausible solution to the historic, unsolved Frome murder case. Relying on this research, it is my conclusion that the Nazi spy ring operating from the San Francisco German consulate, with a key link in El Paso, had the means, motive, and opportunity to murder Hazel and Nancy Frome in the West Texas desert in 1938. The German consul, Baron Manfred von Killinger, ordered the executions. The deep-cover Nazi spy, Wolfgang Ebell of El Paso, orchestrated the operation. Two unknown but expertly trained hit men, German American or White Russian thugs, were, most likely, the actual triggermen.

The *means* was a readily available cadre of trained German agents operating in deepest cover in the American West, abetted by White Russian Fascist criminals or fanatical German-American Bund members who were eager to do anything, even murder, in furtherance of Hitler's ambitions for world domination.

The *motive* was initially to coerce the Frome women to cooperate in opening the industrial secrets of Atlas Powder Company to pilferage, after the intransigent head of the family and Atlas executive, Weston G. Frome, had rebuffed the spies' blackmail threats. The failed attempt to co-opt the mother and daughter led to the second motive: to protect the valuable spy network from exposure.

The *opportunity* was the unexpected and unfortunate happenstance of the women crossing paths with this ruthless gang of Nazi spies, when they

were temporarily stranded in the geographically remote border town of
El Paso.

Here, then, is my theory of what happened, in the murders of Hazel
and Nancy Frome:

The temporary stranding was only a momentary nuisance to the San
Francisco Bay Area socialite and her beautiful daughter, who arrived after
business hours at the Hotel Cortez. Nancy Frome was suffering from a
severe cold and leg cramps. Since the regular hotel physician had left for
the weekend, a Mexican bellboy summoned an outsider doctor, who gave
generous tips for such referrals.

The mother, as usual, chatted away about her husband's important position in the explosives industry, while the visiting physician examined
and treated her daughter. Since the doctor spoke with a German accent, it
was natural for Hazel to mention that her husband was also full-blooded
German. Unfortunately for the women, Wolfgang Ebell was more than a
simple, down-at-the-heels physician forced to make after-hours room calls
for extra money. He was the key, deep-cover link in a well-organized Nazi
spy chain, operating from the German consulate in San Francisco, via Latin
America, to Abwehr headquarters in Berlin.

When Ebell telephoned his boss, Baron Manfred von Killinger, at
the German consulate in San Francisco, to report his chance encounter
with the women, the fanatical Nazi spymaster immediately recognized
the Frome name. His agents in the Bay Area had been trying for months
to penetrate Atlas Powder Company, which they knew was a major U.S.
munitions-component manufacturer. Even a blackmail scheme involving
an affair with a young German showgirl had failed to budge the tough old
executive, Weston Frome, into collaboration.

Now, two seemingly vulnerable family members had serendipitously
landed in the Nazi web of intrigue. An excited von Killinger ordered Ebell
to employ any ruse possible to exploit the stranded women who had fallen
victim, first to car trouble, and then to illness, which revealed their plight
to the Nazi spies.

But time to act was short. Trained agents from the West Coast might not
arrive before the women's car was repaired and they were off again and out
of reach, on their cross-country drive. Ebell had to use the resources at hand.

A White Russian con man named Romano Trotsky was in El Paso, pestering Ebell for back fees owed for illicit medical services. Another mysterious Russian or Ukrainian named G. N. Gepge was also in town, peddling stolen mining equipment. Both claimed to be pro-Fascist, former tsarist royalty; both were reputed ladies' men; and both were desperately broke. They had collaborated with the Nazis on minor jobs before, so Ebell quickly enlisted them to get close to the women and paid for their rooms at the posh hotel where the Fromes had taken refuge.

The self-proclaimed royal lotharios approached the women several times in the darkened nightclubs of Juarez, trying to entice them to dance and party. Hazel was overheard telling one of them that she believed she had met him before in California. (Trotsky had spent several years practicing in the Bay Area and had even given horse-riding lessons there.) But the sophisticated mother and daughter were more bemused than beguiled by the sleazy womanizers.

The pressure was stepped up, and the women were stalked by the Nazi lackeys in El Paso, while waiting for their car to be repaired. As the time to close a deal rapidly approached, Mrs. Frome was accosted outside a beauty salon where she had her hair done. Mild coercion had failed, too.

The spy Ebell needed to come up with a more sinister approach to recruit them. A mysterious letter threatening to expose Pop Frome's peccadillos was surreptitiously dropped at the hotel's front desk for Hazel. The letter panicked the women, but they could not seek help from the police or the company man Harold White, without revealing its contents. More afraid of a family scandal than of their stalkers, Hazel and Nancy chose flight rather than fight, as they prepared to leave El Paso. Before taking off, Hazel tried, unsuccessfully, to get a travel companion to accompany them.

Either Trotsky or Gepge observed the delivery of the women's repaired Packard to the hotel and their luggage to the lobby. Ebell had to hurriedly come up with an emergency plan to delay or waylay them. With only one route east out of town, it would be easy to intercept a car on the long, lonely stretch of highway.

Ebell, by this time, had summoned more reliable accomplices from his list of fellow Nazi agents working both sides of the border, but the replacements had not yet arrived. So Ebell and an unidentified redheaded woman drove out of town in a dark sedan, while Trotsky and Gepge proceeded in Trotsky's older-model, green Cadillac roadster to a prearranged rendezvous point somewhere east of El Paso. Once on Highway 80, the silver Packard had to be stopped.

When approached by the smaller dark car driven by Ebell or the redhead, the Frome women, experienced drivers, just sped up. To stop them, Trotsky's heavier car staged a minor fender bender at high speed. While the damage was slight, it forced the Frome car off the road long enough for Ebell and the woman to join the Russians. Once Hazel and Nancy were stopped, it was a simple matter to use a firearm to detain them.

Trotsky, who had little or no personal loyalty to Hitler's cause, likewise had no stomach for the violence he guessed was about to be inflicted upon the women. He also knew there would be dire repercussions for this confrontation. The con man sped off to nearby New Mexico, where he could establish an alibi. He called on a few doctors for whom he had provided questionable services in the past. He also had his green car painted yellow and black, after the dented fender, streaked with silver paint from the Packard, was repaired.

Ebell and the remaining Russian henchman, Gepge, took control of the Fromes on the side of the highway. The scene of one black car parked behind the Packard and the bug-eyed Ebell was described by witnesses. Then the two men piled into the Frome Packard and guarded the women at gunpoint, forcing Nancy to drive. The red-haired woman followed in the smaller, dark car. This was the entourage observed by several witnesses driving in tandem, at high speeds, at a number of points along the highway. The Fromes were taken to an isolated structure, probably one of the several abandoned ranch houses in the vicinity of Van Horn. The victims and their captors were met by other Nazi conspirators, previously summoned by Ebell. The women were left with these thugs for interrogation and torture.

One man, probably Ebell, and possibly Gepge, drove the luggage-laden Packard, followed by the red-haired lady, to a location marked by a caliche pit, well known to the Nazi gang for its relative isolation, six miles east of Van Horn. They planned to search the Frome belongings for the telltale, threatening letter. But the usually lonely area was busy that day with unemployed oil worker Bill Tripp building a livestock watering tank nearby and his girlfriend, Juanita Elliott, honking her car horn from the highway to signal him. So the Packard was moved to an even more isolated spot, where the search continued. Still failing to find the incriminating letter, the perpetrators took all the belongings with them for a later, more thorough, search. The Packard was driven to the junction of US Highways 80 and 290, near Balmorhea. There, the car was wiped clean of fingerprints and abandoned with the keys in the ignition and fuel in the tank, in hopes that some hungry hitchhiker would steal it and drive it far away.

That did not happen, and the car was discovered sooner than the spies had hoped. The alarm for the missing women was sounded. Meanwhile, Hazel and Nancy were held for a day or two after their abduction and subjected to more horrific treatment. But they were even more stubborn than the family head of household. When it became clear that the attempt to recruit them was futile, Ebell, who had by this time returned to El Paso with the redhead, called von Killinger to report the bungled attempt.

The ruthless Nazi spymaster told Ebell the only solution was to eliminate the captive women rather than risk exposure of the spy network. The clandestine organization had taken years to perfect and was producing a trove of valuable U.S. military and industrial secrets.

A day or two after their kidnapping, the barely conscious Frome women were driven by their captors unseen, under cover of darkness, to a spot six miles east of Van Horn and not far from where they were being held. The site was close to the area where witnesses saw the Frome Packard off in the brush the day the women vanished.

Their executioners were professional killers who had been sent from either Mexico or San Francisco by the spymaster. The women were shot to death in the caliche pit where their bodies were soon to be discovered. Nancy was killed by a type of 7.65 mm bullet, manufactured only in Germany and not sold in North America.

To clean up loose ends, the Mexican bellhop who had summoned Ebell to the Hotel Cortez in the first place, and the only outsider who could connect the spy with the Fromes, was kidnapped by Nazi agents, taken into Mexico, murdered, and buried.

In effect, what started as an ill-conceived attempt to recruit the women quickly became a fiasco, ending in murders that were never originally intended.

For the perpetrators, it turned out to be a perfect crime. There was only one other potential glitch the Nazis had not counted on. That was Sheriff Chris Fox. When the Texan showed up in the Bay Area snooping for a motive for the killings closer to the Frome home and offices of Atlas Powder, it caused the Nazis in the spy nest at the San Francisco consulate their own moment of panic. The instigators were terrified of being connected to the, by then, infamous crime. Baron von Killinger was quietly recalled to Germany, where he would be forever out of reach and beyond questioning, should the evil deeds occurring in El Paso shortly before the outbreak of World War II be uncovered.

When Wolfgang Ebell was arrested in December 1941, days after Pearl Harbor, a reporter described him as "pop-eyed." But the Frome investigation was a cold case by then.

Petty jurisdictional jealousies on the part of Texas lawmen, and the feds' unwillingness to share their clandestine, counterespionage activities — most of which were extralegal — greatly contributed to the Frome murders becoming one of the biggest unsolved crimes in the history of the Southwest. In spite of the roadblocks, El Paso sheriff Chris P. Fox came closer to the answers than he ever knew.

ACKNOWLEDGMENTS

The accurate telling of a long-ago incident, after all eyewitnesses have passed on, depends on the work of the few who dedicate their lives to what may seem the mundane work of preserving records of the past. They are writers' best friends, the archivists, who toil without recognition in America's few institutions that still have the commitment and good sense to preserve history in order to build a better future.

My research into the unsolved Frome murders was made vastly easier by the assistance of valuable resource people at opposite ends of a small city in Far West Texas. In 1995, Claudia Rivers, head of Special Collections at the University of Texas at El Paso (UTEP) library, introduced me to a treasure of letters and documents retained in that extraordinary facility; and most recently, archivist Laura Hollingsed rounded out UTEP's contribution to this book.

The most important contribution to never-before-published information in *Fetch the Devil* came from a dusty warehouse. The late sheriff of El Paso Leo Samaniego and his administrative deputy at the time, Sergeant Jose Dominguez, responded to my Texas Open Records Act request by unearthing what is probably the only complete case file of the historic Frome murders still in existence, since the unfortunate destruction of case files once held by the Texas Department of Public Safety.

Custodians of records at the American Medical Association, Robert K. Williamson, records administrator, and Amber Dushman, senior archivist, were especially helpful in locating records of unusual events occurring during this pre–World War II period. Research librarians too numerous to identify individually at the Dolph Briscoe Center for American History and Perry-Casteñeda Library at the University of Texas, the Lyndon B. Johnson Library in Austin, and the FBI's Information Resources Division in Washington, D.C., were always willing to help locate the most obscure fact or data.

Alison (née Dodge) Knope, Tri Delta sorority sister, who did not want her dear friend to be forgotten, provided letters from the twenty-three-year-old Nancy Frome that she had saved her whole life, as well as extensive interview time.

Norman B. and Mary Lou Wilson advised on technology, mores, and lifestyle in Texas in the 1930s. W. H. Peterson III, grandson of Chris Fox, provided useful insights into the life of his famous forebear. Michael Grace's fascination with history provided a unique understanding of little-known events of the prewar years.

My literary agent, John Talbot of the Talbot Fortune Agency, was undaunted by the headwinds buffeting the publishing industry and brought this work into the safe harbor of just the right publisher. Johanna Farrand reviewed an early draft and encouraged development of the project.

My editor, Stephen Hull, was steadfastly committed to this book, from acquiring it for the University Press of New England (UPNE), to his insightful suggestions, and shepherding it through to completion. He and UPNE director Michael Burton assembled a similarly dedicated team. My thanks to managing editor Amanda Dupuis, production editor Ann Brash, copy editor Naomi Burns, production assistant Sara Rutan, publicity and rights manager Barbara Briggs, media-marketing coordinator Katy Grabill, sales-exhibits manager Sherri Strickland, marketing-sales director David Corey, and senior designer Mindy Hill.

This book would never have come to pass had I not been one of those fortunate few writers who find that rare companion willing to endure the sacrifices required for a writing life. Judith Morison, my wife and a career writer herself, has been that person. One day I came home and announced I wanted to quit a well-paying job and return to my original calling in journalism. She didn't ask how I expected to earn a living but instead bought me an IBM Selectric typewriter and a new dictionary. And then she joined me as a full partner in a freelance career that has now spanned thirty years. Ten published nonfiction books and countless magazine stories later, we are bringing *Fetch the Devil* to print.

If there are any words in this book that, evading the eagle eyes of my editors, look something like this: xx9xj3;g, I have the rascally Bengal, Bugs, to thank for that. She's been loyally uncritical, patiently sleeping on my desk beside the computer through thousands of hours of writing and rewriting, waking only occasionally to walk across the keyboard to generously contribute her undecipherable code into the text or to strew newspaper clippings and loose pages of government documents about my office, in search of a missed cat treat.

And finally, but not lastly, I thank my sons, Doug, Mark, and especially Caleb, and daughters-in-law Yumi and Lisa. Without their stalwart support during two unbearable events that occurred while I was writing this book, it never would have been finished. Those tragedies were the untimely deaths of their siblings, my daughter Dr. Joy Richmond, theatre director and professor at Trinity Valley Community College in Athens, Texas, and my son Jonas Richmond, recently discharged army sergeant who survived combat in both Iraq wars. Jonas died in a car-truck accident on an icy bridge in 2011 and was buried with military honors at Arlington Memorial Cemetery. Joy died after a heroic battle with cancer in 2012 and was interred in the beautiful piney-wood hills of East Texas, the source of both her and my inspiration to create.

NOTEſ

1. "Nancy Frome Engagement Broken," *El Paso Times*, April 6, 1938, 1. Original newspaper (OR) archives, Dolph Briscoe Center for American History, University of Texas at Austin (UT).

2. Peter Watson, *The German Genius* (New York: HarperCollins, 2010), 324.

3. "Recalled as Teacher," *Oshkosh Daily Northwestern*, April 5, 1938, 2, Newspaper Archive, http://newspaperarchive.com.

4. J. Harrison, genealogy research for author, Austin, TX, December 12, 1994.

5. Evelyn Rose, "The Giant Powder Company," *Glen Park News* (Winter 2007/2008), FoundSF, accessed July 14, 2013, http://www.foundsf.org.

6. Jean H. Hall, close friend and sorority sister of Nancy and Mada Frome, interview by author, Lafayette, CA, February 10, 1995.

7. U.S. Census Bureau, 1940 Census, last updated January 14, 2013, http://www.census.gov/1940census.

8. *Blue and Gold* (yearbook), Class of 1935 (Berkeley: University of California, 1935).

9. Society Section, *Oakland Tribune*, May 13, 1934, 19, Newspaper Archive, http://newspaperarchive.com.

10. Sailing Schedule, 1934–35, Dollar Steamship Lines and American Mail Lines, Round-the-World, accessed April 4, 2008, http://www.timetableimages.com.

11. Mrs. Alison (Dodge) Knope, close friend and former Tri Delta sorority sister of Nancy and Mada Frome, interviews, correspondence, and clippings from personal scrapbook provided to author, Lakeland, Florida, October 1995–January 1996.

12. "Rewards for Killers Swell," *El Paso Herald-Post*, April 5, 1938, 1, OR archives, Briscoe Center, UT.

13. Rosters of 1934 and 1935 Cal Golden Bears football team, University of California, Berkeley.

14. Mrs. T. B. Chattam of Mexia, TX, letter to Chris Fox, May 21, 1938, El Paso County Sheriff's Office (EPSO), case file 9628.

15. Weston G. Frome, interview by Texas Ranger Hugh J. Pharies at Richmond, California, November 5, 1940, transcript, EPSO, case file 9628.

16. Ibid.

17. Daniel Yergin, *The Prize* (New York: Simon & Schuster, 1991), 208.

18. *Get the "Plus" of a Packard in 1937*, sales brochure (Detroit: Packard Motor Car

Company, September 2, 1936), accessed September 9, 2009, http://www.classyauto
.com.

19. Energy Information Administration, U.S. Department of Energy, *History of Gasoline Prices*, pamphlet (Washington, DC: Government Printing Office, July 2009).

20. Chattam, letter.

21. Texas Department of Public Safety, Special Bulletin to all Peace Officers, April 18, 1938, describing the wardrobes, jewelry, and luggage missing from the Frome vehicle, EPSO, case file 9628.

22. W. G. Frome, interview.

23. Nancy Frome, letter to close friend Alison Dodge, mailed from El Paso, TX, March 28, 1938, Alison (Dodge) Knope correspondence with author.

24. W. G. Frome, interview.

25. Nancy Frome, letter to friend Alison Dodge on Hotel Cortez stationery, March 25, 1938, copy provided to author by Alison (Dodge) Knope, January 11, 1996.

26. "Academy Award Winners and History 1929–39," Academy of Motion Picture Arts and Sciences, Beverly Hills, California, accessed July 15, 2009, http://www.oscars .org/awards/academyawards/about/history.html.

27. Charles Higham, *Errol Flynn: The Untold Story* (New York: Dell, 1980), 169.

28. Chris Fox, notes, EPSO, case file 9628.

29. Fox, notes.

30. Harold White, El Paso manager of Atlas Powder, interview by Chris Fox, in Fox, notes.

31. "Oil Cars Seized in Juarez," *El Paso Herald-Post*, March 25, 1938, 1, OR archives, Briscoe Center, UT.

32. Bill Hollum, mechanic, interview by El Paso sheriff's investigator, EPSO, case file 9628.

33. Betsy Hagans, brochure describing Hotel Cortez restoration (Cactus Points, 1983).

34. "Mother, Daughter Slain in Vicinity of Van Horn," *El Paso Herald-Post*, April 4, 1938, 2, OR archives, Briscoe Center, UT.

35. N. Frome, letter to A. Dodge, March 28, 1938.

36. "Mother, Daughter Slain," 9.

37. Tex Riccard, Cortez doorman, interview with sheriff's deputy, Fox notes, EPSO, case file 9628.

38. "Ranger Holds Abandoned Car," *El Paso Herald-Post*, April 7, 1938, 1, OR archives, Briscoe Center, UT.

39. "Foul Play Feared after Car Found," *Dallas Morning News*, April 4, 1938, 1, *Dallas Morning News* (*DMN*) archives, accessed September 13, 2006, http://nl.newsbank .com.

40. Fox, notes.

41. "El Paso Women Visitors Disappear," *El Paso Times*, April 3, 1938, 1, OR archives, Briscoe Center, UT.

42. Ibid.

43. W. G. Frome, interview.

44. "Mother, Daughter Slain," 1.

45. Ibid.

46. Ibid.

47. Andy Edwards, vocational agriculture teacher, Benavides, TX, sworn statement, taken May 2, 1938, EPSO, case file 9628.

48. N. D. Collear, inspector in charge, El Paso district Immigration and Naturalization Service, letter to Chris Fox, April 28, 1938, EPSO, case file 9628.

49. "Report of Post-Mortem Examination," autopsy conducted April 4, 1938, at Peak-Hagedon Undertaking Parlor by Office of City-County Health Department, EPSO, case file 9628.

50. "Mother, Daughter Slain," 1.

51. Ibid.

52. Hollace Weiner and Kenneth Roseman, *Lone Star of David* (Waltham, MA: February 1, 2007), 233–38.

53. "Allred Offers $1000 Reward For Slayers," *El Paso Herald-Post*, April 4, 1938, 1, OR archives, Briscoe Center, UT.

54. "Mrs. DeBolt's Slaying in 1933 Is Recalled by Frome Murders," *El Paso Herald-Post*, April 4, 1938, 3, OR archives, Briscoe Center, UT.

55. Emile C. Schnurmacher, "Wire That Photo," *Popular Mechanics*, July 1937, 393–95.

56. AP Wirephoto service was launched in the United States in 1935. Associated Press, "The Modern Cooperative Grows," AP History 1901–1950, accessed June 30, 2010, http://www.ap.org.

57. Jim Milam, eyewitness account taken by Sheriff Anderson, EPSO, case file 9628.

58. "Report of Post-Mortem Examination."

59. Ibid.

60. Ibid.

61. Ibid.

62. Ibid.

63. "Manhunt for Fiendish Attackers Is Organized," *El Paso Herald-Post*, April 4, 1938, 1, OR archives, Briscoe Center, UT.

64. "Locate Place Where Trunks Were Looted," *El Paso Herald-Post*, April 5, 1938, 7, OR archives, Briscoe Center, UT.

65. Ibid.

66. H. S. Michael, Side-Bar Remarks, *El Paso Times*, August 5, 1937, 4, OR archives, Briscoe Center, UT.

67. Photographs of Chris Fox, Special Collections, University of Texas at El Paso (UTEP) Library.

68. U.S. Senate, Final Report of Select Committee to Study Governmental Operations with Respect to Intelligence Activities ("Church Committee"), book 3, April 23, 1974, Office of Naval Intelligence.

69. "Gang Car Theft Blow Is Struck," *El Paso Herald-Post*, October 7, 1936, 4, OR archives, Briscoe Center, UT.

70. "Fox Is Athletic Idealist," *El Paso Herald-Post*, July 23, 1932, 1, OR archives, Briscoe Center, UT.

71. "Fox Puts Armstrong Deputies on the Spot," *El Paso Times*, June 6, 1932, 31, OR archives, Briscoe Center, UT.

72. "Our 'Inexperienced Sheriff,'" editorial, *El Paso Herald-Post*, December 1, 1933, 4, OR archives, Briscoe Center, UT.

73. "Van Horn Victim Cleveland Woman," *San Antonio Express*, December 9, 1933, 14, Newspaper Archive, http://newspaperarchive.com.

74. "Plane Speeds Dillinger to Fort Worth," *San Antonio Light*, January 30, 1934, 1, Newspaper Archive, http://newspaperarchive.com.

75. QFINANCE, "Definition of Bucket Trading," accessed July 10, 2013, http://www.qfinance.com/dictionary/bucket-trading.

76. "17 Go to Penitentiary in Bucket Shop Inquiry Started by El Pasoans," *El Paso Herald-Post*, March 26, 1935, 1, OR archives, Briscoe Center, UT.

77. "El Paso Protests Rangers Activity," *Abilene Daily Reporter*, April 1, 1936, 1, Newspaper Archive, http://newspaperarchive.com.

78. "Berkeley Police Chief and Frome Request Aid of El Paso Sheriff," *El Paso Times*, April 5, 1938, 1, OR archives, Briscoe Center, UT.

79. Christina Smith, research librarian, Texas Ranger Hall of Fame and Museum, online info service, Waco, October 13, 2009.

80. Al Eason, *Boom Town* (Kilgore, TX: Kilgore Chamber of Commerce, 1980), 5.

81. "FBI History: The New Deal, 1933 to Late 1930s," accessed October 14, 2009, http://www.fbi.gov.

82. Silver belly is a term used to describe the most common color of cowboy hats. (The fur used in felt was originally from the soft-haired underbelly of a beaver.) The neutral, almost off-white tone can vary slightly from very light beige to silver gray.

83. Chris Fox, investigation summary, EPSO, case file 9628.

84. Bill Tripp, interview by Rangers at Van Horn, TX, EPSO, case file 9628.

85. "Rewards for Killers Swelled to $1,650," *El Paso Times*, April 5, 1938, 1, OR archives, Briscoe Center, UT.

86. Frances Hammer, interview by Chris Fox, May 17, 1938, summary of transcript, EPSO, case file 9628.

87. "Slain Bodies Arrive Home," *Oakland Tribune*, April 6, 1938, 1, Newspaper Archive, http://newspaperarchive.com.

88. "Bay Friends Aid in Frome Quiz," *Oakland Tribune*, April 6, 1938, 1, Newspaper Archive, http://newspaperarchive.com.

89. H. Joaquin Jackson and James L. Haley, *One Ranger Returns* (Austin: University of Texas Press, 2009), 49.

90. "Bay Friends Aid in Frome Quiz," *Oakland Tribune*, April 6, 1938, 1, Newspaper Archive, http://newspaperarchive.com.

91. "Seek Ex-Convicts, Blonde, in Murder," *El Paso Times*, April 6, 1938, 1, OR archives, Briscoe Center, UT.

92. "Blonde Woman Flees from Sonora, Texas," *El Paso Herald-Post*, April 9, 1938, 1, OR archives, Briscoe Center, UT.

93. "Fox Thinks He Struck Slayer's Trail in West Texas," *El Paso Herald-Post*, April 9, 1938, 1, OR archives, Briscoe Center, UT.

94. Brownson Malsch, *"Lone Wolf" Gonzaullas, Texas Ranger* (Norman: University of Oklahoma Press, 1998), 129–30.

95. "Can You Give Sheriff Fox a Tip?" *El Paso Herald-Post*, April 12, 1938, 8, OR archives, Briscoe Center, UT.

96. M. K. Graham, statement to Chris Fox, April 26, 1938, EPSO, case file 9628.

97. Ibid.

98. C. H. Stone, chief of Criminal Investigation Division, California State Bureau of Investigation, Sacramento, letter to Chris Fox, February 6, 1942, Chris Fox archive, Special Collections, UTEP.

99. Chris Fox, letter to DPS director H. H. Carmichael, June 13, 1938, EPSO, case file 9628.

100. Maria Baca, interview by Captain Stanley Shea, EPSO, case file 9628.

101. Chris Fox, summary report, April 26, 1938, EPSO, case file 9628.

102. Ibid.

103. E. L. Bradford, interview by deputy sheriff, EPSO, case file 9628.

104. Allie Gillespie, summary of interviews by El Paso Sheriff's Office, May 12, 1938, EPSO, case file 9628.

105. "E. P. Seer Who 'Told Fortune' of Mrs. Frome Says Murderers Are Still in City or Nearby," *El Paso Herald-Post*, May 3, 1938, 1, 8, OR archives, Briscoe Center, UT.

106. B. N. Gist, interview by Chris Fox, May 1, 1938, EPSO, case file 9628.

107. Keno Smith, interview by Chris Fox and Stanley Shea, Juarez, Mexico, EPSO, case file 9628.

108. Ibid.

109. Ibid.

110. Fox, investigation summary.

111. Toby Martin, interview by Fox, EPSO, case file 9628.

112. "Ranger Doubts Frome Women Were Tortured," *El Paso Herald-Post*, April 11, 1938, 8, OR archives, Briscoe Center, UT.

113. "Sheriff and Investigators Travel Along Trail Leading to Murders," *El Paso Herald-Post*, April 12, 1938, 1, OR archives, Briscoe Center, UT.

114. Ibid.

115. Fox, investigation summary.

116. "Mystery Coupe Chief Clue to Agony Killers," *Dallas Morning News*, April 5, 1938, 1, *DMN* archives.

117. Jonathan Worchester, *The Worchester Family: The Descendants of Rev. William Worchester* (Lynn, MA: W. W. Kellogg, 1895), 1. Revised and reprinted, 1914 by Sarah Worchester, Hudson Printing, Hudson, MA; last modification, January 16, 2005.

118. Chauncey Worchester, interview by FBI, April 29, 1938, EPSO, case file 9628.

119. Ibid.

120. Ibid.

121. Hammer, interview, EPSO, case file 9628.

122. Chris Fox, investigation report, EPSO, case file 9628.

123. Chris Fox, investigation report summary, EPSO, case file 9628.

124. Ibid.

125. Ibid.

126. Ibid.

127. Ibid.

128. U.S. Department of Labor, Immigration and Naturalization "Wanted" bulletin, sent to Chris Fox by H. C. Horsley, agent in charge, New Mexico district, April 1938, EPSO, case file 9628.

129. Pete Crawford, summary of Ranger's report to Chris Fox, EPSO, case file 9628.

130. The Fence, *El Paso Herald-Post*, April 9, 1937, OR archives, Briscoe Center, UT.

131. Mrs. Helga Dorn Lukian, a wife of suspect Romano Trotsky, interview by Chris Fox and Stanley Shea, Las Cruces, NM, EPSO, case file 9628.

132. FBI, Ballistic Report requested by Texas DPS, April 12, 1938, EPSO, case file 9628.

133. Chris Fox, memo to other agencies of the investigation team, April 26, 1938, EPSO, case file 9628.

134. Summary of report, El Paso Sheriff's Office investigation of guest at Hotel Cortez, EPSO, case file 9628.

135. Ibid.

136. Summary reports, Texas Ranger interviews of witnesses in Benavides area, EPSO, case file 9628.

137. T. P. Hunter, special agent, California Board of Medical Examiners, letter to ADA Myron R. Adams, Reno, NV, December 14, 1940, Department of Records Management and Archives, American Medical Association (AMA), Chicago.

138. Ibid.

139. Summary, Texas Ranger interviews, EPSO, case file 9628.

140. Chris Fox, bulletin, April 30, 1938, EPSO, case file 9628.

141. "Frome Suspect Held in San Angelo," *Dallas Morning News*, May 1, 1938, 14, *DMN* archives.

142. "No Clues Yet Link New Frome Suspect," *Dallas Morning News*, May 2, 1938, 8, *DMN* archives.

143. "Californian Jailed in Frome Murder Case," *Oakland Tribune*, May 1, 1938, 1, 8, Newspaper Archive, http://newspaperarchive.com.

144. Ibid.

145. "Trotsky Is Eliminated from Investigation of Killings," *El Paso Herald-Post*, May 2, 1938, 1, OR archives, Briscoe Center, UT.

146. San Angelo is a picturesque town in the Texas Hill Country. In the 1930s, it was not located on any main routes and was best known as the home of historic Fort Concho, where the famed U.S. black cavalrymen known as buffalo soldiers sallied forth during the closing days of the frontier, to drive the last of the hostile Indians from Texas.

147. "Dr. Trotsky Arrested by San Angelo Officers in Frome Murder Quiz," *El Paso Times*, May 1, 1938, 1, OR archives, Briscoe Center, UT.

148. Ibid.

149. DPS officers, interrogation summary of R. Trotsky, EPSO, case file 9628.

150. Agent Pat Taliafarro, Department of Public Safety Criminal Investigation Division, report on alibi witnesses of suspect Trotsky or Romano Lukian, March 30 and March 31, 1938, EPSO, case file 9628.

151. Ibid.

152. Dr. J. L. Cavanagh, Carlsbad, NM, interview by DPS agent Taliafarro, EPSO, case file 9628.

153. "No Clues Yet," 1.

154. "Wife Does Not Suspect Husband," *El Paso Herald-Post*, May 2, 1938, 1, OR archives, Briscoe Center, UT.

155. Chris Fox, letter to Culberson County sheriff Albert Anderson, May 2, 1938, EPSO, case file 9628.

156. Federal Bureau of Investigation, Romano Trotsky file 47-5683 and 62-HQ-34838, accessed via author's request under Freedom of Information and Privacy Act (FOIA).

157. Andy Edwards, vocational agriculture teacher, Benavides, TX, interview by DPS, EPSO, case file 9628.

158. Dr. Ferdinand Schmitter, New York City, interview by FBI agent R. E. Vatrelli at FBI offices in U.S. courthouse, May 1, 1938, EPSO, case file 9628.

159. International News Service report, *Charleston Gazette*, May 1, 1938, 1, Newspaper Archive, http://newspaperarchive.com.

160. Investigative reports, Bureau of Investigation AMA, for a period from 1929 to 1942, R. N. Trotsky file, AMA archives, July 18, 1995.

161. Ibid.

162. Document seized from Dr. Romano Trotsky upon his arrest by San Francisco detectives for State of California, Board of Medical Examiners, and transmitted to AMA with cover letter on January 19, 1937, AMA archives.

163. Investigation of U.S. Public Health Service, U.S. Bureau of Investigation, April 19, 1935, FBI Romano Trotsky file, FOIA.

164. Ibid.

165. R. N. Trotsky, letter to J. Edgar Hoover, November 17, 1934, FBI Romano Trotsky file, FOIA.

166. Bureau of Investigation, "R. N. Trotsky: Deportable Alien with Many Aliases and a Criminal Record," *JAMA* 103, no. 25 (December 22, 1934): 1966–68, AMA archives.

167. Ibid., 1966.

168. Ibid., 1966.

169. "Court Castigates Trotzky on Record," *Twin Falls (ID) Daily News*, August 22, 1933, Newspaper Archive, http://newspaperarchive.com.

170. "Sobrino de Trotzky Detendo," *El Dia* (Mexico City), August 3, 1935, 1, AMA archives.

171. George L. Mosse, *The Crisis of German Ideology: Intellectual Origins of the Third Reich* (New York: Grosset & Dunlap, Universal Library, 1964), 110.

172. "Sobrino de Trotzky Detendo."

173. "Sobrino de Trotzky," *El Dia* (Mexico City), August 13, 1935, 1, AMA archives.

174. T. P. Hunter, special agent, California Board of Medical Examiners, letters to Chris Fox and Jack Greening, May 3, 1938, EPSO, case file 9628.

175. C. F. Cline, investigator, National Automobile Theft Bureau, Pacific Coast Division headquarters, San Francisco, letter to Chris Fox, April 18, 1938, EPSO, case file 9628.

176. Chris Fox, letter to Jack Greening, May 25, 1938, EPSO, case file 9628.

177. Ibid.

178. Ibid.

179. Ibid.

180. Ibid.

181. Chris Fox, investigation summary, EPSO, case file 9628.

182. Ibid.

183. Ibid.

184. Fox, letter to Greening.

185. Ibid.

186. Thomas Brightbill, California Historic Landmarks, Site of the Giant Powder Company, accessed March 28, 2008, http://www.brightbill.net.

187. Ibid.

188. C. F. Cline, letter to Chris Fox concerning activities of Weston Frome, EPSO, case file 9628.

189. R. H. Colvin, FBI agent, El Paso office, confidential letter to Chris Fox, May 12, 1938, EPSO, case file 9628.

190. Report on trial of Nazi era spies, *Wisconsin State Journal* (Madison), May 3, 1948, 10, Newspaper Archive, http://newspaperarchive.com.

191. Louella Parsons, Louella Parsons column, *Modesto Bee and News-Herald*, February 27, 1938, 10, Newspaper Archive, http://newspaperarchive.com.

192. Testimony of FBI informant, Committee on Military Affairs, House of Representatives, 78th Congress, interim report on Investigations of the National War Effort, June 14, 1944.

193. M. L. Britt, National Automobile Theft Bureau (NATB) agent, investigative report to Chris Fox, August 30, 1941, EPSO, case file 9628.

194. FBI, field report, Wilhelm Rohl file, FOIA, December 10, 1942.

195. FBI, Internal Security, July 7, 1941, declassified July 14, 1982, Wilhelm Rohl file, FOIA.

196. Testimony of Biltmore Hotel staff to FBI, Committee on Military Affairs, House of Representatives, 78th Congress, interim report on Investigations of the National War Effort, June 14, 1944.

197. J. B. Turner, Atlas Powder Company official, interview by Sergeant Charlie Baumhauer, California Highway Patrol detective, in report from M. L. Britt, NATB San Francisco investigator, February 23, 1940, EPSO, case file 9628.

198. Lieutenant L. J. Hurst, detective, Los Angeles Police Department, memorandum to Chris Fox, May 12, 1938, EPSO, case file 9628.

199. Chris Fox, telex to Berkeley police chief Jack A. Greening, May 25, 1938, EPSO, case file 9628.

200. Jack A. Greening, confidential response to Chris Fox, May 28, 1938, EPSO, case file 9628.

201. Chris Fox, response by telex to Jack A. Greening, May 31, 1938, EPSO, case file 9628.

202. Ibid.

203. Chris Fox, telex to Greening, May 31, 1938, EPSO, case file 9628.

204. Jack A. Greening, confidential letter to Chris Fox, June 3, 1938, EPSO, case file 9628.

205. Chris Fox, notes from telephone conversation with Berkeley police chief, June 3, 1938, EPSO, case file 9628.

206. Trotsky, who was freed as a suspect, prematurely in Fox's opinion, was a habitué of the West Texas oil fields.

207. Chris Fox, private letter to friend and NATB agent M. L. Britt, July 30, 1938, EPSO, case file 9628.

208. Ibid.

209. Chris Fox, letter to Ranger Mills, July 11, 1938, EPSO, case file 9628.

210. Chris Fox, letter to Coast Guard Lt. Lyons, July 18, 1938, EPSO, case file 9628.

211. Albert Anderson, letter to Chris Fox, July 23, 1938, EPSO, case file 9628.

212. Chris Fox, letter to Albert Anderson, August 3, 1938, EPSO, case file 9628.

213. Ibid.

214. Chris Fox, letter to DPS director Homer Garrison, October 31, 1938, EPSO, case file 9628.

215. DPS director Homer Garrison, letter to Chris Fox, November 9, 1938, EPSO, case file 9628.

216. Chris Fox, notes on investigation, January 18, 1939, EPSO, case file 9628.

217. Chris Fox, letters to Albert Anderson et al., June 29, 1938, EPSO, case file 9628.

218. "Frome Murder Suspects Released in Juarez," *Albuquerque Journal*, April 13, 1939, 11, Newspaper Archive, http://newspaperarchive.com.

219. "Frome Murder Clue Sought in Juarez," *Dallas Morning News*, April 14, 1939, 4, *DMN* archives.

220. James J. Biggins, Chicago district supervisor, Federal Bureau of Narcotics, letter to Chris Fox, February 15, 1939, EPSO, case file 9628.

221. Steven J. Ross, "Warner's War: Politics, Pop Culture and Propaganda in Wartime Hollywood," Norman Lear Center, accessed July 5, 2010, http://www.learcenter .org.

222. Michael Sayers and Albert E. Kahn, *Sabotage! The Secret War against America* (New York: Harper & Brothers, 1942), 141.

223. Alan Hynd, *Passport to Treason: The Inside Story of Spies in America* (New York: Robert M. McBride, 1943), 46–50.

224. Sander A. Diamond, *Nazi Movement in the United States, 1924–41* (Ithaca, NY: Cornell University Press, 1974), 28.

225. Ibid., 37.

226. George Gallup, founder, in 1935, of the American Institute of Public Opinion, began doing national surveys that greatly influenced American policy makers.

227. Sayers and Kahn, *Sabotage!* foreword.

228. William L. Shirer, *The Rise and Fall of the Third Reich*, vol. 1, *The Rise* (New York: Touchstone by Simon & Schuster), 307.

229. FBI, synopsis of facts, Wolfgang Ebell file, December 29, 1941, FOIA.

230. Ladislas Farago, *The Game of the Foxes: The Untold Story of German Espionage in the United States and Great Britain during World War II* (New York: David McKay, 1971), 571.

231. Transcript, Investigation of Un-American Propaganda in the United States, Special Committee on Un-American Activities, House of Representatives, 75th Congress, 1938, Internet Archive, accessed September 15, 2010, http://www.archive .org.

232. Farago, *Game of the Foxes*, 571.

233. "Oakland Bund Nazi Link," *Oakland Tribune*, September 29, 1938, 1, Newspaper Archive, http://newspaperarchive.com.

234. Transcript, Investigation of Un-American Propaganda.

235. Federal Bureau of Investigation, "Vonsiatsky Espionage," FBI History of Famous Cases, accessed April 16, 2010, http://www.fbi.gov.

236. Chris Fox, letter to DPS director Homer Garrison, October 31, 1938, EPSO, case file 9628.

237. "Secret Berlin-Tokyo Pact Revealed by Ex-Soviet Agent," *Oakland Tribune*, March 5, 1939, 3, Newspaper Archive, http://newspaperarchive.com.

238. United Press wire service, "Capt. Wiedemann, Close Adviser of Nazi Leader, Says He Knows He Will Be Closely Watched," *Corpus Christi Times*, March 8, 1939, 3, Newspaper Archive, http://newspaperarchive.com.

239. "She's Ousted—" *Kingsport (TN) Times*, December 20, 1940, 1, Newspaper Archive, http://newspaperarchive.com.

240. Sayers and Kahn, *Sabotage!* 211–14.

241. "Naturalized Germans Ask Consul's Removal," *Middleton Times* (New York), March 21, 1939, 4, Newspaper Archive, http://newspaperarchive.com.

242. U.S. Department of State Bulletin, "Proclamation of Unlimited National Emergency," May 27, 1941, reference to September 8, 1939, Limited National Emergency, accessed July 9, 2013, http://www.ibiblio.org.

243. "Deserter Bares Nazi Spy Plot," *Standard Examiner* (Ogden, UT), October 18, 1938, 1 (testimony in the first large Nazi spy trial in the United States), Newspaper Archive, http://newspaperarchive.com.

244. Guenther Gustav Rumrich, one of the first important spies caught by the FBI, testified at his trial in New York City in October 1938 that "Nazi Germany's interests shifted from American military secrets late in 1937 to industrial information" (Ibid., 2).

245. *Moody's Manual of Investments, American and Foreign: Industrial Securities* (New York: Moody's Investors Service, 1938), 257–59.

246. William Bradford Williams, *History of the Manufacture of Explosives for the World War, 1917–1918* (Chicago: University of Chicago Press, 1920), 39–47, Google Play.

247. Chris Fox, notes, May 1938, EPSO, case file 9628.

248. Hynd, *Passport to Treason*, 47, 153, 199.

249. Arthur Landis, *The Abraham Lincoln Brigade* (New York: Citadel, 1967), 208.

250. "Lessons of People's War in Spain 1936–1939," *Progressive Labor* 9, no. 5 (October–November 1974): 109.

251. Sayers and Kahn, *Sabotage!* 22–23.

252. Erik Larson, *In the Garden of Beasts* (New York: Crown, 2011), 265.

253. Diamond, *Nazi Movement*, 20–31.

254. Chris Fox, letter to W. E. Shoppe, NATB, San Francisco, March 28, 1940, EPSO, case file 9628.

255. Chris Fox, letter to CBI chief Owen Kessel, EPSO, case file 9628.

256. Fox, correspondence with NATB agents, EPSO, case file 9628.

257. Clipping from the *San Francisco Call Bulletin*, March 26, 1940, in Fox, notes.

258. "Mystery Coupe," 1.

259. Chris Fox, letter to Harry Hooper, NATB Phoenix, AZ, April 6, 1940, EPSO, case file 9628.

260. M. L. Britt, NATB San Francisco agent, unofficial report to Chris Fox, April 23, 1941, EPSO, case file 9628.

261. Chris Fox, personal notation appended to Frome file, March 23, 1940, EPSO, case file 9628.

262. "Intelligence Activities and the Rights of Americans," U.S. Senate Select Committee on Intelligence Activities, Final Report, book 2, April 14, 1976, 27.

263. "Introduction," in "The Development of FBI Domestic Intelligence Investigations," U.S. Senate Select Committee to Study Governmental Operations with Respect to Intelligence Activities, Final Report, book 3, April 14, 1976.

264. Ibid.

265. Ibid.

266. "Dies Committee Enters Texas Red Investigation," *Oakland Tribune*, March 8, 1940, 11, Newspaper Archive, http://newspaperarchive.com.

267. FBI, teletype from FBI headquarters, Washington, DC, to special agent in charge, Salt Lake City, and resident agent at Reno, Romano Trotsky file, FOIA.

268. FBI, Field Report, October 26, 1940, Romano Trotsky file, FOIA.

269. Hynd, *Passport to Treason*, 187–88.

270. Ibid., 189.

271. Ibid., 190.

272. Chris Fox, notes on conversation with Hugh J. Pharies, EPSO, case file 9628.

273. Hugh J. Pharies, undated notes from report to DPS director Homer Garrison, EPSO, case file 9628.

274. Ibid.

275. Hugh Pharies, letter to Chris Fox, July 22, 1940, EPSO, case file 9628.

276. Ibid.

277. Homer Garrison, transmittal letter to Chris Fox, December 21, 1940, with transcript of Ranger Pharies's interview of Weston Frome conducted in Richmond, California, on November 5, 1940, EPSO, case file 9628.

278. Ibid.

279. The National Academy of the FBI was created in the early 1930s as the FBI Police Training School. FBI, "The National Academy," accessed April 25, 2011, http://www.fbi.gov.

280. Garrison, transmittal letter.

281. Jackson and Haley, *One Ranger Returns*, 54.

282. Garrison, transmittal letter.

283. Confidential FBI Report, November 11, 1946, Subject: Espionage, Dr. Wolfgang Ebell, declassified April 20, 1989, Wolfgang Ebell file, FOIA.

284. Wolfgang Ebell, Immigration and Naturalization Service, case file 753, Confidential Abstract of Consolidated File, April 22, 1942, FOIA.

285. Farago, *Game of the Foxes*, 31.

286. John Weiss, *Ideology of Death* (Chicago: Ivan R. Dee, 1996), 259.

287. FBI, Intelligence Report, detailed document referred to the FBI by Immigration and Naturalization Service, undated, Wolfgang Ebell file, FOIA.

288. Ibid., 268.

289. Special Inspection Division of Immigration and Naturalization, synopsis of case files from 1930 through 1941, on Wolfgang Ebell, Document for Cancellation of Citizenship, January 19, 1942, FOIA.

290. Ibid.

291. Ben F. Foster, U.S. attorney, El Paso office of the Department of Justice, transmittal letter to FBI, May 27, 1942, FBI Wolfgang Ebell file, FOIA.

292. Ibid.

293. "Oakland Bund, Nazi Linked," *Oakland Tribune*, September 29, 1938, 1, Newspaper Archive, http://newspaperarchive.com.

294. Foster, letter.

295. Weiss, *Ideology of Death*, 296, 378.

296. Chris Fox, advisory to FBI El Paso office, concerning unethical practices of Wolfgang Ebell, FBI Wolfgang Ebell file, FOIA.

297. Immigration and Naturalization Service, Confidential Abstract and Consolidated File, Department of Justice, April 22, 1942, FBI Wolfgang Ebell file, FOIA.

298. Rosa Prieto et al., "The Mexican Repatriation in 1930s Is Little Known," Borderlands annual publication, an El Paso Community College Local History Project, El Paso Community College, 2001–2009.

299. Chris Fox, notes about investigators' frustration with being unable to locate the Hotel Cortez bellhop and the physician who might have attended to Nancy Frome, EPSO, case file 9628.

300. FBI, Investigation Report, April 4, 1940, interview with a twenty-two-year-old bellhop (name redacted) working at Hilton Hotel in El Paso, stating that he had known Ebell since 1936, FBI, Wolfgang Ebell file, FOIA.

301. Hugh Pharies, letter to Chris Fox, June 4, 1941, Chris P. Fox archives, Special Collections, UTEP.

302. FBI, interrogation of arrested Nazi agent (name redacted), January 29, 1942, Synopsis of Facts, Wolfgang Ebell file, FOIA.

303. FBI, Report Synopsis, December 29, 1941, Wolfgang Ebell file, FOIA.

304. FBI, Confidential Memorandum for the Director, December 18, 1941, declassified February 4, 1999, Wolfgang Ebell file, FOIA.

305. FBI, Confidential Summary Report, December 1941, declassified February 2, 1999, Wolfgang Ebell file, FOIA.

306. FBI, Espionage Case on Dr. Hermann F. Erben, March 18, 1940, Errol Flynn file, FOIA.

307. FBI, Field Report letter, May 4, 1944, to FBI director from New York SAC E. E. Conroy, Errol Flynn file, FOIA.

308. H. R. Duffey, FBI special agent in charge, El Paso, transmittal letter to FBI director, reporting on intercept of a transmitting radio, September 23, 1940, Wolfgang Ebell file, FOIA.

309. D. A. Bryce, FBI special agent in charge, El Paso office, letter to director, November 19, 1941, Wolfgang Ebell file, FOIA.

310. H. R. Duffey, FBI special agent in charge, El Paso, confidential report, August 15, 1940, declassified January 21, 1999, Wolfgang Ebell file, FOIA.

311. FBI Chicago Office, investigative report, March 20, 1941, Wolfgang Ebell file, FOIA.

312. H. R. Duffey, FBI special agent in charge, El Paso, letter to FBI director, January 31, 1940, Wolfgang Ebell file, FOIA.

313. U.S. Justice Department, Criminal Division, summary of proceedings of cancellation of citizenship, May 27, 1942, FBI Wolfgang Ebell file, FOIA.

314. Edward C. Ezell, *Handguns of the World: Military Revolvers and Self-Loaders from 1870 to 1945* (New York: Barnes & Noble, 1981), 424.

315. "Much Contraband Seized Here in Round-Up of Enemy Aliens," *El Paso Herald-Post*, March 1, 1942, 1, OR archives, Briscoe Center, UT.

316. Chris Fox, letter to DPS director Homer Garrison, April 30, 1941, Special Collections, UTEP.

317. Chris Fox, letter to DPS director Homer Garrison, February 21, 1941, EPSO, case file 9628.

318. Homer Garrison, letter to Chris Fox, February 25, 1941, EPSO, case file 9628.

319. Felix McKnight, "Texas Rangers Still Scourge of Outlaws," *Dallas Morning News*, September 10, 1941, *DMN* archives.

320. Jackson and Haley, *One Ranger Returns*, 57.

321. "3 Suspects Set Free in Frome Killings," *Dallas Morning News*, January 1, 1942, 1, *DMN* archives.

322. Chris Fox, letter to C. W. B. Long, chief inspector, U.S. Post Office, Dallas, January 24, 1942, Special Collections, UTEP.

323. "Vonsiatsky Espionage," Famous FBI Cases, 12–17, accessed July, 11, 2000, http://www.fbi.gov.

324. Chris Fox, letter to game warden W. B. Stubblefield of Ysleta, April 26, 1941, EPSO, case file 9628.

325. Sayers and Kahn, *Sabotage!* 31.

326. FBI, Confidential Field Report, Hawaiian Contracting Company, October 29, 1942, Wilhelm Rohl file, declassified December 30, 1985, FOIA.

327. FBI, "William Sebold: An FBI Plant in Nazi Spy Ring," Famous Cases, accessed March 21, 2008, http://www.fbi.gov.

328. "Report of the Commission Protecting and Reducing Government Secrecy," appendix A: "The Experience of the Second World War," accessed July 26, 2010, http://www.fas.org.

329. Gordon W. Prange, Donald M. Goldstein, and Katherine Dillon (copyright Anne R. Prange), *At Dawn We Slept* (New York: McGraw-Hill, Penguin, 1981), 151.

330. Sayers and Kahn, *Sabotage!* 12.

331. FBI, teletype cover and memo to Director J. Edgar Hoover from agent in charge, Salt Lake City, March 14, 1941, Romano Trotsky file, FOIA.

332. Ibid.

333. FBI, Field Report, Romano Trotsky file, June 16, 1941, FOIA.

334. Chris Fox, letter to FBI director J. Edgar Hoover, May 1, 1941, Special Collections, UTEP.

335. Chris Fox, letter to FBI agent Hugh J. Pharies, June 20, 1941, Special Collections, UTEP.

336. Chris Fox, letter to Herbert S. Bursley, special consul on smuggling, U.S. State Department, May 5, 1941, Special Collections, UTEP.

337. Farago, *Game of the Foxes*, 569.

338. FBI, "The FBI's Most Famous Closed Cases," chap. 35, "Vonsiatsky Espionage," Office of Public and Congressional Affairs, 17, accessed July 11, 2000, http://www.fbi.gov.

339. Sayers and Kahn, *Sabotage!* 79.

340. Hynd, *Passport to Treason*, 199–203.

341. Gerhard Wilhelm Kunze, confidential transcript of interrogation in New York Field Office, July 14, 1942, FBI German-American Bund file, declassified May 29, 1998, FOIA.

342. Charles Lindbergh, speech at America First Rally, Des Moines, IA, UP wire report, *Florence Alabama Times*, December 12, 1941, Newspaper Archive, http://newspaperarchive.com.

343. FBI, Field Report, Wolfgang Ebell file, FOIA, July 7, 1942.

344. C. H. Carson, attorney, Department of Justice, memo to D. M. Ladd, FBI headquarters, December 8, 1941, declassified March 2, 1999, Wolfgang Ebell file, FOIA.

345. FBI, reconstruction of events concerning the spy trip made by Gerhard Wil-

helm Kunze and Otto Willumeit in the fall of 1941, March 4, 1942, Wolfgang Ebell file, FOIA.

346. FBI, Synopsis of Facts, December 12, 1941, Wolfgang Ebell file, FOIA.

347. Ibid.

348. Department of Justice, El Paso office, summary, FBI Wolfgang Ebell file, June 5, 1942, FOIA.

349. Hynd, *Passport to Treason*, 216–18.

350. Wilhelm G. Kunze, letter to Fernando Goeldner, undated, Department of Justice, El Paso office, FBI Wolfgang Ebell file, FOIA.

351. Ibid.

352. J. Michael Miller, "Concentration at Mariveles," in *From Shanghai to Corregidor: Marines in Defense of the Philippines*, Marines in World War II Commemorative Series (Washington, DC: Marine Corps Historical Center, 1997), accessed September 30, 2006, http://www.nps.gov.

353. Gerhard Wilhelm Kunze, letter to Wolfgang Ebell, December 8, 1942, *United States of America vs. Ebell*, Civil Action no. 165, Court of U.S. District Judge Charles A. Boynton, El Paso, TX, March 28, 1942, FBI Wolfgang Ebell file, FOIA.

354. Ibid.

355. FBI, summary of charges against five Nazi agents, January 6, 1943, declassified February 9, 1999, Wolfgang Ebell file, FOIA.

356. "Fort Bliss: History," Military Bases, accessed July 10, 2013, http://www.militarybases.us.

357. Chris Fox, correspondence with C. H. Stone, chief of Criminal Investigation Division, California Bureau of Investigation, Sacramento, February 10, 1942, Chris P. Fox archives, Special Collections, UTEP.

358. Ibid.

359. Chris Fox wrote a letter to W. H. Richardson noting the "many, many problems" law enforcement agencies had "trying to keep your personnel established," because of the war's drain of young policemen joining the war effort. Chris Fox, letter to W. H. Richardson Jr., Texas Commissioner of Public Safety, January 4, 1943; Fox archives, Special Collections, UTEP.

360. D. M. Ladd, FBI legal counsel to Justice Department, classified FBI memo to E. A. Tamm, FBI supervisor in Washington, DC, December 17, 1941, declassified February 4, 1999, Wolfgang Ebell file, FOIA.

361. D. A. Bryce, teletype to J. Edgar Hoover, December 17, 1941, declassified February 4, 1999, FBI Wolfgang Ebell file, FOIA.

362. "El Paso Raids Seize Enemy Guns, Cameras, Radios," *El Paso Herald-Post*, February 28, 1942, 1, OR archives, Briscoe Center, UT.

363. D. M. Ladd, FBI legal counsel to Justice Department, confidential memo ex-

plaining why the agent escaped capture in the roundups, January 9, 1941, declassified February 4, 1999, Wolfgang Ebell file, FOIA.

364. "Indictment On German Gestapo Agent Returned," *Denison (TX) Press*, January 7, 1942, 1, Portal of Texas History, accessed September 18, 2013, http://texashistory.unt.edu.

365. Lawrence Smith, Defense Unit Confidential Memorandum, March 24, 1942, FBI Wolfgang Ebell file, declassified February 4, 1999, FOIA.

366. John Edgar Hoover, letter to special agent in charge, El Paso, April 15, 1942, enclosing two copies of the presidential warrant for arrest of Wolfgang Ebell for citizenship revocation, signed by Attorney General Francis Biddle, April 2, 1942, FBI Wolfgang Ebell file, FOIA.

367. Associated Press wire report of the ongoing Vonsiatsky spy trial from Hartford, CT, August 8, 1942, "Dr. Wolfgang Ebell, 43-year-old, pop-eyed El Paso physician," *El Paso Times*, 1, OR archives, Briscoe Center, UT.

368. FBI, case summary, Wolfgang Ebell file, January 6, 1943, FOIA.

369. "FBI Conducts Further Raids on El Paso Aliens," *El Paso Times*, March 4, 1942, 1, OR archives, Briscoe Center, UT.

370. FBI, "History Timeline," accessed April 13, 2010, http://www.fbi.gov.

371. "Alien Contraband Seized," photo, *El Paso Times*, March 1, 1942, 1, OR archives, Briscoe Center, UT.

372. Steven Finacom, "Berkeley, A Look Back: City shocked by sensational double murder," *San Jose Mercury News*, April 4, 2013, accessed April 4, 2013, http://www.mercurynews.com.

373. Dawson Duncan, "Frome Double Murder State's Biggest Mystery," *Dallas Morning News*, February 1, 1953, 1, *DMN* archives.

374. Homer Garrison, interview with Associated Press reporter Ed Overholser, *Amarillo Globe-Times*, October 5, 1959, 1, Newspaper Archive, http://newspaperarchive.com.

375. Ibid.

376. Office of Naval Intelligence, Headquarters Eighth Naval District, correspondence by agent named "Joe" with Chris Fox, who was then the general manager of the El Paso Chamber of Commerce, May 11, 1942, Special Collections, UTEP.

377. Colonel C. M. Adams, commander, 273rd Infantry Regiment, letter to family, March 6, 1945, Chris P. Fox archives, Special Collections, UTEP.

378. Chris Fox, letter to Rex McMorris, March 21, 1945, Chris P. Fox archives, Special Collections, UTEP.

379. J. Michael Miller, *From Shanghai to Corregidor: Marines in the Defense of the Philippines*, Marines in World War II Commemorative Series (Washington, DC: Marine Corps Historical Center, 1997), accessed September 30, 2006, http://www.nps.gov.

380. "Japanese POW Hell Ships of World War II: Historical Content," *Oryoku Maru* Online, accessed September 30, 2006, http://www.oryokumaruonline.org.

381. Mada M. McGill, letter to author declining to discuss that period of her life because of the grief still evoked, February 4, 1996.

382. "Weston Frome, Atlas Powder Founder Dies," *Oakland Tribune*, July 4, 1973, 18, Newspaper Archive, http://newspaperarchive.com.

383. "War Probers Want Former Nazi Official," *Charleston (WV) Gazette*, August 28, 1946, 1, Newspaper Archive, http://newspaperarchive.com.

384. "King Traded Shots With Enemy in Exciting Coup," *Moberly (MO) Monitor-Index*, September 9, 1944, 1, Newspaper Archive, http://newspaperarchive.com.

385. "Fritz Wiedemann Fined $600 for Part in Nazisms," *Dunkirk-Fredonia (NY) Evening Observer*, November 17, 1948, 8, Newspaper Archive, http://newspaper archive.com.

386. J. Edgar Hoover, memorandum to Lawrence M. C. Smith, chief, special defense unit, October 18, 1941, FBI Romano Trotsky file, FOIA.

387. A. H. Belmont, advisory to L. V. Broadman, U.S. Immigration Service, forwarded to the FBI on March 12, 1958, FBI Romano Trotsky file, FOIA.

388. Alexis Romanoff, letter to FBI director J. Edgar Hoover, March 7, 1958, FBI Romano Trotsky file, FOIA.

389. Senate bill 3422, 86th Congress, 2nd Session, April 25, 1960, FBI Romano Trotsky file, FOIA.

390. Jackson and Haley, *One Ranger Returns*, 63.

391. Ibid., 47.

392. Joaquin Jackson, interview by Nancy Ray and Eddie Ray at his home in Alpine, TX, September 15, 2008, living history archives at Texas Ranger Hall of Fame and Museum, Waco.

393. Jackson and Haley, *One Ranger Returns*, 62.

INDEX

Federal Bureau of Investigation (FBI): enlists Fox for counterintelligence, 238; investigation of Trotsky, 159, 160, 166–68, 239; expanded surveillance powers, 236–37; on Frome case, 38–39, 69, 98, 125, 130, 143, 209; spy sweeps, 277–80, 300–301, 302–3; surveillance of Ebell/Vonsiatsky spy ring, 240–42, 269, 280, 285–87, 288–91, 293–95; surveillance of Plack/Rohl (and the Biltmore), 185–86, 187–90

Ferguson, Miriam "Ma," 86

Finacom, Stephen, 307

Flagstaff, AZ, 170

Flippin, Jack, and gang, 98–99

Flynn, Errol, 20, 185, 221, 268

Fort Bliss, TX, 72, 73, 112, 169, 258, 260, 270, 295, 304

Fort Hancock, TX, 122, 126

fortune-teller. See Gillespie, Allie

Forty-eighters, 7

Fox, Chris P., 71–80; at autopsy, 59, 64; in Berkeley, 175–80; blackmail revelation in LA, 191–94; career after law enforcement, 283–84, 296; conflict with other lawmen, 81–82, 106, 118, 159, 200–201; cooperation with other agencies, 72–73, 183–84, 230–31; as coordinator of Frome case, 71, 81, 82, 83, 85–86, 90, 95, 132; elected sheriff, 71, 75; family of, 76, 293, 310; frustration with Frome, 175–76, 179–80, 196–97; other notable cases of, 55, 73, 77–80, 238; relationship with Hoover, 72, 238 (see also Hoover); retraces Frome trip, 119–23; and surveillance of Ebell, 242, 255, 265, 269–72, 276–77; theory of Frome case, 68,

95–97, 102, 117, 174–75, 198, 235, 230; tracking Trotsky, 131–32, (see also Lukian, Helga); and Trotsky arrest, 147–48, 151, 154, 155, 156, 159; and turf wars, 81–82, 85–86, 106, 156, 200, 205. See also Fox correspondence

Fox correspondence with: AMA, 160, 173; Anderson, 156, 202, 203–4, 208; Bursley, 284; Carmichael, 106; Garrison, 204–5, 273–74; Greening, 179–80, 194–95, 196; Hoover, 143, 283; Lyons, 201; Mills, 201; NATB, 174–75, 200, 231–32, 233–34; Pharies, 264, 284

Fox Jr., Chris P. (son), 293, 310

Freikorps, 257, 271

Frome family: finances, 7, 245; home, 5–6; social status, 6, 8, 11; women's past travels, 11–13, 17, 30–31, 246–47. See also individual Frome names

Frome, Hazel Eva (née Johnson), 8, 9, 12–13, 16, 19, 226; Pop Frome on, 246–49, 250, 252, 253. See also Frome family; Frome women's fateful trip

Frome, Mada Margaret, 6, 8, 9, 10, 12–13, 18, 53, 226; as Mada McGill, 311; as Mada McMakin, 94, 292, 311; Pop Frome on, 246–47, 248. See also Frome family

Frome, Nancy Eudora, 5, 8, 9–10, 19, 226; Pop Frome on, 246–48, 249–50, 251–52, 253. See also Frome family; Frome women's fateful trip

Frome, Weston G. "Pop," 6–8, 227; at Atlas Powder, 181, 194, 224–25, 245–46, 311–12; and Biltmore Hotel, 19, 189; blackmail of, 192–99, 202, 227–29; denial of Frome women in LA, 94, 95, 177, 183, 192, 231–32, 249;